Principles of Interactive Multimedia

Mark Elsom-Cook

School of Computing & Mathematics
University of Northumbria
Newcastle Upon Tyne, UK

Principles of Interactive Multimedia

The McGraw-Hill Companies

London • Burr Ridge, IL • New York • St Louis • San Francisco • Auckland
Bogotá • Caracas • Lisbon • Madrid • Mexico • Milan • Montreal • New Delhi
Panama • Paris • San Juan • São Paulo • Singapore • Tokyo • Toronto

Published by
McGraw-Hill Publishing Company
SHOPPENHANGERS ROAD, MAIDENHEAD, BERKSHIRE, SL6 2QL, ENGLAND
Telephone: +44(0) 1628 502500
Fax: +44(0) 1628 770224
Web site: http://www.mcgraw-hill.co.uk

British Library Cataloguing in Publication Data
A catalogue record for this book is available from the British Library

ISBN 007 709610 X

Library of Congress cataloguing in publication data
The LOC data for this book has been applied for and may be obtained from the
Library of Congress, Washington, D.C.

Web site address: http://www.mcgraw-hill.co.uk/textbooks/elsom-cook

Publisher: David Hatter
Page design: Mike Cotterell
Typesetting: Mouse Nous
Illustration origination: Fin McMorran
Production: Steven Gardiner Ltd
Cover: Hybert Design

The **McGraw·Hill** *Companies*

Printed in Great Britain by Bell & Bain Ltd. Glasgow
1   2   3   5   BB   4   3   2   1   0

For Tamsin

Contents

Colour Plates   following page 178

1. Clearway and a few red bordered circles.
2. Black and white no entry.
3. Yield sign.
4. Train, quayside.
5. One-way signs.

Preface

What is *Interactive Multimedia*? This is the question that should be in your mind when you first pick up this book. I am not going to tell you, because I don't know; indeed, I don't believe that anyone knows, although many of us have ideas about what it can and will mean. This book will help you explore those ideas, discover for yourself, and develop your own understanding of the terms. It will do this by examining the broad range of contributory disciplines which feed into the area and showing how they relate to practice and potential future developments. This is exciting because *Interactive Multimedia* is a field in its infancy, and it is people such as ourselves who are in the process of creating the specialism of research, design and development. It is a major revolution in computing which is inevitable but, despite what some people may think, hasn't happened yet. So far, what we see described as *Interactive Multimedia* is a collection of toys and exploratory systems.

Let me expand upon that. Multimedia has been around for a long time. It has origins far older than computers. Books which used words and pictures are, by one definition, multimedia. The Open University in the 1970s pioneered multimedia teaching-using text books and study guides, television, radio programmes, cassette tapes and video tapes. There wasn't a computer in sight, but it was still a multimedia system. It was not *Interactive Multimedia* however, since the interactions were provided by people

By enabling us to combine and control various technologies from a single box, *computers* have enabled us to integrate these media more closely, but they have not taken our thinking beyond the things that we could do with these older technologies. They have made it easier and more accessible, but not novel and innovative. In the same way that early support for text enabled authors to put books on-screen, but didn't lead them to think about the advantages or otherwise of such a strategy, *multimedia* is an enabling technology, but not a guiding one.

In the late 1980s I was visiting Apple Computer with a group of academics and, for the first time, we were given a demonstration of how you could take a running piece of video and paste it into a spreadsheet. 'Very interesting' was our reaction, 'but what is it *for*?' The Apple response was 'We make it possible. *You* tell *us* what it is *for*.'

In a sense, this book is an approach to answering that question. It assumes the technology of multimedia and invites the reader to think differently about what to do with it. This is achieved through taking an alternative perspective on *multimedia*, and through examining the nature of interactions more closely. This book will not teach you how to use authoring tools or how to produce graphical effects. It will not tell you much about how to program or how to integrate video. What it will do is introduce you to a different way of thinking that will enable you to radically reorient your approach to the use of the computer in the future, breaking away from current practice and examining just what we could do with a computer (or several) and what they could do for us.

To this end, there are two main strands to the book. The first requires one to realize that the various media are not, of themselves, new. They have a long history and the processes of creation and interpretation of a medium in the past cannot be ignored. It is painfully apparent when a developer utilizes a medium without being aware of its history and meaning. The result is almost invariably crude and stilted. A parallel can be found in the uses of the early Apple Macintosh:

Before the Mac, computers had *a* screen which had *a* font. This was normally a fixed width, typewriter style font. You could not change size, colour, face or emphasis. The only people who used fonts were those who worked in the areas of typography, and they did not use computers. With the advent of the Mac, there were suddenly, for the first time, hundreds of fonts available in many different formats and everybody wanted to use them. Consequently, there was a huge upsurge in the use of fonts by people who had no idea about why fonts evolved, how they work, what effects they have on the reader, or whether they are even readable. Often you would find 20 fonts on one page with every possible effect applied to them. It was horrendous. You could tell a Mac tyro a mile away by looking at anything they printed and counting the fonts – 'Oh yes, you must be a Mac user.'

Barely 15 years on, such typographic aberrations are thankfully rare. Once the novelty wore off and people started to learn or discover about typography, a general improvement in document layout and readability occurred. This happened because the basic typographic knowledge has disseminated far beyond the original restricted, specialized audience and into the community at large. If you fail to take account of typeface and readability in your software designs these days you are laughed at. If that can happen with typography, what about Art, graphic design, film, video, sound – all areas in which the general public already has a much higher awareness than they did with typography. Multimedia developers may share this public awareness of the personal effect of these media upon them, but are often lacking in the historical knowledge and expertise to design with these media. Consequently, if we wish to avoid repeating the errors of over-simplicity and naivety we cannot move ourselves forward in multimedia until we have understood the background of these contributing fields.

The second major strand of the book is *Interaction*. As you will find out, 'interacting' with computers is much more recent than the development of computers themselves, and our ideas about what is and is not possible, or useful, are still evolving. Computers are still not fully 'interactive' in the sense that will be introduced here, and the term is often badly misused elsewhere. By drawing on models of interaction from a variety of disciplines we will ground our thinking about interactions in a much richer context.

If all this sounds far too theoretical,

Don't panic.

The book leads you through these areas in a comfortable manner (I hope!), with pointers to places where you can find out more about the things that interest you, and suggestions for how you might incorporate some of these ideas into your own work. It leads towards an integration in which a design process is outlined that takes account of the various needs. There are plenty of examples and anecdotes around to lighten the tone of things.

Bear in mind that developing an *Interactive Multimedia* system is not a one person process. Because of the complexity involved you will inevitably work as part of a team. Between them, the team needs to understand all the issues raised in this book thoroughly, but one individual needs only some awareness of all the areas, and can focus in the particular one that interests them. Whether you are a developer, a programmer, a designer, a manager or a user, there are parts of this book that are for you. Don't feel you have to read the whole thing, but you really should if you want to get the big picture. Remember that our objectives are not about how to use the tools of multimedia, but are about what to do with them. It is like the difference between a course that teaches you how to use water colours and a course which helps you develop into a painter.

Structure of the book

The book is divided into three sections. The first addresses the fundamental issues that we need to think about in the design of an *Interactive Multimedia* system before we even consider the nature of the media that we might use. Chapter 1 clarifies and, to some extent, defines what we mean by *Interactive Multimedia* and why it is a different approach from multimedia. The other chapters in section one introduce the three key components that we must consider in a system design: Communicative Interaction (Chapter 2), knowledge of the subject content (Chapter 3), knowledge about the user (Chapter 4) and issues in the design of computer interfaces (Chapter 5).

In the second section we progress to examining the media content (assets) in more detail. We do this by introducing the idea of a set of languages for describing the different media. The unifying theme is Semiotics (Chapter 6), and this is followed by a more detailed examination of communication with four key media: text, sound, still and moving images (Chapters 7–10).

In the final section of the book we deal with issues which help us to integrate what we have learnt into the design and development of system. Chapters 11–13 explore teamworking, product design and project design in greater detail, providing a concrete approach to development based upon the earlier chapters. In Chapter 14 a certain amount of tentative predicting of the future takes place.

You can read any of the three sections independently, and most chapters can stand independently once you have read Chapter 1. To genuinely get a feel for the whole subject area, however, it is recommended that you follow the whole book, but perhaps only pursue the readings associated with chapters that are of special interest to you. I hope you enjoy it.

Acknowledgement

I would like to thank all the students who have been subjected to various versions of this material over the years, and have often provided quite insightful comments. I would like to thank my academic colleagues – particularly Stuart Allison and Graham Watts – who read and commented on drafts. Angela Lin very kindly provided the Chinese component. I am also extremely grateful to the following, who contributed content that I could not have produced myself:

Andrew King (Music Technology, University of Hull) – co-author of the chapter on Sound (Chapter 8).

Fin McMorran (School of Computing and Mathematics, University of Northumbria) – co-author of the chapter on Text (Chapter 7), and the chapter on Still Image (Chapter 9). More significantly, Fin generated all the artwork which I feel adds an indefinable something to the whole volume. Some of the characters may yet get their own animated cartoons on the web!

Many thanks to Mike Cotterell at Mouse Nous for extremely helpful and sympathetic type-setting of the book, and to the staff at McGraw-Hill for putting up with my various problems in getting it finished.

1

What is interactive multimedia?

1.1 Introduction

If you have read the Preface, you will be aware that this book is seeking to determine specifically what is meant by *Interactive Multimedia*. It is not possible (or desirable) to give a precise definition, but the objective is to provide readers with sufficient understanding of various areas to develop their own model and to understand why *Interactive Multimedia* is quite clearly distinct from *multimedia*. This understanding will only be achieved once you have mastered the various areas covered by the book, but in this chapter we will seek to motivate that discovery and to give a feel for what we mean by *Interactive Multimedia*.

We will do this by examining each of the components in detail. To begin with we will explore what *multimedia* means to the person on the street and introduce some key concepts and questions about what *multimedia* might be. We will then turn to examining *interaction* and try and clarify what we intend the term to embrace. This is particularly interesting because there are many views of what interaction is, which are not in day-to-day usage. Having explored these issues in general, we turn to their specific relationship with computers: first examining the history of computers and multimedia, and then turning to the history of computers and interaction. The chapter is concluded by two sections of a more practical nature. The first describes some examples of multimedia systems to give us a feel for what these packages encompass. The second comes as close as we will get to offering a definition of *Interactive Multimedia* as an alternative to multimedia.

1.2 Multimedia

In any technical or scientific field there is a tendency to define specialist terms. Sometimes this appears to be purely for the purpose of obfuscation, but often the reason for such terms is to allow workers in that field to talk precisely and concisely about what they are doing in a meaningful way. In typography, for example, there is talk about *fonts*, *faces*, *kerning*, and *serifs*. Some of the terms do not arise in everyday language, and have meanings that are only understood within that community (e.g. kerning). Some of the terms refer to words that do exist in everyday language, but provides those words with entirely different meanings (e.g. face). Sometimes the technical term has a meaning which is very similar to its day-to-day usage, but which has been made more precise in the specialized usage of the field.

Given this situation, and the comparative youth of the field of *Interactive Multimedia*, we are still in a position where there is a confusion over terms. Different people may use the same words to mean different things or to provide different levels of specificity. We will therefore try to clarify what we mean by multimedia as precisely as possible.

An obvious starting point is to examine what multimedia means to the general public. This awareness has grown up since the late 1980s. In common usage people will typically describe a multimedia experience as one involving pictures, sound, and video. They tend to think of it as a combination of stimuli such as this, often taking place in a specialized area (such as a 'multimedia experience' at a theme park or gallery). Individuals who use computers also commonly equate multimedia with CDs. In neither of these areas is interaction a key aspect of the term. People have tended to see themselves as recipients of a multimedia experience – passive observers of the time-based experiences that unfold before them.

However, this view of multimedia is limited by the fact that it is based upon the experience of what is commonly available now, rather than being informed by what will become available in the future. There is little reference to tactile or olfactory multimedia, for example. Equally, there is a tendency to ignore the more obvious multimedia systems. A television programme might well use moving pictures, subtitles, spoken words, music, and sound effects. This would certainly appear to qualify as a multimedia experience, but it is not perceived as such by the general public. We therefore need to go beyond this intuitive idea if we are to arrive at a description of what multimedia is that is suitable for us to work with as designers and developers.

Our definition will depend upon an understanding of three interrelated terms: the *modality*, *channel*, and *medium*. We will explore each term in detail before bringing them together into multimedia.

1.2.1 Modalities

There is one clear-cut way of dividing up the components of a multimedia activity: the sensory system through which that activity occurs (*modality*). We can determine unambiguously whether something is communicated through our sense of sight, hearing, touch, taste, or smell. This applies to both communications of which we are the recipient and communications of which we are the initiator. Music, speech, and sound effects are all received by us through the auditory modality (hearing). The keyboard, mouse, and touch screen are all communications that we would make through the tactile modality. If there is a speech input system for a computer then communication through an auditory modality to the machine is possible. From these observations we will therefore assert that the first (and easiest) question to ask about a multimedia system is which modalities it can or does utilize. Remember the formal names for the five modalities:

- tactile – touch;

- gustatory – taste;

- visual – sight;

- auditory – hearing;

- olfactory – smell.

1.2.2 Channels

While the division of multimedia activity into modalities is clear, it is obviously not sufficient for us to be able to distinguish adequately between different sorts of multimedia artefact. If we consider the auditory modality, for example, there is something fundamentally different about receiving spoken communication, hearing noises, or listening to music. Yet they all operate within the same modality. We need to introduce something more sophisticated.

This additional concept is the idea of a *channel* of communication. A channel of communication exists within a single modality, but one modality may contain many channels of communication. We can regard a channel as something like a form of encoding of the information within a particular modality. This has a number of implications.

- The first implication is that for there to be an encoding there must exist an encoder and we, as the recipient of the multimedia input must be able to operate as a decoder for the particular channel that we are receiving. This can be simply illustrated. At the moment you, the reader of this book, are receiving a communication through your visual modality (that is, you are reading this page). Within that modality you are using a channel which is encoded as printed text in English. I can safely assume that you have a decoder for this channel inside your head since you have got this far into the book. However, 如果我開始寫中文,大多數的讀者們將不會明白我的意思.

So, what went wrong there? Nothing, for some readers, but most of us would suddenly find that communication was no longer happening. This is because I switched to a channel coded as printed text in Chinese. If you, as a reader, do not have a decoder for that channel then you cannot understand it. I would be a very poor author if I relied upon channels that I cannot expect my audience to be able to use. Note that I remained very firmly in the same modality while switching channels.

- The next key concept that we must consider is that of *bandwidth*. As we shall see in a subsequent chapter, bandwidth is a strict mathematical idea that indicates how much information can be carried by a certain encoding. It is quite common to talk about the bandwidth of different modalities: for example, to indicate that the visual modality has a much higher bandwidth than the auditory modality. In fact, while there are such absolute limits on the bandwidth of given modalities, most people who make such comments are talking about the bandwidth of specific channels. One can suggest, for example, that we can read words at the rate of 100 words per minute, whereas we can listen to words at the rate of 500 words per minute. This is not a comparison of the visual modality with the auditory modality, but a comparison of the printed text channel in the visual modality with the spoken text channel in the auditory modality. This is a very different thing.

  A further point to remember about bandwidth is that it is a theoretical maximum level at which information can be transferred through a channel. It is something that we are rarely likely to reach in practice.

- The reason that the bandwidth indicates a level that we are unlikely to see is that it assumes the perfect encoder and decoder. These are processes which are unambiguous and take zero time, so that the only constraint is movement of information along the channel. When we are dealing with humans this is unlikely to be the case. In particular, later chapters of this book will demonstrate that this decoding process is very much dependent on the individual. We will emphasize the importance of the psychology of interpretation as it applies to different individuals and different channels. A thorough understanding of the psychology of your intended audience and the subject knowledge that you are trying to communicate to them will allow the selection of appropriate channels and is key to the design of a successful multimedia artefact.

1.2.3 Medium

We can build upon these ideas to arrive at a description of what we mean by a *medium* (i.e. the singular of media). In general usage, something like a television is referred to as a medium. How can we usefully encompass that within our set of definitions? It is apparent that a television programme uses multiple modalities (auditory and visual) and multiple channels (moving picture, written text, spoken word, music, etc.). So what is it that makes it a single entity? We will define a medium to mean:

> A set of co-ordinated channels spanning one or more modality which have come, by convention, to be referred to as a unitary whole, and which possess a cross-channel language of interpretation.

Our definition makes several important points.

- Our medium must contain at least one channel or no communication happens. Spoken word radio is an example of a one-channel medium. The captionless cartoon (i.e. drawn not animated) is another example. Typically, however, we will expect there to be more than one channel in our medium. Radio is a medium which includes spoken word, music, and sound effects, on the channels which it encompasses. These channels are all in one modality, but our example of a television (above) shows a medium which has several channels operating across several modalities.

- Where we are dealing with more than one channel in a medium, our definition states that the channels are *co-ordinated* and that there is a *cross-channel language of interpretation*. These two properties are interconnected. The first means that a true medium must display some form of relationship between the channels. If you are watching pictures on television with the sound turned down while your partner is berating you for failing to do the washing up then this combination of channels is *not* a medium. This is because the channels are not co-ordinated: There is no intention for them to interrelate and indeed they are in competition.

- The *cross-channel language* indicates that this co-ordination of the channels adds an additional communicative feature which can only be understood through a combination of the individual channels. If I hear a character say 'Let me take that plate for you' followed by a breaking noise, then I know that a plate has been broken by combining the information from the two channels used. If I heard either alone, I would not realize its significance. This is an example of co-ordinated channels with a language of interpretation additional to that of either channel alone.

- The final important point in our definition is that this medium comes into being by *convention*. Television, a book, a radio, a newspaper, a film: each of these is a combination of channels which constitutes a *medium*. You, the reader, could immediately identify the modalities and channels utilized by each of these media. You would also possess a language of interpretation for each, although you may not be conscious of it or able to introspect about it. As we will see later, there is nothing about a particular combination of channels which makes them inherently comprehensible: it is something that we, the interpreters, construct over time. Early viewers of film did not know how to interpret what they saw and hence, by our definition, film was *not* a medium in the early days.

This last point has a particular significance for us. If I define a particular combination of channels, it need not correspond to an accepted medium, and as such may not be easily interpreted by an audience. A major claim of subsequent chapters is that *Interactive Multimedia* is exactly about the creation of a new medium and a new language of interpretation.

Well, that was a lot of long words. What do we actually mean by it? Perhaps a picture (change of channel) will help.

In Figure 1.1 we are looking at two modalities: auditory and visual. These are represented by the ear and eye at the left. We are then considering six channels of communication (in the centre) of which three are in the *auditory* modality and three in the *visual*. The former are *spoken word*, *music*, and *sound effects*. The latter are *written words*, *images*, and *diagrams*. Each channel belongs to one modality only. To the

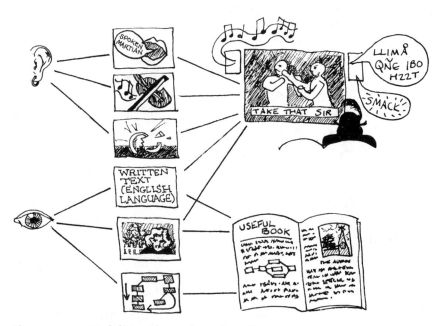

Figure 1.1　Modalities channels and media.

right of the diagram, we see two different media. The medium of film, at the top, utilizes five channels of communication across two modalities. The medium of the book, at the bottom, uses three channels of communication, all of which lie within the visual modality.

1.2.4   So what is multimedia?

Given this set of terminology, we can now return to our original question and see what we mean by *multimedia*. To some extent we have already reached this definition by excluding certain other possibilities. We know that multimedia is not the same as a modality, a channel, or a medium. Our definition of a *medium* encompasses many things that people tend to refer to as *multimedia*. We are left with our definition almost by a default:

> Multimedia is the combination of a variety of communication channels into a co-ordinated communicative experience for which an integrated cross-channel language of interpretation does not exist.

From this we can see that there are essentially two ways to create something which is multimedia. The first is to take more than one conventional medium and utilize them together in a co-ordinated manner. This is how the Open University became multimedia: it combined accepted media such as books, videos, and study guides, but had to create a language of interpretation because they were co-ordinated in a novel manner. The Open University students learn this co-ordination, but it is still novel for the rest of us.

The second way to create multimedia is to take a combination of channels which have not previously acquired unification as a medium, put them together in a co-ordinated form, and develop a language for them.

This definition has an interesting implication for us. It defines multimedia in terms of convention and the novelty of the co-ordination and cross-communication between the constituent channels. This means that multimedia is necessarily an evolving thing. A particular combination of channels may be initially novel, and hence multimedia, but as they gain in acceptance and popularity, they cease to be multimedia for their user group and become a single medium. In this very real sense multimedia is the process of the creation of new media. We shall learn more of the importance of this evolutionary approach later.

1.2.5   Summary

In this section we have moved from an intuitive definition of multimedia to a formal one. This was achieved by first identifying *modalities*, and then defining *channels of communication* within a modality. This enabled us to define a *medium* in terms of channels together with a cross-channel language of interpretation. Finally, we arrived at the specific definition of multimedia based upon these terms.

While *communication* is fundamental to these definitions, *interaction* is not. In the following section we will explore ideas of interaction that take us beyond multimedia to *Interactive Multimedia*.

1.3　Interaction

Our discussion so far has given us a working definition of what *multimedia* is. We have been very careful to couch this in terms which permit multimedia to be a one-way experience. The assumption has been of some sort of multimedia artefact which, at its simplest, may deliver information in some form to an observer. That observer may decode and interpret the information, but have no control over it. There are certainly many multimedia systems that conform to this model. What is missing from this view is the component of interaction. This is the essential element which takes us beyond traditional models and into a truly new realm of systems. The revolution starts here.

While we can ask the person on the street what is meant by multimedia, it is much harder to do this with *interaction*. It makes more sense for us to approach the question of defining interaction by examining the previous models and seeing how well they capture the desired range of meanings for the field of *Interactive Multimedia*.

1.3.1　Action and interaction

Let us begin with a simplistic division between three sorts of activity that a human being can engage in: thought, action, and interaction.

- *Thought* is something that you do to yourself. An individual can engage in some sort of internal process (of a mental nature) which has an outcome of changing their internal (mental) state.

- *Action* is something that you do to an object in the world. The effect is that something in the world has changed. An obvious example would be opening a door or pressing a key or clicking a mouse button. The change that arises in the world is a direct consequence of your action. Actions may also be performed upon yourself (e.g. biting your fingernails) or on other humans (e.g. kicking someone in the shin). However, it should be clear that for our purposes you, or the other person, are an object in this case. It is irrelevant whether you are capable of thinking or not.

- *Interaction* is a somewhat more complicated phenomenon. We can clearly state that it involves the participant in going outside the individual. It is not possible to interact with yourself! It is more than action in that it implies a two-way process. You act upon something

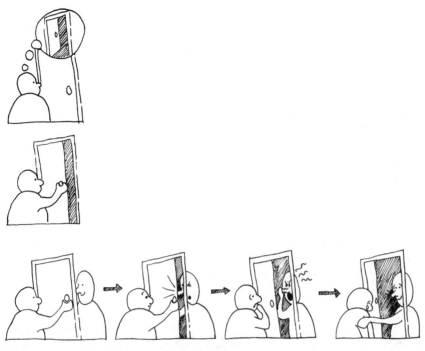

Figure 1.2 Thought, action, interaction.

and it acts upon you. At a simple level, you can interact with an object: I can turn the wheel of my car and it can resist me. This is the most basic form of interaction. At a more sophisticated level (but still non-human) I can give a query to a search engine which can return an outcome from my search, which I can then refine to produce a new query. This is, at some level, interaction. A more sophisticated sense is the interaction which occurs between two human beings. I can engage in some activity in order to bring about a change in the internal state of some other human. That person can respond by trying to modify my internal state. This is another level of interaction and is different from two humans thumping each other on the football pitch.

These are complex issues which will be explored in more detail in the appropriate chapter, but for the moment it is important to recognize that interaction is complex and that there are several definitions typically in use within the multimedia field. In particular, we will distinguish between *physical interaction* and *communicative interaction*. *Physical* interaction corresponds to things which achieve related changes in state in the physical world (e.g. I hit you, you hit me). *Communicative* interaction concerns things which could achieve changes of state in the mental world (e.g. I tell you my own life story, you tell me not to be so miserable).

From the way that we have used these terms, it is clearly the case that objects can act upon each other and can have *physical interaction*, but not *communicative interaction*. Humans can engage in communicative interaction, but quite commonly resort to *physical interactions*! Computers add an extra level to the discussion. Do they behave like objects or like humans? Can we talk about them as communicating? Do they have something equivalent to a mental state? In order to achieve a meaningful interaction with a multimedia system, we would wish to move away from the physical to the communicative definition of interaction. This is one of the fundamental drives towards *Interactive Multimedia*.

1.3.2   Physical interaction

We will clarify this term in the context of multimedia. Many people who talk about interactive systems have a model which encompasses the physical level of the system. It is possible to take a set of written text and place it upon a screen with controls (commonly labelled *previous* and *next*) which allow you to move through the pages. In fact, many people have done exactly this without worrying about why they do it or whether it is interesting. In effect, they have created a worse medium than the one that they started with. If you can only turn to the previous or next page, you would be better off with a book that you can stick book marks in or hold open with your thumb. Even at this level it is possible to produce high quality physical interaction, but we should bear in mind that this is not making use of the potential of the computer as a controlling mechanism. It is emulating the physical world and treating the computer as an object. This is not to imply that all systems that work at such a level are pointless, but that careful thought needs to be put into their design. For the purposes of *Interactive Multimedia*, a system that provides only physical interaction is not sufficient. It is not, in our terms, acting at a level which enables the development of a radically new sort of artefact.

We have discussed observers who are recipients of multimedia information. They are normally active in the decoding and interpretation of that information. In going beyond a multimedia delivery system, our next level must be a system that permits physical interaction with the information channels. Bear in mind that these channels are, to some extent, co-ordinated in a multimedia system, and hence the physical interaction is likely to control multiple channels together rather than a single channel. Much multimedia consists of giving the observer a level of physical interaction with these channels. Providing 'video recorder' type controls, simple navigational controls, etc. is interaction at this basic level. For the purposes of *Interactive Multimedia*, such active observation is not interactive in the desired sense. We are interested in *communicative interaction*.

1.3.3 Communicative interaction

Let us assume, for the moment, that *communicative interaction* can only occur between two *agents* (where an agent is something with an intentionality and an internal 'mental' state). In order to fully understand the sort of interaction to which we aspire, we need a better model of the communicative process itself. Without going into too much detail at this stage, Figure 1.3 illustrates a simple model.

In this cartoon, the agent in the white hat (Agent 1) is intending to communicate with the agent in the black hat (Agent 2). Each agent has a *role*: Agent 1 is the *teller* who is trying to communicate to someone else and Agent 2 is the *hearer* – the recipient of the communication. While the agent names remain fixed, their role may change many times throughout the interaction.

1. In the first frame we see the basic situation: Agent 1 has something inside his head – in this case the idea of [a broken computer mouse]. This is the thing that it wants to communicate to the other agent. Unfortunately, this thing is in a form that is specific to Agent 1: it is whatever form the agent keeps his thoughts in. He cannot simply reach into his own head and extract this thought and glue it into the head of Agent 2. Instead, he must use a channel of communication.

2. The first step is to translate that internal belief into something that is not personal. This is a process of dissociating the information from the internal context and representation into something that is potentially communicable. In this case the initial idea has been transformed to the communicable belief 'pointer 1 = faulty'.

3. The next step is to choose a communication channel, to encode the information in the form appropriate for that channel and to transmit it. Our agent has to make a decision about whether to assume that a given channel can be received and decoded by the intended hearer. Once this is done and the encoding has taken place, Agent 1 transmits it along the relevant channel. This is an action that affects the

Figure 1.3 Knowledge transfer model.

world (e.g. by wobbling the air to make sounds). The thing that goes out along the communication channel is 'my mouse is a sticky'.

4. Now Agent 2, receives the communication from the given channel and decodes it to get a new representation. In this case the representation is 'Rodent is glue-covered'. This is referred to as the *received belief*.

5. The process is completed by Agent 2 interpreting that received belief into his own internal representation: the idea of an animal in glue. Our communication is complete: information has been transferred from one agent to another.

This is communication. Like most communication it was not successful. It did not achieve its desired effect. We can imagine that these agents will be at cross-purposes until Agent 2 initiates a new discussion to clarify the meaning of the original utterance. Because the process can proceed in both directions, it constitutes interaction. Because it is about affecting the internal state of another agent, it constitutes communicative interaction.

1.3.4 Summary

This concise introduction to interaction will be pursued more thoroughly in Chapter 2. For the present we will provide a historical perspective on both multimedia and interaction in the context of computers so that subsequent chapters can be more easily related to practical examples.

1.4 A brief history of computers and multimedia

While not making any attempt at being comprehensive or balanced, this section will describe a few multimedia applications to try and give a more concrete form to some of the issues that we have been discussing. We will present a number of examples and show where they fit in the spectrum of multimedia.

1.4.1 Tape control devices

Prior to the advent of computers, other devices were used to control multimedia presentations. A range of devices, which could display particular media, were linked together via an electronic controller. This was typically a multi-channel audio tape recorder which combined audio channels with a number of control channels. Each control channel would manage a particular device by sending simple electronic signals to it. The simplest such device was the synchronized slide show. In these systems an electronically controlled slide projector was filled with a set of 35-mm slides. A tape was then produced containing, for example, a lecture presented through spoken word, music, and sound effects. A control channel was added to the tape which simply sent a 'move to next slide' message at particular points during the presentation. This ensured that the slides were synchronized with the audio track (Figure 1.4).

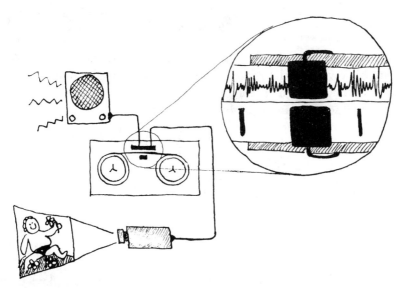

Figure 1.4   Slide system.

What makes this multimedia? It is a combination of two existing media: the slide and the audio tape. Slides give us access to a range of channels in the visual modality such as written text, diagrams, photographs, etc. Audio tape gives us access to channels in the auditory modality such as spoken words and music. This satisfies our definition of multimedia by being a novel combination of these media. They are co-ordinated through the synchronization of the controlling device and provide a cross-channel language through the interpretation of a given slide in the context of the current auditory activity.

More sophisticated versions of this approach extended the number of devices that could be used. A development which is still in use today is the 'multimedia slide wall' (Figure 1.5). In these systems a large number of slide projectors are organized so that each projects onto one square in a grid of projection screens. This vastly increases the potential of the medium because it enables more complex co-ordination and a more sophisticated language of interpretation. For example, slides can fade in and out on the same screen, can overlay each other, or can be changing simultaneously in different parts of the presentation screen. The complexities achievable with such a system have still not been fully explored. Even today (1999) there are examples of this which have quite high profiles, such as the 'Dublin multimedia experience' at Trinity College, Dublin.

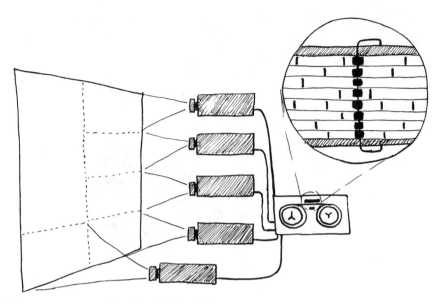

Figure 1.5   Multimedia slide wall.

It is possible to extend this model using more display devices of different types and an increasing range of complexity of control messages. It is worthy of note that MIDI (Musical Instrument Digital Interface) is essentially a highly sophisticated version of this, allowing the linear synchronization of a large number of event types on a large number of channels. MIDI will be discussed further in Chapter 8.

1.4.2   Branching systems

It is possible to move beyond linear presentation even without the use of a computer. This can be achieved by the use of a system which permits branching. In its simplest form, branching is a means of combining linear presentation segments such that there is a mechanism to choose between different segments at different points. Between branch points the system is still the sort of linear presentation discussed above. The easiest way to produce such a system is to give users a simple interface which they can operate at decision points to choose which of these linear presentations they wish to follow next. A simple map of a branching presentation might appear as shown in Figure 1.6.

An entertaining example of this from the early 1980s was a purely mechanical ATM (cash dispenser machine).

I used a particular machine at a bank in Coventry, UK. You placed your card into the machine as with a modern instance. There was a simple mechanical keyboard with numbers and a long roll of black cloth on which text messages were written. When you first came to the machine,

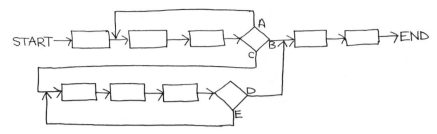

Figure 1.6　Branching flow chart.

the cloth would be positioned to show the message 'please enter your number'. If you did this successfully then the cloth would scroll up or down (literally, with little motors) until it displayed the message 'what service do you require?'. If you chose 'withdraw cash' then it would scroll to a message which said 'please enter the amount', but if you chose 'display balance' it would move to another part of the cloth which said 'your balance is …'.

This sort of interaction can also be controlled by tape – particularly if you have a tape recorder of the sort which can give itself instructions to move backwards and forwards along the reel of tape. This can be used with slide projectors to produce a branching visual experience, but because of the slowness of the projectors you either had to wait while the system went around until it found the correct slide, or you had to have a separate projector already loaded with the slides for each individual subsequence. There were severe practical limitations to this approach.

A further difficulty arises from the branching nature of the system. It is necessary to provide the linear sequence for each option that might be selected, but most of these may never be seen by a particular user. This makes the cost of such systems significantly higher than a simple linear system. There is also a problem in that one could potentially design an infinite (or at least a very large) range of options and costs could quickly become prohibitive, as could be the time needed for development. Consequently, mechanically controlled branching systems had a limited range of applications.

Can these systems fit our definition of multimedia? Of course they can. We can control a number of channels in different modalities to achieve co-ordination of channels. However, not all branching systems are automatically multimedia, as can be seen from the *teaching robot* example in the section on interaction.

1.4.3 Computer presented media

The above examples have the common feature that a set of media presentation devices (such as a slide projector) are controlled by a central device such as a tape recorder. This tape recorder could be replaced by a computer with no significant change to the multimedia nature of the systems (although there would be a significant change in the interaction). The step which permitted the computer to introduce a new form of multimedia (as opposed to *Interactive Multimedia*) was when the media moved from outside the computer to inside.

The prerequisite for moving beyond the simple controller model is that the media must be stored in a way in which the computer can have direct access, and the computer must be equipped with devices internally which permit it to display those media. There were two major changes required for this to happen: the *digitization of media* and the drastic *price reduction* of digital storage systems.

- *Digitization* of media means converting from other forms of storage, which are analogue, to represent media as a set of binary data which can be manipulated by the machine. There is one level at which text has been digital since the advent of computers, although text with print-like features did not become available until much later. Audio came next with the advent of digital studios, then still images began to move to digital formats, and the same process is now in progress with video.

- *Reduction in the price* of digital storage was key to this new phase in media. As far as multimedia is concerned, the big advantage of digitized media is that it can be accessed instantly by the controlling computer so there are no time lags in the display of particular combinations of media. This can only be achieved if the price of the storage mechanisms is sufficiently low to enable such storage. This is one of the main reasons why the sequence went text, audio, still image, video. Each requires a significantly greater amount of storage to be available than the previous one.

These are the major changes, so did they change multimedia? Remember that we are not talking about interaction yet. The change was due to instant access to the data. Digitized materials could be combined by the computer at speeds which were not possible with separate display devices, and could be integrated into a single whole. This speed meant that designers could do the previously impossible. With these facilities, a computer can now operate in a number of modalities and with quite a wide range of communication channels without having to resort to specialist devices. This permits a closer integration which also increases the range of potential methods for co-ordination of the channels and a more sophisticated cross-channel language of interpretation.

A related development is that digitization also meant that the cost of producing and copying various materials was significantly reduced, and hence the overall cost of a multimedia artefact became lower.

1.5   A brief history of computers and interaction

In this section we will briefly review some key aspects of computer interaction. We will start a long time before the first computers, in order to get a perspective on what it is that makes a computer a special kind of object, and will come up to the present. We will achieve this with a sequence of historical examples.

1.5.1   External memory

When human beings try to carry out a complex activity, one of the limitations upon their performance is the amount that they can hold in their memory at a given time. From the earliest points of human history humankind has sought to overcome this limitation by providing some form of external representation which can be used to augment the human memory. Simple graphical depictions and the development of written language can both be regarded as forms of memory. I may not be able to name all the states in the USA, but I know where to find a book which lists them for me. Consequently, my memory can be said to be extended by the contents of that book. Systems such as this can be regarded as analogous to human long-term memory, i.e. a place where things are stored which are intended to be retained for a very long period.

There is a somewhat different sort of memory, which is needed to retain things for a short period of time such as during the course of a calculation. It is reasonable to expect a human to multiply two two-digit numbers in their head, but not two 20-digit numbers. If we wish to do something like this, then we need to have another sort of external memory to help us. In the case of mathematics it is common to write down intermediate results on a scrap pad. This pad is thrown away when the calculation is complete, because the notes only have a meaning in the context of that calculation. The difference between the two sorts of memory is a bit like the difference between a mathematics reference book and a piece of scrap paper.

A famous example of a device created to be a form of external memory is the abacus. The positions of the beads on the different rows have a particular meaning which can be interpreted by the human user. They are like using a piece of scrap paper during a calculation. There are not many people who understand how to use an abacus these days. The reason is that it requires understanding of specific *algorithms* which are no longer commonly taught. An algorithm is a set of rules or procedures which tell us how to behave in order to get a certain effect. Many of us learnt to do multiplication through memorizing rules about 'borrowing' and 'carrying', but without really understanding what this meant. In effect, we have learnt an algorithm which we can apply but which we do not understand. Using an abacus is just applying a different algorithm (together with an external memory device) to the same end.

The idea of something (in this case human) which can *store* and *execute* an algorithm is the second key component to the behaviour of the sort of systems in which we are interested. Given an abacus and a human who knows the algorithms, they can together solve problems which neither component could solve individually. The whole is greater than the sum of its parts!

The seventeenth century saw the advent of the logarithm. This proved extremely important, because it enabled us to take a complex algorithm (multiplication) and replace it with a simple one (addition). Instead of trying to multiply two very large numbers, we could look up the logarithms and add them, then convert the result back into a number. This certainly made things easier for humans, but it had another important effect. It enabled mechanical devices to be constructed which could perform multiplication.

1.5.2 External algorithms

One device for performing multiplication mechanically is the slide rule (Figure 1.7). All a slide rule actually does is add lengths together. As an addition device it is not very exciting: 3 cm plus 5 cm equals 8 cm. However, when these lengths are marked with logarithmic scales we can add the lengths and say 3 cm times 5 cm is 15 cm. An important change has taken place here: the human is carrying out a simple mechanical task, while the object is doing the equivalent of a complex multiplication. In a sense the algorithm has become embodied in the artefact itself. The physical machine is a frozen algorithm.

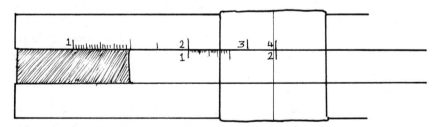

Figure 1.7 Slide rule.

The construction of a physical machine which embodies an algorithm, hence turning a complex task into a simple one for a human assisted by the machine, is a major step forward. It has the disadvantage, however, that it is necessary to construct a new machine for each specific algorithm that we want to execute. This can be a very costly process. The solution to this problem arose in the nineteenth century with the development of the *Jacquard loom*. A basic loom is a device which

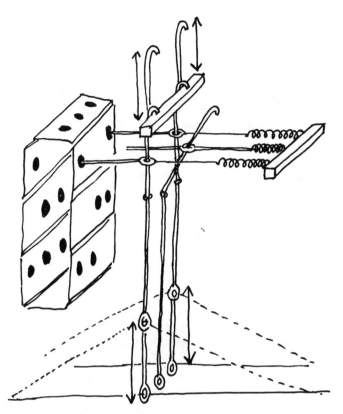

Figure 1.8   A Jacquard loom.

permits a human to weave a piece of cloth (Figure 1.8). Complex looms which were powered by humans permitted the user to create individual and unique patterns. The advent of machine-powered looms meant that weaving was faster, but patterns could not be varied because the machine had a fixed sequence of working. In effect, the problem was that the loom had been built to embody a fixed algorithm.

This was changed by the Jacquard loom. These looms were designed to be powered, but general purpose in that their motions were controlled by a stack of cards which had punched holes in them corresponding to the actions which should be performed (Figure 1.9). In order to change the pattern to which the loom was weaving, it was necessary to create a new set of cards with punched holes in them – this is much cheaper than building a new machine.

This idea – controlling the behaviour of a machine with a replaceable stack of cards – has had a remarkable longevity and has been applied across a number of areas. Most readers will be familiar with the steam-powered fairground organs which use a punch card system to control which tunes they play. It would be ridiculous to build a separate organ for each tune. Figure 1.10 shows an example of a card from such an organ.

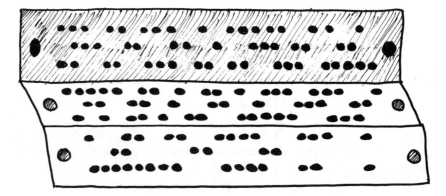

Figure 1.9   Loom punch card.

Moving across the card represents the passage of time, and a hole in the card indicates an action to be performed. What that action is is determined by the position across the width of the card. The top track, for example, may be a bass drum and the next may be a cymbal.

Fairground organs are something of a novelty now, but punchcards are still in use. In the 1990s there are still knitting machines which are controlled by punchcards in exactly the same way as the original loom. More surprisingly perhaps, the large computers of the 1950s used similar cards as a way of storing their programmes. This continued to be an important mechanism for computer programming until the early 1980s. We will return to this point later.

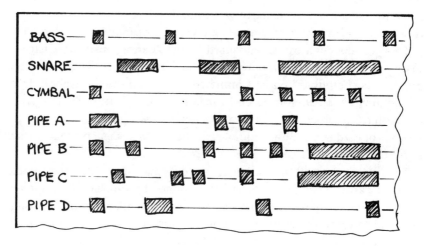

Figure 1.10   Organ punch card.

1.5.3 The first computer

It is generally agreed that the first 'computer' can be attributed to Charles Babbage in the nineteenth century. His first machine, the Difference Engine, was motivated by the need to produce accurate mathematical tables for purposes such as the navigation of ships. These tables were previously produced by hand and were slow to make and prone to error. Babbage realized that the mathematical equations which produced these tables could be embodied in a physical device which could then execute the calculations automatically. Although designed in the 1820s, the Difference Engine was not built until 1991, to mark the 200th anniversary of Babbage's birth. It was found that the drawings for the machine were almost perfect, with only two minor errors. The machine was not completed within the lifetime of its designer partly through lack of funds, and partly because it required mechanical components of a precision that had not been previously available. The attempts to produce it did much to advance approaches to precision engineering, however.

While the Difference Engine performed a particular calculation, Babbage went further and realized that it was possible to create a machine that would be capable of performing *any* mathematical operation. This machine, called the Analytical Engine, was even more difficult to construct and more expensive than the Difference Engine. It is important because it embodied the idea of a machine whose behaviour could be changed to carry out different calculations (i.e. it was programmable).

1.5.4 The electric brain

In the 1930s and 1940s the term 'computer' was commonly used to refer to a person who was employed to carry out repetitive mathematical calculations using a pen and a piece of paper. Companies would often employ rooms full of people whose job was to sit at a desk and carry out whatever calculations were given to them. During the same period, however, a significant step forward was made in the idea of what constitutes computation or a computer. Alan Turing in the UK and John von Neumann in the USA both came up with models which form the basis of modern computer science. They described a special sort of mathematics which encompassed the idea of a Universal Machine which could carry out any possible algorithm.

The combination of these theoretical insights with innovations in the new field of electronics (particularly the vacuum tube) and the urgency brought about by a wartime situation led to investment being made in the development, first of special purpose electronic calculating engines, and then of the first general purpose computers. These monsters were often called Electric Brains, Giant Brains, or Thinking Machines.

While there is not space to examine the history of this fascinating area in detail, it is worth commenting that the question of who produced the 'first' computer of the electronic age is much contested but essentially irrelevant. Within a period of four years, four machines were built, each of which was in some way 'first' because of its design. The computers of this era were COLOSSUS (1943), ENIAC (1946), BABY (1948), and EDSAC (1949). Despite their differences, they all contained core components recognizable as essential to a modern computer.

These machines had memory (short and long term), could store and execute algorithms, and had some means of interacting with a user. The machines were huge, clumsy, expensive, and unreliable. No one anticipated the changes in technology which would make such systems cheaper. Consequently it was not expected that there would ever be many computers in the world. The head of IBM (which used to make general office machinery) said:

> I think there is a world market for maybe five computers.
>
> Thomas Watson, Chairman of IBM, 1943

and in a moment of foresight, *Popular Mechanics* predicted:

> Computers in the future may weigh no more than 1.5 tons.
>
> *Popular Mechanics*, 1949

Because of the rarity of the machines and the cost of maintaining them, being a computer operator was a very specialized and rare job. It was not possible for just anyone to use a computer. Many science fiction books of the time envisage a future in which computer operators are the new aristocracy: an elite above the computer illiterate. One of the reasons that the job was so specialized was that these computers were extremely difficult to operate and to understand. The rarity and unreliability of machines meant that computer time was very expensive. As a consequence it needed to be devoted to the business of running algorithms which got results. There was no point in wasting computer time on trying to make the input and output more understandable to human beings. Humans were cheaper than a computer, and could learn to adapt to what the computer wanted rather than the other way around.

It is from this period that our original idea of a computer program arrives. It seems very strange these days to realize that these first computers were not in any sense interactive. If you were permitted to use a computer, then you first had to prepare your program – through a rather arcane process (which normally involved punching holes in cards or onto paper tape) – and then hand it over to the computer operators. At some point, when they and the machine had time, your program would be fed into the computer and executed. Your program would run and would produce some data which was then printed out. This would be sent back to you. Cycles such as this commonly took several days or sometimes weeks, and the normal result was to find that your program had not worked correctly because of some silly error that you had made, so you corrected this and started the cycle over again. This model of computing, in which each program was a job submitted by a user, and these jobs were put together and executed in groups called a batch was known as a batch processing. The term is still used for certain types of data processing activity.

During the 1950s and 1960s, computers became somewhat more common and computer time became less expensive. These machines were still the size of a room or two, and also required all sorts of specialized air conditioning, power supplies, and other facilities, but the proliferation of such systems meant that it was possible to look at other ways of using them. This is when the first interactive use of computers occurs. A large computer can optimize the use of its time by switching between several different jobs on a very small time scale. Hence a single processor can run several programs in 'simulated' parallel. By using a similar process, it is possible for several different users to talk to the same computer simultaneously, and for each user to believe that he or she has exclusive use of the machine. This is particularly the case when the interaction which the user can perform is so slow or restricted that the bottleneck which slows the system down is the user's ability to think and interact rather than the computer's ability to process. This feature, called 'time sharing' on a large machine enabled the move away from batch models to the first interactive processes.

The interface with the computer still included such items as a card reader and a paper tape punch, but now there was also a way of communicating data directly to the mainframe and getting responses from it as soon as it was ready with them. Initially the device used for such purposes was the teletype, which had already been developed for the telephone communications industry. In this system, the teletype consisted of an integrated keyboard and printer. Things that were typed on the keyboard were sent to the computer, and responses from the computer were printed on the printer (Figure 1.11).

This seems extremely primitive, but led to a drastic change in the use of computing technology. We still retain the legacy of the systems today with things such as the idea of a carriage return and a linefeed as two separate operations on a monitor (cathode ray tube) where they mean nothing, and the use of an 80-character wide screen. There is even a character in the normal computer character set which corresponds to ringing a bell to indicate that you have reached the end of the carriage on your printer! (Figure 1.12).

The major change resulting from all this innovation was that it was no longer the case that one wrote a program, ran it, and then received the results. It became possible to start a program, and for that program to interact with the user *while* it was still running. This meant that the

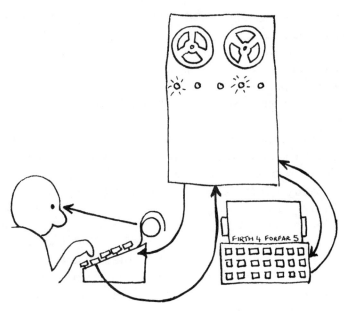

Figure 1.11   Teletype talks to computer.

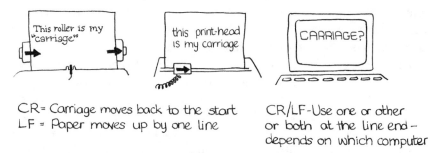

Figure 1.12   What do carriage return and line feed mean?

behaviour of the program could be changed during the course of its execution by interaction with the user. Until this point there had been no need for programming languages to include commands which obtained data from a user-controlled input device, because such things were not previously possible.

Initially, interaction progressed through the use of keyboard and printer on the teletype. The computer could, for example, print questions, to which the user responded via the keyboard. This permitted a broader range of interaction, but was still severely limited. The next important step was the move away from the teletype to a cathode ray tube (CRT) based monitor. These were still divided into 80 characters width and 25 characters high in emulation of the printer, but soon special commands were being added, which enabled programs to control where text appeared on the screen. This meant that the idea of a scrolling screen of text could be removed as it became possible to overwrite different regions to provide visual organization (Figure 1.13).

Prior to the first visually oriented interfaces, all computers operated via a command line (Figure 1.14). The user had to have a detailed model of how the machine worked and a good memory for all the things that they could do. There are still command lines under the DOS and Unix operating systems, but they are no longer the only (or even the main) way of interacting with a computer.

While the command line permitted a user to issue instructions to a computer which were immediately carried out, it required users to have a lot of specialist knowledge, and hence did not make the computer widely accessible. The importance of visually oriented interfaces is that they can provide an on-screen reminder of key commands and options (Figure 1.15). This makes it easier for a less expert user, or one with a poorer memory, to use the computer. Simple text-based, but visually organized interfaces made the computer much more accessible. Interaction, while still via the keyboard, normally used special keys to modify the behaviour of the alphabetic keys and turn them into short

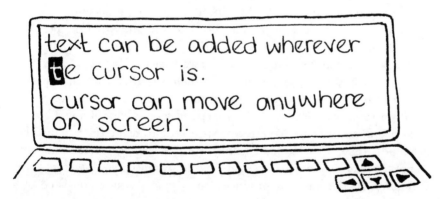

Figure 1.13   A screen.

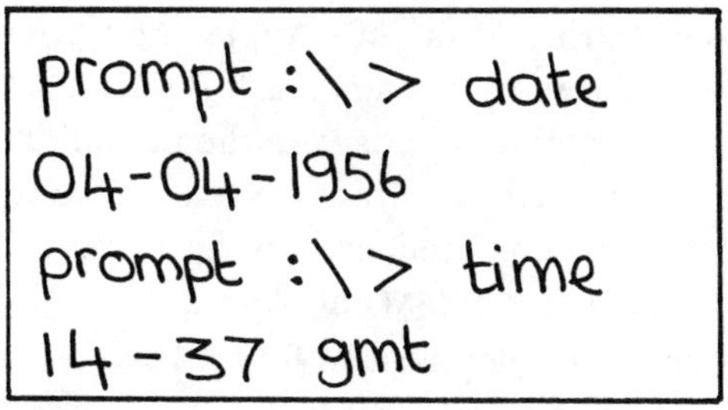

prompt :\\> date
04-04-1956
prompt :\\> time
14-37 gmt

Figure 1.14   A command line interface.

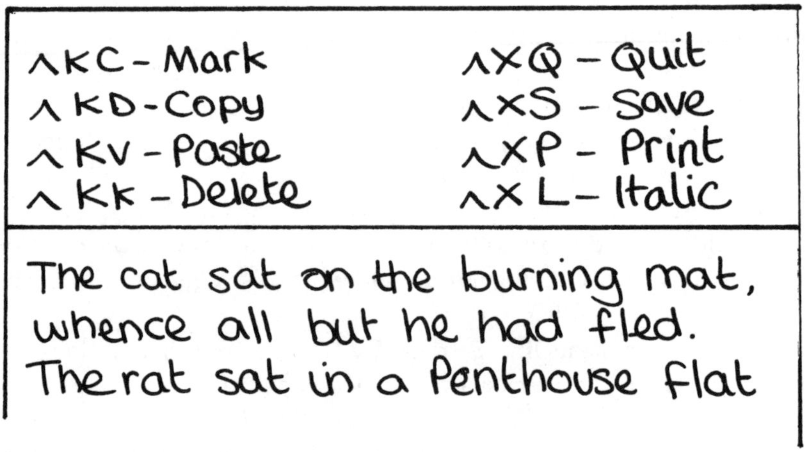

Figure 1.15   Visually organized interface.

commands. Even more exciting was the introduction of cursor keys which enabled the user to move around the screen to different points.

Specialist computers did have the possibility to produce simple graphics via a plotter or a sophisticated screen, but these were not widely available. A big transformation happened in the computing market when the conjunction of reduced computing costs and increased technological awareness resulted in the birth and growth of the personal computer market. Beginning in the early 1970s, a number of companies produced personal computers which were basically boxes of electronic components and a circuit board to put them together with. It appealed only to people whose hobby was electronics. The computers were very small (in terms of memory and power) and were almost impossible for most people to operate. No attempt was made to make the use of these machines easy for inexpert humans. The move towards making computers more widely accessible was essentially due to Apple Computer. In the 1970s it produced the *Apple I* which consisted of a computer on a single board (Figure 1.16 and Figure 1.17), hidden away in a nice plastic box with curly corners, a built-in keyboard, and a wire to connect to your television. Suddenly people other than hobbyists were buying personal computers, despite their excessive price. Other companies followed the lead of Apple and the market grew phenomenally fast. Subsequent versions of this machine introduced colour to the monitor, simple sounds, and the possibility of printing out what you saw on the screen. Gradually, the number of companies producing personal computers reduced until it became effectively a two-company competition between IBM and Apple.

The most significant development to follow this, was the introduction of the Apple Macintosh (Figure 1.18). Just as Apple had led the way with computers that had customer friendly packaging, it led the way with the

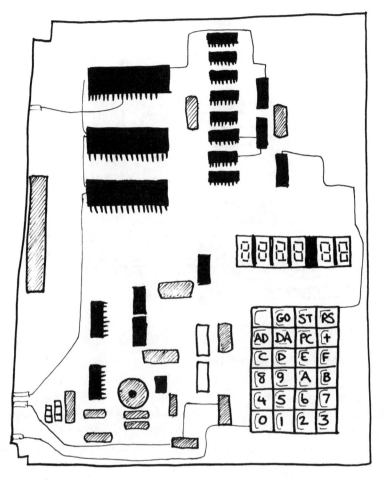

Figure 1.16   A computer on a board.

Figure 1.17   An Apple I or II.

Figure 1.18   Apple Mac, screen and box.

Mac by taking a number of design principles from Xerox and putting them into a mass market computer for the first time. We shall learn more about these in Chapter 5, but for the moment we should note that this was the first application of a desktop metaphor designed to appeal to non-computer users. It introduced the idea of *windows* on the screen, dividing it into regions. It introduced *icons* to symbolize different commands. It introduced *menus* to provide the visual groupings of commands. It introduced the *pointing device* – most commonly a mouse these days, but a class which includes joystick, touch pad, trackball, etc.

These are still the main interface devices that are with us at the moment, and we have not fully exploited the range of interactions that can be achieved with them. However, for the future there are many more possibilities. Being able to talk to a computer, gesture and to move around physically, use facial expression and handwriting, are all existing technologies which are changing the way we work (Figure 1.19). The story of how to interact with computers is certainly not completed yet.

1.6   So – what is IMM?

In this chapter, we have explored the two main components of *Interactive Multimedia*. First, we have examined the idea of multimedia and a brief history of the use of multimedia. Subsequently, we have looked at an idea of interaction and a brief history of how the user can interact with a computer. The idea of *Interactive Multimedia* as an evolving subject has been introduced. More specifically, we are

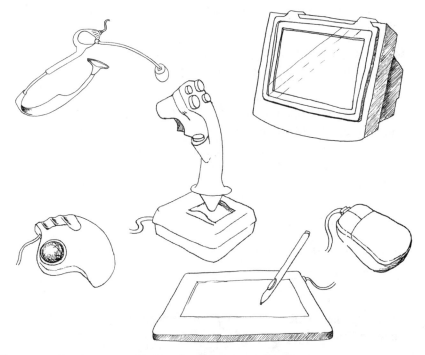

Figure 1.19 A range of input devices on a computer.

proposing that it is the interaction itself which is key to the existence of systems in this category, and, as we shall see, that this interaction is the defining feature of the *Interactive Multimedia* system. It was stated at the beginning of the book that we would not provide a definition of *Interactive Multimedia*, but would seek to help readers discover it for themselves. We have provided much of the background in this chapter, and Chapters 2 to 5 examine in more detail the components of such a system. We will commence with a more detailed exploration of *communicative interaction*.

1.7 Exercises

Each of the following exercises relates to material in particular sections of this chapter. They are each intended to open up general areas of discussion and are best tackled in a group, if possible.

Exercise 1.1 Note down some of the communications that you received during the course of a day. For each one, identify the modality or modalities in which they operate. How many of these communications would you regard as being a single 'medium'?

Exercise 1.2 Pick some activities that are going on around you during the day and involve some form of communication. See if you can identify which channels of communication they are using. How long would it take you to write a comprehensive list of all the channels of communication that exist?

Exercise 1.3 It is often suggested that 'a picture is worth a thousand words'. Is there anything in this chapter to support or disprove that view?

Exercise 1.4 Identify a number of things that are generally referred to as a medium. You could write a list yourself, or try asking other people for their ideas. How many of them fit with the definitions in this chapter? For each of them, can you identify the modalities and channels of communication? Which are one way, and which are interactive?

1.8 Further reading

Paul E. Ceruzzi, *A History of Modern Computing*, MIT Press, 2000

Martin Campbell-Kelly and William Aspray, *Computer: A History of the Information Machine*, Basic Books, 1997

Herman H. Goldstine, *The computer from Pascal to Von Neumann*, Princeton University Press, 1980

Andrew Hodges, *Alan Turing: The Enigma*, Vintage Paperback, 1992
   A biography of Turing, but it helps to give a flavour of British work in computing and balance the over-American perspective of the other texts.

2

Communicative interaction

2.1 Introduction

In the previous chapter we introduced some historical ideas related to multimedia and Interactive Systems, and provided a definition of multimedia which was based around the use of modalities and channels of communication. The definition of multimedia offered was perfectly capable of encompassing one-way multimedia experiences, in which the human is a 'recipient' of an experience provided by some multimedia device such as a computer. We briefly outlined an idea of types of interaction more sophisticated than a simple 'next' button and alluded to the way that these interactions require a model of the participants as 'agents'.

In this chapter we will take these issues further, examining the nature of interaction in more detail and exploring the communication processes essential to a successful interaction between any two agents. The way that examples from the human world impact upon the development of multimedia will be explained. Through these approaches we will demonstrate the central importance of interaction in the design of any multimedia system. We will then expand upon mechanisms which can be used to design and implement such interactions, managing the channels of communication effectively.

In general terms, the argument will be that interaction is the central component of any multimedia system, as shown in Figure 2.1. The nature and requirements of other components of our system are all determined by the needs of the interaction and the way that the components are applied in that interaction. This chapter places a great emphasis on the idea of language, because this is a key way to think of

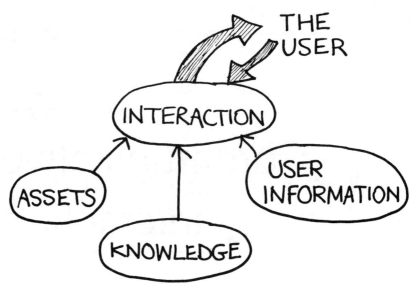

Figure 2.1   Components of interactive multimedia.

interaction, and will be applied in a variety of forms to every component of our system.

2.2   Objects and agents

In Chapter 1 we briefly introduced an idea of what is meant by *interaction*, which attempted to be more precise than the commonly used definitions. In particular, we made a distinction between *thoughts*, *actions*, and *interactions*. We then went further and divided interaction into two types: *physical* and *communicative*. In making this distinction the idea of an *agent* was simply assumed. This section will explore these ideas in more detail as the basis for our definition of Communicative Interaction (Figure 2.2).

Consider the following terms, which have been arranged in increasing order of complexity:

Passive – being acted upon by something else. Inert.
Reactive – acting in response to a stimulus (an action by something else).
Active – initiating activity spontaneously. Independent.
Pro-active – initiating activity based upon anticipation of future events.
Interactive – mutual influence or interaction between two or more systems.

If we reconsider the distinctions of the previous chapter, we separated thought, action, and interaction partly by distinguishing the worlds in which they had effects. Some things have an effect in the physical world

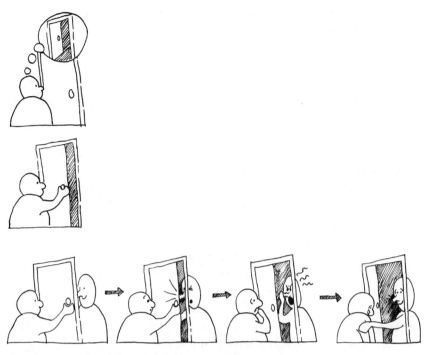

Figure 2.2 Thought, action, interaction.

(*actions*), some in the mental world (*thoughts*), but some (*interactions*) can potentially have effects in both.

A *passive* system remains in a state of doing nothing until some other system acts upon it. A rock is pretty passive. It does nothing. If you kick it, it moves but that is not a reaction, just a consequence of your action (as is the pain in your foot!).

A *reactive* system is something which does something in response to an action upon it. An example might be a thermostat, which switches on or off depending upon the temperature. The thermostat is reacting to the change in temperature.

An *active* system is capable of engaging in actions without it being the direct response to an action performed on the system. An alarm clock might be such a system, since it can suddenly start ringing. If you take the system apart, however, you find that the bits are not necessarily active – the bell is reactive and the hands set off a trigger. What this system has is some sort of *internal state* which can trigger actions. In this case it is a spring unwinding, but it could be sand falling through a glass, or water dripping, or a computer clock – the point is that the system maintains some sort of dynamic state internally, and changes in that internal state can trigger actions.

A *pro-active* system is much more complicated. This is a system which responds not to actions performed upon it, or to some simple internal state, but to some anticipated future state (either internal or external). These systems carry out actions intending to bring about, or to prevent, that future state. They must therefore have an internal state, and some sort of reasoning mechanism which can be applied to that state to determine future possibilities and their desirability or otherwise. In short, they must have *goals*, and *actively plan* to achieve those goals. We will refer to systems which possess an internal state about which they can reason as systems with a *mental state*.

In summary then, we are concluding that interaction requires two or more systems which are, at the absolute minimum, reactive. It is more likely that at least one of them will be active. This is the minimum requirement for physical interaction. When we are considering Communicative Interaction, we additionally require that each system has a *mental state*, and the interacting systems have definite *intentions* with regard to achieving changes in the internal state of other systems. This combination of an internal state and a structure of intentions constitutes a class of system which we will refer to as an *agent*.

For most of history it has been assumed that humans were the only systems with these properties (apart from essentially 'human' mythological figures, such as gods). Studies in the behaviour of animals have indicated that there is a powerful distinction between animals which have an accessible mental state, and those which do not. Our close relatives, the apes, and creatures such as dolphins and whales, all demonstrate an awareness of themselves as individuals, recognize others as separate, have concepts of 'life' and 'death', and possess language skills, which indicate a sophisticated knowledge of the self and hence an internal mental state. Other animals, such as dogs and cats, possess simple intentions (e.g. 'I want this human to feed me'), but there is no indication of self-awareness. Simpler animals seem to be even more lacking in these regards.

The twentieth century has seen the introduction of an extra level of complication, which has made our idea of agent necessary. This is the idea of the computer. The computer itself is just a box of bits which has certain actions built into it, and which is purely reactive. When software is added the behaviour changes. The resulting combination of hardware and software may still be reactive, or it may now have become active or pro-active depending on how the software is written and what it does. Significantly, it may, with some pieces of software, acquire an internal mental state and a set of intentions. In other words, *some* combinations of computer hardware and software are capable of acting as *agents*, and it is these systems that are capable of engaging in *Communicative Interaction* (Figure 2.3). There is no reason to suppose that humans are significantly different from these systems, and our term *agent* may encompass humans, certain computer systems, and certain higher animals (and probably little grey aliens).

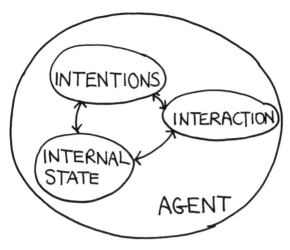

Figure 2.3   Components of an agent.

2.3   Channels of communication

Having now established what we mean by the term agent, we can return
to a clarification of the concepts in the previous chapter.

Our definition of multimedia relied upon the use of the idea of *channels
of communication*. It is essential to be precise about the use of this term if
the definition is to be meaningfully applied. Now that we have the idea
of interaction between two (or more) agents we can expand our
definition based upon an extremely precise view of the channel of
communication.

The essential concept is that some agent, which has something that it
wishes to communicate to another agent (i.e. an intention to communicate), selects a single modality through which to transmit the
information, encodes it in a particular form, and transmits it. Another
agent (the recipient) receives the encoded signal and engages in a process
of decoding to turn it back into a comprehensible form. Simple examples
might be encoding something in Morse code for transmission over an
analogue radio frequency, utilizing semaphore code with flags over the
visual modality, or speaking in English in the auditory modality. In this
process we are assuming that both the agents have access to an encoder
and decoder which is effectively perfect and that no errors arise during
the process of transmission. This means that the input which the first
agent sends into its encoder should be identical with the output that the
second agent receives from its decoder – there is no question of a process
of 'interpretation' here. The interpretation is performed outside the
channel of communication as we define it.

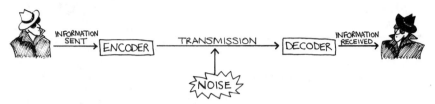

Figure 2.4   Shannon and Weaver model.

This idea derives from the field of information theory which was popular in the late 1950s and early 1960s. The classic definition of a similar system is that of Shannon and Weaver, illustrated in Figure 2.4. Here, a source sends a signal through an encoder to create a message which is transmitted along a channel. At the other end of the channel a decoder translates the message into a form which is given to the receiver. An additional component in this diagram, which we have not been considering, is a source of 'noise' – basically a cause of errors occurring during the communication process. Being able to equate our channels of communication with the equivalent in information theory provides a precise base because the information theoretic model is highly mathematical and can be used to examine many properties of our channels. We do not have the space to go into detail here, but bear in mind that information theory underpins many aspects of electronics and telecommunications. Concepts which we use daily, such as *bandwidth* or *signal-to-noise ratio* are actually information theoretic terms.

Channels must exist between our agents in both directions if interaction is to take place. This does not require, however, that any given channel must be bi-directional. If Agent 1 can talk to Agent 2 in English, and be understood, whereas Agent 2 talks in Spanish and is still understood by Agent 1, we have a potential communicative interaction, even though neither of the actual channels used is bi-directional.

Information theory does not require the concept of an agent in order to have an information channel: only a source and receiver. For our definition we do require agents because our idea of Communicative Interaction also requires that the received messages are *interpreted*, that some change in mental state happens, and that (probably) some corresponding communication is generated as a response.

Rather than trying to extend our idea of a channel, we will assume that the channel remains simple, but that a process of interpretation works upon the output messages from this channel. To understand what we mean by a process of interpretation we will turn to another key idea in communication: that of language. The following two sections explore the classes of *artificial* languages, which humans have created and the class of *natural* languages, which humans learn as they grow up.

2.4 Artificial languages

The previous section clarified the idea of a channel of communication in information theory terms. This concentrated upon the transmission of information between a source and destination, and the processes of encoding and decoding which occur at those respective locations. The model provides a useful underpinning to our interactive systems, but is of limited use until we can relate the received information to some sort of interpretation which gives it meaning. To this end we will examine the space of languages in greater detail.

2.4.1 What is an artificial language?

An artificial language consists of a set of symbols, which have been defined by someone as constituting a language. There will be rules to tell you which symbols are allowed in the language, rules describing ways that the symbols may be combined, and rules that enable the meaning of symbols and combinations of symbols to be determined. Anyone can make up a set of such rules, but we are normally only interested in systems which have a certain level of consistency and expressive power – a language which satisfies the requirements of being a formal system. When we are talking about a formal system we expect it to be clearly defined such that it is unambiguous and so that the scope of it is clearly delimited. We will normally expect there to be some way of reasoning about the system to prove its consistency, expressiveness, and power.

We all use formal languages on a regular basis. The most obvious is mathematics. We recognize 3 + 4 as a legal piece of mathematics with a meaning, but × + / is not acceptable (in day-to-day mathematics). Other examples of formal languages are programming languages and logics.

In every case, we can divide the definition of our formal language into three components: lexicon, syntax, and semantics.

2.4.1.1 Lexicon

The lexicon defines the primitive symbols that we are allowed to have in our language. It is a bit like a dictionary, but contains less, because there are no definitions of words and no information about how they fit together. In some cases, it may just be an exhaustive list of symbols which cover everything in the language, for example:

A, the, dog, ball, red, hamster, furry, sandwich

but it is more common to also have a small number of terms which can be defined by the user. In these cases the way that the terms are constructed is defined by rules such as:

```
basic-integer ::= [0..9]
integer ::= basic-integer *
```

This translates as 'An integer is one or more basic-integers in sequence. A basic-integer is one of 0, 1, 2, 3, 4, 5, 6, 7, 8, 9'.

Most languages have some sort of thing that can be named, such as variables, functions, etc. The rules for these things (which are often called atoms) are generally something like:

Atom ::= [a..z][a..z | 0..9]*

Which would translate as 'an atom consists of a lower-case alphabetic character followed by any number of things which are either lower-case alphabetic characters or numbers'.

We will use rules similar to these very extensively throughout the book, so it is worth getting used to them now. They consist of a left-hand side and a right-hand side separated by some dividing character (in this case ::=) and can generally be read as 'The thing on the left consists of the thing(s) on the right'. There may be things on the right which are also defined by their own rule (as in our integer example) or 'literals', such as 1 or X. These can be combined using a variety of special symbols which we will explore later in this chapter, but which have meanings like 'and', 'or', 'repeat zero or more times'.

In summary, every language will have a lexicon which consists of some list of literal symbols to be included in the language and possibly some rules describing how certain other symbols can be created legally.

2.4.1.2   Syntax

While the lexicon tells us which symbols can be used in a language, it doesn't tell us how we can combine those symbols to produce bigger things. In English we can say:

The red dog

But with the same lexicon we can say:

Dog red the, dog the red, the dog red, etc.

and these are not English. Any language is controlled by a set of rules that put constraints upon the order in which the symbols can be combined to produce bigger structures in the language (such as sentences). This typically involves assigning each symbol to a *syntactic category* (e.g. noun or verb in English) and then providing a set of rules which determine how the different categories can be combined. These rules are called the *grammar* of the language.

In our tiny bit of English, we can assign the following syntactic categories:

Determiner (det) : The, a
Adjective (Adj) : red, furry, cabin
Noun (N): boy, dog, hamster
Proper_Noun (pnoun): Roger, Lucinda

You probably recall from school that a noun is a word which names something, while a proper noun is a name for a particular person. An adjective describes something and a determiner identifies how many of it there is and whether it is a specific or general thing. To produce a grammar which describes the legal combination of these categories we could use a single rule which is:

Noun_Phrase ::= pnoun | (det adj N)

This rule translates to 'A noun phrase consists of a proper noun or a determiner followed by an adjective followed by a noun'. It will allow us to say *the red dog*, but will prevent us from saying *the dog red* because dog is not an adjective and red is not a noun. It is normal to express the way that the rules are applied to a particular sentence in the language with a diagram called a parse tree, which shows how the rules are used on a particular occasion. Figure 2.5 illustrates this for our current English subset, giving two different noun phrases 'Roger', 'The cabin boy'.

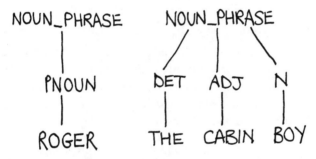

Figure 2.5   Simple English parse tree.

Exactly the same approach of rules can be applied in mathematics. Here is a simple grammar for arithmetic expressions:

Exp ::= (exp op exp) | integer
Op ::= + | − | × | /

And so the expression $2 \times 3 + 4 \times 5$ would appear as in Figure 2.6.

We can use exactly the same approach with an artificial language such as a programming language. Consider this fragment:

```
For i = 1 to 10
{print i;
print i*i}
```

Whole programming languages are quite easily defined with a grammar, but here we will just use a small fragment. For clarity we have shown the terminal symbols (those which do not have rules for them) in bold.

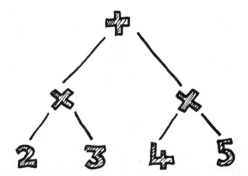

Figure 2.6   Simple maths parse tree.

> For_loop ::= **For** var **=** int **to** int cmd_block
> Cmd_block ::= **{** cmd [**;** cmd] **}**
> Cmd ::= **print** exp

Notice that special keywords like 'For' and symbols like '{' are part of the lexicon. This grammar would produce the parse tree in Figure 2.7.

2.4.1.3   Semantics

The grammar of the language tells us which combinations of lexical items are syntactically correct or incorrect. Consequently, it is possible to identify things which are 'wrong' because they do not follow the rules of the grammar. Syntax does not help us, however, when we are confronted with a sentence such as:

> Angry refrigerators knit aluminium socks

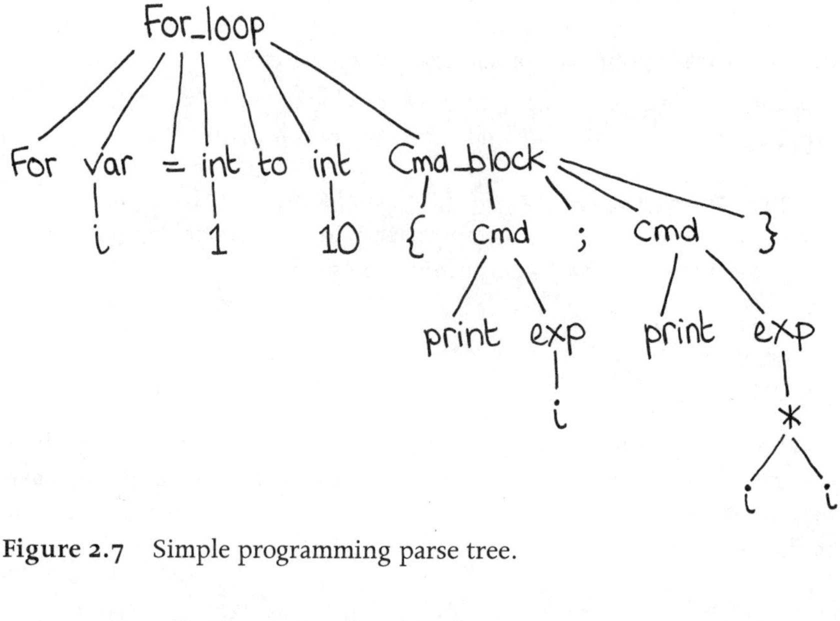

Figure 2.7   Simple programming parse tree.

In this case the sentence is correct from the grammatical point of view. All the verbs, nouns, adjectives, etc. are in the right order and have been combined legally. The sentence fails to work not because of the syntax, but because no meaning can be determined from it. In order to understand how languages work at this level, it is necessary to extend our model by adding another component – the *semantics* or the *theory of meaning*.

The semantics permits us to assign meaning to individual items in our lexicon, and to combinations of such items. Note that any individual lexical items will probably have more than one meaning and that in most cases meaning can only be determined by examining the context in which a particular word is used. Formally representing and describing semantics is much more difficult than syntax. We will introduce two basic approaches to semantics used in computer science.

Operational semantics describes the meaning of something in terms of 'operations'. It works on the idea that we describe some primitive set of actions which we know how to carry out, and the semantics of an expression in any programming language is then expressed as the set of actions in our primitive set which would do the corresponding thing. This is a fundamental idea in computing and one which is actually a lot more complicated than it looks: the semantics should be such that a *for* loop, a *while* loop and a *repeat* loop that do the same thing in a particular case should translate into the same set of primitive actions. None the less, we can ignore some of these complexities and just assume for the moment that operational semantics is about translating everything into a set of primitive actions.

Axiomatic semantics are systems based upon a mathematical logic. These systems also assume that there is a world, which is in some sort of 'state'. The meaning of an expression is given as a set of logical rules which express the difference between the state of the world before the action is executed and the state afterwards. The meaning of a large program is determined by reasoning about the combined effect of the meanings of its components upon the state of the world.

2.4.2 Types of formal language

The distinction between the different sorts of semantics used in the previous section enables us to divide languages into distinct categories. In particular, we can distinguish *procedural* languages in which the lexical units and sentences have a meaning which corresponds to a set of actions, from *declarative* languages in which the meaning is, in effect, a description of something.

Procedural languages   include most of the languages that are understood by a computer and are referred to as *programming languages*. These languages are ways of giving instructions to the computer about actions which it should perform. The machine already knows how to carry out a 'primitive' set of actions (which are written into the hardware of the CPU) and these languages group such actions together in novel ways in order to achieve larger and more complex objectives. For example, the language LOGO would define a new action to draw a square as:

```
to square :side
Repeat 4
Forward :side
Right 90
End repeat
```

Declarative languages are more concerned with expressing statements about things and the relationships between things. These languages require some particular process of *interpretation* to be applied if it is expected that an agent will take some action based upon these languages. Declarative languages and processes of interpretation are central to our model of communicative interaction.

Currently the most familiar examples of declarative languages would be the set of *page description languages*. For most people, this would mean something such as HTML. The majority of people are now aware of this language, which lies behind the world-wide web. HTML itself is a declarative language which describes the nature of the elements which appear on a web page and the relationship between them. It captures structural ideas such as *paragraph*, *heading*, or *table entry*. It has a clear and simple lexicon, a simple syntax, and a precise semantics. HTML is not a language in which the elements automatically have a meaning in terms of the actions of the computer. Lexical items such as *H*1 ('A heading of importance 1') may be interpreted on one machine to mean a centred 14-point heading in Arial Black, and on another machine to be 12-point red italic heading in Times. In either case, the HTML is unchanged because it is describing elements and the relationship between them. The actions which our computer performs in order to display something based upon HTML is the result of an *interpreter* which examines the declarative language and makes its own decisions about how it wishes to display the page described by that language. This interpreter is called a *web browser*. Differences of interpretation in different browsers mean that it is perfectly possible for the same browser on two different hardware platforms to produce different visual renderings of a page, or for two different browsers on the same platform to produce different renderings. It is also the case that the interpreter used to produce a rendering on the screen is different from that which is used if you try to print a web page on paper. Special function browsers, such as purely auditory ones for the visually impaired, or Braille output browsers, will interpret the HTML in a very different way from a conventional screen-based browser. The important point here is that in all cases the descriptive language (HTML description of the page) remains unchanged. It is the interpretation made of that language which causes the variations.

```
<table>
<tr><th>Date</th><th>Time</th></tr>
<tr><td>12-5-00</td><td>11.00</td></tr>
<tr><td>12-6-00</td><td>15.00</td></tr>
</tabe>
```

This description basically says: A table with two columns, one called 'Date' and one called 'Time', then two rows, each of which contains two pieces of data. The point is that this is a description of the structure. It does not say how it is to be interpreted or displayed, or indicate any actions to be performed. It is purely a declarative language.

2.5 'Natural' communication

Formal languages form a basis for communication which can be used to interpret the meanings on a single channel of communication. They also have the advantage that, because they are precisely defined, we can reasonably hope to create a computer that can use these languages. Interacting with a computer (or getting it to talk to you) in mathematics, programming languages, or simplified 'English-like' languages as described above is perfectly plausible, although by no means all the problems of these formal languages have been resolved. However, each of these languages is only accessible to the humans who understand it. Even for people who have learnt one of these languages it is often difficult to communicate with a computer – for example, it is easier to tell another human how to perform a complex calculation than it is to program a computer to do the same thing. Humans allow you to use shorthand and applies their intelligence to understanding what you mean, rather than what you literally say. Consequently, the interaction is generally shorter, and apparently easier and more effective. For this reason, among others, it seems sensible to look at the way human beings communicate between themselves and to see whether we can get the computer to participate in the same process.

This idea of examining 'natural' communication between humans and applying it to computers was very popular in the 1960s. As with many things which were attempted as part of artificial intelligence, speaking seems so simple and natural for human beings that it was initially imagined that making a computer do the same thing would be straightforward. In fact, after billions of dollars was spent, the major outcome was to discover that the problem was much harder than was originally imagined. Even today most of the issues surrounding computational models of human–human communication are still in flux.

None the less, there are still aspects of human dialogue that can inform our design of communication systems for interactive multimedia. We will now examine some of these issues.

2.5.1 Psycholinguistic models of communication

The approaches to studying natural language (i.e. the languages which human beings speak) are primarily based upon concepts similar to those that are used in formal languages, but have differences of detail, complexity, and stage of development.

Our first step must be to identify the channels of communication through which natural language is communicated. We may be referring to spoken language or written language. In each case, we are assuming that the sender is putting a message onto the channel and the receiver is obtaining it and decoding it. Even at this stage, before any interpretation has taken place, there are problems. Loosely speaking, people do not speak and write in the same way, even if they are communicating the same thing.

A written-text channel is the only communication between sender and receiver. It can (normally) be reviewed by either party to see previous history (e.g. flicking back a couple of pages in the book) but it is an isolated channel which does not relate to others. By contrast, the spoken channel is a linear stream of noise which cannot be 'wound back' to hear what the speaker said three minutes ago. This means that there tends to be a greater redundancy of information when using this channel, and the speaker tends to encourage more interaction, checking that the hearer is following what is said by breaking things into smaller segments and seeking feedback from them frequently. In addition, the spoken channel is not (typically) used alone, but in conjunction with other channels such as facial and body gestures which transmit synchronized information. The channel also includes details of intonation, pauses, etc., which provide an additional richness of communication over the written word. The following channels all communicate words of natural language, but they are all using different channels with different properties which affect what can be said and understood effectively.

- *Textbook*: printed page – random access (can go back and forth), large quantity of connected/related material which is carefully organized and prepared for a particular audience with particular needs in mind. High-quality, grammatical English.

- *Email*: short, fairly informal, often ungrammatical, has developed certain special conventions to replace things that cannot be otherwise communicated :=).

- *Simple 'chat' facility* (without a history): ephemeral world in which a typed sentence is lost forever. Very slow, so much use of abbreviations and almost never complete sentences.

- *Chat room*: as above but multiple users can participate and there is a transcript of what has happened so you can refer back easily. Lots of potential for interruption and confusion.

- *Telephone*: almost perfect turn taking. Words are augmented by inflection and prosody information.

- *Video telephone*: surprisingly, the video image adds little to the communication of a phone, since the screens are too small to see much facial expression and the body language is still not visible.

- *Face to face*: words with prosody and intonation, enhanced by spatial expressions, body language, and the ability of the listener to communicate with the hearer through other channels without speaking (e.g. an 'I am bored' expression).

One further point will serve to illustrate this. When we listen to our 'mother tongue' (i.e. the first natural language that we learn) being spoken by someone, we think that we hear separate words. It is as though the words we would read on a page are coming into our ears one at a time, with pauses between them. In reality, if you look at the waveform produced by someone speaking a natural language, it is continuous – the 'pauses' that we hear between words do not really exist. Try listening to a fluent speaker of a language you do not know, and you will quickly realize how difficult it is to tell where one word ends and another begins if you do not understand the words. One of the things that was discovered in the 1960s was that this recognition of 'gaps' is a major problem which can only be solved by clever reasoning, and much money was invested in trying to get computers to identify the gaps between words. It was not until the late 1990s that this technology became accurate enough and cheap enough for most people to have access to it, however, and the computer is still not understanding natural language, but transcoding it, from a channel on which it is coded as audio waves to a channel on which it is coded as ASCII text (Figure 2.8). All this channel processing needs to be done before we can even examine the language itself.

As with the formal languages, natural languages are regarded as having a lexicon and a syntax. Unlike formal languages, however, both of these aspects change over time (though slowly).

From the lexical perspective, each new edition of the *Oxford English Dictionary* will include a few hundred new words that have joined the language, or words whose meaning has changed. Some words will be dropped because they are no longer in use. In some countries (e.g. France, Iceland) there are formal committees who meet regularly to consider words and decide whether to admit them into the official language. Certain adopted English words are problematic in French (e.g. 'Le Parking', 'Le Weekend', 'Le Zapper') and may not be used in official

Figure 2.8 Transcoding diagram.

documents, though it is much harder to prevent people using them day to day. By contrast, such a policy could not possibly be adopted in English since the entire vocabulary seems to have been stolen from other languages!

The grammar of English is complex and has not been completely codified. Most everyday English has been expressed as a grammar, but there remain a few rare and bizarre constructions that are still areas of research and debate. This need not concern us here. More significantly, the English which has been formally specified is still unlike the English that many of us use most of the time. There is a 'correct' English – which we get closest to when we write in an official context, but there are the 'real' versions of English that we use day to day. Listen to someone talk for example, and see how often you hear sentences without verbs, or sentences which never end. Psycholinguists distinguish between 'competence' and 'performance' in a language – between the 'perfect' model and the actual language used by an individual.

As with formal languages, semantics is a difficult problem in English. It is not always apparent that the meaning of a sentence can be constructed from the meanings of its constituent parts. Interpretations seem to be highly dependent upon the context in which words are used. Consequently, while there is considerable work on semantic approaches to natural languages, there is also a range of approaches based upon recognizing that what the sentence appears to mean (the 'surface form') is often quite different from the way it is intended to be used (the 'deep structure'). This distinction between the way the language appears to work and what is actually being communicated is something which does not happen in the formal languages that we have presented earlier (indeed, they are designed specifically to avoid such differences). This process is very human, and is important in all aspects of human communication, so we shall examine it further in the next section.

2.5.2 Beyond surface form

We are all familiar with situations in which miscommunication occurs, but there are certain cases that are worth examining more closely because of the clue that they give about how we use language. Children are fond of jokes such as when one person says 'Have you got the time?' and the other replies 'Yes' and walks away. An alternative example is when sitting at table and someone asks 'Can you pass the salt?' and you reply 'Yes' rather than doing it. What is interesting in these cases is that there seems to be nothing wrong at first sight – 'Can you pass the salt?' is a question, and 'Yes' is an answer. If the communication had been 'Pass the salt' then it would have been an *instruction* and carrying out the action would have been the right thing to do. What these examples tell us is that, even with an understanding of syntax and semantics, we are not reaching the complete story about human language.

An important concept in understanding this form of communication is 'speech acts'. These are actions which are achieved by the use of words. One of the most obvious examples is naming a ship – by saying the words 'I name this ship the Black Pig' you are actually carrying out the naming action. It becomes apparent that the role which these utterances serve is something separate from the words that are used and, in particular, there are certain *intentions* behind them which are communicated. Sometimes the intentions can be derived from the syntax and semantics, but often it depends upon context and upon conventions which have arisen around our use of language. These larger structures in language were identified as having a major effect on the meaning of any communication. One example is the (apparently obvious, but actually complex) idea that a question is generally followed by an answer.

Consider these:

Example 1:   (A) Are you coming to the movies?
                      (B) Yes.

Example 2:   (A) Are you coming to the movies?
                      (B) What's on?
                      (A) Creature from the Black Lagoon.
                      (B) Yes.

Example 3:   (A) Are you coming to the movies?
                      (B) When did Captain Scott go to the Antarctic?
                      (A) 1910.
                      (B) Yes.

The first example is a question followed by an answer, and we can see that they are related. The answer responds to an issue raised in the question. In the second example, the response to the question is not an answer, but another question. However, we can see that this question might be legitimate in preparing an answer to the first question. It might be seeking more information, and so the first questioner answers it and person (B) then answers the original question. We have, in effect, a subsidiary question and answer within the outer pair – the first and last statement constitute a question–answer pair, and there is another question–answer pair inside it. In the third example, this all goes wrong. The question–answer structure is exactly the same as in the previous example, but the middle question feels wrong because it is not relevant – it is not contributing to deciding the answer to the first question.

A model for dealing with this is to assume that conversation is all about achieving *goals*, or *intentions*, and that there are structures within our interaction which are larger than a sentence, and not necessarily explicitly visible, but which correspond to methods for achieving certain sorts of goals. These are often referred to as *dialogue games*.

2.5.3 Dialogue games

Dialogue games are interesting to us because they attempt to model units of communication which have a goal, and which are bigger than a sentence. They also allow us to examine other ways by which the game may be achieved, which need not necessarily use natural language. Games can generally be divided into a small number of components in an organized manner. The hybrid we use here consists of goal, roles, content, actions, and effects.

Name: Impart
Goal: Change information in hearer's head
Roles: Teller (T), Hearer (H)
Content: P (some logical expression)
Actions: T says P
Effects: H knows P, T knows H knows P

This suggests a simple game for imparting information. In this case a teller simply states some content to a hearer and the effect is that the hearer knows that content, and the teller knows that the hearer knows that content. One example of a more structured turn taking relates to questions.

Name: Info-seek
Goal: Gain information in questioner's head
Roles: Questioner (Q), Informer (I)
Content: P
Actions: Q says 'Tell me P'
I says P
Effects: Q knows P

Name: Info-probe
Goal: Gain information about questioner's head
Roles: Questioner (Q), Informer (I)
Content: P
Actions: Q says 'Tell me P'
I says P
Effects: Q knows I knows P

These two are almost identical. The difference is in the effects. In either case, someone asks a question and the other responds. In the first place, however, the first person now knows something that he did not previously know, whereas in the second place he knows that the person he asked knows something. This is an important difference, particularly in the educational context, where 'What is 2 plus 3?' from a teacher does not normally imply that she doesn't know the answer, but that she wants to find out whether the student knows the answer. In each of the examples above I have assumed that things go according to plan. There are alternatives for when you ask a question and the other person does not know the answer, or similar situations. These examples should give a sufficient flavour of the idea and the further readings will provide more detail. The relationship of multimedia to dialogue games will appear in later chapters.

2.6   Meta-languages

Earlier in this chapter we introduced the idea of syntax and started writing down rules to express the syntax of a particular language. We did not stop to explain what the symbols were that we were using to describe grammars with, or the meanings that they have. This was an unavoidable deception. The point is that to describe a language in a clear and formal way, the only way to do it is in another language! There are special declarative languages designed purely for the purpose of expressing other languages, and they are known as meta-languages. Two well-known examples will suffice for our needs.

In computing generally, programming language syntax is normally described using *Backus–Naur Form* (BNF). This is a model using rules which relate a left-hand side to a right-hand side. The elements used are either 'terminal symbols' – things which are to be interpreted literally or from an obvious set (e.g. integers) or non-terminal symbols – things made up from rules. The language consists of very few components and is very simple. People tend to use small variations on it for different purposes (as I do throughout the book) but most of it remains the same. Typically, it consists of a set of symbols close to the following:

• Terminals – appear in quotes e.g. 'for'.

- Non-terminals – any other words – must have corresponding rules to explain them.

- Rules – symbol ::= divides the two sides of a rule, e.g. RHS ::= LHS can be interpreted as RHS consists of LHS.

- And – symbol , (comma) indicates that each of the things around the comma must happen.

- OR – symbol | (vertical bar) indicates that either the thing to the left or the thing to the right happens.

- Optional – symbol [ ] indicates that things in square brackets can be omitted.

- Repeat – symbol * indicates the thing to the left can be repeated an arbitrary number of times.

- Group – symbol ( ) indicates things within parentheses belong together. Not technically required, but handy in conjunction with |.

Using these definitions, we can create things like:

XX ::= "a", "b", "c"
XX ::= "a", [b], "c"
XX ::= "a" | "b", "c"
XX ::= "a" | ("b", "c")

See the exercises for more examples and explanations.

The second common meta-language is related to HTML. In Section 2.4 we saw that HTML is a declarative language which can describe a page of hypertext. HTML consists of a set of rules saying what would or would not constitute a particular legal page. It is a language for page description. There are many other possible page description languages, and if we were trying to describe a legal book chapter (e.g. there is only one chapter heading) then HTML would not do the job, because it does not know about chapters. There would be another language for describing book chapters. This could be terrible because we would have to write a new language for every sort of thing that we wanted to describe. In fact, it is not too bad, because there is a meta-language called SGML (Standard Generalized Mark-up Language). This meta-language is good for describing a huge space of possible declarative languages. Something like HTML is actually a definition within SGML of a language that applies to a restricted sort of document. HTML is an instance of an SGML DTD (Document Type Descriptor).

2.7 Components of interactive multimedia systems

This chapter has presented a number of ideas intended to provide a clearer and more precise basis for our application of the term *interaction* in the context of interactive multimedia systems. We have introduced the notion of *agents* with *intention* and *mental states*. Following this, communication between agents has been defined by utilizing a combination of the idea of a *channel of communication* as presented in information theory and a *language of interpretation* as it is understood with certain formal languages and natural languages. This can be regarded as the core model upon which the whole of this book is based. The implications for the basic idea of interactive multimedia can be illustrated as shown in Figure 2.9.

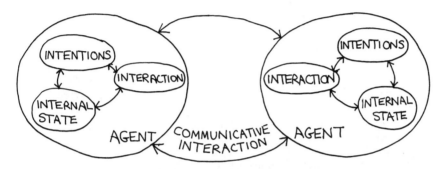

Figure 2.9 Interacting agents.

The diagram is similar to notions in the previous chapter. The difference is primarily that the communication must be bi-directional, and that we are explicitly representing the idea of intentions and a mental state in each of the participants. From this we can derive a definition which encompasses the terms introduced in the first two chapters of this book:

Interactive multimedia is:

Two (or more) agents engaging in communicative interaction utilizing multimedia communications.

For this definition to make sense we have to acknowledge three important things:

1. The definition of an agent as a system with an internal state and a set of intentions.

2. The definition of communicative interaction as agents coding, decoding, and interpreting messages with the intention of changing the mental states of the other agents in a bi-directional process.

3. The definition of multimedia presented in the previous chapter.

In future chapters we will expand upon the implications of this definition for the design of multimedia systems and for the skills that we require in order to develop them.

2.8 Exercises

Exercise 2.1 Categorize each of the following as passive, reactive, active, pro-active or interactive, and explain why in each case:

> stone, tortoise, door, lift (elevator), taxi, quiz show,
> television, robot, pokemon, telephone, dolphin

Exercise 2.2 Create a lexicon and grammar which is just sufficient to allow the following sentences and no others:

> A blue bucket, A chicken dinner, A frozen bucket,
> A blue dinner, A chicken bucket, A frozen dinner.

Now draw parse trees for a few of the sentences above.

Exercise 2.3 Extend the grammar to allow sentences such as 'A frozen chicken dinner'. Write out some sample sentences and parse trees.

Exercise 2.4 Describe some aspect of your life using declarative statements in English.

Exercise 2.5 Describe some aspect of your life using procedural sentences in English.

2.9 Further reading

Claude E. Shannon, Warren Weaver, *The mathematical theory of communication*, University of Illinois Press, 1949

This is a classic text which laid the foundations of the mathematical field which is the basis of what is referred to as 'Information theory' or 'Communication theory' from a strict mathematical perspective.

David Crowley, David Mitchell (eds), *Communication theory today*, Polity Press, 1994

This offers the alternative common use of the term: Communication theory as a sociological and psychological phenomenon.

Jean-Pierre Koenig (ed), *Discourse and cognition*, Centre for the Study of Linguistics and Information, 1998

A collection of papers which help to establish the relationship of ideas about language and ideas thinking.

Alan Davies, *An introduction to applied linguistics*, Edinburgh University Press, 1999

Good general introduction from the more sociologically oriented perspective.

Friedrich Ungerer and Hans-Jorge Schmid, *An introduction to cognitive linguistics*, Longman Higher Education, 1996

By comparison with the previous text, a much more psychologically oriented text with some interesting inter-disciplinary links.

M. Coulthard, *An introduction to discourse analysis*, Longman Higher Education, 1985
A classic introduction to one approach to examining discourse.

Stuart C. Pool, *An introduction to linguistics*, Macmillan 1999
Clear, general introduction.

Rachel Reichman, *Getting computers to talk like you and me*, CIT Press, 1985
One of the most accessible of the introductions to Artificial Intelligence related issues in language.

Ernest Lepore, *Meaning and argument: an introduction to logic through language*, Blackwell, 1999
An interesting approach to showing why logic is necessary and relating formal and natural languages.

Howard Pospesel and William Lycan, *Introduction to logic*, Prentice-Hall, 1997
There are a variety of good introductory texts on logics. This is just one of them.

3

Knowledge

3.1 Introduction

The previous chapter concluded with a description of the components of an *Interactive Multimedia* system and a definition of the key features that such a system must have. In this chapter we will investigate one of those components in more detail: *knowledge*. For the purposes of our discussion, this is taken to mean the content of the system in terms of subject matter. As we shall see, this may be something which is explicitly present in our final system, or it may just be something that we utilize in the design process in order to come up with a well-informed structure for our system. In either case, an understanding of the knowledge content of the system is crucial to a successful design. It is important to be clear that the knowledge content is not the same as the content in terms of multimedia *assets*: several different aspects of the knowledge may be involved in a well-designed asset.

This chapter will introduce some ideas about why knowledge is important, and how it is structured, before moving on to a fairly pragmatic approach, which introduces techniques for describing and representing the knowledge of our system. This is followed by a section intended to assist in the complicated process of extracting subject-matter knowledge from an expert in some field.

3.2 Why does knowledge matter?

Our definition of *Interactive Multimedia* has stressed that the systems that we are designing concern the communication of information between agents in some form. It also specified that for this communication to be effective the participants must know what they are doing. A simple electronic book which presents pages is not achieving communicative interaction in the sense that we are interested in, because it does not know what it is doing or why. An interactive system may have a detailed (deep) knowledge of the subject area in which it operates, or it may be sufficient for it to be provided with a comparatively shallow knowledge provided that a deeper model was used in the design process. In either case, there are four major reasons why we would wish to utilize knowledge in the development of our system.

1. *Structure*. As we shall see in subsequent sections, a body of knowledge consists not simply of a jumbled collection of 'facts', but of an organized and ordered structure of inter-relationships between those 'facts'. Some organizations are preferable to others, in that they facilitate *understanding* or *learning* or *generalization* from the existing knowledge of the user. While the structure of our implementation is unlikely to reflect the structure of the knowledge itself, it must nevertheless take it into account if it is to provide a successful model of the system to the user. At the very least, we must ensure that the model offered by our system is not in direct opposition to that of the user.

2. *Planning*. No one develops *Interactive Multimedia* systems on his or her own. It is always necessary to work as part of a team, and to interact with clients and potentially subject-matter experts. Many of these conversations will be about the 'content' of the system that is being designed. In order to have such discussions, and to plan the system successfully before implementation takes place, it is essential to have a language in which to talk about the content of the system. This is a language for describing knowledge. Effective use of descriptive representations of different sorts of knowledge is key to the success of the team interactions that result in our system design.

3. *Abstraction*. Of the many ways of organizing and relating knowledge, one very important one is that of abstraction: identifying common features across a range of instances and separating them out. This improves the accessibility and learnability of that knowledge, and can also be used to simplify the design and structure of our *Interactive Multimedia* system to facilitate its effective use. This facility will be particularly apparent in our discussion of navigational approaches.

4. *Adaptation and generation*. Not all systems will have the ability to adapt their interaction to different users, but it is something that the designers should aspire to. In order to maximize the possibilities for adaptation, the potential for the generation of interactive and communicative components needs to be examined. The development of either of these features is dependent upon the system having some encoding of knowledge which it can reason about and utilize as part of the process of interaction.

In subsequent sections we will return to each of these features and show how they can have a practical effect upon what we do with the system.

3.3　The basic idea of knowledge

In the previous section we used words such as 'knowledge' and 'facts' rather loosely. This was a pity, but unavoidable since it was not until we reached this point that we were able to come close to giving a definition of what we are going to use the terms to mean. We can begin to do this now.

3.3.1　Information, knowledge and belief

The main point that we will make is to distinguish between three different things: information, knowledge, and belief.

Information was discussed fairly thoroughly when we talked about channels of communication. The key point about it is that it is a property of the channel and is independent of any interpretive process by either the generator or the receiver of the information. It is a purely mathematical measure, and is related to the idea of levels of organization of sets of symbols. It can be thought of in terms of producing an encoding for the sake of the code itself.

In order to talk about a communicative process we must go beyond this simple model of information and introduce something that takes account of the agents that are engaged in the communicative act. For this purpose we will examine the idea of *knowledge*. This is a very complex area, upon which we can only touch briefly, but it is worth noting that there is a substantial body of philosophical literature on the nature of knowledge, and an equally substantial body of psychological literature on the field. We will draw upon both of these sources.

We can begin by examining the way that the idea of *knowing* is used in day-to-day conversation. I can say that I 'know' the time of the next bus or the telephone number of Aunt Maisie. We can talk about whether a child 'knows' how to do multiplication. In all these cases there is an idea that something is either right or wrong. If I think that the next bus is at 8:32 and you think that it is at 8:47, then we cannot both be correct. There is some external authority (in this case a timetable) to which we can appeal. This seems fairly straightforward. Unfortunately, we also use the term for things where this is not the case. I might 'know' that it will rain today, or 'know' that all programmers live on coffee and pizza or 'know' that crop circles are created by little grey aliens. In this case, there is no way of telling whether I am correct – the answer is *not* out there. It is also possible to have an idea of 'knowing' that relates to the views of a group or majority. There are various things which members of the Flat Earth Society 'know' and take as obvious, but which the rest of us might question. Models of the development of scientific thought within a community also now acknowledge that the acceptance of an idea into this community is part of it becoming accredited. Ideas must be demonstrated (proved) and must also become widely accepted in order to be 'known' by the group. These variations in the way that we use the term everyday reflect some of the debates that exist within the study of the philosophy of knowledge. For the purposes of this book, we will make a strong distinction between *knowledge* and *belief* and provide a working definition for ourselves on pragmatic grounds.

The first idea of knowledge that we introduced was that in which something is either right or wrong. There is a sense in which an *absolute truth* exists, and some arbiter in the world can determine this for us. We can know the time that the bus is scheduled to leave, or we can be wrong about it, but in any case there is a source of external knowledge independent of any individual to which we can refer. There is a fairly trivial case in which this is obvious: if we are dealing with an artificial system with a limited number of possibilities, and if we limit the terms of our question carefully, then we can have an absolute knowledge of the subject. It is possible (though extremely boring) to know the bus timetable. In London, 'The knowledge' is the name given to the encyclopaedic understanding of street names and locations which must be possessed by taxi drivers in order to gain their licence. This is delimited in some sense by the range of streets that constitute London. Each of these is an artificial system, and, as we shall see below, is essentially a factual one. In the philosophy of knowledge, the idea of knowledge as absolute truth can be traced back to Plato. His model was rather more grand and all encompassing. He suggested that there is an ultimate truth to everything in the universe – the *perfect knowledge*. This is also known as *Platonic knowledge*. His basic approach was to suggest that such a knowledge exists, but that humans are a long way from being able to see it. Life is about trying to remove the veils that shroud our vision and so uncover the knowledge that explains everything to us.

This idea is very appealing, because it seems to have an inherent simplicity. It becomes problematic in areas where we can find alternative views, where there is no arbiter and nothing to make one view 'more true' than the other. It is also problematic in that even the language we use may be a source of dispute between us. As we discovered in previous chapters, agents cannot see inside each other's heads. They must use a means of communication to determine what is there. Consequently, you and I may both say that the sky is blue, but our individual perceptions and representations of this will be specific to us and can be entirely different. If one accepts this difficulty with absolute truth, and the importance of communication and distinctions between individual knowledge, then one moves towards an alternative approach that works in terms of *belief*.

Models of belief start from the axiom that the only thing that individual agents can know is what they have internal to themselves. This can be called a *personal belief*. Such a belief cannot be shared, and does not become part of the community. However, it can be communicated in some other form. This refers back to our early diagram of communication (Figure 1.2) in which the two agents discussing the mouse have different things in their heads. These are the beliefs of the two individuals. In this model we do not have the idea of an absolute truth, so we have to arrive at a similar conception in a different manner. If we take our two agents, then through a process of communication they can try and establish beliefs that are compatible. This does not imply that the beliefs are identical in the heads of the individuals, but that they are communicated in a form that is compatible with the beliefs of both individuals. If this is achieved, then we say that the agents have a *shared belief* or *mutual belief*. In effect, we are saying that one agent believes that the other agent believes something compatible with a belief of the first agent. Obviously, there is much room for misunderstanding in this model. We can extend this idea beyond two agents into a larger group and produce a 'community of agents' who have established a set of shared beliefs in this form. This does not imply that these beliefs are 'right' but that they are commonly accepted (Figure 3.1). This enables us to model conflicts of belief between different groups, and changes of belief over time. The belief that the world was flat, or that the sun revolved around the earth are both examples of beliefs which were held by a large society and which are no longer tenable. This view lets us explore the idea of changes in the knowledge of the individual or the group.

3.3.2 Organization of knowledge

The previous section introduced a discussion of the epistemological nature of what is inside the head of a single agent, but it did not explore

Figure 3.1   Community of agents.

the form that this thing in a person's head might take. In this section we will clarify some ideas about what the structure and organization of knowledge might be. Note that the terms introduced are useful for describing properties of knowledge whether represented in a person, on a computer, or on a piece of paper. There is no claim that things exactly like this exist inside the head of a human being (i.e. there is no suggestion of a psychological validity).

In a number of examples that we have given, such as the bus timetable, we are dealing with what are commonly referred to as 'facts'. These are unitary pieces of knowledge which are either present or absent. I can know that the bus time is 8:32. This is a fact. However, it is useful to extend this idea beyond things which have a simple right or wrong value, or which can be tested. This extended set of things still share the common property that they can all be couched as statements of some form. This general group will be referred to as declarative knowledge. It covers everything that could be phrased as a declaration or statement, e.g. 'There is a high probability that it will rain today', 'All presidents are corrupt', 'Jane believes I come from China'.

We can join together individual statements to make more complex declarations, e.g. 'it is raining' AND 'I am outside'. We can also use statements to express relationships between other statements, e.g. 'I am wet' BECAUSE 'it is raining' AND 'I am outside'. This is important because it allows us to move beyond the simple idea of a statement as being an independent unit that is either present or absent, and express a connection to other statements. This can be used as the basis of a *reasoning process*.

We can perform reasoning upon declarative knowledge in order to determine things which are not explicitly represented, or to create new statements based upon the ones which we already know. These processes of reasoning are discussed later, but for now we simply need to be clear that reasoning is a process which can operate on declarative knowledge. Reasoning is not itself declarative.

This combination of a reasoning process and some declarative knowledge about which to reason is sufficient to enable us to construct an argument (Figure 3.2). An argument, in this sense, is taken to be some statement that is provided with a justification by applying a reasoning process to a set of declarative statements.

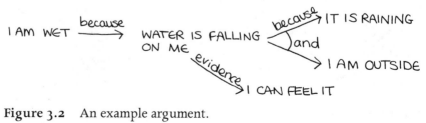

Figure 3.2   An example argument.

In the section on knowledge representation we will see the various ways in which declarative knowledge can be organized, and ways in which we can draw and represent it.

While declarative knowledge captures statements about things, the commonly used alternative, *procedural knowledge*, describes procedures or 'how to do things'. I know how to open a door, drive the car, or ride a bicycle. I cannot necessarily reason about these things, but I can do them. If I were asked to explain how I ride a bicycle I would find that there are many things involved which I cannot adequately talk about. Not all procedural knowledge is so inaccessible, however. If someone asks me how to travel from Edinburgh to Leeds then I can tell that person the various actions that must be performed in order to achieve this. In effect I have successfully transferred my procedural knowledge to another agent (assuming that the destination is reached). One of the most important ideas about procedural knowledge is that it is possible to combine various small procedures to achieve something that could not be achieved through a single procedure alone. Ways in which such procedures can be combined will be explored further in the section on knowledge representation.

3.4 A working definition

The earlier discussion raised a few issues in the understanding of the nature of knowledge. These are primarily intended to illustrate that this is a very complex area. While there are occasions when one might need to delve further into these issues, we will take a pragmatic approach and choose a definition which is likely to be effective in most day-to-day instances. Specifically, we will work with *Socially defined Platonic knowledge*.

Socially defined Platonic knowledge is a property of a community of agents who are 'expert practitioners' in a particular subject area. This knowledge is taken to be that area of shared belief which is mutually established among the members of the group. No individual 'possesses' this knowledge, but all have beliefs that are compatible with it. As long as the group, and the beliefs of the group, can be regarded as stable, then this knowledge can effectively be treated as though it was Platonic.

If we accept this definition, then we can continue to use an idea of knowledge as though it was absolute, provided that we acknowledge that this is only a working assumption which will sometimes be incorrect. This also allows us to include a model of belief of an individual, and how that may change over time with respect to the deep knowledge of the group (Figure 3.3).

In terms of defining our systems, we have already agreed that a primary purpose of these systems is *Communicative Interaction*. We can now go further, and suggest that the *Interactive Multimedia* system

Figure 3.3   Socially defined platonic knowledge.

represents or embodies the Socially Defined Platonic Knowledge in a particular area. We will treat this knowledge as though it is 'correct'. The individual will possess a set of his or her own beliefs, which will be in some relationship to this knowledge: it may have compatible components and incompatible components; it may cover a broader area or a smaller one. The purpose of our *Interactive Multimedia* system is to ensure that individuals hold beliefs compatible with their goals and with the knowledge of the area. Note that we are still distinguishing knowledge and belief – there is no assumption that the things in the head of the agent are identical to the knowledge, just that they are compatible with it.

We will clarify this with a couple of small examples.

1. Let us imagine a simple tourist information system which consists of a kiosk (in the centre of a town for example) with which visitors can interact. There will be details of the layout of the town, the facilities offered, landmarks, sites of interest, restaurants, pubs, etc. In our model this will be described as the knowledge embodied in the system. Our tourists will have some set of beliefs, and by choosing to use the system they are indicating that they wish to change or extend some aspect of those beliefs. They do not necessarily want to be told everything that the system knows but just, for example, where they could find a Malaysian restaurant. In this instance we need to provide an interface which enables tourists to express the area of their understanding which they want to emend and permits the *Interactive Multimedia* system to communicate the relevant information to them.

2. Similarly, we could imagine a system for providing five-year-old children with experiences to help them develop an understanding of three-dimensional objects and their relationship to two-dimensional structures (e.g. relating circles to spheres). In this case the system still embodies a fairly powerful knowledge, but the communication that it is trying to achieve is not so obviously information oriented. The experiential nature means that the interaction may well be less focused. Nonetheless, the purpose of the system concerns the communication, in some form, of the knowledge in the system (or part of it) to the learner who is constructing an experience from it.

3.5 Techniques of knowledge representation

Having established a perspective on what we mean by knowledge, this section turns to the more pragmatic question of how we utilize knowledge within our systems. We will begin by introducing some general features, and then move on to explore declarative and procedural representation in more detail.

It will not come as any surprise to realize that when we are talking about knowledge representation, what we are referring to is a mechanism for describing knowledge in a strict way which can be understood by humans and by computers: we are talking about a *language* for representing knowledge. In fact, this is slightly deceptive because it is our intention to encourage the idea that there are many simple languages which can be used (or invented) to describe aspects of knowledge. It is not necessarily the case that we are seeking a single all-encompassing knowledge representation method.

In the previous chapter we established the terms of what we mean by a language. In particular, we discussed the lexicon (which identifies the base set of symbols), the syntax (which tells us what the legal combinations of symbols are), and the semantics (which tells us how to interpret those symbols). We will make use of these components repeatedly in this section. Remember that the most important thing is to be consistent in the way you notate and use symbols, rather than necessarily sticking to a particular official language. There are many complex techniques of knowledge representation, but we will avoid them here. We will restrict ourselves to a small number of simple methods which are very powerful and are likely to encompass everything that an *Interactive Multimedia* designer will typically encounter. We will also restrict ourselves to techniques that have a very obvious graphical depiction, such that they can easily be used among humans to communicate knowledge. A further point that we will emphasize is the existence of a precise formal mapping between the symbols and the graphical depiction. You should ensure that you are thoroughly comfortable with this in each of the techniques discussed below.

3.5.1 Declarative knowledge

Declarative knowledge concerns making declarative statements and expressing relationships between statements. The simplest form was the disconnected fact, unrelated to anything else. Let us we consider our bus timetable:

'a bus leaves at 8:32', 'another bus leaves at 8:54', 'there is a bus at 8:59'

These are statements, and they are disconnected. There is no particular relationship between them. I could change the time of any one bus and the others would be unaffected. Each of these statements means the same sort of thing, but because they are expressed differently in a language (English) it is difficult to see that they are the same in meaning. Because there are different symbols, the computer would treat them differently unless it understood English. It is also apparent that communication among humans may be adversely affected by letting the same thing be expressed in a number of different ways. Consequently, it is normal to try and simplify the language in which we are talking so that it is unambiguous, and any two things that have the same meaning are expressed in the same manner. In this case, we could create a special lexical item called *bus_departs* which takes a single argument that is the time. Our three sentences would now appear as:

bus_departs(8:32), bus_departs(8:54), bus_departs(8:59)

This is a big improvement. We can clearly see that all these statements contain the same sort of information and we can imagine how easy this would make it to include a reasoning process in the computer. We could, for example, create a program that can tell us all the buses leaving between particular times by searching through the different instances of bus_departs. This was not possible until we made our description consistent. We will refer to the linking relationship bus_departs as a *predicate* and refer to the things that it connects as *arguments*. In the above example we have chosen to adopt a standard notation in which the predicate comes first followed by a pair of round brackets that contain as many arguments as are required, separated by commas. This is just a convention that we have chosen. We could equally well have selected:

[bd$8:32]-[bd$8:54]-[bd$8.59]

However, this is probably less understandable to humans (though just as meaningful to computers). Remaining within the same representation, we could extend it to add information such as the destination of the bus (quite useful!) and whether it is an express or local service. In doing this the important thing is to remain consistent. If we add a destination to one of our statements, then we must do the same to all of them, otherwise we are introducing ambiguity into our language once more.

```
bus_departs(8:32, Liverpool, Express)
bus_departs(8:54, Leeds, Local)
bus_departs(8:59, Glasgow, Express)
```

It is also important to note that not only does each *instance* of the predicate have the same number of arguments, but also that they appear in the same order. It is up to you as the creator of the language to decide what this order should be and how to interpret it, but you must remain consistent. You cannot change the order arbitrarily for different statements. This is all there is to say about disconnected statements. The main point is that even in this case it is important to develop a consistent language for describing statements if you wish to reason about them or manipulate them. It is also true that there is little point in drawing diagrams of the knowledge representation in this case because they are uninformative.

Declarative representations become much more interesting as soon as we start to express relationships among the statements. When this happens we need to think even more carefully about our language, and about what it is that we are trying to represent. This will often depend upon the sort of reasoning that we want to do with this knowledge. Let us consider expanding our bus example to enable users to explore the information in different ways. We can imagine that some potential passengers would only travel on buses if they serve drinks or show videos or have toilets. We could attempt to add this information to every single departure in our list, but this would not be very efficient and would not be easy to change. Instead, we could create some related statements about different sorts of buses and express a relationship between those buses and the departure events. Let us suppose that all buses are one of three varieties, which we will call *variety1* to *variety3*. Each variety has certain properties and any bus of that variety also has those properties. Here are some classes of bus:

```
isa(variety1, bus)
isa(variety2, bus)
isa(variety3, bus)
isa(freds_bus,variety1)
isa(sues_bus, variety2)

has(variety1, video)
has(variety1, toilet)
has(variety1, drinks)
```

In these statements we have done two things:

1. expressed a relationship between a particular object (e.g. freds_bus), a class of objects (e.g. variety1), and a more general group of things (buses);

2. described some of the properties associated with a class of things (variety1).

We can immediately make this clearer with some diagrams. First, we can draw a picture where the links correspond to isa relationships, and the arguments to these predicates are the nodes. This is a simple tree hierarchy (Figure 3.4).

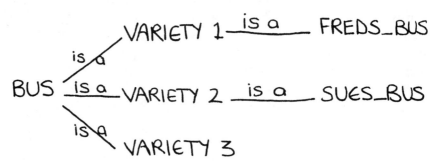

Figure 3.4   isa diagram.

The choice of predicate names is very important. We could have used predicates called kind_of_bus and example_of_bus or anything else. However, because we chose to use predicates which were all called the same thing (isa) we have created a tree structure since the links are all of the same type. This means that we can create ways of reasoning with the structure which makes use of this nomenclature. There is a statement that tells us that Sue's bus is of variety 2 and a statement which tells us that variety 2 is a sort of bus. There is not a statement that tells us that Sue's bus is a bus. We could make up a general reasoning rule, however, which would allow us to deduce this from the relationships. Such a rule would look like:

IF (isa(?A, ?B) AND isa(?B, ?C)) THEN isa(?A, ?C)

This is a sort of inference rule to use with tree relationships. In this case we can use it to join two of the existing isa statements together to create a third. This is useful, but it can be even more useful if we can combine our tree with links to other things. The has relationship tells us about things that go with a bus of variety 1. It is not part of the tree organization because the relations have a different name, but none the less we can express it on the same diagram if we bear in mind that only part of the diagram is a tree structure (Figure 3.5).

We can clearly see that a bus of variety 1 has a video and could answer this question directly by looking at the statements. There is not a statement that tells us whether Fred's bus has a video but we could make up a reasoning rule that would allow us to deduce it from the existing statements. Such a rule would appear like this:

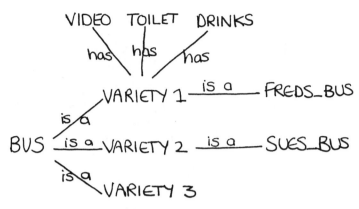

Figure 3.5 isa and has.

IF (isa(?A, ?B) AND has(?B, ?C)) THEN has(?A, ?C)

This is extremely powerful. Without such inference and tree structures we would explicitly have to say what properties each individual bus has. By using the tree structure to group the buses into classes and associating properties with those classes we only have to state these things once. Consequently this is a much more concise representation which is easier to change or add to, and which enables us to cope with many more queries. In fact, these representations ultimately let us describe an infinite number of statements without having to write them all down.

We can complete our bus representation by modifying the initial departures to say whose bus is on each journey. This is achieved by extending the bus_departs predicate to include an additional argument, and allows us to answer questions such as 'Is there a bus going to Edinburgh which has a video on it?'.

    bus_departs(8:32, Liverpool, Express, sues_bus)
    bus_departs(8:54, Leeds, Local, janes_bus)
    bus_departs(8:59, Glasgow, Express, freds_bus)

We could draw this as shown in Figure 3.6.

This is essentially all there is to creating declarative knowledge representations and depicting them graphically. Other key points to remember are as follows.

- Try to identify a small number of objects to talk about (small lexicon) [conciseness].

- Be precise with your syntactic construction. In particular, remember that all instances of a predicate must have the same number of arguments in the same order – consistency is key [consistency].

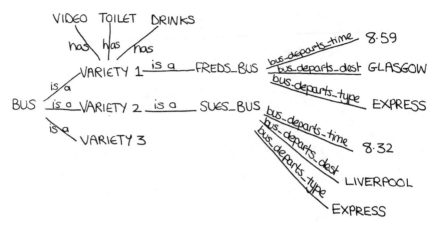

Figure 3.6   Full bus picture.

- Use as few relationship names (predicates) as possible, and make them work hard [conciseness].

- Think about what the representation will be used for and try and group things accordingly [organization].

- Try to think of good graphical representations for your notations [depiction].

- Identify places where inference rules could be created which would save a lot of repetitive statements [reasoning].

- Organize things to be as concise as possible [conciseness].

3.5.2 Procedural knowledge

We will now consider procedural knowledge: knowledge about doing things. This is significantly different from declarative knowledge in a number of ways. A key difference is that while declarative representations make statements about which we can reason, procedural representations are primarily about actions which we can perform. They may or may not be able to be inspected, so in some cases we may reason about them, but in general we use procedural representations to represent how to carry out some piece of behaviour. In particular procedural representations are commonly used to provide a set of small actions which can be joined together to construct bigger actions.

An important consequence of this is that almost all procedural representations have implicit or explicit within them a temporal component which is absent in declarative representation. We can illustrate many of these ideas through a simple example.

Consider the problems involved in that major task of getting up and out of the house on the way to work each morning. We can immediately say that there are certain things that we have to do. An example might be:

get_up, have_breakfast, go_to_work

We can see that there is a temporal element here. There is no point in going to work before you have got up, especially if you do not like wearing pyjamas in bed! We will not concern ourselves over much about the situation in which some of these things could overlap, but will return to it later. Each of these actions has a period of time that it lasts, and the actions are carried out in a certain order. However, simply telling someone to 'have breakfast' is not necessarily explicit enough. It depends how well you know the person, and whether they like eggs or toast or cereal or a cigarette for breakfast (or, indeed, a combination of all these). We can see that 'have breakfast' is simply a high level description of action, and that that action can be broken into a number of things at a lower level. We could break our instruction to 'get up' into three components:

Get_out_of_bed, take_shower, get_dressed

This improves upon the level of detail, but may still not be sufficient: perhaps we should break down 'take shower' into:

Go_to_bathroom, set_water_temperature, enter_shower,
apply_soap, exit_shower, get_dry

But suppose that the person does not know where the bathroom is? Then we would have to make this more detailed again:

Stand_up, left 45°, forward 2m, extend_hand, grasp_doorknob, ...

But they might not think in metric and so fail to understand 2 m. The point of this example is that we can break down high level tasks into lower level tasks, but that ultimately there comes a point at which we must stop and assume that these actions are in some sense *primitive*, and are understood by whoever (or whatever) is interpreting our procedural representation. If we do not do this, then we can go on forever! A further point to note is that we have composed these actions into a hierarchical structure, so naturally we can draw them as a tree (Figure 3.7).

We can see that this could immediately be a very useful way of controlling things that need to be done. How difficult would it be to express this in a symbolic language that the computer can work with? Quite easy, actually.

Go_out <= get_up, have_breakfast, go_to_work
Get_up <= get_out_of_bed, take_shower, get_dressed
Take_shower <= go_to_bathroom, set_water_temperature, enter_shower,
apply_soap, exit_shower, get_dry

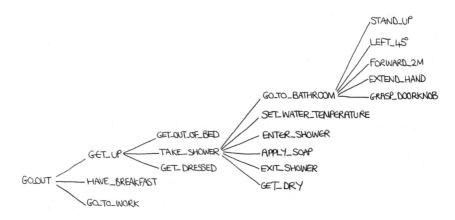

Figure 3.7   Breakfast tree.

Go_to_bathroom <= Stand_up, left 45°, forward 2m, extend_hand, grasp_doorknob, ...

In this notation we have taken a fairly simple decision that a procedure is described with its name, followed by some symbol, and then the names of all its sub-procedures separated by commas. We can read it as 'In order to do {the thing on the left} do each of {the things on the right}'. Note that we can have different numbers of sub-procedures on the right on each occasion. At some point we will need to have procedures that do not break down into sub-procedures, so we will give them no right-hand side, for example:

Stand_up <=
Enter_shower <=

We can think of these rules as a substitution grammar which allows us to replace the things on the left with the things on the right. We can usefully talk about things at the higher levels, but if we actually replace each thing in a rule repeatedly with the components that make it up until we are left with procedures which have no subparts, then we turn the tree into a sequence of primitive actions which can be carried out.

When we use a graphical depiction of a tree to describe procedural information it is conventionally agreed that there is a temporal ordering implied by the way that the tree is structured. This ordering normally goes from left to right or from top to bottom depending upon which way round the tree is drawn (Figure 3.8).

While the tree is read as time in one dimension, the perpendicular dimension is read to indicate sub-procedures in the hierarchy. Because of the temporal element, it is commonly assumed that a similar interpretation is made in the formal notation. On a given level of the hierarchy, things which are higher up the written page occur earlier (i.e. to the left in the diagram) than things appearing below them.

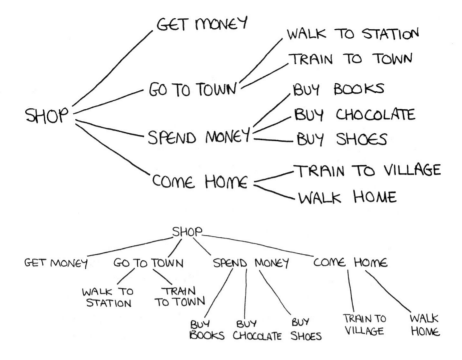

Figure 3.8 Examples of trees in both directions.

While the grammar rules given above are fairly clear, there are many other ways to represent procedures. We will now switch to one in which all procedures are represented by a predicate (Proc) which expresses a relationship between a procedure name and a set of sub-procedures. This will make things easier later:

Proc(go_out, [get_up, have_breakast, go_to_work])
Proc(Get_up, [get_out_of_bed, take_shower, get_dressed])
Proc(Take_shower, [go_to_bathroom, set_water_temperature,
enter_shower, apply_soap, exit_shower, get_dry])Proc(Go_to_bathroom,
[Stand_up, left 45°, forward 2m, extend_hand, grasp_doorknob,·])
Proc(stand_up, [])
Proc(enter_shower, [])

Make sure that you are comfortable with this and the earlier notation. All we have done is change syntax. The structure and meaning are the same.

The representation so far is sufficient to describe a hierarchy of actions in which all actions must be undertaken whenever we do something. As we noted earlier, however, there are times when actions are alternative – I may like different sorts of breakfast on different occasions. We can deal with this by introducing an extra component to our formal notation which tells us when to perform certain actions. The resulting formalism might look like this:

Proc(name, condition, sub-procedures)

And our semantics would be that the procedure is used if it is asked for and the *condition* is fulfilled.

Proc(have_breakfast, [Saturday], [have_eggs])
Proc(have_breakfast, [feel_hungry], [have_toast])
Proc(have_breakfast, [feel_healthy], [have_cereal])
Proc(have_breakfast, [late_for_work], [have_cigarette])

These predicates deal with the choice of breakfasts. Note that they are all called have_breakfast, so that we can tell that they are alternative ways of doing the same thing. There are different conditions which enable us to distinguish when different options apply. Each is distinguished by taking different actions if the condition is appropriate, for example having a cigarette for breakfast if one is late for work.

We can slightly extend our notation for drawing trees to encompass this, as shown in Figure 3.9.

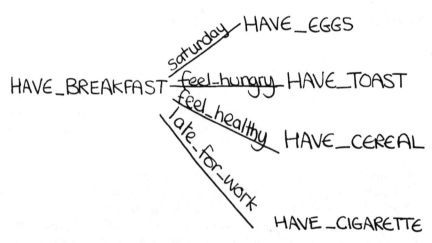

Figure 3.9 Graphic of having breakfast.

What are these conditions, exactly? They are predicates (or collections of statements) which are true or false. They achieve their value by looking at the 'world' in which we carry out our procedures. For humans they are things that we could ask them to check (e.g. look out of the window to see if it is raining). Within a computer or a formal system, we can describe that world by sets of declarative information which can be changed over time.

It is not always neatest to depict procedures as a tree. Sometimes a network notation is more appropriate. In this model we provide a set of

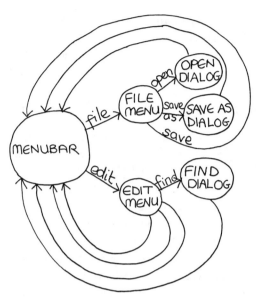

Figure 3.10   Transition networks.

links between nodes where the links represent the conditions under which we can move to those nodes. Figure 3.10 provides a small example.

We will study this technique more in Chapter 5.

3.5.3 When do procedures become declarative?

While the distinction between declarative and procedural was probably fairly clear when we started, I suspect that some people may be becoming a little confused by now. Surely we have been reasoning about procedures, so doesn't that make them declarative? The answer is yes and no. We can make a distinction that is generally quite clear, but we can change our usage of the things that we represent. Procedural knowledge may become declarative when we reason about it. More likely, in fact, is that the reverse will happen. There are various psychological theories which suggest that as humans we initially learn things in a declarative manner, and subsequently turn them into procedures so that we can carry them out more quickly, and later still we 'compile' these procedures and throw away the declarative knowledge from which they were built. This means that we can no longer inspect them.

Schoolchildren think fairly explicitly about what they are learning, but soon it either gets forgotten or becomes so automatic that they are no longer aware that they are doing it. This is the compilation process. We do it all the time. In particular, experts in a specialist field tend to forget what they learnt and find it hard to talk about it, although they can do it. This is one reason why being good at something does not necessarily mean that you are good at teaching it. It is also a reason why as multimedia designers one of our hardest jobs is getting information out of subject experts, as we shall discover in the next section.

3.6 Techniques of knowledge elicitation

We have established that one of the aspects of a multimedia system which makes it significantly different from other computer applications is that it is necessarily concerned with communicative interaction between the computer and a human being. Furthermore, we have recognized the obvious consequence that communication requires content and hence that the development of multimedia systems must incorporate the analysis of the knowledge about which they are intended to communicate. Since we, as system designers, cannot possibly be experts in every subject, it follows that we will often be required to develop systems in areas of which we have no personal knowledge. It is therefore essential that we learn and practise techniques which are necessary to acquire relevant knowledge from appropriate sources. This includes existing physical resources such as books and manuals, and human resources such as experts and practitioners in the appropriate field.

Particular problems exist when we need to use experts as our source of knowledge. It is extremely difficult, in many circumstances, to get information out of an expert practitioner. This is not normally because they are awkward and difficult people (though that *is* sometimes the case) but more often because they do not know what they know. In the previous section we mentioned the idea of knowledge compilation in which understanding that used to be explicit and accessible becomes automatic and ceases to be available for introspection. This is often the situation that arises with experts – they have been applying their expertise for so long that they have forgotten how difficult it is to learn or what it is that they know. To overcome this it is necessary for us to utilize a range of techniques designed to help both the expert and ourselves in the process of communicating and extracting knowledge. This systematic method of extracting information from expert sources is often referred to as *knowledge elicitation*.

3.6.1 Existing sources

Before beginning the process of getting information from experts in the subject area, it is important to examine existing sources that can inform you about the subject content of your multimedia system. There are two reasons for doing this: first, it helps you to limit the scope of the system – that is, to determine the range of information that will fall within the system and that which will be outside the focus of your interest; and second, because experts are much more receptive and helpful if you appear to understand at least the basics of the field in which they are operating.

This process of determining the scope of the system (both in the breadth of coverage and depth of detail) will depend at least partly upon the intended users of the system. Understanding these users is the focus of the following chapter, and the interdependence between understanding of the users and understanding the knowledge content means that both these aspects of the system design must normally be pursued in parallel.

At this stage in the elicitation process we are predominantly concerned with written information. The exact sources will depend upon the type of system being constructed, but system manuals, office procedures, text books, help systems, and introductions to new staff are just some of the sources that may be available to you. At this early stage in the elicitation process you should read these sources in order to get a general feel for the area – to identify key issues, to exclude certain aspects, and to become familiar with some of the basic terminology of the area. You should also seek to identify in very rough terms a list of the concepts that seem to be necessary in the domain and the particular processes or procedures that will be the concern of your system. You will probably find that there are certain sources which are very detailed and specific but which probably go into too much detail for you to understand at present. These 'definitive' sources should be retained for use later in the elicitation process.

From this information you can construct some starting set of loose and general questions which can be directed to experts as part of an informal interview.

3.6.2 Techniques

One of the first observations to make is that the process of knowledge elicitation never works correctly the first time. It is simply not possible to ask another person a number of questions and to obtain answers that are both perfectly correct and complete. The expert will make incorrect assumptions about what the audience knows, and you will be unclear of the relevance of various aspects of the knowledge to the system which you are attempting to design. This need not be a source of difficulty, as long as you recognize that this is the nature of the process. The first attempt at getting information from an expert will normally result in a very vague and general model of what is going on – this model may be full of inaccuracies, inconsistencies and misunderstanding. This is a good starting point: as soon as you have anything which is in some form outside the experts' head (e.g. in writing) then it can be a topic for debate. It is a lot easier to get someone to tell you why something is wrong or how it should be changed than to provide you with some knowledge in the first place. Consequently, it is best to look upon knowledge elicitation as a process of *successive refinement* of a model of the subject area.

While there are various approaches to knowledge elicitation which are suited to different groups of users and subject areas, the following steps are typical.

1. **Brain storming**

The initial phase simply depends upon getting something, anything, out into the shared space between the experts and the person engaged in the elicitation process. There is no point in worrying at this stage whether what you have is correct, or at a sufficient level of detail, or even comprehensible to you. The only objective initially is to get the ball rolling. Once you have something, you can always revisit it later in the process to expand upon it and refine it. This construction process is often referred to as brainstorming. Questions such as 'Tell me all about your job' or 'Tell me about your subject' are normally unproductive because they do not help users to focus their activity in any form. Instead, you might try things such as 'What would you expect a new person to know if they were joining this company?' or focused questions in time ('What do you do first thing?') or activity ('What would I need to start task X?').

At this stage you should not try to get any structure or relationship into the information that you are receiving – just get it all down on a piece of paper or similar medium. The outcome from this phase will normally be something like a list of words which are unstructured and disorganized. This is an appropriate input to the next phase of the process.

2. **Organizing**

The second stage of the process is to impose some sort of organization on your collected words. There will be a lot of variation here depending on how you choose to design a system, the sort of area in which you are operating, and the relative abilities of your experts to communicate. One of the most important distinctions is to separate the terms out into different sorts of knowledge – things that are conceptual or declarative should be clearly identified, as should procedural and process components. This is quite difficult to do in the presence of an expert, so don't expect to treat this clarification as a single activity, but be prepared to insert these sorts of questions wherever is appropriate in other organizational exercises.

The second major part of this process concerns grouping together terms which are related such as concepts whose definitions are interdependent, processes which utilize other processes, and concepts which need to be understood in order to carry out certain processes. The form that this organization will take depends both on the nature of the activities in which the expert engages, and in the nature of the multimedia system that you are trying to produce. For example, if your expert knows how to operate a particular piece of equipment then his or her knowledge is structured in a certain way. However, the way that you might wish to organize the knowledge to produce an introductory system for novices who have not previously met the equipment would be very different from the way that you would organize it if the system were intended as a troubleshooting aid for experts. Consequently, at this stage in the process you need to have some fairly clear ideas about the nature of the use that you will make of the knowledge being elicited.

Grouping things in this manner can often be aided by some fairly straightforward techniques based on the idea of clustering things together. One approach is to write each of the words on a separate card and to throw these down in a heap. The expert can then be asked to divide up this heap of cards in ways that are appropriate or meaningful. Afterwards you can ask them how they chose to organize the cards. An alternative is to suggest particular ways of organizing the cards such as things that you do at the same time, things involved in the same task or activity, things which occur in the same location, things that are done frequently (or rarely), things which involve particular people or equipment. The details will depend upon the context.

There are also a variety of simple diagrammatic techniques you might explore in this area which are useful for communicating vague ideas between humans but which are too imprecise to be used with a computer. These techniques often appear under such terms as 'cluster diagrams', 'concept mapping' or 'mind mapping'.

3. Diagramming

While there are a range of diagrammatic techniques which are useful for communication in an imprecise form between humans, some of them can also be gradually refined into a form which is sufficiently exact to be understood by the computer. A major focus of this chapter has been to introduce some ways of describing knowledge which are fairly natural such as tree or network diagrams, but which can also be encoded into a notation which could be represented directly by machines. Depending upon the nature and the level of expertise that you require you may well engage in a process of modifying the informal diagrams or developing new formal diagrams, such that they match the notations given in this chapter. These diagrams can then become a process for discussion between yourself and the expert, enabling you to ensure that the coverage of the subject area is sufficiently *comprehensive*, *accurate*, and *detailed* for the purposes to which it is intended to be put. In a number of fields you will find that the experts quickly learn to interpret these diagrams and can begin to use them as tools of communication with you. This is particularly valuable if you are working with the same experts over an extended period.

4. **Structured interviews**

Structured interviewing is a common technique of knowledge elicitation, something between a questionnaire (very organized, but no scope to go off in directions which seem important but were unplanned) and an open interview (often too undirected to get effective results). Structured interviews involve the interviewers having a good understanding of the area, and a range of questions which they want to use to get answers, but are able to recognize something which is important coming from the expert and to pursue it opportunistically, even though it is not on their list of questions. This is often used as a technique in later stages where a good general understanding of the subject exists, but there are clear gaps in coverage or detail. Asking questions about the missing information will help, but if it reveals a complete set of other connections or knowledge then the interview must be prepared to go along that route and end up with (potentially) something entirely different from that which was expected at the start of the interview.

All the techniques above, and many more, have been explored in great detail in the literature on knowledge elicitation, and it is important to understand them thoroughly before you engage in these processes. Details can be found in the further readings.

3.7 Summary

In this chapter we have dwelt on the subject of knowledge, which is not generally covered in texts on multimedia. We have established that these systems are different from many other sorts of computer software because they have *content* in relation to some subject area, about which they must engage in Communicative Interaction. Creating effective multimedia systems therefore requires at least some understanding of this knowledge, which is not generally in an area where the designers are expert.

To facilitate this we discussed the nature of knowledge and belief, introduced a range of graphical and formal notations for describing knowledge, and introduced some of the issues concerned with how to elicit such knowledge from an expert in some subject area. By engaging in this process we will be better able to make an effective system design, specify (and produce) multimedia assets, and implement appropriate interaction methods. The following chapter explores the relationship between this knowledge of the subject area, and the knowledge of the user of the system.

3.8 Exercises

These exercises are fairly open-ended, since there are a variety of ways to represent equivalent knowledge structures and diagrams or notations.

Exercise 3.1 Imagine a supporter of Manchester United and a fan of Newcastle United watching a match between the two teams. What information, knowledge, and beliefs might exist in this situation? What belongs to which category? Which of these things will be shared between the fans and which will be (or might be) different?

Exercise 3.2 Write down the conceptual knowledge involved in making a cup of tea.

Exercise 3.3 Write down the procedural knowledge involved in making a cup of tea.

Exercise 3.4 Fred, Jane, and Norma each own a dog. Fred and Norma have terriers, Jane has a bulldog. Fred's dog is called Pluto, Jane's is called Beefsteak and Norma's is called Tomato. The dogs of Fred and Jane are black. That of Norma is ginger. Represent this in a formal notation.

Exercise 3.5 Represent the information from Exercise 3.4 as an isa/has diagram.

Exercise 3.6 Most people have a collection of CDs. There are various CDs which could be grouped by artist, record company, date, or style (genre) of music. Artists could be grouped by style (genre), sort of artist (female vocal, rock band, jazz singer, dead, etc.)

   Pick a few CDs and represent the above information about them in a notation.

Exercise 3.7 Repeat Exercise 3.6 representing the information as a diagram.

Exercise 3.8 Get a recipe from a recipe book. Represent what you have to do as a tree diagram of a set of procedures.

Exercise 3.9 Translate the tree from Exercise 3.8 into the proc(...) notation used in this chapter.

Exercise 3.10 You can probably get to work by several different methods and combinations of methods (e.g. walking, driving, taxi, train, plane). Represent this as a tree and/or procedure notation including conditional statements to determine which method to use on a given occasion.

Exercise 3.11 Imagine you are required to write a multimedia tourist information system about Whitby, UK. How would you set about finding sources of information?

Exercise 3.12 Identify the key concepts and processes involved in the production of *shoddy* and *mungo*. Clue: they are old methods of recycling material.

Exercise 3.13 Find a friend who has a hobby about which you know nothing. Interview him or her to obtain suitable information to create a multimedia introduction to that hobby.

3.9 Further reading

The first three readings cover the general context of thinking about knowledge:

Adam Morton, *A guide through the theory of knowledge*, Blackwell, 1997
   Good introduction to the basic issues in thinking about Knowledge.

Robert Audi, *Epistemology*, Routledge, 1997
   More advanced text on issues in the Philosophy of Knowledge.

J. Angelo Corlett, *Analyzing social knowledge*, Rowman and Littlefield, 1996
   About the relationship of knowledge and belief to individuals and groups.

These 6 books provide introductions to knowledge representation techniques at a variety of levels:

E. Rich and K. Knight, *Artificial intelligence*, McGraw-Hill, 1991
   General introduction.

Stuart Russell and Peter Norvig, *Artificial intelligence: a modern approach*, Prentice-Hall, 1995
   General introduction.

Nils Nillson, *Artificial intelligence: a new synthesis*, Morgan Kaufmann, 1998
   General introduction.

John F. Sowa, *Knowledge representation: logical, philosophical and computational foundations*, 1999
   Quite sophisticated, and mixing many similar ideas to this chapter.

Arthur Markman, *Knowledge representation*, Lawrence Erlbaum, 1998

Han Reichgelt, *Knowledge representation*, Intellect Books, 1991

Knowledge elicitation or knowledge acquisition are concerned with getting information from experts:

Alison Kidd, *Knowledge acquisition for expert systems: a practical handbook*, Plenum, 1987

J. H. Boose and B. R. Gaines (eds), *The foundations of knowledge acquisition*, Academic, 1990

4

Understanding users

4.1 Why are users important?

As we saw in Chapter 1, users were not important in the early days of computing. Computers were very large and expensive machines which ran programs that generated some sort of output. There was no opportunity for interaction. The people who worked with the computers were specially trained, normally to work with one specific machine or one specific program. It was much cheaper to train a person to adapt to the idiosyncrasies of the computer than to waste time trying to make the computer more usable for humans.

Things have changed since that time. As computers have become much cheaper, and more widespread, there has been a great increase in the variety of people using them. Until the 1970s it was still regarded as quite acceptable for the computer to be extremely difficult to learn and for significant effort to be required on the part of the user. Subsequent to this, the computer began to move into areas where the users would not be trained specifically for computer operation. It began to become important to construct programs which could actually be used by the general public. This provided a major change in focus and emphasis in the design of software. We can illustrate this with a simple comparison. There have been algorithms for calculating mathematical formulae since the very early days of computing. It would be typical of an early implementation that users would create a text file containing all the data that they wanted the program to use, in a format which the program expected, and the software would then read this data, process it, and output results to another file. One hundred per cent of the program code was devoted to carrying out the computational tasks that the program was intended to solve. By comparison, a modern equivalent might be a symbolic mathematics package in a GUI environment. There will still be code to execute the mathematical algorithms, and it will almost certainly be much more powerful and flexible than on those early machines, but it will be a very small part of the overall program. Where initially there would have been no effort put into the interface, it is typical that two-thirds of a modern computer program will be code concerned purely with the maintenance of the interface. The purpose of all this code is to make life easier for the people using the software, at the expense of increased complexity and effort for the computer (and the programmers) (Figure 4.1).

Figure 4.1   Typical code components and sizes.

This change of emphasis in the relationship between the *functionality* of a program and the *usability* of a program, brought on by the increased availability of cheap computer power, has led to a radical change in the way that we think about and design computer software. Previously, it was possible to specify a program purely in terms of the inputs and outputs: a program consisted of some data and some algorithms for manipulating that data (Figure 4.2). By introducing the user into this equation, our needs become more complex: not only must the software achieve a required functionality (do something specific) but it must also achieve a certain level of usability (do things in a way that the intended users can work with) (Figure 4.3). Almost all software design has moved towards this perspective, and with *Interactive Multimedia*, where our focus is upon *Communicative Interaction*, this aspect is even more central. Without a powerful and meaningful interaction with the user, we cannot hope to achieve the goals that we set for our designs.

In earlier chapters we saw the importance of *Communicative Interaction* to our design process and learnt that a key part of achieving such interaction was to have some sort of model or appreciation of the other agent involved. In subsequent chapters we will see that the design and selection of multimedia content is also dependent upon an understanding of the range of languages with which our users are familiar. In both of these dimensions an understanding of the user is key to the development of a successful system. Hence, this chapter is devoted to trying to explain what users might be like, what we might want to know about users, how to acquire such knowledge, and how to

Figure 4.2   Program = algorithm + data.

Figure 4.3   Program = algorithm + data + interaction.

apply it to our system. We will conclude with some examples of detailed techniques that we can adopt to describe our users. The chapter emphasizes the importance of *user-centred design* within our systems.

4.2   Things you might know about a user

The discussion so far has probably created an image of *a* user interacting with *a* computer. These two players are in a one-to-one relationship like the agents of Chapter 2, and when we talk about 'knowing' the user we appear to be talking about this one individual who is actually sitting in front of the computer. This was, indeed, the original conception of user-centred design. Subsequently it has been recognized that there are many players who have an influence on the needs and objectives of this interaction and the participants within it. It is common to initiate any design process with a *stakeholder analysis* (Figure 4.4) which seeks first to identify the individuals or groups whose needs may influence a design, and then to identify those needs and the ways in which they interact and complement each other (or conflict) when they are brought

Figure 4.4   Stakeholder analysis.

together into a set of design objectives. We will examine this in more detail in the later sections, but for the moment will satisfy ourselves with identifying a small number of common groups to consider.

The most obvious stakeholder is the person sitting in front of the computer, interacting with our system. It should be borne in mind that this may be an individual, or may be two or more people together. This influences what we know about them. It is likely that a cash machine will have a single user at a given time, but a tourist information system may have a whole family or similar group clamouring to interact with it and satisfy their needs through the system. Even if we are dealing with one individual at a time, they may well be one representative of a particular group or class of individual users who wish to get different things out of our system. An integrated management computing system in a retail car showroom may be used by sales people, accountants, senior management, and the person who washes the cars. Each of these groups will have different objectives and it is essential to our design that we identify the needs, strengths, and weaknesses of each group and cater for them effectively if our system is to be generally accepted.

There are other players who may never go near our *Interactive Multimedia* system but who nevertheless have a profound influence on the design and the success or failure of the software. The most obvious of these is the *client*, a term which is being used here to indicate the person who is paying for the development of the system. As we shall see in Chapter 11, this is a particularly difficult stakeholder group. They often have either hazy and extremely ill-formed ideas or very clear and ill-formed ideas. This group often think they know what the users need, but typically have little insight into actual requirements, as opposed to what they fancy the requirements should be. Their influence needs dealing with in special ways discussed later. Further details on stakeholder analysis can be found in the key references. For the remainder of this chapter we will concentrate only on issues related to those individuals who will be in direct contact with the computer system, and hence will be engaging in *Communicative Interaction*.

4.2.1 Task models

In earlier chapters we decided that *Interactive Multimedia* is purposeful – interactions are pursued in order to achieve goals of some form. It is common in most software design to take a similar view. The major difference is that in other software the goals are those of the human, and they are oriented towards actions – achieving something in the world. It is common to refer to this as a *task model* approach to design, and it has something particular to offer to our understanding of users and what we need to know about them.

Imagine yourself sitting in front of a word processor. You have some task: writing a letter to your grandma; handing in your resignation; complaining about the price of fish. Each of these is a task that you want to achieve using the computer. To carry out these tasks you are constrained by the facilities offered by the interface of the word processor that you are working with. It probably does not have a button for 'write a letter to grandma' but it might have something to insert an address, and almost certainly has something to start a new paragraph or leave a space. This is the functionality which is accessible through the interface. It is possible to have a program in two versions with identical functionality but different interfaces which are completely different in their usability, because they make different things easy or difficult. To maximize the usability of our program, we wish to provide as close a mapping between the facilities of the interface and the tasks of the user (or users), as possible. We can illustrate this as shown in Figure 4.5.

In Figure 4.5 we see, on the left, a user who has a set of tasks which he or she wishes to achieve, and on the right, a computer which has a particular functionality and some interface which provides a means of communicating that functionality between the two participants in the interaction. We can describe the *usability* in terms of how well the two sides work together. There is a translation and mapping process not unlike that which we described between our agents: the user decides to

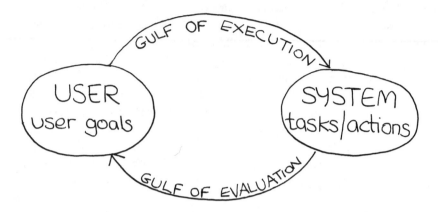

Figure 4.5 Gulf of execution and evaluation.

achieve a task, examines the computer to see what actions can be performed upon it, and performs those tasks, causing the computer to behave in certain ways and potentially provide feedback as a way of communicating with the user.

There may be a gap between the tasks that the user wishes to complete and the immediately accessible functionality being offered. This gap has been named the 'Gulf of Execution' because it describes the (often enormous) gulf between what the user wants to do and actually putting those wants into practice (executing them) with this machine.

There is a similar communication problem in the reverse direction. The computer will report on what it has achieved, and its successes or failures, in a language related to the way it was programmed and of the inbuilt model which it follows. This will not necessarily be the same as that of the user, so again there is a translation process required. This has been named the 'Gulf of Evaluation' because it describes the process of the user receiving the feedback from the machine and attempting to work out what it means (evaluate it). It is important to note a significant difference between this model and our model of what *Communicative Interaction* is. In the current case we can try and improve the mapping between the tasks of the user and the accessible functionality of the system, and try and make our feedback as close to the user's expectation as possible, but ultimately the active process of trying to leap across the Gulf of Execution or Evaluation is carried out by the user. By contrast, in *Communicative Interaction* both agents endeavour to clarify and adapt this communicative process in order to achieve their goals.

4.2.2 What is a user?

Before we start discussing the sort of knowledge we need to acquire about users, we should be clearer about what a human being is like. This is the domain of psychology. There are many different varieties of psychological models and different approaches to understanding what humans are. We will concentrate upon cognitive models: those which focus upon mental processes and reasoning. From within these we will examine a well-known model often referred to as the *Human Information Processor* (Figure 4.6). This has been chosen because it is compatible with much of the previous discussion.

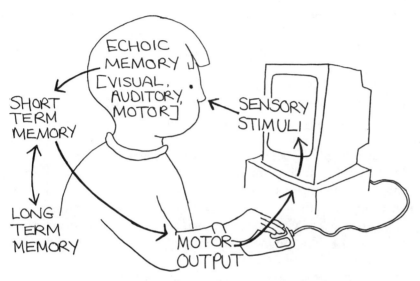

Figure 4.6 Human information processor.

Figure 4.6 shows the basic components of this model in its simplest form. To the left we see the sensory stimuli through which input comes to the brain. The different senses, as we have already established, can be thought of as the modalities of communication with the human. These sensory stimuli transfer directly to small, specialist information stores which are referred to as echoic memory. This part of memory is very short-term storage which simply retains the image in an unprocessed form. It is like remembering a number by shouting across a valley and waiting to hear the number echoed back to you – hence the name. There are different echoic memories for each modality, and they have slightly different properties in terms of how much they can store and how quickly they can be updated. It is the use of these systems which enable us, for example, to perceive a moving image out of the individual still frames of a film.

The next element in our diagram is the working memory or short-term memory. This is a place with a larger, but still limited, capacity for storage. It can be thought of as analogous to the scrap of paper that one may produce workings on while calculating a complex sum. It is a key component in any conscious, active reasoning processes in which we engage. For our purposes, a very important point is that this information is encoded in some form – it is no longer the raw stimulus that was in echoic memory. Consequently, some translation has gone on between echoic and short-term memory. A process has been applied which took the raw data, decoded it in some way and re-encoded it in a format suitable for humans to keep in their memory. There may have been several such decoding processes operating upon one echoic memory. There might, for example, be a speech analysis process, a music understanding process, and a sound effect interpreting process all operating to decode the auditory stimulus. This idea should be very familiar: these are the channels of communication which we discussed in Chapter 1.

The decoding process is also constrained by the available size of short-term memory. There is a famous result in psychology which claims that short-term memory can contain seven things. This is known as 'the magic number 7 plus or minus 2'. Various implications of this for interface design will be discussed in the following chapter and it is an important factor in designing the content of our multimedia systems. In particular, while there are seven 'things' in the short-term memory, the actual nature of a thing is less clearly defined. By careful organization we can group simpler items into more complex ones and the more complex one becomes a thing, so more information can be accessed in the short-term memory. This process of gluing things together is referred to as chunking and the things are commonly called chunks (Figure 4.7).

Figure 4.7   Grouping things into chunks.

The third component in our diagram is the long-term memory. This is where humans store things which they retain over significant periods of time. The learning process involves making changes to what is in this memory. When we are engaged in reasoning, the model suggests that we retrieve information and procedures from long-term memory into short-term memory and carry out our reasoning using those components. When we 'forget' something and are able to recall it later, it is because we are temporarily unable to find it in the long-term memory. As you can imagine, there are a lot of things in there, and it is easy to put something down and forget where you have left it. Consequently, ways of organizing and structuring this knowledge are extremely important to our effectiveness as reasoning machines. This is one reason why it is necessary for us to understand ideas about the organization of knowledge: ultimately, we wish our multimedia systems to be compatible with the organization and constraints of our users' knowledge.

We will simply note that all of the output channels of the human being are contained in the *motor output* box. Whether we talk or kick, the effect is still achieved through muscular control.

4.2.3 Organizing user knowledge

We can now turn to a discussion of the sorts of knowledge that we might wish to acquire about our users and the way that it is organized. In a sense this section should really be read in the parallel with the section on applying user knowledge: understanding of what we wish to know and how we are going to apply it are intimately related aspects of our design. The particular organizing principle that should be borne in mind is 'Don't model what you can't use'. Collection of data about users is expensive, and if you have no way of using it in your system then there is no point in collecting it. You can ask what the first language of your target audience is, but if you can only build the system in English then it is a pointless question. Nonetheless, this illustrates the interconnectedness of these issues. We might build our systems for multiple languages, only to find that the audience is exclusively English speaking, so there is something of a chicken-and-egg problem in the relationship between the analysis and design at this stage.

Perhaps the most basic question that we need to ask is 'Who is it that we are modelling?' This is a question concerning the granularity (level of detail) of the information that we will collect, and hence of the level of variation in our system. The simplest form is to assume that there is a group of people called 'the users' who are a homogeneous mass. If we work with this level of modelling, then we can use it to fit our system to the needs of the group in advance, but cannot provide any variation in behaviour for different individuals or subgroups. A model of a group typically consists of a number of very general features expressed either as properties (which are either present or absent) or pairs of elements consisting of some attribute and a value for that attribute. Examples might be:

First language: French
Reading level: 3
Computer skills: 8
Sense of humour: 1

As we will see below, this sort of information allows us to ensure that our design matches this user group – for example, by ensuring that all our text is at an appropriate level of reading difficulty. It is important to note that simply by choosing to define a user group in this manner, we are also excluding certain users from the system. This does not mean that they will necessarily be prevented from trying to use it, but that the interactions may not be appropriate for them. A good technique for identifying your user group is often to work out who the system is *not* for. Sometimes groups simply have to be excluded: there are few systems which support the visually impaired, for example. It is important to make these exclusions explicit in your design process and documentation.

The next level of adaptation that can be considered is where some gross variation is permitted in the system. This involves us having knowledge of more than one user group. We can use this approach when we identify a number of groups in our intended audience which have significantly different needs and knowledge. These might be distinct groups separated by, for example, job descriptions (managers, the sales staff, accountants) or they might be groups corresponding to stages which an individual may pass through over time (beginner, intermediate, advanced, irritating). Once again, we can use a similar sort of methodology to that which identified a single user group, but need to pay particular attention to areas of similarity and difference. It is often the case that, among a large number of small differences in groups, there are one or two features which account for most of the variation. If such features can be identified then providing adaptation in only those respects can be very cost effective and will suit most of the users most of the time.

The third level that we consider is modelling the user as an individual. Each potential user of the system must be provided with a representation of their knowledge and objectives. Because we are focusing on individuals, this method allows us to collect very detailed information – often more detailed than can be utilized. It is necessary to think about how the information will be used very carefully in this instance. A further problem is the acquisition and maintenance of this level of information. It is much harder to obtain detailed knowledge about what is in the head of an individual than to obtain a general knowledge about a group. Also, while individuals in a group will change over time, we would normally expect that the general characteristics of that group change either very slowly or not at all. In the case of an individual's user model the knowledge can be changing on a moment-to-moment basis. This means that such modelling cannot be a one-off process, but must include a mechanism for continuously updating and maintaining the user knowledge.

Bearing these things in mind, we can now explore the sorts of knowledge we want to obtain about our users in more detail. These issues apply whether we are dealing with individuals, groups, or a homogeneous audience.

4.2.3.1 Background and foreground knowledge
The first distinction that we wish to make is in the relationship of the user knowledge that we are studying to the content of the system that we are implementing: a key difference between *background* and *foreground* knowledge (Figure 4.8).

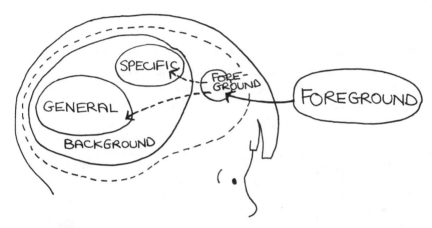

Figure 4.8   Background and foreground.

Background knowledge refers to knowledge which the users possess before they come to the system. It is the background from which they are starting and is independent of the subject area or content of the system. Obvious possible components of background knowledge are things such as: the level of computing skills (which could be divided into mouse skills, keyboard skills, etc.); familiarity with the sorts of issues and problems raised by the system; language skills (what language is spoken, what levels, reading abilities); mathematical skills. These issues can have a significant impact upon the way in which we design the system, irrespective of what the system is for and what the subject matter is.

There is a second aspect to background knowledge which is related to the content of the system. It is intended to answer the question 'What can we assume the user knows about the subject area?' This question can be answered using the same sorts of techniques that would be used for foreground knowledge (see next section).

Foreground knowledge, by contrast, is specifically concerned with what the user knows about the subject matter of the system and what might happen to that knowledge during the interaction with the computer. In the case of a tourist information system this concerns the content of the area in which the system is operating (e.g. social life in Edinburgh, the classical statues of Neasden, cultural life in Milton Keynes). It is in the area of foreground knowledge that most possibility for individualization within the system exists. If it is possible to identify exactly what the users know of the foreground when they begin to use the system, and what their needs and objectives are, then it is in principle possible to provide a totally individualized interaction adjusted to those needs. This is one of the objectives to which we want to move with *Communicative Interaction*.

Having introduced this basic distinction we can now look in more detail at the sorts of knowledge that might be involved in each case.

4.2.3.2 Cognitive, conative, and affective components

There is a tendency when modelling users to focus only on those aspects which are easy to model, and to ignore the rest, but it is important to be aware of the bigger picture. We will divide knowledge about the user into three categories: *cognitive*, *conative*, and *affective* (Figure 4.9).

Figure 4.9   Cognitive, conative and affective components.

Cognitive   Cognitive information is concerned primarily with the sorts of knowledge that we discussed in the previous chapter: procedural and declarative knowledge, reasoning processes, etc. Within this category we will also include what might be thought of as 'mental skills'. If, for example, we are considering our tourist information system, then this will involve information about the language skills of the users, their knowledge of the local area, what knowledge they may have as to the range of facilities that are likely to be available, etc. For an educational *Interactive Multimedia* system, cognitive knowledge in the background is likely to be the relevant learning that we will assume the user already has, while cognitive knowledge in the foreground is linked to what we wish the user to acquire from the system. If we wish to teach multi-column subtraction then we probably assume single-digit subtraction is already known: single-digit subtraction is part of the cognitive background knowledge and multi-column subtraction (including borrowing, carrying, etc.) is foreground cognitive knowledge. Most attempts at modelling or adapting to the user concern themselves only with things in the cognitive domain.

Conative   Conative knowledge is very important if we wish to move towards genuine *Communicative Interaction*. It is rarely discussed in software design, except in the field of *intelligent agents* where it is seen to be of key significance. Conative factors are those concerned with the motivations of the user (not to be confused with emotion, see below). Conative knowledge refers to an understanding of the drives of the user. In everyday English these would commonly be referred to by terms such as *wants*, *needs*, or *desires*. This provides a way of representing what it is the user is trying to achieve, and what the status of these objectives are. It is richer than task-oriented models, because instead of just assuming that the user wishes to achieve an effect which is a particular goal, it allows other factors to influence whether that goal is pursued and, if so, in what manner.

I could, for example, wish to decline an invitation to go out to the cinema with a friend. My goal is simply to avoid going to the cinema (or rather, to communicate this to my friend). However, there are many ways in which this could be achieved. Consider:

'I would love to but I'm otherwise engaged'
'Sorry, but I am washing my hair that night'
'Sorry, but I am washing my hair every night for the next century'
'Me? Go to the cinema with you? Don't make me laugh!'
'Bog off, you creep'
'Look, do you want me to call the police?'
'No'
'NO!'

Each of these phrases, hopefully, satisfies the objective of communicating that I do not wish to go to the cinema, but we can clearly see that they have other communicative effects as well. We can only explain those effects by taking multiple factors into account regarding what it is that I am trying to achieve through the communication. Sometimes I am wanting to support my friend (and perhaps encourage an invitation at another date), at other times I am clearly wanting to completely discourage the friend or even terminate our relationship. In accounting for these differences in communication we need a model of the intentions of the speaker which go considerably beyond a simple task and goal based model. This is why we try to build a model of *wants*, *desires*, and *needs*.

This is clearly a difficult area to model and one where limited work has been done. For *Interactive Multimedia* systems in practice, we must restrict ourselves to very simple models at present. Since it is also very difficult for a computer to recognize these things automatically, we are reduced to explicitly asking the user for information through an interface that restricts the user to only those possibilities that we are able to implement. A simple example might be asking questions such as 'Do you prefer explanations to be verbose or concise?' and adjusting the interaction accordingly.

Affective   The third key component to our model of the user is the affective one. Affect is a technical term relating to the emotional state of the individual. It covers issues related to arousal, excitement, boredom, enthusiasm, etc. This is an area where there is a range of psychological studies about the measurement of, and impact of, affective state, but where there is comparatively little work on how to deal with these differences in affect within the design for a system. All we can really do at present is acknowledge that such issues exist and attempt to deal with them on a general level. Most of the emotional influences on our users will be from external factors which our software cannot be aware of or react to, so there is little adjustment that can be made. If a user has just had a row with the boss, or it is their birthday, we cannot know this (and even if we knew it was their birthday, we could not know whether they are the sort of person that loves birthdays or hates them). Some systems have included interfaces which allow the users to answer questions such as 'How bored are you?' on a rating scale, but this information is normally used only to speed up or slow down the interaction, whereas the boredom might be for entirely different reasons.

It is worth mentioning one other aspect of affect in computer usage – the external measurement issues. Since it is often difficult to test whether a computer is 'more effective' or users are 'learning better' or 'performing more efficiently', designers have often resorted to testing whether users 'like' the system. This can be valuable, since an unpopular system will not be used, but it is necessary to be very careful about such conclusions. In the first place, we have the effect that people who are being watched will often work harder, and people who are answering questionnaires will be anxious to please. This means that the results are unreliable. In the second place we have an edge effect consequent upon the novelty of the system. Since people are naturally more interested in something new, they will be attracted by the novelty and hence enjoy it. The test only really works if you come back later and see if the system is still popular after the novelty has worn off. It is not many years ago since the effect of seeing a picture on a computer screen (just a still image, not a movie) was so novel that everyone loved any system that had pictures, even if they were entirely gratuitous pictures in an entirely useless system!

	COGNITIVE	CONATIVE	AFFECTIVE
BACKGROUND	what you know	Desires in life	How you feel
FOREGROUND	knowledge gained from system	Purpose of interacting with system	How you feel when using the system

Figure 4.10   Background/foreground vs cognitive/conative/affective.

4.3   How to apply user knowledge

Having outlined a way to analyse the knowledge that we might wish to acquire about the user, this section looks at the way in which we might change the design of our *Interactive Multimedia* system to take account of what we have learnt. You may wish to move backwards and forwards between these two sections to get a feeling for the inter-relationship between the knowledge and the adaptation.

Bear in mind that when we talk about the user we are referring only to the individual directly engaged in *Communicative Interaction* with our system. Other aspects of human–computer interaction (HCI) are considered elsewhere. We will first consider the general areas that we might adjust for different users, and then examine three specific approaches: user-centred design, adapted (tailored) systems, and adaptive systems.

4.3.1   What can be adjusted?

By using knowledge about the user in our design, we are seeking to achieve a variety of objectives, all of which can loosely be categorized under of the heading of 'maximizing the effectiveness of the interaction'. Three key factors in this process are *usability, learnability,* and *accessibility*. By usability we mean ensuring that users can achieve their own goals through interaction with the system. By accessibility we mean that it should be as easy and transparent as possible for users to achieve these goals. By learnability we mean that, as far as possible, users should be able to engage in this purposeful interaction without an overhead of additional learning.

Since we are regarding *Interactive Multimedia* systems as being focused around *Communicative Interaction*, the ways in which we can utilize knowledge about the user are focused upon improving this interaction and hence the communicative value of the system. These issues can be loosely divided into those concerned with the structure

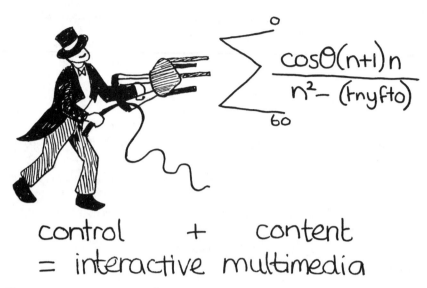

Figure 4.11   IM = control + content.

and organization of the interaction, and those concerned with the content of the interaction (Figure 4.11).

In terms of control we are concerned that the mechanisms by which the interaction is organized are meaningful to the user, and that both user and system have appropriate control over these processes. These belong to a communicative metalevel concerned with the interaction itself – rather than the subject area of the interaction. This metalevel includes such devices as navigational mechanisms and structural dialogue components. It also relates to issues of the *locus of control* in the interaction and ways that this may be adjusted.

Content is clearly an important part of *Interactive Multimedia*. To maximize the effectiveness of communication it is necessary to make judicious selection of the content in the system and the manner in which it is made available to the user through various multimedia assets. This can loosely be equated to asking the two questions: 'What do I say?' and 'How do I say it?' The former is an epistemological question concerned with identifying the subject-matter content (as opposed to media content) which is appropriate at a given point in the interaction. The latter is concerned with the style in which this content is communicated. This may involve choices of media, combinations of media, and various communicative techniques within an individual medium. In short, this is really a question of selecting the appropriate channels of communication at any given moment in the interaction.

The way in which this communication is effected via multimedia assets and the meanings and encodings with which they are associated is the subject of the second half of this book. For the remainder of this chapter we will focus upon the impact of this information on the general system design, interaction, and control structures.

4.3.2 User-centred design

The most basic way in which to use knowledge about the user is to follow a process for developing your system known as *user-centred design*. This is a methodology which has become increasingly common since the early 1980s and is now regarded as key in almost all aspects of system development. In Chapter 1 we explained how the early computers, due to cost of computer time, were developed in a purely problem-oriented manner: a statement of a problem (typically mathematical in nature) was produced and an algorithm was developed which satisfied that specification of the problem. In this approach there is no need to take account of users because they will adjust to the needs of the system. A consequence of the increased usage of machines by a less technical audience was a change of the balance between the process of solving a problem and the process of enabling the user to work with and understand the machine that was solving the problem. Consequent upon this there is an implied need for a change in the design approach to be used for any system intended to reach a large audience. This change is, in essence, user-centred design.

The basis of this approach is to put the user at the centre of the design process. There may be an initial problem specification, such as providing a tool to do the company accounts, but at this stage it is quite general. It is not possible to understand the problem fully until we understand our users: the object is not to produce a system which solves a problem, but to produce a system which solves a problem in a way which is understandable by, and accessible to, the target user group. The key phases in this approach could be described as:

- work out a general problem outline;

- study the user groups;

- work out what the user group wants to achieve and how they wish to achieve it;

- design and build a system around the outcome of this process;

- evaluate the system with the users and redevelop as a appropriate.

Clearly, this is a very general outline of the sort of thing that is involved in this approach, and more detailed explanations of it can be found in the various readings. For our purposes the main thing to note is the centrality of knowledge about the user within this process. This is emphasized even further when we are aspiring to systems which achieve *Communicative Interaction*. It becomes a primary purpose of our system that interaction with the user is successful and effective – even more so than whether anything is achieved as an outcome of the interaction! Notice that the study of the user groups and the closer development of a design for the program are commonly interlinked processes rather than sequential. Since users do not necessarily know what can be achieved by using a computer, the things that you learn from the users about their objectives and how they currently achieve them will be limited by their current understanding. It is often the case that a certain degree of user education has to be included in the process of working with the user groups. A further aspect to note is that this process is interactive: having built the system you return to the user group and evaluate it to see whether it achieves the objectives of usability, and it may be necessary to engage in redesign as a result of that evaluation. This area is discussed further in the following chapter.

Having identified the process that we would engage in for user-centred design, and emphasized the importance of knowledge in this design, what do we actually do with that knowledge? The idea of this approach is that what we have learnt about the user is embodied in the artefact itself – there is no variability in the artefact for different user groups or different individuals. Knowledge about the user is implicit in the final system rather than being explicitly present and manipulable.

The most obvious application of this knowledge is in adjusting the interface in a manner that is appropriate to the user group. Managers and sales people may use different languages to refer to the same things, and something as simple as an appropriate choice of language can make a significant difference to the usability of the system. These different user groups may belong to different linguistic communities with different socially defined Platonic knowledge, and a system which fails to take account of the conventions of that knowledge will be considerably less usable.

An example of this is the early tools for doing graphics on a computer. These tools were developed by programmers to enable them to create simple images, and display very clearly their programmatic origins. They were not tools which professional artists or graphic designers would use. Tools for graphic designers are now one of the biggest markets in software. Much of the functionality is the same as those early tools, but it is expressed in a different way. The original language refers to things in terms of their implementation method, whereas the modern language of design interfaces refers to the more traditional language of the graphic design community. A similar evolution has taken place in the relationship between publishing and desktop publishing, and in the move from analogue to digital music operation. Each field has taken control of the language used in its equivalent computer-based community.

The language is only one part of the communicative process. A second, which we emphasized early on, is the model of what is to be achieved. It is important to make frequent tasks easy, even at the expense of making less frequent tasks more difficult. This is the concern of narrowing the gulf of execution and we shall return to it in a later chapter.

When we consider the multimedia component of our system, it is also important to ensure that this achieves the appropriate effects for the intended community of users. Specifically, we need to ensure that we are utilizing channels of communication suitable for our expected audience: the type and level of content should be appropriate, the style and method of presentation should be appropriate, and the encoding and decoding processes of the selected channels should be familiar to our users. This covers everything from ensuring that text is written for the appropriate reading age in appropriate language, to utilizing a film theory model of communication. Each of these asset-related areas is explored in the later part of the book.

4.3.3 Adapted (customized) systems

An adapted system is really a variation on the user-centred approach. It employs all the same methods and techniques, but goes slightly further by enabling the system to be presented in more than one way. This is particularly important if there is a great diversity in the user group or some particular aspect of behaviour in the users which would preclude a large percentage of the group from working with the system. In essence the basis of this approach is to work as above, but to provide more than one version of certain parts of the design. These alternative versions can then be invoked via a 'user profile' which specifies the properties of a particular user of the system at a given time.

A very obvious example is systems that may have to deal with users that have different first-language skills: English and Russian, for example. It is not adequate to produce an English interface and assume that the Russian audience will be able to work with it, and even less adequate to produce a Russian interface and expect an English audience to understand it (given the notoriety of the English for learning no language except their own). This is a clear case in which there must be an adaptation of the system to different users. Almost the first thing that must happen is the provision of some selection mechanism to enable users to identify their preferred language. This may not even be explicitly necessary: cash dispenser machines (ATMs) which accept cards from various countries often have the capability to automatically switch their interface into the language of the country in which the card was issued. You can be in the centre of Paris and find a machine speaking English to you − a very unnerving experience. In a primitive way these users are carrying their own 'user profile' around with them on this card. When they give the card to the machine it recognizes the characteristics of the user and adjusts itself to them accordingly.

Obviously there is the potential to make it adapt in more than one simple way, but in general the features which can be adapted are large-scale gross changes. This is because we are dealing with gross variations in groups of users rather than genuinely dealing with each individual. It also happens because the expense of producing huge variability is rarely justified.

Typically, when we conduct our user analysis and design a system, we will identify a small number of subgroups within our user group. We might name each category (e.g. accountant, rally driver) and identify the set of features that will be available to people in that category. Commonly, there will be some sort of data file which contains the mapping between the category name and the features which are available in that category. We write our software in such a way that it reads from this file whenever it meets a new user, and selects the appropriate features for that user. This is normally a one-off process which is carried out whenever the system is initiated, but is not repeated during the course of an interaction – there is no *dynamic adaptation* to the user.

This being the case, there are typically three methods by which we can select between the different profiles: we can remember individual users as members of a particular profile (which is what the international cash card does); we can ask users to identify themselves with a profile (either by explicitly choosing one themselves, or by answering questions which enable us to determine the appropriate profile); or, in some circumstances, we can set the system to a particular context (e.g. the computer on the manager's desk is in the manager mode and the computer in the lions' den is in lion-keeper mode).

In practice this level of adaptation is as far as current technology will let us go in most *Interactive Multimedia* applications. The future, however, will see an increasing use of adaptive systems, as we shall see in the next section.

4.3.4　Adaptive systems

Adaptive systems take us into the field of artificial intelligence. These systems will normally conform to the process of user-centred design and they may well include some form of initial profile which gives them a gross expectation of user knowledge at the beginning of the interaction. What makes them different, however, is that during the course of the interaction they dynamically construct and maintain some representation of the users' knowledge and make use of that representation to try and change and adapt the interaction in real time as the communicative processes continue. The potential of this approach is great but it is difficult to achieve. Most of the work in this field has been referred to by the terms 'user modelling' or 'student modelling'.

The modelling process requires that there are algorithms within the *Interactive Multimedia* system which watch the interaction with the user. Through observation of the interaction and potentially through asking explicit diagnostic questions, the computer builds an understanding of what users know, what they want to achieve, etc. A complete model of this form would include cognitive, conative, and affective components. The content of such a model is likely to be finer grain compared to the other methods and enables us to talk for the first time about genuinely adapting our system to an individual user. We can approximate aspects of the knowledge of one person and potentially construct our interaction at a level of detail suited to that one individual. To achieve this our system must contain generative algorithms which can make use of the information provided by the user model. There are several key aspects to the *Communicative Interaction* which may be adjusted in response to such a model.

Most software has some sort of interface with which users interact, and which they gradually learn as they use the software more and more. In use, the person working with the system is continuously learning about that interface: trying to build a model of the way of interacting with the machine which has been encapsulated in the design. A well-designed interface makes this as easy as possible, while a poor design of interface can be impossible to learn. An alternative, and initially appealing, proposal is that the interface should adjust itself to fit in with what the users need. If, for example, they always do the same thing at the beginning of an interaction then this should be automated and carried out for them. If they never use certain commands available on the menus, then those commands could be eliminated so that there is less to remember. Things that they do extremely frequently could be made very obvious. All this could be available for each user as part of the individual model changing over time. The difficulty, of course, is that users have a hard time building a model of a fixed interface. If the interface that they are trying to model changes as the user is trying to model it, then they are in the hopeless situation of trying to build a model of an unstable target. This is virtually impossible in all but the simplest cases. Consequently, dynamic interfaces remain an area of research and should be approached with caution. The most obvious guideline in this area is that any change that is occurring within the interface should be flagged to the users (and preferably approved by them). Changing the interface behind the scenes when no one is looking is unlikely to be a successful strategy. Having said that, there are some tools on the market which do indeed add and remove functionality depending on what the designers think the user needs rather than on what the user actually needs. Second-guessing users who very probably do not even understand their own minds is an ambitious task to set oneself!

The most significant area in which we can make use of user models to provide an adapted system is in the dynamic control of the content of our system. We have already established that the subject-matter content is a key component of our design and a key part of the interaction. There may be wide variation in what users already know about their subject matter and in what it is that they need to learn about the subject matter. If we simply present everything that we know then the user will sit through a lot of irrelevant material and probably give up. Instead, the object is to match the content of the interactions to the needs of the user as closely as possible and as quickly as possible. This is clearly something which can be facilitated by a dynamic user model. If a user selects restaurants from an information system then over a period of time we will have enough information to discover that this person only ever eats in Indian restaurants or Vietnamese or Thai perhaps, hence when they next come to look for a restaurant, we can make these the initial preferred areas of search and hence, hopefully fit the user's needs more easily. This does not mean we should exclude English food, but that it should be lower down our priority list. In a multimedia system the simplest version of the generative approach that would utilize such adaptation is something that can make a choice between large numbers of multimedia assets to select those which are appropriate for the knowledge content that it believes is appropriate at a given time. A more sophisticated approach would be to have a computer which can dynamically create the multimedia itself. Progress is being made in this direction but it is slow.

The third area in which we can adapt is the way by which we present things to our user. We can think of things in terms of different dialogue acts such as *illustration, example, definition, explanation*, etc. Over time it is likely that we will acquire data that shows that certain of these methods are preferred by our user. Equally, we are likely to find that certain communication channels or combinations of channels are preferred by our user. This can be used to try and make general changes in the presentation style so that it is more suited to this individual. Some of the issues surrounding this will be explored in a later chapter.

In conclusion, let as just reiterate one point: *do not model what you cannot use*. It is very tempting, particularly in the case of adaptive systems, to include all sorts of information in the user model. There is no point in doing this and it is wasted effort unless you can create corresponding generative mechanisms that will make use of the information in the model.

Now that we know what sort of knowledge we want about the user and how we are going to apply it to the design of a system we can turn to the third big question of user modelling: *how do we acquire knowledge about the user?*

4.4   How to acquire user knowledge

Just as in the previous chapter we explored techniques for acquiring knowledge about a subject area, there is a range of techniques that we can adapt to gain knowledge about our group of users.

4.4.1   Research – background – demographics

The most basic information about the user must be acquired for any system you design, whether it is adaptive or not. It is essential to recognize the specific nature of the users of your system and to design appropriate interactions and media content for this group of users. To this end any system design must proceed from the basis of research into the general nature of the likely user groups. Previous sections of this chapter should indicate to you *what* it is that you wish to know about the users, so here we are concerned with the mechanisms for acquiring the information.

The obvious starting point is previously published work about groups of users similar to those in which you are interested. You may discover published academic papers regarding the users of similar systems. Once you can identify some general statements about your user group (such as age range, level of education, etc.) there are various sources of demographic information which you can use to identify key characteristics of the population (e.g. how many are likely to be computer literate, what the typical level of reading skill is, etc.). These sorts of surveys and books can provide a valuable clue to designing the system and, for some systems, this may be all that you need to do.

If you wish to match the system more accurately to your user group then you are likely to have to engage in some empirical activities yourself in order to get a more detailed model. One of the simplest approaches is to design a set of *questionnaires* which should be given to individuals who are typical of the group that you think will be users of your system. These questionnaires should seek to answer some of the basic questions about sorts of interactions, needs of users, levels of understanding, etc. Questionnaires are not appropriate in all cases, and in some cases it is helpful to augment them with other empirical methods. In work-related activities it is common to use *observation studies* in which you watch the potential users engaging in the tasks that they will subsequently carry out in conjunction with your computer software. This can provide you with information about the task and the users' ability to do it which is not available to the users themselves or to the people around them. An additional technique that might be applied is the use of interviews with a small sample of people typical of the range of users, in which you can seek further clarification of issues which have arisen from questionnaire studies, observation studies, or other aspects of your system design.

All these techniques can be drawn together into a report which seeks to describe the nature of your user group in the terms that we have discussed earlier in this chapter. This can then be used as a design document, and *every* decision which you make that impacts upon the user (such as choice of interaction style or design of multimedia assets) should be justified with reference to this user definition document.

4.4.2 Pre-testing

Pre-testing is an approach which is typically used when you design a piece of software which is adaptive through the use of user profiles. In these systems you have already determined the basic range of users, but within that space there is the possibility of a certain degree of variation depending upon the strengths and weaknesses of the individual user (or subgroup). In order to successfully apply the system it is therefore necessary to engage in some sort of testing and analysis process that enables the correct selection of different user profiles.

The simplest form of user profile divides the range of users into perhaps three or four categories (e.g. management, secretarial, sales, customer). Pre-testing can be used with a number of people from one of these groups in order to determine the profile of a 'typical' member of that group and hence define the system interaction for that group as a whole. If this approach is used then the pre-test is something which will only be done during the system design process and it can be quite lengthy and detailed. When users come to interact with the final system they will simply be asked to select which of a number of predetermined groups they are a member of. This technique is a little like the use of questionnaires when conducting background research except that the questions which are used refer specifically to aspects of the system which can be changed to fit the needs of different user groups.

The more sophisticated form of user profiling involves constructing a profile for each individual that will use the system. The technique is not dissimilar to that for defining groups, though it must be borne in mind that there are constraints of time and energy upon this use of pre-testing. While a group profile will only require a given individual to select the group to which they belong, individual profiling may require a lengthy process in order to develop the relevant information for each user. In an application such as a voice recognition system an hour spent on the pre-tests to build up a user profile may be considered worth the effort given the usefulness of the final application. A minute spent building a profile before you can use a basic calculator would be considered far too much. As a consequence, the design of pre-tests for the two situations has to be significantly different.

Since pre-tests are normally analysed by humans (and are often administered on paper), there is normally a delay between the user taking the test and being able to use the software. In some cases it may be possible to design a computer-based pre-test which also does the analysis and gives the user access to the system, but these are currently rare.

4.4.3 Asking

The previous two techniques have been appropriate for systems which are either fixed in behaviour but designed with users in mind, or which can be adapted to different user groups via profiles. We will now turn to techniques which can be used to determine information about users while they are interacting with the system. This enables us to produce systems which adapt dynamically during the course of the interaction.

The most obvious way to find out about users while they are interacting with the system is to ask them. Strangely, this approach has been little used in interactive systems: most approaches have attempted to guess what users are trying to do or what they do or do not understand using indirect information. Directly asking users whether they understand, whether they would like more or less detailed explanation, etc., somehow seems a rather obvious way to provide adaptation.

Despite the apparent simplicity of this approach, there are certain difficulties to be aware of when creating an interaction of this form. The first issue is determining how to phrase the question so that the user will understand and answer it appropriately. In an educational system this is often a problem because you are asking users whether they understand something or not, and it is difficult for them to assess that for themselves. In other systems uses of terminology or particular phrases may confuse the users or cause them to misunderstand the questions asked. Even if users correctly understand the question it is necessary to examine their answers very carefully – is the user telling you something which is a matter of fact, or something which is their personal belief, or perhaps simply what they think it is that you would like to hear? These are all possible responses and require both that the interaction is designed carefully and that the interpretation which is placed upon responses given by the users is thought about carefully rather than just accepting what they say.

It has also been found to be the case with a number of systems of this type that the user will deliberately lie or give 'wrong' answers in order to see what the computer will do. Users perceive the system as something that they are exploring and playing with, so it is not unreasonable to expect them to try out different things, not because they really mean them, but in order to determine their effect. There was a famous computer-assisted learning package from the Open University concerning basic numerical ideas. It was widely used but, surprisingly the number of students making errors in basic mathematics went up, rather than down, as they used the package. Further examination revealed that while the package simply said 'well done' if users got their sums right, it gave a very entertaining animation of a puffin bouncing along a number line if they got the answer wrong. Consequently, many users deliberately got their mathematics wrong in order to be entertained by the puffin.

The overall conclusion is that while asking the user may be simple and can be quite a powerful technique, the meaning of the answers to your questions must be interpreted with caution.

4.4.4 Testing during interaction

The previous section suggested that we ask questions explicitly of the users. These would be general questions such as asking them if they understood something, how they were feeling, etc. A more practical alternative in many cases is the use of explicit testing within the interaction. This differs from the previous techniques in that the users are given tasks to do or problems to solve which rely upon them being able to understand and apply certain knowledge. With careful design this is much less error prone than the previous technique because the computer can tell unambiguously whether the task has been completed correctly or not and hence whether the user has accurately understood the relevant information. These techniques can give very accurate, up-to-the-minute data, allowing the system to adapt to the user on a second-by-second basis and, potentially, provide highly individualized interactions.

The main objections to this are twofold: first, that the technique can be very intrusive; and second that some things simply cannot be tested by this method. On the first point, it is often the case that when users are engaged in a particular task or in solving a particular problem they do not wish to be distracted into other activities whose sole purpose is to enable the computer to understand what they are up to. They see this as a distraction from their main purpose in using the package. In certain situations, such as with some classes of educational software, this is not too much of a problem, but for general-purpose interactive systems it can be a cumbersome technique to use. The approach can also be intrusive because it may require a lot of diagnostic tasks to obtain accurate information about a comparatively small piece of the user's understanding. The second issue is quite apparent given a little thought. It is easy to test the typing skills of users, or their ability to do addition or subtraction. It is much more difficult to frame an appropriate diagnostic test that will determine their concept of 'freedom' or their ability to construct a moral argument.

The techniques of *diagnostic* testing are somewhat different from those of *assessment*. In the former case we are attempting to understand what is in a person's head, whereas in the latter we are attempting an evaluation relative to some criteria – as though that person was taking an exam or trying to pass a test. For the purposes of making our systems adaptive, the diagnostic approach is what we are primarily interested in and this has been most widely explored by techniques of student modelling in the field of artificial intelligence and education. Some of these techniques are introduced in Section 4.6.

4.4.5 Inference

The final range of techniques that can be used for gaining knowledge of the user takes us firmly into the field of artificial intelligence, and will only be briefly mentioned here. These are techniques which require the computer to engage in inference processes based on observations of the user. It is expected that the users of software will engage with the system and carry out the normal tasks that they would wish to perform. While they are doing this the computer observes them and attempts to apply a range of sophisticated techniques to enable it to learn from the observations that it makes of the users. This is a non-intrusive technique because at no point is the user asked any explicit questions or set any diagnostic tasks, but it is also an extremely challenging one from the point of view of computer science. There is an entire academic field known as machine learning which deals with the techniques that might be applicable to inferring the state of the user from this sort of information. Even if we had perfect machine-learning techniques (which we don't) we are still confronted by other problems based on the limited amount of data we can collect from the user during a single interaction with the machine. While these matters are of great interest from the research perspective, they are too far beyond the scope of what is currently feasible in practice to be further discussed within this book.

4.5 Techniques: user profiling

User profiling is a fairly straightforward technique to implement in practice. The difficulty, as described above, is in first deciding what to include in the profile and what to change within your software. To include this method within your program you need to do three things:

1. Set up some sort of file containing the data about the user.

2. Include some initialization code in your program to read from this file and set up appropriate variables within your system.

3. Include code at relevant points in the program to select between alternatives based upon the values of these variables.

In a simple form, this is exactly the same process which is used to store user preferences. In a Microsoft Windows program, for example, each piece of software typically has a file in the system folder which has the extension .ini. This is called an initialization file and serves just this purpose. Specifically, any choices which the user made during the installation process (such as where to put the software) or subsequently made through selection options such as *Preferences*, *Options*, or *Customize* are stored in this file. Each time the program starts it uses this information to configure itself. Here is an example from the Dragon Dictate package:

```
[HARDWARE]
DRAGDEV=dragmedi.dll
[DSP]
IOADDRESS=0x310
INTERRUPT=0
ControlVolume=Yes
Interface=MMLevel
Maximum Number of Blocks Needed=80
Current Number of Blocks Needed=80
[Installed]
DDWin1=D:\DEVTOOLS\DRAGON,809
DDWin2=D:\PROGRA~1\DRAGON,809
```

As is apparent, this file is stored as ASCII text. This makes it a lot easier to read and understand. The convention adopted in Windows is that the file is divided into sections. Each section begins with its name in a pair of square brackets. Lines following that consist of a property name, an equals sign, and a value for that property. This is probably as sophisticated as a user profile needs to get. We could imagine applying this approach to our software with a profile such as this:

```
[General]
Name=default user
[IT skills]
Computer=3
Mouse=0
Keyboard=4
[Language skills]
Language=English
Reading Level=8
[Background knowledge]
Restaurants=yes
Wool mills=no
Trains=yes
Balloons=no
```

In this example we have chosen a file which represents the properties of a single user group and that divides their attributes into sections. If we wish to change all the properties of this group we could edit the file or replace it with another file that we have created for a different group. Alternatively, we could imagine dividing the file into several sections such that each section corresponded to one of our user groups. This would enable us to initialize our software by displaying a list of alternative user groups and asking the user to pick the one that is most appropriate.

```
[User 1]
Name=manager
Computer=1
Understanding=1
Language=English
[User 2]
Name=shop floor
Computer=3
Understanding=10
Language=French
[User 3]
Name=Technical Support
Computer=100
Understanding=5
Language=Geek_speak
```

During initialization of our program we would read the relevant files and assign values to variables corresponding to the information in the file. Subsequently, at points where we had made adaptation possible in our software, we would provide a conditional statement which utilized those variables. For example:

```
if (reading_level < 5)
    Then explain('simple/explain255')
else if (reading_level <10)
    Then explain('middle/explain255')
else
    Explain('top/explain255')

If (mouse==0)
    Then
        Give_mousetutorial();
Start_package()
```

This is the basis of user profiling. It can be used to achieve a remarkably sophisticated behaviour without becoming any more complex in form than the examples above.

4.6   Techniques: user modelling

We will now turn our attention to techniques of user modelling. These are more sophisticated than user profiling, enabling us to make changes in our software for individual users, and to dynamically change the behaviour of the system in response to activities of the user during the interaction. User modelling is a technique which originated in work on artificial intelligence and education, although it has been applied to other fields (such as HCI) subsequently. It is an area in which there is much research, particularly regarding the fact that the model of a user is rarely perfectly accurate and may be drastically different from that of the people who created the software or the 'expert practitioner' in the field. Readers who are interested in these areas are recommended to examine the further readings. We will finesse these problems by returning to our definition of socially defined Platonic knowledge. Since we can, in some sense, refer to this as the 'correct' or 'expert' knowledge of the domain, and since we wish our users to move towards this knowledge, we can make the simplifying assumptions that we are only interested in modelling users in terms of their state relative to that expert knowledge. Consequently, there are two basic techniques available to us: *subset modelling* or *perturbation modelling*.

4.6.1   Subset modelling

The subset model is exactly what it sounds like: persons using the system are represented as *subsets* of the expert knowledge that we wish them to possess if they had the complete information from the system. For this model to work we must regard the knowledge embodied within the system as being separable into a number of small, discrete units. Each of these is then assumed to be something that can be acquired independently of the others. We can also think of this as the bucket model of the user.

In Figure 4.12 our expert is represented by a bucket which is full of all the bits of knowledge. Our user is represented by another bucket which is not full. The object of the system is to add bits from the expert bucket into the user bucket until the specific needs of the user are satisfied or the user bucket contains everything that the expert bucket contains, in which case the user cannot be helped any further by this system. We can make the initial assumption that the user has no knowledge about the domain (a *tabula rasa*) in which case the bucket is initially empty, or we can assume that the user has some knowledge and there are already a few things in the bucket. We could make a slightly more formal diagram of this as a set and subset (Figure 4.13).

This form of modelling is clearly related very closely to the way in which we have defined our knowledge of the domain. Each unit of the user model corresponds to some small part of our declarative or

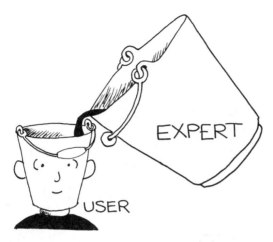

Figure 4.12 Subset.

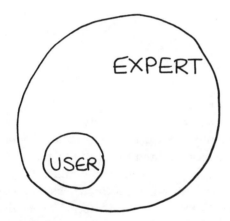

Figure 4.13 Set and subset.

procedural knowledge. Since we work on the assumption that the user either has or does not have each small piece of knowledge we can represent the user model diagrammatically by extending our diagrams of knowledge to include some simple Boolean property (e.g. a tick) attached to each small part within the representation. Figure 4.14 shows a declarative network with a simple subset model added.

There are various ways to extend this modelling approach which are further discussed in Section 4.6.3.

4.6.2 Perturbation modelling

The extension from subset modelling to perturbation modelling is based upon the simple observation that not everything in the head of a user is also in the head of an expert. Whereas the previous approach assumed

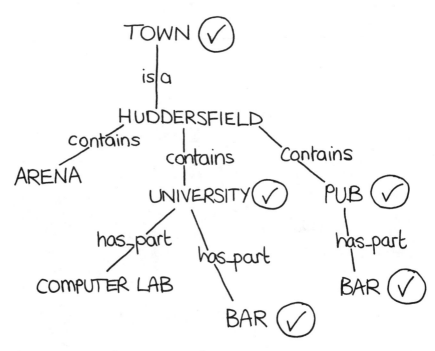

Figure 4.14 Declarative network.

that the user either had the correct knowledge or did not have any knowledge in a particular area, observation and research clearly shows that users frequently construct explanations which gives them 'knowledge' that is incorrect and hence unlike that of the expert. These faulty bits of knowledge are commonly called 'bugs'. An *error* is a mistake that users make in their behaviour as a consequence of having some bugs in their knowledge. In a procedural model, bugs are also sometimes called malrules. The appropriate modelling technique in this case is to use a perturbation. The implication of the term is that the user conforms to the expert model in some ways, but has anomalous knowledge (perturbations) in other cases. With systems based upon this approach, the objectives involve not only conveying correct pieces on knowledge, but also removing incorrect pieces of knowledge from the user. This corresponds to correcting their misconceptions or misunderstandings. We can visualize this type of user model as in Figure 4.15.

An immediate complaint about perturbation modelling might be that while there is only one 'correct' model there are many, many errors. Consequently we would expect that the modelling problem is massive by comparison. Certainly, if we wish to encompass every conceivable misunderstanding then it would be difficult in many domains and impossible in many more. What makes the approach plausible is that our users are, on the whole, using very similar reasoning processes and so

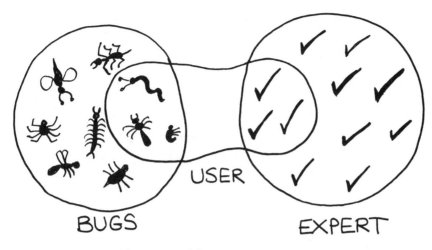

Figure 4.15 Perturbation model.

there is a remarkable consistency in the sorts of error which they generate. Consider the following subtraction problem:

$$\begin{array}{r} 23 \\ -\ 17 \\ \hline 6 \end{array}$$

We can immediately see that there is only one correct answer to this problem, 6. A naive view would expect that children who are learning subtraction would get any other answer with equal probability if it was wrong. In fact almost all the errors are accounted for by only two other answers: 10 or 14. These are *errors*, i.e. surface behaviours which are incorrect. To explain why they are the common answers we must seek to understand the underlying knowledge which the user has in order to create these errors – specifically we are looking for the *bugs* in the knowledge which generate them.

$$\begin{array}{r} 23 \\ -\ 17 \\ \hline 6 \end{array} \qquad\qquad \begin{array}{r} 23 \\ -\ 17 \\ \hline 14 \end{array}$$

In this case it is fairly easy since we have chosen subtraction which is a rule-based procedure. The problem arises because in this case the top digit in the right-hand column is smaller than the bottom digit and hence requires the student to *borrow* (or some similar procedure). They could be perfectly capable of doing two-column subtraction in all cases where the top numbers are larger than the bottom but be at a loss in this case. If they can solve these sums correctly then they have the piece of knowledge which tells them to borrow if the top number is smaller (and presumably tells them how to do this). If they do not have this knowledge then they have to substitute some other piece in order to get an answer. The answer 14 is easily explained as a misapplication of commutativity. Students know that 2 plus 7 is the same as 7 plus 2 and, on finding that they cannot solve the sum 3 minus 7 replace it with 7 minus 3 in the right-hand column resulting in the answer 14.

The answer 10 is arrived at by a modification of the process of counting down. We commonly teach children to count and subtract using physical objects: 5 apples take away 3 apples leaves 2 apples, etc. These rules can also be applied to counting with fingers to do subtraction in a concrete form, and we can immediately see that 3 fingers take away 7 fingers is a problem. If you count down then you run out of fingers. The student may assume that this means that the answer is 0 and hence the answer to the whole sum is 10. More formally we could describe this with the following three rules:

```
If right_top <right_bottom then borrow
* If right_top <right_bottom then answer = 0
* If right_top < right_bottom then answer = right_bottom – right_top
```

The first rule represents the correct situation and is part of our expert knowledge, while those marked with * represent incorrect rules which could be applied in the same context. These are malrules or bugs or perturbations. Formerly within our system we would represent our user as a set of correct rules and a set of perturbations. We would have actions to inform them of rules which they did not appear to possess and actions to correct malrules which they did have.

This is a very appealing approach which can give a remarkably sophisticated interaction. The primary difficulty is in establishing the perturbations themselves. This involves some fairly significant psychological work to understand how people operate in the knowledge domain with which the system is concerned. When the technique can be applied, however, it is extremely useful.

4.6.3   Extending the user models

Without going into sophisticated student modelling approaches which utilize techniques such as *granularity* and *machine learning*, there are two significant extensions which can be applied to each of the models described above.

The first extension is to go beyond the constraint on independence of the knowledge components. So far we have assumed that each piece of knowledge can be acquired separately from any other and hence can be modelled separately. In fact there are very few domains where this is the case, although it can often be taken as a pragmatic assumption. It is much more common for there to be dependencies between components of knowledge in a subject area. This has the implication that some things have to be known before others can be told to the user. If these dependencies are included in our knowledge representation then we can also model them and use this information in representing our user. The common example is the case where certain pieces of knowledge are prerequisites to other pieces: it is impossible for users to acquire the later piece until they have the earlier pieces. For example, a user of my information system may request the address of an Indian restaurant and the system could respond by telling them about a Malaysian restaurant. This looks like a mistake by the system if the user is unaware of the similarities between certain Indian and Malaysian dishes. Consequently, the system should really deal with the prerequisite knowledge by telling the user about this relationship before suggesting a Malaysian restaurant.

The second extension, which is related to the first, is that we can move away from the simple idea of representing each piece of knowledge as something the user either has or does not have. In fact, there are two distinct problems here – the first is to represent the idea that a user has partially acquired some knowledge (e.g. they know something but not everything about Indian-style restaurants), and the second is to represent that the system is unsure about the status of the user's knowledge. Both of these aspects introduce a level of uncertainty into the system.

To represent the partial acquisition of knowledge by the user, we could use a structure such as prerequisites and assign a percentage known value to aggregate concepts which represent groupings of these knowledge units. Alternatively, we could use simple numerical measures which make a crude estimate of the frequency with which the users can apply a particular piece of knowledge appropriately.

The issue of confidence in our knowledge of the user is more complex. Most tractable solutions are simply compromises. A human being does not normally have a 'correct' model of another human being but has a model which is close enough for the purpose that is needed to apply it to. Without going too far into this, we can use the idea of a confidence value to represent such a thing.

A single-tail user model of this sort would associate a number with each piece of knowledge which varied over a range (e.g. 0 to 1) (Figure 4.16). The bottom of the range (0) means that the student knows nothing or we do not know what the student knows. The top of the range (1) means that the student definitely knows everything about this piece of knowledge. The more evidence we have for the student understanding the knowledge, the closer the model will get to the top limit, and the more reluctant we will be to accept evidence of misunderstanding.

It should be apparent that this model conflates the two issues: we require both a measure of the level of student understanding and a

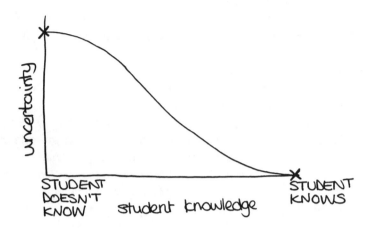

Figure 4.16   Graph of one-tail model.

measure of our confidence in it. One way to handle this is to introduce a scale associated with each piece of knowledge which has a mid-point (e.g. ranges from −1 to +1) (Figure 4.17). In this case the mid-point (0) represents the state in which the system has no knowledge about the understanding of the user. As we move towards one extreme or the other we are representing an indication that the user does or does not understand, and a level of confidence in our belief. The most extreme negative point on the scale indicates that we are sure that the user does not understand this piece of knowledge while the most extreme positive point indicates that we are sure that the user does understand.

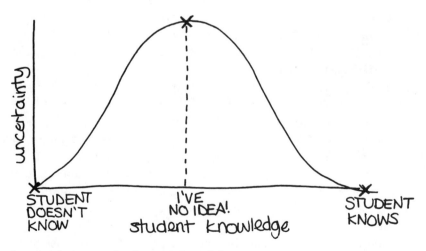

Figure 4.17   Graph of two-tail model.

4.7 Summary

This chapter has introduced the single most important element in multimedia system design: the user. We have presented issues relating to the way that systems should be designed for users, and a variety of approaches to making systems adaptive to different users. In all cases, understanding of users, and particularly their cognitive state, is central to a successful system. To support a designer in developing in this field we have examined the nature of user knowledge, looked at ways to acquire and apply it, and introduced a few techniques which can be embodied within a system that takes account of the user.

The following chapter will examine one of the critical parts of the relationship between user and computer: the interface.

4.8 Exercises

Exercise 4.1 You are intending to design a new website which is for fans of British films of the 1940s and 1950s. Who are the stakeholders? Why?

Exercise 4.2 You are asked to design a bank website that lets customers view their accounts and pay their bills. Who are the stakeholders? Why?

Exercise 4.3 Identify a list of likely background knowledge for users of the system in Exercise 4.1.

Exercise 4.4 Identify a list of likely foreground knowledge for users of the system in Exercise 4.1.

Exercise 4.5 Identify a list of likely background knowledge for users of the system in Exercise 4.2.

Exercise 4.6 Identify a list of likely foreground knowledge for users of the system in Exercise 4.2.

Exercise 4.7 Categorize each of the following according to whether it is primarily cognitive, conative, or affective: I want to be a millionaire; The square root of 4 is 2; Never used a computer before; I'm having a bad day; Sausages would be nice; That hat is on backwards; Your shirt is ugly; Isn't life wonderful; Tuesdays always make me miserable; I'm down; I'm hot; I'm cool; Never clean the window with a soft-boiled egg.

Exercise 4.8 For the system in Exercise 4.1 or the system in Exercise 4.2, identify at least 2 and possibly 3 distinct groups of users for whom the system could be adapted to behave differently.

Exercise 4.9 For each group identified in Exercise 4.8, write down a list of the key assumptions you could make about the user knowledge, similarities and differences between groups.

4.9 Further reading

User modelling is most often referred to in journals and conferences, but you will also find it included in books on Human Computer Interaction, including:

Alan Dix (*et al.*), *Human computer interaction*, Prentice-Hall, 1997

Jenny Preece (*et al.*), *Human computer interaction*, Addison-Wesley, 1994

Ben Shneiderman, *Designing the user interface*, Addison-Wesley, 1998

Joann Hackos and Janice Redish, *User and task analysis for interface design*, Wiley, 1998

5

Interaction and the interface

5.1 Introduction

At the start of this book we introduced the idea of computers and talked about the way they were in the 1940s and 1950s. These were big and expensive machines with a severely limited lifespan. They were complex to operate and there was no prospect of them being made available to the general public. It took a long time to become a competent 'computer operator', let alone a programmer. The machines were unreliable, required special rooms, huge amounts of power and cooling, and continuous access to maintenance teams. In this era, *computer time* was expensive. If we calculate the total cost of a machine over its working life then a computer of this period would have an effective cost in the region of $30,000 per hour of use. By comparison, a modern desktop machine (which is much more powerful) has a cost which is significantly less than $1 per hour. In the 1950s a typical human wage was something like 50¢ per hour.

Simply by looking at these costings it is apparent that there was no point in making computers easy to use. The phenomenal cost of computing time meant that it was expended only on the core of an algorithm – the part that only a computer could do – while humans were trained to manipulate and interpret its somewhat cryptic operation for the rest of the world. This made sense because human time was much cheaper than computer time. Throughout the 1950s and into the 1960s computer operators were people trained in this esoteric and arcane process of manipulation and there was no access for other users. A computer was a big machine – physically and electronically inaccessible to all but a few. Mere mortals (i.e. most programmers) were doomed to communicate with the system only through paper (punchcards, tapes, and printouts) which were actually input and output by the operators. The idea of an untrained user being able to even send a program to a computer, let alone operate one, was unheard of.

In the 1960s there was some research on the way that people operated in conjunction with a computer, but it focused primarily on the organizational aspects of large teams and could have applied to any organization. It was not until the end of the 1960s that the subject of the *psychology of programming* first gained mention. The first text to propose the study of users interacting with computers was still concentrating on professional programmers (and mostly, upon programmers in a batch programming environment). Nonetheless, this is one of the first indications that the way that humans approached and understood computers was worthy of examination in itself.

Through the 1960s and the 1970s the market for computers grew. Technology improved, prices came down and consequently more people were able to gain access to machines. By the mid-1970s computers were beginning to reach people who did not study computing, and these users began to use programs instead of writing them. They began to notice that some computers were quicker and easier to use than others, or had particular software that they wanted which was not available on other machines. What was being achieved was that users without detailed computer expertise were beginning to gain access to computers and expected to be able to use them, and the drastic reductions in cost of hardware meant that for the first time it was becoming economically viable to try and make a computer do some of that work. Instead of expert users operating cryptic machines, some manufacturers started trying to make software which was actually suited to the needs of the new users.

This interest in (and possibility of) making computers that fitted with the needs of users was a major revolution in software (and hardware) design which has permeated throughout the computer industry in less than 30 years. From the time when computer software consisted entirely of 'the works' and made no effort to be comprehensible to users, the balance has swung to the point where the vast majority of code in almost any piece of software is dedicated to making the user able to operate the software effectively, rather than executing algorithms in the traditional sense of calculations.

The subject area concerned with users and their ability to use computers is called *human–computer interaction* (HCI).

5.2 Traditional HCI

Prior to the use of computers there was a subject area concerned with setting up an appropriate working environment for human beings. This included many things that we take for granted these days such as desks and chairs of the correct height to prevent back strain, comfortable layout of controls in our cars, appropriate lighting in the office, and door handles that are comfortable to hold. This field was known as *ergonomics* – the study of the relationship between workers and the environment (Figure 5.1). The studies focused primarily on physical well being in the workplace. Later, a branch devoted to the mental well being of the worker in the environment developed and was called *cognitive ergonomics*. This concerned the way that the environment related to what humans thought about, or expected from, the objects around them. This could relate to items such as the meaning given to door handles, control panels, knobs, levers, switches, etc. The importance lay in the fact that it was not concerned with the physical effect (is this knob easy to turn?) but with the mental effect (does turning this knob make *sense*?).

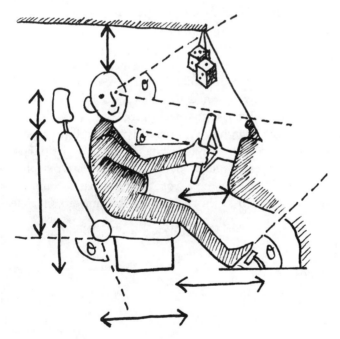

Figure 5.1 Ergonomics.

This was an important leap because it moved ergonomics from the realm of physical interaction into the realm of cognition. Suddenly, the subject area was concerned with how the object was interpreted by the brain. It recognized the importance of a process of communication (albeit one way) between the environment and the human. The advent of the computer and the consideration of the way that the user was affected by the design of the software and hardware was a natural extension of this form of ergonomics.

5.2.1 The ergonomics of computing

Ergonomics and computers sits between the physical and mental worlds. It includes very traditional ergonomics of the work environment – which has slightly different constraints upon it when there are computers present, but also examines things specific to the physical interaction with computers such as the visual display characteristics, noise, and radiation issues.

5.2.1.1   Physical

The most obvious physical effect of working with a computer is that it limits the amount of movement or different working positions that users occupy over the course of a day: they spend much time staring at a screen with hands on keyboard and mouse. This contrasts with a pre-computer environment where the same range of activities might involve writing with a pen, drawing, using a typewriter, going to filing cabinets to get data, telephoning people, and visiting other offices. In the earlier period there was a variety of changes of posture which do not occur in modern workplaces. Consequently, there is an increase in problems related to the static or constrained range of postures and movements. When our bodies are restrained like this, muscles are under constant tension and this can give rise to certain problems. The most obvious are back and neck pains, together with repetitive strain injury/carpal tunnel syndrome in our mouse and keyboard hands. It is not the purpose of this section to explore these issues in detail since they are peripheral to the main thrust of the text, but it is worth noting that for any desk-based computing environment, the following parameters (at least) are considered important:

- desk height;

- chair height;

- desk-to-chair distance;

- angle of chair back;

- height of chair back;

- distance from table edge to keyboard;

- distance from table edge to VDU;

- height and angle of keyboard relative to hands;

- height and angle of VDU relative to line of sight.

In addition, for the keyboard itself there is considerable work which suggests better possible designs and layouts (such as split keyboards, different character arrangements, etc.) but for a 'standard' keyboard there is more or less universal agreement about the correct values for:

- keyboard front height above desk;
- keyboard rear height above desk;
- angle of inclination;
- distance between keys;
- size of keys;
- key depression distance;
- key resistance;
- tactile feedback distance.

This traditional approach to ergonomics (Figure 5.2) has identified a range of factors which may affect computer use and we have not even got to the point of looking at a screen yet!

Figure 5.2   Computer ergonomics.

5.2.1.2   Visual

Visual aspects of ergonomics of computers concentrate on making it easy to read the screen without causing too much eye strain. There are three basic aspects to this: the external environment; properties of the CRT (cathode ray tube, or equivalent) itself; and properties of the software in use.

External environment refers to factors around the computer and user that affect the visibility of the screen. This includes the type, quality, positioning, and brightness of the artificial lighting. It includes the location and orientation of windows and other natural light sources. It includes the interior design as it affects the ambient light – such as the colours and levels of reflectivity of the surfaces around the user and machine. The objective in arranging the lighting (or more often, moving the computer around in order to minimize the effects of poor lighting) is to achieve:

• sufficient brightness for non-computer areas;

• no excessive variation in brightness between looking at the screen and looking away;

• no 'hot spots' of excessive brightness;

• stable flicker-free light sources;

• no glare or reflection on the screen.

Properties of the CRT refer to aspects of the screen which cannot be changed by software but are inherent in the physical display hardware. The image on a CRT is created (much like a television) by the movement of an electron beam which repeatedly scans across and down the screen, changing in intensity to cause small pieces of the phosphor coating of the screen to glow. This phosphor continues to glow (persists) for a short time after the beam has moved on, therefore giving the impression of a stable image on the screen, although it is actually constantly oscillating in intensity. Newer technologies such as LCD screens have a different set of issues associated with them, but for the CRT we need to consider at least:

• **Flicker** – The screen is not really at a constant level of luminance, but is constantly oscillating through a process of being refreshed and fading calculated by the phosphor persistence. Minimizing flicker requires a *fast refresh rate* and an *appropriate phosphor persistence* (too short a persistence and the display flickers too long and there is a 'ghosting' effect). There is an additional problem when the computer is being used in a room with lighting that flickers (notably fluorescent tubes) since the interaction between the speed of the lighting and the speed of the screen refresh can cause a perceived flickering which can be very disturbing. This is much the same process that caused the wheels to go backwards on wagons in old cowboy movies.

• **Sharpness** – The accuracy of the beam position (particularly horizontally) controls the apparent preciseness of the luminant areas of the screen, and hence can make a line, edge, or character appear more or less sharp. This is more commonly a problem horizontally than vertically, with characters on cheap screens potentially having fuzzy edges. Higher quality screens with better quality components are generally sharper in the image. Note that this is not the same as the resolution of the screen, which is a question of how many pixels the video drivers decide to divide the screen into. Sharper screens can support higher resolutions, but all screens reach a point at which a higher resolution would become so fuzzy as to be unacceptable.

- **Jitter** – Particularly with cheap or old screens, there can be a tendency for the electron beam to waver vertically over the course of a scan. This can result in horizontal lines which are not horizontal, but wobbly, and which potentially move up and down over time.

Properties of the software covers anything that can be manipulated and managed by ourselves as software designers. This includes pretty much anything that does not fall into the categories above. Some of these which are examined in ergonomics are:

- typeface choices and sizes;

- display contrast;

- display brightness;

- colour choices;

- amount on screen.

There are many aspects of this area of visual ergonomics that are of importance to interface designers, and we will return to them in a later section.

5.2.1.3   Other aspects

There are other aspects of computers which appear from time to time, particularly those related to health and safety. Although we rarely think about it, most PCs have cooling fans which make a continuous noise quite near to our heads, and this must be kept within reasonable limits. There are also levels of electromagnetic radiation emitted by monitors which must be kept within safe limits. Happily there are good international safety standards in this area and although there have occasionally been suggestions that the radiation might relate to causing cataracts, higher levels of miscarriage in pregnancy, and various other health issues, there is no evidence that there are health risks associated with computer radiation. The level of radiation from computers is significantly lower than that from other everyday sources.

I have always blamed the fact that I had white hair by the time I was 30 on spending my life in front of VDUs. This seems to make sense to me since astronauts on moon shots had hairs which turned white owing to radiation. I must concede, however, that the fact that both my father and grandfather had white hair by the time they were 30 may affect the validity of this excuse.

One further aspect of ergonomics of the workplace is the way that the job itself is designed and how this affects the activities of the users. This has been taken up as a major part of recent work in HCI and expanded drastically. Where the ergonomic issues focus on fine details, the large-scale end of HCI now examines the very broad context in which the system operates. We will consider this context in the following section.

5.2.2   Computing in context

The opposite extreme of approaches to HCI concentrates on the larger picture. The basic point is that any software (or indeed, any other sort of object or innovation) exists in a context. If someone is trying to do a job in an organization, then that job affects (and is affected by) not only the person doing the job, but also all the people around who supply input to the job, or use output from the job. It affects people who maintain the infrastructure that makes the job possible, and people who employ those people. It affects policy makers and is affected by changes in policy. Not only are all these different actors affected by the job, but they are also affected by any change in the job such as the adoption of a new tool. This implies that if we are attempting to design a new piece of software for such an environment, it potentially affects all these people in addition to the actual user who is operating with it. These other people are termed stakeholders in this process and are the subject of a process known as soft systems engineering, which attempts to understand their impact and relationships.

This approach to HCI involves starting with a big model of the organization and context and working down to the individual user and requirements for the software and the interface needs. This is a useful part of the design process, but too large scale to relate directly to our model of Interactive Multimedia as a system of Communicative Interaction. These processes are further explored in Chapter 11.

5.2.3   HCI as communication

The most common approach between the two forms of HCI described above is the one that interests us: the idea of HCI as a communication between a (single) user and a computer. This approach traditionally concentrates on the idea of an *interface*, which is a mechanism by which users communicate their goals and objectives, and some instructions, to the computer, while the computer communicates its current state, activities, and related information to the users. This idea is akin to the processes of communication that we have already introduced – particularly that of channels of communication. Traditional HCI does not consider the issues of media raised in this text, so we will treat the interface as a group of channels of communication between user and computer which exist alongside our multimedia channels. As we shall see below, many interface styles have now acquired a conventional language of interpretation which means that we could regard them as a *medium* in terms of our definition. We shall return to this in Section 5.4.

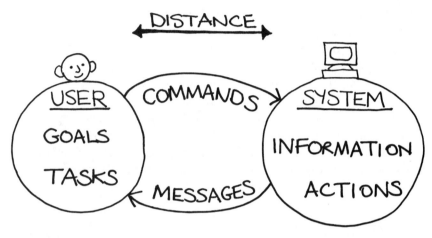

Figure 5.3   The gulf.

It is worth expanding this model of the interface as communication by using a rather famous distinction: the gulf between computer and user. Figure 5.3 illustrates this approach, which is typical of approaches to software design based upon recognition of the importance of the user in the process. The basic assumption behind the diagram is that on the left there is a user who has goals that need to be achieved (or tasks that need to be completed) therefore the user must try and issue appropriate communications (e.g. commands, data, etc.) to the computer. The computer is on the other side of the gulf and it receives commands, interprets them (to a greater or lesser degree), and executes them. The result is then (hopefully) communicated back to the user across the gulf.

Work at the University of California at San Diego went further and divided this gulf into two components: the gulf of execution and the gulf of evaluation. The former is the 'distance' (in some cognitive sense) between what the user wishes to do and what the computer is able to understand. If the two match well, then the gulf is narrow and the communication via the interface can be effective. The latter is the gap between what the computer 'says' and what the user understands by it. If the computer meaning is always clear then this gap is small and communication from computer to human is effective. A larger gap means that the user is having greater difficulty in understanding what is going on. If we treat the interface as a single channel of communication (which is bi-directional) then we can immediately see a relationship to the effectiveness or otherwise of the encodings and decodings that we discussed as part of Communicative Interaction. In practice, we will find that the interface is more effectively regarded as a collection of channels of communication, and that these channels form only a small part of the communication between computer and user: the rest is communication related to the *multimedia content*.

While it is obviously important to emphasize the view of HCI as being primarily concerned with the idea of communication in the interface, it should also be noted that in order to study this effectively, HCI embraces a variety of aspects related to this interaction. Key components are understanding the user, and working with the knowledge content and task structure of the subject area in which the system is to operate. These fields are of such importance that they have been explored in separate chapters, and hence we are able to focus our attention on a more restrictive view of HCI in this chapter. The other aspect of our focus in this chapter is that we are separating HCI from issues concerned with the *multimedia content* of our system.

5.2.4 Multimedia content

Historically, software consisted of algorithms to achieve some result. The interface was concerned with providing a method whereby a user could have access to the software to control these algorithms and manipulate the results. Since it originated in these sorts of systems, HCI has historically focused upon the idea of goal-directed systems. The idea, in essence, is that there is some sort of task to be carried out, by the user, the computer or, more likely, both, and each has a range of actions that they can engage in to achieve the completion of that task. This approach makes sense for almost all sorts of software, but more recently it is beginning to be questioned as new approaches to software become possible. There are several changes happening here.

- There is potentially an increase in autonomy within the software (intelligent agents, etc.) and this does not necessarily match the sort of 'master' and 'slave' model which has applied to most approaches to interaction of a human and a computer.

- The application of the computer in domains that are not task-oriented is being explored, and hence researchers are trying to suggest radically new metaphors and mechanisms for interaction (e.g. the computer as theatre).

- Mixtures of complex narrative channels (such as film, soundtrack, etc.) imply a new form of communication which has not been previously considered in the work on HCI. We now find that we are looking at interfaces which can 'tell a story' and in which the meaning of the interaction is open to broader interpretation than a traditional text-based or graphical user interface.

While certain researchers are attempting to extend the scope of HCI to encompass the above changes, the approach that we will take is to remain with a very traditional model of HCI and deal with multimedia content as a range of other communicative activities which exist in parallel with the interface. This will be seen in later chapters to make sense because we can explore the interface in terms of fairly well-understood formal languages and techniques (discussed later in this chapter), whereas the exploration of the meaning of the multimedia content will lead us into a different sort of range of languages, typified by a common thread of semiotics (Chapter 6).Having established our restricted definition of HCI as referring to the interface as being one among a set of media in our system, we will now examine what approaches we can bring to designing and understanding this interface (Figure 5.4).

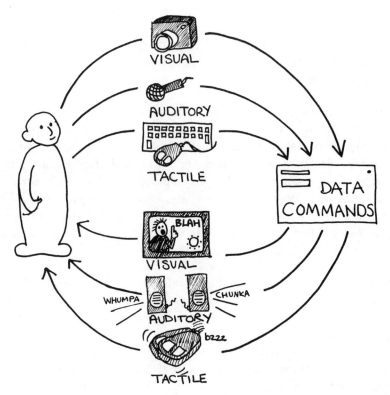

Figure 5.4　Interface as medium.

5.3   Modalities and the interface

The first step in examining the issues of the interface is to relate them to our existing definitions of *modalities* and *channels of communication*. In doing this we should first note that we are assuming that the modalities are only effective if they fit our model to the extent that the participants in the interaction (computer and user) both have appropriate encoders and decoders to work with the modality and 'understand' it. Reproduction without understanding in a modality does not permit its inclusion in our interface (though it might appear as *multimedia content* in the system).

In terms of modalities, most computers, and most researchers in HCI, deal with a very restricted range. These communications are not symmetrical (i.e. the computer does not have the same options of communication as the user) so it is necessary to separate input and output modalities.

5.3.1   Input modalities:

- **Tactile** – The vast majority of input to the computer is tactile. Historically, this has been through devices such as the keyboard (and, more recently, the mouse). Newer work includes the use of touch screens and special keyboards and devices such as tactile clothes and floor mats. There is also a number of movement sensors (such as air wands, with which you can conduct) that react directly to tactile contact with the body.

- **Auditory** – Auditory input has been a goal of computer interaction since the 1960s. It was intended to be one of the first 'easy' problems solved by artificial intelligence methods. The problem turned out to be much harder than most researchers envisaged, but we are finally reaching the point at which the computer can listen to speech and recognize what many of the words are. This does not, however, imply that it is understanding speech. Attaching actions to discrete words is possible, but getting a computer to work out the meaning of a spoken (or written) sentence is still a significant problem.

- **Visual** – Some work in artificial intelligence has concentrated on visual recognition of pictures and videos. This is still at the level of fairly basic research, but some work is beginning to bear fruit. The most obvious possibilities in this area are gestural interfaces (in which the computer watches your movements through a camera and recognizes activities such as pointing) and eye-movement systems which can carry out actions depending on where your eyes are focusing.

5.3.2 Output modalities:

- **Visual** – Historically almost all output from computers has been in the visual modality. It has concentrated primarily on the use of textual information (even in a graphical user interface the information content is primarily textual), with some use of spatial layout (GUIs, menus, icons, etc. are essentially spatial organizations of the visual modality). Research on generating diagrams is making progress, but the use of photographs, film, and similar rich visual communications is severely restricted by the problem of ensuring that the computer 'understands' what it is doing or saying. Simply using the computer as a playback machine for video does not satisfy our requirement for the interface to be a communication activity.

- **Auditory** – Auditory output in terms of the use of sounds to represent activities and to communicate states of the computer has been explored for a considerable period of time, particularly in environments such as factories or aeroplane cockpits, where practical constraints upon the visual modality of the user (such as being unable to look at two things simultaneously) make additional forms of communication necessary. Generation of spoken 'natural' language is slightly more complex than generating written text, and can be done with understanding in restricted language areas, but it is still a difficult problem in general. As with playing a film, playing a pre-recorded speech does not satisfy the communication requirements of our interface.

- **Tactile** – Tactile interfaces exist in restricted domains and have mostly been explored for users with special needs, particularly the visually impaired. Braille displays (which have moving dots to represent letters of the Braille alphabet) are commercially available, and work on mapping visual images to sensations on sections of the body (arrays of pins) are also being explored. Some effectively tactile interfaces are appearing in the games world in the form of devices which attach to the body and vibrate when there are low frequency sounds (such as explosions) during a game.

To the best of my knowledge there are currently no olfactory or gustatory interface devices but this is a current area of research interest.

Each of the above modalities can be used, but in each there is still much further work to be done. Most 'mainstream' HCI still focuses upon tactile input and visual output. The innovations in the use of modalities are coming from more esoteric fields: notably from work on users with disabilities, work on hostile environments (such as factories), and some areas of the games industry.

5.4   Channels of communication and the interface

Having clarified the modalities we can now turn to considering the most appropriate way to regard an interface in terms of channels of communication. While there are some things which we might regard as primitive (such as pressing a key), other things seem to be made up of many parts and to have an interpretation which is dependent upon understanding those parts. Different styles of interface would be examples of this: Macintosh house style is different from Microsoft house style (although they have a lot in common) and interface guidelines for a different platform such as the Palm Pilot are different again. We will explore this by starting with the 'primitive' components and building up to interface styles.

5.4.1   Interface channels

5.4.1.1   The text channel

The *keyboard* has been the primary way to interact with a computer for more than 40 years. It satisfies our definition of a channel of communication very precisely. The users have some idea of a character (e.g. 'A') in their head. They use a keyboard as an encoding system to convert this into a set of binary digits. This is transmitted along the channel (in this case, some sort of physical hardware bus) and a process somewhere inside the computer knows how to interpret this as a character from a given character set. The exact character set chosen will depend on the sort of keyboard and the particular physical key. The corresponding character can be more than just one from the printable character set – it may include control characters and other special keys. This description excludes any question of interpretation – there is no notion of what the computer will understand by the character or do with it.

By convention we have come to associate this textual input channel with a visual output channel. In general, when we press a key on a keyboard, we expect to see a corresponding letter appear on the screen of the machine. This does not have to happen – in the early days of batch processing there was often no feedback for the characters that were typed at a keyboard. Equally, it is only generally true of 'printable' characters – we accept that modified characters (such as control sequences) may not have a simple visual appearance on the screen, but may have complex effects which differ from package to package. Nevertheless, it has become such a common convention of computing that pressing a key on the keyboard results in a visual representation of a character on the screen, that we will group the keyboard input channel and the visual text output channel together, and refer to the two in a group as the *text channel* (Figure 5.5).

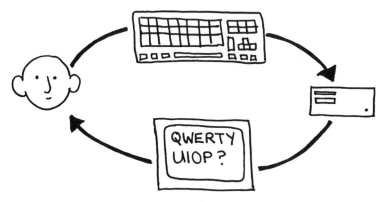

Figure 5.5 Text channel.

5.4.1.2 The spatial position channel

Prior to the late 1970s, spatial location was hardly used in the interface. Command line interfaces (Section 4.2.1) were the norm, and if a positioning device existed at all on the keyboard, it was a set of arrow keys. Behaviour of the computer was independent of the part of the screen on which one operated. Beginning with the cursor keys, and later moving to the mouse (or similar 'pointing device') an entirely new means of communication with the computer has evolved which depends upon the position of an action as well as the action itself. This had firmly established itself by the 1990s as the primary means of interaction for most users.

As with the text channel, we are considering two distinct, but related, channels of communication here. The first is the *pointer input* channel. With this channel the user moves a physical device in a two-dimensional space (e.g. on a desk). This movement is encoded and transmitted (normally as a sequence of positional information) to the computer. This information is then decoded as either a *relative* movement of the device from its previous position (typical of a mouse) or a change to a new *absolute* position (as with a graphics tablet). This information has no inherent meaning and it is almost never used in this form. Instead, the position is mapped into some other sort of two-dimensional space (such as the objects which appear on the screen) and the meaning of the movement is related to the position resulting from the mapping into this other space. For communication to be successful, this meaning in the second space must be accessible to the users, so that they can know the meaning of the action that they have made (or know how to perform a movement to communicate a meaning that they want to communicate). For this reason, the pointer input channel is, almost invariably, associated with the *cursor output* channel. This channel provides a visual representation of the position in the screen space of the computer, and the meaning of the pointing movement can only be decoded with access to this information.

This grouping is conventional (e.g. visually impaired users may use mice without a visible cursor), but is such a strong linking between the channels that we will in future group them together and refer to them as the *spatial position channel* (Figure 5.6).

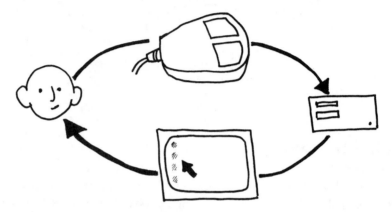

Figure 5.6   Spatial position channel.

5.4.1.3   Other channels

There are many other channels that could be defined in the interface. Many are restricted to particular packages and contexts. We have restricted ourselves to a minimal set of modalities and channels that represents the most common set of interface communications. The vast majority of current interfaces can be described using just the two combined channels described above. Other channels can be constructed or introduced as required.

The next stage in understanding the role of the interface in our model is to relate these channels to higher levels of interpretation. These group channels together and provide a way of interpreting them that has evolved as a conventional language of interpretation. This means that these can be called 'media' in terms of our definition. They correspond to what have historically been called 'styles' of interface.

5.4.2   Conventional interfaces

Interfaces have evolved over a period of 40 years. As the power of the computer, the flexibility of the graphics, and the availability of different physical devices have progressed, the ways of interacting have changed to cope with this. While there have been many different and novel approaches, most of these have fallen by the wayside and, in practical terms, there have only been a few different styles of interaction with computers that have achieved the status of a convention. There are three main types of interface, each of which corresponds to placing a particular form of interpretation of the channels of interaction described above. These are the communication 'media' of the interface.

5.4.2.1 The command line interface

The command line interface (Figure 5.7) is the most basic method for working with an interactive computer. These systems are entirely text-

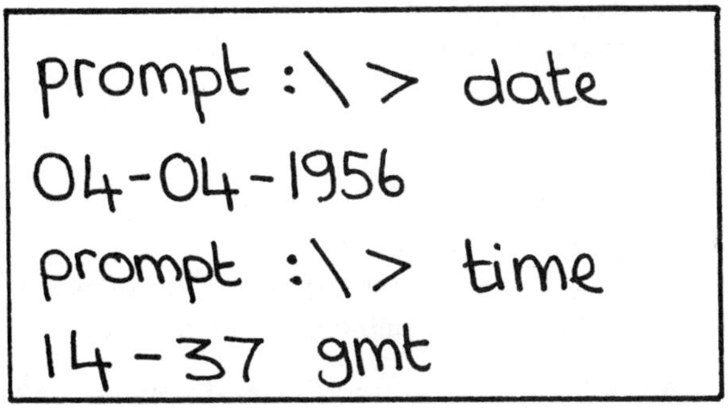

```
prompt :\> date
04-04-1956
prompt :\> time
14-37 gmt
```

Figure 5.7   The command line interface.

based and there is no utilization of spatial information. Most computer operating systems, even if they possess a modern graphical interface, have a command line interface somewhere within them. Currently, the most widely known are Unix and DOS. Command line interfaces can also arise within specific packages in an otherwise graphical environment (such as versions of NetWare). The two key components of these interfaces are as follows.

1. **Turn taking** – These interfaces have a single point at which interaction occurs (such as the bottom of the screen). This means that only one thing can be happening at a time: either the user can communicate to the computer or vice versa. It is essential to take turns. Normally, the computer will display a special symbol (called a *prompt*) to indicate that it is waiting for a command from the user. The user types this command and presses a key (normally *enter*) to indicate completion and it is now time for the computer to deal with whatever the user typed. Whether this takes a fraction of a second, or a day, it remains the computer's 'turn' while it calculates and displays information to the user. The user cannot interact again until the computer indicates that it has finished its turn by displaying another *prompt*.

2. **Command line syntax** – While there are few conventions governing what the computer says to the user, almost all command line interfaces use the same basic structure to the command line. There are

three components: a *command*; some *arguments*; and some *parameters*. The *command* is an instruction to the computer about an action to carry out, the *arguments* are things that the command is to be done to, and the *parameters* are things that modify the way in which the command is carried out. In linguistic terms, we can think of these components as a verb (an action), some nouns (references to things), and some adverbs (modify the meaning of the action).

The following are examples of command lines (command name is in bold and the parameters are italic):

ls	%% list a directory
ls *-l*	%% list directory with long details
ls fred	%% list directory called fred
ls fred *-l*	%% list fred with long details
cp * ..	%% copy everything to the directory above
ls jane *-R*	%% list jane and directories inside it

In terms of our definitions, this interface is simply defined. It uses the *text channel* (only), with two additional conventions of interpretation: (i) computer and user take alternate turns, with completion of a turn indicated by displaying a *prompt* or pressing the *enter* key, respectively (ii) user communication to the computer consists of a *command*, zero or more *arguments*, and zero or more *parameters*.

Beyond these conventions the meaning of a command line interface depends upon the particular package or system in use. Interpretation of individual command meanings and the nature of the communication from computer to user are outside the general definition of this form of interface.

5.4.2.2   Spatial textual interfaces

Spatial textual interfaces (Figure 5.8) followed from the increased use of CRT monitors (as opposed to paper-based output devices such as teletypes). The teletype only permitted turn-taking command line interaction. The CRT permitted the use of spatial position, but initially all applications used it as a sort of paperless teletype, with information always appearing at the bottom of the screen and scrolling up. Computers of this period had only a single, fixed width font and no graphics capabilities. Consequently, the spatial layout of a screen could only be used in terms of character locations. A screen was (typically) 80 characters wide and 25 high. The computer was able to move to arbitrary parts of the screen to write text, and the user could also move around the screen (though not necessarily with complete freedom) using *cursor* keys or *tab* keys.

The primary use of this spatial positioning was to enrich the communication from computer to user so that strict turn taking was no longer necessary, and information could be always present to help the

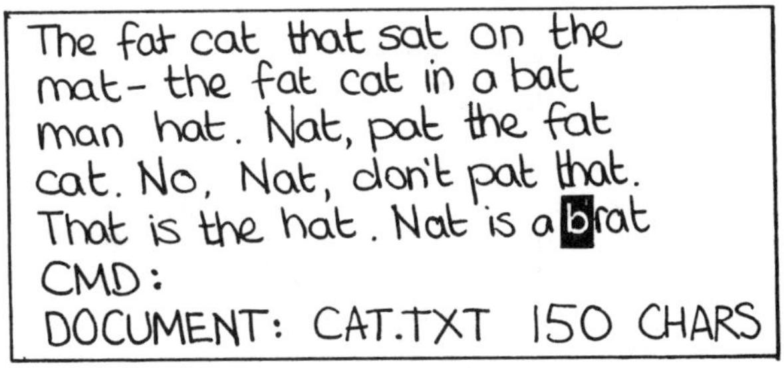

The fat cat that sat on the mat – the fat cat in a bat man hat. Nat, pat the fat cat. No, Nat, don't pat that. That is the hat. Nat is a **b**rat
CMD:
DOCUMENT: CAT.TXT 150 CHARS

Figure 5.8 Basic spatial textual interface.

users and require them to remember less. These systems came in a number of varieties over a period of years, but would normally include one or more of the following.

- **Working area** – Most applications included an area which displayed information related to the main file or activity that the user was engaged in. For example, a text-processor where the working area allowed you to see the document that you were working on (previously you would have been able to see no more than a line at a time!).

- **Command line** – The command line did not go away. Users still manipulated the software by issuing commands using either typed sequences of printable characters or sets of control characters. Most applications had a single line on the screen (which remained at a fixed location, e.g. the bottom or the top) and the user would go to this line and type to issue commands. The same typing did not work in the same way if the cursor was not positioned on the command line.

- **Information areas** – Various areas of the screen could be set aside to provide information to the user, for example lists of available commands, the status of the current document (whether it had been saved, how big it was, etc.). These information areas persist as status lines in most modern applications.

- **Form screens** – Forms are a specific example of one way to structure a working area (Figure 5.9). These were commonly used for tasks related to data entry or examination. There would be certain areas of the screen which were fixed (such as names of sorts of data – the 'fields') and other areas which could be changed (which contained the actual data – the 'values'). Users could move to a particular part of the screen and type to indicate that what they were typing was information of a certain kind. This was determined by the field on the area of screen where they were typing. This is still commonly used with databases and other information tasks.

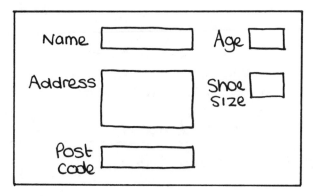

Figure 5.9   Form interface.

- **Menus** – Although rare, some systems introduced simple menus for executing commands. Whereas many systems included lists of commands visible on screen, to remind you what you had to type, some systems enabled you to move the cursor to the place on the screen where a particular command name was written and press a key (e.g. enter) to indicate the command to be carried out. These menus normally occupied a fixed part of the screen but in later systems there were the first attempts at a menu bar across the top of the screen which allowed the user to issue one command (press a key over a menu name) to see a menu, and another command (press a key over an item on that menu) to issue the command (Figure 5.10). This became popular because it offered a way to give the user a greater range of commands to use without typing. These interfaces were quickly superseded as bitmap displays and graphical interfaces became possible.

These interfaces utilize our *text* channel together with a simple *spatial position* channel consisting of a small number of locations, horizontal or vertical movement using cursor keys. These channels work together to produce a communication which has a *language of interpretation* that derives a meaning from the combination of channels. The interpretation

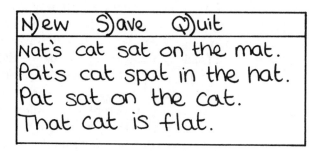

Figure 5.10   Menubar interface.

of the user input upon the text channel is dependent upon the location of the cursor. This gives an interface with different modes from which we can usefully separate four separate types: *passive* areas, *command* areas, *selection* areas, *data* areas.

- Passive areas – user input is ignored.

- Command areas – input treated as command line.

- Selection areas – input treated as command chosen from list.

- Data areas – input treated as information given to computer.

Equally, the output from the system to the user can now be divided into: *permanent* information, *dynamic* information and *transient* information, depending upon where it appears on the screen.

- Permanent – always present and the same (e.g. command list).

- Dynamic – changes depending upon mode/context (e.g. content of document).

- Transient – immediate response to user (like turn taking).

While there are few spatial textual interfaces still in use, these distinctions, which form the basis of interpretation of the interfaces are still applied in many graphical user interfaces today, so it is important to understand them clearly.

5.4.2.3   Graphical user interfaces

Almost all readers of this book will be familiar with graphical user interfaces (Figure 5.11) – probably more so than the interfaces described earlier. These interfaces were originally referred to as WIMPs, and this is still the best way to remember what distinguishes them: *Windows, Icons, Menus,* and *Pointers.*

Figure 5.11   GUI.

WIMPs became possible with the improvements in graphics and monitors which meant that computers could move away from character-based interaction and begin to regard the screen as an array of points (pixels) which could be turned on or off individually. This made it feasible to draw things with precision and accuracy. A single character was made up of a collection of dots and while it initially looked worse than its pre-graphics counterparts, the advantages of being able to draw previously impossible things (such as fairly good circles) and to create and change fonts and graphics, far outweighed the initial disadvantages. As pixel resolution improved these disadvantages ceased to exist.

A WIMP interface utilizes the *text* channel and *spatial position* channel. In essence it still preserves the distinction between different areas and information types which existed in the spatial textual interface, but the ability to use a more accurate pointer (referring to individual pixels rather than characters) and to draw high quality graphics means that the range of activity has been extended. The interpretation of these interfaces revolves around the four key aspects in the name.

- **Window** – An area of screen dedicated to a particular purpose. Windows can (often) be moved, grown, shrunk, hidden behind things, etc. There will generally be many windows on a screen.

- **Icon** – An area of screen where a particular action can be initiated by clicking a mouse button.

- **Menu** – An area containing a range of alternative selections from which one is chosen.

- **Pointer** – A physical device represented by a pointer on the screen which communicates location information.

Although these are the main components, they are not the complete set of functionality in a WIMP. The conventions of interpretations of these systems have resulted in a set of common communicative units (both from user to computer and vice versa) which have become a convention, and each of which has the same basic interpretation across a range of environments and platforms. These are often referred to as *interface widgets*. Some of the most common are listed below.

Selection widgets (items you can select with a location and key press) (Figure 5.12):

- icons;
- buttons;
- simple buttons;
- check boxes;
- radio buttons;
- menu items.

Figure 5.12   Selection widgets.

Groups of selection widgets (ways to organize selection widgets into meaningful combinations) (Figure 5.13):

- menubar;

- menu;

- toolbar;

- palette.

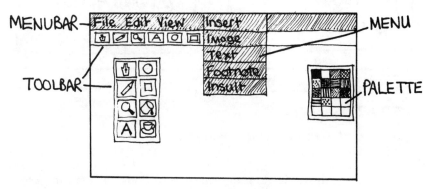

Figure 5.13   Selection grouping widgets.

Data input widgets (allow the user to provide open-ended input from the keyboard) (Figure 5.14):

- fields;

- windows;

- dialogs.

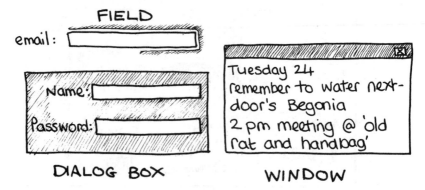

Figure 5.14   Data input widgets.

Information output widgets (system communicates open-ended information to user) (Figure 5.15):

- status line;

- system dialogs;

- fixed fields.

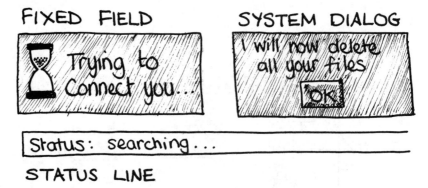

Figure 5.15   Information output widgets.

In this section we have provided descriptions of two important channels of communication for interfaces, and illustrated the three main categories of interface that utilize those channels. The following section will examine the design of specific interfaces in more detail.

5.5 Functionality and usability

The previous sections concentrated on explaining the way that the interface relates to our model of Communicative Interaction. We have established the general components of a modern interface, but in order to design a system it is necessary to go into detail about the specific interfaces with which we are working. This section will introduce some techniques for describing interfaces, and for understanding how they are likely to be used. These will be incorporated into our design process later in the book. Throughout the book we acknowledge the importance of the communicative nature of the systems which we are designing, and hence the importance of understanding the user. This is also key in the interface, and to distinguish it further we will distinguish between *functionality* and *usability* of the interface.

Functionality represents what the interface can do. A system which lets us use only two commands has less functionality than one which lets us use 2000. But remember, more is not always better.

Usability represents the ease with which the user can learn and utilize the interface. A system where all the commands can be selected from menus is likely to be more usable than one where there is just a command line and the user has to remember everything.

These descriptions are a gross simplification. The design of a system will depend upon who the users are, what the knowledge content is, the context in which the system will be used, etc. In general, there will be a certain range of functions which are better suited to these particular users and this particular context than others, and it is not necessarily the most functionality that is most useful. Equally, the easiest interfaces to use, which will probably be most learnable and suitable for novices, are not necessarily the fastest, and so may be inappropriate for experts. There will be a trade-off between the functionality and usability in any interface. The next sections explore these issues in more detail.

5.5.1 Functionality: defining the interface

Previous chapters have focused on ideas of language and different ways to represent and use language in understanding communication. It will probably come as no surprise to learn that the interface to a piece of software can be represented as a language. There are only certain things that a user can do, and only certain items to which the user can do things – these constitute a lexicon of the interface. Equally, at any moment there are only certain of these actions and items that are available to the user. The rules which describe what can be done when describing a grammar of the language. By writing down this language we can specify how we would like our interface to be implemented and what it should do. We can even test certain aspects, such as whether it is consistent and allows all the functionality we wish before we build it. It is very important to be able to describe an interface in this way.

5.5.1.1 Lexicon of the interface

The interface permits a user to issue certain commands (verbs) to refer to certain things (nouns) and to provide various additional pieces of information. We can represent the lexicon of the interface by listing all the nouns and verbs which are available to the user. The exact level of detail that we use will depend upon the particular requirements of our interface definition, but we are quite likely to use a level which is close to the 'conventional' level of units referred to in our description of a GUI given above. For a GUI, a typical range of actions might be: key press, mouse-click, mouse-double-click, mouse-down, mouse-up, mouse-enter, mouse-leave. Note that these are not all primitive. Some (e.g. mouse-click, mouse-double-click) can be described in terms of others (mouse-click = mouse-down, mouse-up). They have been chosen to represent a convenient level of description of our interface. Clearly complex actions could be broken down into simpler ones if we needed to do so.

On a similar basis, our things in the interface (which we will refer to as *objects*) can be defined using both primitive objects (e.g. button), special cases of objects (e.g. OK-button), and groupings of objects (e.g. edit-menu, file-dialog-box). Typical examples might be: menubar, file-menu, edit-menu, save-as-menu-item, open-dialog-box, user-prompt-box, alert-message-box, status-line. Once again, the complex items can be broken down into their components if necessary, but it is convenient to group together items which appear together as a single entity.

5.5.1.2   Grammar of the interface

Having described our lexicon, the next stage is to create a grammar to describe the way they can be combined within the interface. The Backus–Naur form which we introduced in a previous chapter is an appropriate way to do this. We will present a modified version of Backus–Naur, which is convenient for use in describing interfaces, and also a graphical notation for state transition networks, which can be developed quite easily and is precisely equivalent. For either notation the important thing is to think of the interface as moving over time from one *state* to another. Each of these states represents a stable point. To travel between states either the user or the computer must perform an *action*. To illustrate:

Current state	Action
Sitting at desk	Stand
Standing by desk	Walk to door
Standing by door	Open door
Standing by open door	Walk through door
Standing outside open door	Close door
Outside	

In this example the left column is a sequence of states in which I exist. I move from one to another by carrying out the action in the second column. The action *stand* takes me from the state of *sitting at desk* to the state of *standing by desk*. This information could also be represented as shown in Figure 5.16.

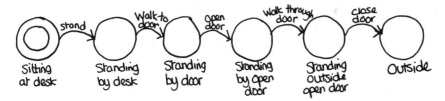

Figure 5.16   Desk STN.

Each state is represented by a circle (node) and each action by a line connecting two circles (an arc). The start state has a double border to indicate that this is the beginning. Each arc is normally labelled with the condition that must be true to pass along it. In our case this is generally the action that is performed by the user. If there is more than one possible way to leave a state, then there will be more than one arc leaving it. I could represent the option of climbing on the desk by adding the following to the diagram as shown in Figure 5.16.

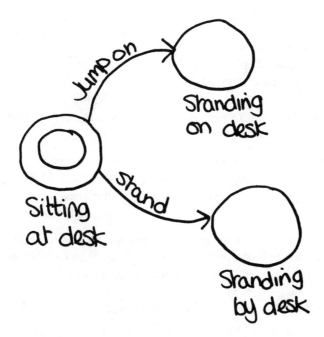

Figure 5.17   Desk STN2.

Normally a state will be labelled with a description of what it is. For our interfaces this may be a description of the interface objects that are available for the user to access in that state.

We can describe the same behaviour in a modified BNF by representing each state as a symbol which has a rule, and by adding the condition for choosing a certain state as a description of the action that one needs to perform to achieve it. In this notation we use a set of three things in brackets after the symbol: the action to carry out, the object to do it to, and any data that might be associated with it. Clicking on an OK button, for example, might be represented as [click, ok-button,]. This means that our lexical interface components are used to describe the conditions on the arcs. The diagram in Figure 5.16 could be described in this notation as:

Sitting-at-desk ::= standing-by-desk[stand, ,]
Standing-by-desk ::= standing-by-door [walk-to, door,] | standing-on-desk [jump-on, desk,]
Standing-by-door ::= standing-by-open-door[open, door,]
Standing-by-open-door ::= standing-outside-open-door [walk-through, door,]
Standing-outside-open-door ::= outside[close, door,]

The following example should clarify how this applies to describing an interface.

5.5.1.3   An example

Imagine a simple interface with a menubar across the top. This is a 'state' of our interface. We could move to the word 'File' on the menubar and click the mouse to display a file menu. This is an action which has taken us to another state – one where the menu is visible. Our next action might be to click on 'open' which takes us to a new state with an 'Open File' dialog. We can represent this interface in terms of states and transitions as:

Menubar ::= filemenu[click, 'file'] | editmenu[click, 'edit'], ...
Filemenu ::= opendialog[click, 'open'] | savedialog[click, 'save'], ...
Opendialog ::= menubar[click, 'OK'] | menubar[click, 'Cancel'] |
                                        opendialog[select, filename]

This can immediately be drawn out as a state transition network in a format such as those shown above, and we can then use this notation in various ways to test our interface before we even build it.

5.5.2   Usability: users and the interface

In exploring the idea of usability we are seeking to determine how well an interface matches the needs and behaviour of the user. As in the question of functionality, we will ignore the bigger picture and concentrate just upon the usability of an interface in terms of a single user interacting with it. We will also assume that we have already understood the nature of our user, our task, and the knowledge content of the system.

In examining usability we will look at several different aspects of the performance of the users: the number of actions they need to perform, the amount that they need to remember, the amount of mental work they need to do to use the interface, and the degree of learnability of the system.

5.5.2.1 Actions

One of the simplest evaluations of the usability of an interface is the number of actions on the interface which are required to carry out certain tasks. For a given task it is easy just to step through the performance of that task and to add up the number of each sort of action that is required (e.g. X clicks, Y key presses, Z mouse movements). Standard reference books are available which indicate how long each of these actions typically takes to perform, and these can be multiplied by the different action types to obtain an approximate time for doing a certain task. This is only a rough assessment, which does not include 'thinking time' of the user (see below). For certain interfaces it may be better to conduct experiments to determine how long actions take than to rely on a standard text.

$$\text{Task time} = \sum_{\text{action-types}} \text{action-count} \times \text{action-time}$$

This would enable us to take a single task (such as *drawing a circle*) and compare how long it would take in different programs. It does not necessarily make sense to try to produce one number for a software package which is 'How long things take' (such as an average across all tasks) because most users will not perform all tasks, and in all cases some tasks will be performed more frequently than others. Consequently, these numbers need to be used with caution.

Techniques such as this can be used to calculate the action load of an interface before it is even built by engaging in this sort of counting exercise on our functional representation (either modified BNF or STN).

5.5.2.2 Mental work

The above approach accounts for the amount of time that is spent in carrying out actions in the interface, but it does not take account of what goes on in the head of the user. This 'thinking time' will depend upon how closely the goals of the user match the structure of the interface. If the user decides that he wishes to do X, and there is a button to press marked 'Do X', then the thinking time is fairly low. It just involves establishing the goal X, recognizing the button, and pressing it. By contrast, if there is no such button, then the user has to go through a process of establishing goals and subgoals until he comes up with a set of goals which will achieve his overall objective and which can be executed using interactions in the interface.

Various formal methods have been developed to model this thinking process and to provide some model of how the user will act in relationship to a particular interface. They all make use of the technique known as production rule modelling to try and capture something of the reasoning processes of the human. The basic approach is quite straightforward, although the details become complex. Two of the best-known models are GOMS and TAG.

In a simplistic form, we can define a mechanism which recognizes that the goal of the user needs to be achieved and can try to achieve it directly through operators or indirectly by establishing new goals.

In the previous case we calculated the total of the action times. In this model we also add up times for the amount of goal setting, and:

$$\text{Total time} = \text{external operator time} + \text{mental operator time}$$

The mental operators are commonly divided into three categories: memory (e.g. remember, forget, add to long-term memory, retrieve from long-term memory); control (e.g. set-goal, remove-goals); mental operators (e.g. read feedback). This enables us to establish a much more accurate model of how much effort is involved in using an interface, not just as actions, but also as the thinking and reasoning involved.

This section is just a quick caricature of a complex process of production rule modelling which attempts to capture aspects of human cognition. The interested reader is strongly recommended to explore some of the more formal models in more detail.

5.5.2.3 Memory loading

Humans can only retain a certain number of things in their memory at the same time. We have discussed models of memory earlier, and particularly the idea of the 'magic number 7 ± 2'. This is often used as a rule of thumb for interface design. The intention is to design an interface such that the number of things that the user has to remember at any given moment is in this region. This can be calculated using the same model as in Section 5.5.2.2 by maintaining a count of the uses of the memory operators within the system. If the total at a given moment goes higher than this value we can expect the interface will cause mistakes because users forget things about it. The other extreme would enable us to minimize the amount that needs to be remembered, but these sorts of interfaces commonly use many extra actions in order to avoid the load on memory, and hence are slower to use. As a result of this most interfaces are a compromise between reducing the memory load and increasing the speed of use.

5.5.2.4 Learnability

The amount that someone needs to learn in an interface can be represented by our syntactic rules and, more specifically, by sets of production rules which relate the goals of the use to the actions in the system. These days it is important to make our systems as easy to learn as possible – most users expect to be able to sit down and use software immediately, and to acquire skills as they go along by experimentation rather than by reading a manual.

Learnability can be separated into a component based upon the learnability within a package and the learnability by transfer from other packages.

To improve internal learnability of a package we need to minimize the number of production rules that describe it. This is equivalent to saying that we try to make it as consistent as possible, so that a rule applied once (and hence learnt) can be applied many more times in other contexts and hence save us from having to learn it again. Having learnt how to operate radio buttons, we do not then need to learn about them every time we see a new set of radio buttons. An interface which uses a smaller number of more powerful rules will be easier to learn.

Learnability by transfer requires linking at the rules which users already have and trying to reuse them in the design of our interface. Some of these will be rules that are grouped into mental models. In this case the idea is to evoke a mental model that the user already has and bring all the rules from that to bear in this new domain. One example is to make a package 'like a book', with previous and next pages, chapters, index, contents, etc. Another attempt to make such a mental model operate across a system is the 'desktop metaphor' which is part of the underlying model behind all current windowing systems (although it has limitations). We can also work on transfer from other software packages. All Microsoft Windows packages, for example, have menus for 'File', 'Edit', and various other things ending with 'Help'. Because this is the same across all application packages we can use one set of rules whenever we approach a new package that conforms to the guidelines.

5.6 Visual appearance and graphic design

In describing an interface we have so far focused on the functionality that it offers. From a formal perspective it is possible to produce interfaces which are functionally identical, but which have a very different effect upon the user because of their appearance. There are issues concerned with the visual design and layout of the interface which change the way it communicates to the user. This includes issues related to how the user perceives the objects in the interface, how they are grouped and structured to make optimum use of the available space, some aspects of providing an overall consistency using things like metaphors (e.g. the computer is like a desk in an office), and visual consistency. These things are generally referred to as the 'look and feel' of the interface. There is no space to consider these issues in detail here, or to explore the underlying psychology on which they are based, so we will simply identify a few useful sources of information in these areas and mention a few key observations about principles, layout, and colour.

5.6.1 Guidelines

There is a range of sources for information which can impact upon the interface design, but there are several specific sources which provide handy practical hints for interface designers. It should be borne in mind that most of these sources provide *rules of thumb* or *guidelines*, and should not be adhered to slavishly. There are three main sources of information:

5.6.1.1 General guidelines

Various research laboratories have produced guidelines at different times which embody the results of their work as a set of recommended design principles. One of the best-known examples is from Xerox laboratories, which were responsible for originating the first GUI and continue to explore new concepts in interface design.

There are also a number of general textbooks which seek to summarize recommendations from a number of sources in a platform independent manner.

5.6.1.2 Standards

Various bodies are beginning to propose standards for interfaces. These are mostly related to health and safety issues and seek to ensure a minimum level among interfaces which make them acceptable in the working environment. They are not hugely helpful in designing interfaces, but they do give an indication of things to consider and things to avoid in the design.

5.6.1.3 Platform guidelines

If you are designing a piece of software for a particular platform, most platform creators provide a set of guidelines for software development which ensure developers maintain a 'look and feel' consistent with the overall design of the operating system interface. This trend began with Apple, but has also been followed by IBM and Microsoft, among others.

5.6.2 Interface principles

Guidelines generally start with a statement of general principles on which the guidelines are based, and then provide a range of more detailed rules which are (at least partly) derived from those principles. Interface guidelines often set out from different points – there is no single 'right way' to design an interface so there is no single correct set of guidelines. As a designer one is often compromising between the suggestions of different guidelines. It is better to try and adhere to a set of general principles which you believe are appropriate for your users, than to try and slavishly follow the detailed rules given in one set of guidelines. Here are some examples of these basic principles.

- **Consistency** – Try to maintain consistency. Ensure that the same thing is done in the same way in different contexts.

- **Conceptual model** – Try to provide a model of the system for the users which relates to their real-world experience.

- **Direct representation** – Provide a visual interface which directly represents to the user what things are and what the state of the system is.

- **Modeless** – Ensure that the same commands always do the same things. If they have to have distinct behaviours, make sure that these different modes are explicitly represented to the user.

- **Closure** – Tasks should have a clear end point indicated to the user.

- **Reversal** – Enable actions which the user carries out to be undone or reversed easily with no loss of data.

- **Feedback** – Ensure that the user is constantly kept informed about what the computer is doing or has done.

- **Selection** – Try to enable users to do most things by selection rather than having to remember and type commands.

5.6.3 Layout

In terms of layout the constant issue is one of screen 'real estate'. There is always more information which the user may need from the software than can be placed on a single screen at a given time. Consequently, the interface is always moving between states where different groupings of information and interface elements are visible at different times. Different strategies are required to manage this information in different sorts of software, and new models and approaches are always being considered. Some rules related to layout are as follows:

- provide a safe 'default' screen to which to return;

- group related interface items together;

- disable rather than remove elements which are not available (e.g. by greying out menu items);

- use left-aligned text;

- use particular font types, sizes, etc. (lots of different rules about this!);

- keep the interface simple and uncluttered.

Screen layout is one of the areas where it is almost impossible to consistently follow a complete set of rules and it is highly likely to be an area of compromise in any real design.

5.6.4 Colour

Colour can be extremely useful because it adds to the information which can be communicated through the visual channel. Having said this it should not be used over-zealously, or gratuitously. Most approaches recommend designing in grey-scale first, and then adding colour on top of it. Colour can be used to relate similar things (such as all word-processor files being the same colour), and to communicate by association (e.g. bright reds may indicate danger), as well as allowing more realistic depictions of real-world objects.

Most of the rules related to colour tell you what not to do. How to use colour well is a more complex question related to many aspects of graphic design. Basic rules for colour include the following.

- Avoid colour combinations that are invisible to colour blind users. There are different sorts of colour blindness – some are just red shades, some are blue shades, and some are red–green–yellow combinations.

- Contrasting colours do not make type more readable.

- Complementary colours can cause flickering effects.

- Intense, saturated colours can cause eye strain when used in quantity.

- Lighter hues are less difficult on the eye.

5.7 Summary

This chapter has introduced human–computer interaction and explained how it relates to some of the issues in other chapters. It has separated out the interface to a system from the multimedia content, and described how the interface maps onto our ideas of channels of communication. Functionality and usability of interfaces have been discussed. These issues will return when we present a design methodology for multimedia systems which encompasses HCI and user-centred design, in Chapter 12.

5.8 Exercises

Exercise 5.1 Examine some pieces of computer software. Which modalities and channels of communication are they using?

Exercise 5.2 Repeat Exercise 5.1 with some interfaces which are non-computer. Try your mobile phone, car controls, television, video, etc.

Exercise 5.3 See if you can find at least three examples each of: a command line interface; a spatial textual interface; a form-based interface; a graphical user interface. Do not expect to find them all in the same place. Consider the interfaces to devices which are not computers.

Exercise 5.4 Considering a (simple) drawing package, write down a list of all the lexical items you can see in the initial interface (i.e. once you have started the package, but before you do anything with it).

Exercise 5.5 With the drawing package, create a circle above a rectangle, and save this as a file. Write down the lexical components you used during this activity.

Exercise 5.6 Write out the sequence of actions you performed in Exercise 5.4.

Exercise 5.7 Draw the actions of Exercise 5.6 as a state transition network, with other options indicated but not drawn out fully.

Exercise 5.8 Write the STN down as a grammar in the notation given in Section 5.5.1.2.

5.9   Further reading

Alan Dix (*et al.*), *Human computer interaction*, Prentice-Hall, 1997

Jenny Preece (*et al.*), *Human computer interaction*, Addison-Wesley, 1994

Ben Shneiderman, *Designing the user interface*, Addison Wesley, 1998

6

Semiotics

6.1 Multimedia content

At the beginning of the book we divided the components of an *Interactive Multimedia* system into those concerned with the *control* and the *interaction* that happens in the system and those which can be directly referred to as *multimedia content*. The chapters prior to this one were concerned with issues relating to the control aspect. For the remainder of the book we will turn to examining principles related to the multimedia content. Bear in mind that this book is concerned with thinking about what we mean and achieve through *Interactive Multimedia* rather than individual techniques of authoring or production, and hence we will be focusing upon those aspects of content which are specifically related to developing and understanding the communication and interaction.

We will focus upon our idea of *channels of communication* within an *Interactive Multimedia* system as the means by which we can discuss different types of media content within the context of *Communicative Interaction*. So far, we have used the idea of *language* as a unifying mechanism by which to explain the diverse components of our systems and their relationship to the interaction. We will continue in this vein, but will have to broaden our definition of language slightly. The new perspective upon language is that corresponding to the field of *semiotics*. This chapter will introduce the ideas behind semiotics while subsequent chapters explore their application, together with other linguistic features, in *text*, *sound*, *pictures*, and *films*.

It will be seen that each of the media that we discuss encompasses a number of communication channels and sometimes incorporates the languages of other media wholesale. This linking of the media is extremely interesting in the context of *Interactive Multimedia* because it indicates a way in which this area is likely to develop. In particular, we will emphasize the way in which this new field lies at the intersection of a variety of disciplines. It involves combining languages of interpretation from a variety of sources and developing new languages of interpretation that operate across a novel combination of channels. This will be seen more clearly after we have introduced the basic ideas of semiotics.

6.2   What is semiotics?

Up to this point we have emphasized formal approaches to the idea of language. We have introduced the concepts of *lexicon*, *syntax*, and *semantics* as well as giving a variety of precise notations that can be utilized to represent these components. We have also introduced the more general dialogic concepts of *goal-based* and *focus-based* systems, together with a notation for these. An introduction to models of communication based on encoding and decoding channels of communication has been outlined, and we have presented our simple two-agent model of the communicative process. In each of these areas we have implicitly worked with a degree of precision implying that there is somehow a 'correct' linguistic system and that any failure to match the system is a failure on the part of one or more of the agents involved in the communicative process.

When we explored knowledge we made the pragmatic decision to focus upon *socially defined Platonic knowledge*. Because of this we are able to talk about 'the knowledge' as though it was absolute and correct. This reinforces the idea that what is being communicated is precise and can be encoded and decoded unambiguously. However, we also introduced the idea of a community of agents where each agent has a relationship to that knowledge and the community. We also noted that no individual will possess precisely the knowledge of the community, although what that individual does have will be to a greater or lesser degree compatible with it.

While these formal and precise models can work very well for interaction between two formally defined systems such as two computers, and are perfect for formal languages which have been created to have the requisite precision (such as predicate calculus), they are not going to prove adequate, given our current state of understanding, for describing the meanings that human beings create from complex combinations of channels of communication. This is not to suggest that it is in principle impossible to describe these interactions at such a level, but only that for the most part it is currently not feasible and in the few cases where it is feasible it is impractical because of the amount of effort required to specify what is going on at this level of detail. If I want to explain how a particular human being interprets a particular communicative act in a precise manner then I require a precise and detailed model of that human being. This is too much to ask!

As with dialogue theory and pragmatics, we accept that there are key elements to the communicative process that cannot be explained simply from rigidly encoding and decoding the symbols on the channel of communication. There is also a question of interpretation of those symbols in a given context. Part of that context will be the environment in which the communication occurred, but part of it will be within the head of the agent who is constructing the interpretation. What we are saying is that the agent who receives a communication is an *active interpreter* and that the interpretation which is constructed is dependent upon unique factors and previous learning. Consequently, the same message on a channel may have a different interpretation for different receivers of that message. In the absence of a complete psychological model we need to introduce the field of semiotics in order to have a way of talking about these issues.

Semiotics is the study of signs and symbols. This definition does not really capture the nature or scope of the term: it only becomes apparent when you realize that semiotics proposes that almost everything in the world can be thought of as a sign in some form. Everything is taken to have some form of interpretation and hence to have a specific impact upon each observer. This seems like an all-encompassing approach and there has indeed been a (fruitless) debate for many years on whether everything (including linguistics) is a subset of semiotics or everything (including semiotics) is a subset of linguistics. We are not concerned with this debate here, but in the application of semiotics to the interpretation of channels of communication.

6.3   The idea of a sign

In order for us to get a clear idea of semiotics and its potential, it is first important for us to establish a clear idea of what a sign is and the relationship of a sign to a meaning. We will do this primarily by example, introducing some very obvious signs. Everybody would accept that a road sign is a sign, take a look at those illustrated in Colour Plate 1.

We probably all understand these signs. The first one, for example, is the *Clearway* sign. Even if we do not know it by that name we probably know that what it means is 'No stopping'. You can probably guess at the others.

We may have learnt the meaning of each of these signs individually, but it is more likely that we have some model of the components of interpretation that can be combined to make up each sign. All these signs are *red*, and red is itself a sign which is traditionally associated with danger (probably because it reminds us of blood and hence death). Consequently, we can see that these signs indicate something dangerous, even if we do not know what that thing is. It is also the case that all the signs shown here are circular. It may not be obvious to all readers, but in the United Kingdom circular road signs are always commands which must be obeyed. Therefore, even without knowing the meaning of a specific sign we can begin to construct some idea of the sort of thing that it indicates. By contrast, this sign shown in Colour Plate 2 clearly has something wrong with it. It has a thin border on the outside and is black and white, but we recognize the symbol to be 'No entry' and hence would expect it to be red with a thick circular border. Our model of road signs and our experience indicates that this is not a proper road sign. We can think of there being a language of road signs within which a particular sign constitutes an utterance in that language. The road sign is such an utterance, but it is itself made up of components which are also signs (e.g. sign shape, size, and colour). These signs which have meanings across a group of other signs allow us to construct an interpretation and themselves form a code to be used in the context of a road sign (Figure 6.1).

Sign ::= shape, border_colour, centre
shape ::= circle | triangle | rectangle
border_colour ::= none | red | white
Centre ::= background_colour, {symbol, symbol_colour}*, {diagonal}*, {text}*
background_colour ::= red | white | blue

Meaning.
Shape = rectangle ⟶ information
        circle ⟶ order
        triangle ⟶ warning
Diagonal ⟶ Do Not

Figure 6.1 Approximate grammar of road signs.

The sign shown in Colour Plate 3 is clearly not acceptable within the language of British road signs. It is an *inverted triangle* (a shape almost never used), it is *yellow* (a colour that is almost never used), and it additionally contains a linguistic symbol, *Yield*, which almost never arises in UK English and never on a UK road sign. The shared knowledge of the community of road users in the UK tells us that the sign is not acceptable: it is outside the culture of the group to which we belong. It would, incidentally, be a perfectly normal and well-recognized road sign for a user in North America. This example illustrates the importance of the cultural context to the interpretation of the sign.

A final point to notice about the signs that we have seen so far is that they are made up of abstracted symbols. There is no way that the signs could be said to look like something which is their meaning. By contrast, consider the British roads signs illustrated in Colour Plate 4.

These signs continue to employ the colour red to indicate danger and use the shape of a triangle, which in the UK indicates a warning. However, they differ significantly from the earlier signs in that they contain a symbol within them which is clearly intended to look like something and to mean the thing that it looks like. In the first case the inner symbol is a train and the sign as a whole means 'Warning – a level crossing without gates or barriers'. In the second case the components are a sign made up of three elements (each of which is itself a sign) which together represent a picture of a car falling into some water. The complete sign means 'Warning – Quayside'. In order to distinguish signs of this type from the previous type, the completely symbolic signs are called 'symbolic signs', whereas the ones which make some representation of the thing which is the meaning are referred to as 'iconic signs'. The construction of these signs is shown in Figures 6.2 and 6.3.

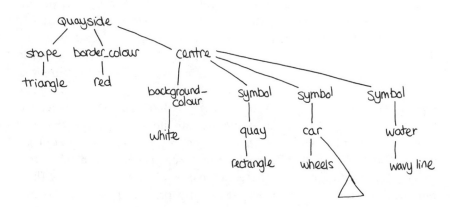

Figure 6.2 Tree model of train sign.

We can also identify a third category of road sign. In these the sign indicates its meaning by pointing at something. All of the signs illustrated in Colour Plate 5 mean 'one-way street', but they would not do so (in any useful sense) unless they had a point, indicating a direction. They indicate the traffic flow, which is their intended meaning, by pointing to it. It is neither represented *symbolically* (the words tell us that there is a specific traffic flow, but not what) nor *iconically* (there is no picture of traffic flow).

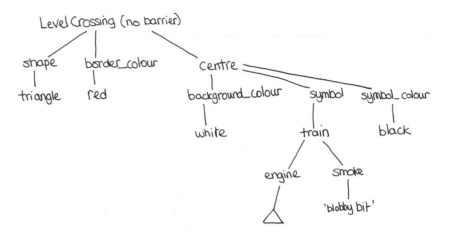

Figure 6.3   Tree model of quay sign.

So far we have described signs which are predominantly familiar to us and come from a set in which there is a code that enables us to interpret novel signs. For contrast, explore Figure 6.4 one frame at a time.

How many frames did it take before you recognized the meaning of the whole sign? Virtually everyone should have figured out by the end that it indicates a customs check point and would hence normally be found in an airport or similar location. If you just take one or two of the component shapes, however, then it is not at all clear what the sign is going to be. It is not until you see the whole picture that you can determine the meaning of the components. The initial two black rectangles could be anything, but by the time we see the full picture it is clear that they are a suitcase. The two blocks with the white diagonal separating them initially appear to be arrow-like, but once we realize that they represent a human being we can immediately see the two components of a belt and infer that it is not only a human, but an official of some sort. This is reinforced by the shapes suggesting a head and peaked cap. Having created these two pieces of meaning, we can then put them together to see an official investigating an open suitcase and

Figure 6.4a   Mystery sign (Frame 1) ...

from this and our experience can determine that this is only likely to happen in the context of passing through customs. This picture clearly illustrates a sign that has a meaning that is not built up from individual components like our previous examples. The meaning of this sign only becomes clear when it emerges from the relationship between the individual images. A new meaning has been created, yet it is almost completely unambiguous.

6.3.1 Terminology

To clarify what we have learnt from the examples given above we will introduce some standard of terminology in a systematic manner. These terms are defined more generally than in the context of road signs, and in the next section you will see how they can be applied to a broader idea of what constitutes a sign.

We have been a little cavalier with the use of terminology such as 'sign' in the previous section, but now we can be more specific. Signifier, signified, and referent (Figure 6.5) represent a key idea in semiotics and can be defined as follows.

- **Signifier:** some object, depiction or other thing which serves the purpose of 'standing for' something else. Typically, something which indicates a particular concept or idea. This is what is frequently referred to as the 'sign'.

- **Signified:** a concept or idea that is indicated by some particular *signifier*. Note that signified can only be defined with respect to signifier. While the concept might exist independent of a signifier it is not signified until there is a signifier indicating it.

- **Referent:** a particular instance of the more general concept indicated by the signified in a particular context. We will explore the relationship to the linguistic idea of reference later, but it is important to realize that while signifier and signified must exist in a pair, there is no need for a referent to be present in every case.

Figure 6.4b   Mystery sign (Frame 2) ...

Figure 6.5 Diagram of three terms.

Example 1: With the 'Dangerous Quayside' road sign, the *signifier* is the bit of metal on a stick beside the road, the *signified* is the idea of a Dangerous Quayside, and the *referent* is the particular Dangerous Quayside just beyond this point that I am about to drive my car off. If you look back up the page, we have a slightly different case here, because the signifier is the picture in the book, the signified is still the Dangerous Quayside, but there is no referent: this sign in this context does not refer to anything more specific than the signified.

Example 2: Imagine a pair of sink taps – one with a red top and one with a blue top. The red colour is the *signifier*, the *signified* is the idea of hotness, and the *referent* is the hot water that will come out of this particular tap. Alternatively, my car has an air-conditioning system with

Figure 6.4c Mystery sign (Frame 3) ...

a knob that has a blue dot at one extreme of motion and a red dot at the other. As with the tap, the signifier is the red colour, the signified is hotness, but the referent is the air that will come out of the system.

Example 3: In conversation I mention the Vice Chancellor. The words Vice Chancellor are the *signifier*. The holder of that office at my university is the *signified*, and the *referent* can vary depending on who the actual incumbent of the post is at the time I say the words.

As well as the fact that a relationship exists between the signifier and signified, the examples have also permitted us to illustrate three different forms which this relationship can take.

- **Symbolic:** the signifier consists of an abstract symbol or symbols that have no inherent relationship to the signified. The meaning is derived entirely through convention.

- **Iconic:** the signifier has some form of depictive quality in which there is a direct relationship between the thing that is depicted in the signifier and the thing which is signified.

- **Indexical:** the signifier indicates the signified neither through an abstract means nor through a depiction, but by 'pointing to' the signified in some manner. This pointing is not necessarily literal and physical, but may be through association or a similar indirect process.

Examples – Symbolic

- Computer: A curved arrow to the left often represents 'Undo'.

- Car: Two wavy lines represent air flow.

Examples – Iconic

- Computer: The printer is represented by a picture of a printer.

- Car: A picture of a window identifies the electric window buttons.

Figure 6.4d   Mystery sign (Frame 4).

Examples – Indexical

- **Computer:** There is a picture of an eraser on the end of a pencil that represents correcting an error in my voice input system. It is indexical because, although the pencil is a real thing, the connection is that the pencil leads me to the idea of erasing, and from here to the idea of correcting a spoken word.

- **Car:** A large triangle indicates my hazard indicators. It is indexical because it is a depiction of the warning triangle you put on the road when your car has broken down, and hence by association leads me to think of breakdowns.

While there is not a direct mapping between the terminologies of linguistics and those of semiotics, we can none the less distinguish between the idea of a general space of things which could be said and a specific thing which is said. Furthermore, we can introduce the idea of a space of related utterances within the overall language which themselves constitute a specific language. For this we can use the following terms:

- **Language:** the large space of possible signs from which particular signs are constructed.

- **Utterance:** a specific communicative event (a unit of signifier and signified).

- **Syntagm:** a combination of utterances juxtaposed in some manner to achieve a larger communicative intent.

- **Code:** a set of interrelated signs which form a 'sublanguage' within the larger space of signs.

These terms have been little used in our examples so far, but they will be clarified by the illustrations in the following section.

6.3.2 Construction of signs

In the simplest case, we can think of a sign as a single entity that signifies something else. This is often adequate for the sorts of analysis that we wish to perform. However, we have also pointed out cases where even signs that are apparently simple are in fact themselves combinations of signs. We will find that this is typical, and normally one of our decisions in semiotic analysis concerns the degree that it is necessary to decompose a sign into components in a given context.

For these compound signs we have identified two distinct ways in which they acquire meaning. The first method is when the overall sign is made up of a number of smaller signs each of which can be given a meaning in the context, and where the meaning of the overall sign can be 'built up' from the meaning of the individual components. This is what we were illustrating with the British road signs and the way that they can be divided into components. The second method is the case in which a sign gains meaning as a result of the relationship between its components, although none of these components could be assigned an individual meaning in isolation. Often, the components acquire a meaning as a consequence of their relationship to the overall sign. This point was illustrated with the 'Customs' sign. The overall meaning of the sign could not be determined until all components were available, but when this happened the meaning was clear and unambiguous, and individual pieces acquired a meaning (e.g. a black rectangle suddenly came to signify the lid of a suitcase).

The third complication is that a simple view suggests that there is a set of things called *signifier* and a set of things called *signified*, and that we can make a direct mapping between items in these two distinct worlds. This is not the case because something that is signified can also be a signifier. There can be extended chains of signifier–signified relationship, and the same sign may play different roles in different contexts.

What constitutes a sign, and what a given sign signifies in a particular context is not absolute. We cannot go to some definitive volume and look up all the signs in the world together with other things that they signify. It is necessary to recognize the importance of several factors in the interpretation of the signifiers with which we are presented.

- **Culture:** the meaning of signs is derived primarily through convention, and is relative to a particular culture. This applies both in the large scale (e.g. Inuit, Celtic, Algerian), and on finer scales referring to a particular community (e.g. physicists, painters) or to some other small grouping with shared experience (e.g. brother and sister). This idea of *cultural dependence* of meaning is something that we should already be happy with, since it is almost the same as our idea of *socially defined Platonic knowledge*.

- **Context:** even within a clearly defined cultural grouping we cannot provide absolute values for signs. The interpretation process will depend upon the context in which the sign exists in a given instance within that culture. An icon of a wine glass, in a bar, might indicate that wine is available, whereas, on the side of a large cardboard box, it indicates that the contents are fragile.

- **Time:** because the interpretation of signs depends upon the above factors, and because these factors change as individuals change, it is also necessary to acknowledge that there is a probability that signs will change in meaning over time. This has less effect than the other components, but it is nevertheless significant. An obvious example would be the word 'green', which now has strong *ecologically friendly* overtones that did not exist 20 years ago. Jeans no longer signify rebellion as they once did. We need to be aware of this when we are attempting to perform a semiotic analysis on materials from a different time, but we also need to be aware of it when dealing with a wide age range of user groups. Signs that mean one thing to the over-60 population may well mean something different to the over-40 age group, something else to the over-20 group and something else to the under-20 group. This is a major concern of advertisers in targeting their materials, and one that we need to remain aware of.

6.4   More complex signs

We have moved quite a long way from our simple introduction of road signs. We have established that a sign is a sort of relationship, that the meaning may not be absolutely determined (there is no single *correct* interpretation), and that anything can be a sign if looked at from the appropriate perspective. Not only the obvious symbols and pictures, but also words, images, sounds, moving pictures can all be signs and collections of signs. We will see how this relates to specific conventional media but what we need to examine first is the way that a signified can itself be a signifier. We will distinguish *denotation* and *connotation*, and use them to introduce an idea of *myth*.

In the previous section we talked about signs which had a referent. In one sense we can think of our sign as being a 'name' or a 'label' for this thing to which it refers. We can say that the sign *denotes* the thing, or that the thing is *denoted* by the sign. It is quite close to the linguistic idea of the *meaning* of an element in a language.

By contrast, the *connotation* of a sign represents not the particular thing, but the associations that may go along with it. This is obviously culturally dependent and can vary quite drastically between different perceivers of the sign. Packages in shops might have a sign on them which denotes a tree, but the intention is to use the connotations of this sign – nature, fresh air, health, etc. – to carry some associations to the perceiver that go beyond the basic meaning. The sign not only tells them that the product is eco-friendly, but it also gives them happy feelings about nature as well (if you happen to like nature, that is). A sign consisting of the word 'eco-friendly' might carry the same meaning, but would not have the same connotations.

A similar sort of example would be the Irish theme pub. These pubs have nothing whatsoever to do with Ireland, but they are a rich source of signs all intended to carry connotations of a quieter, peaceful, but basically cheerful rural life which probably never existed. Plain wooden floors have connotations of simplicity. Prominent Guinness pumps make you feel that you are somewhere different. Some places even have peat-flavour air freshener to try and make you think of rural Ireland with an olfactory sign!

This example is taking us into an area in which signs are being used in conjunction in order to create a 'story' or feeling in the perceiver. Each sign has connotations of its own, but when they are put together they can emphasize certain aspects of each other's meaning and connotation until we have created a complete set of connotations for the perceiver which could not be produced by one sign alone. Our rough wooden floor may make us feel happily rural in the context of the other signs in an Irish theme pub, but placed in a doctor's surgery, the message would be quite different. In this context it would be harking back to days before properly developed antiseptics, surgical methods, etc. and would tend to imply a doctor who was not up to date with the latest techniques. Of course, a highly polished and expensive wooden floor would have different connotations, suggesting that the doctor is making lots of money. How you feel about that depends on whether you believe in private healthcare, I expect.

We should emphasize that the combination of signs into myth is not simply a question of including all the associations of all the signs. The signs may share connotations, may emphasize certain aspects of each other, and may create new connotations from the interaction of their associations. This is a case where the whole may be greater than the sum of its parts. Just ponder, for the moment, the potential meaning of a sign consisting of a photograph of an ice-cream cone with a razor blade in it instead of a chocolate stick.

6.5　Semiotics and media

You can probably see that the idea of myth is very powerful, but also potentially very complex. We had enough difficulty trying to explain the meaning of one sign at these various levels, without starting to think of combinations of signs. This is exactly what we will have to do in subsequent chapters, however. We have introduced our channels of communication and talked about cross-channel languages of interpretation. We have used formal language models to approach the description of these languages of interpretation in areas of interaction and interfaces. When we now turn to media content we find that the formal language techniques will no longer apply. The complexity and cultural and contextual sensitivity of an artefact such as a book or painting is not amenable to existing formal models. This is where we start to use semiotics as our unifying language to talk about the meaning of media. Because the area is so large there are people who specialize in the semiotic understanding of particular small areas of it. In particular, we find that there are people interested in the semiotic structure of texts, of pictures and paintings, of films, of the 'traditional media' (the press), of television, and of advertising. Each of these fields has its own devotees, and they rarely work across more than one of these 'media' (in our usage of the word).

Of all these areas, advertising is in many ways the most fruitful to explore. Advertisers are restricted to a very limited channel of communication (e.g. a billboard can only hold so many words, a TV commercial can only be 30 seconds) and hence want to communicate their message to their intended audience as efficiently as possible. They use all the tricks in the semiotic field (and others besides) to try and reach their audience. These small but densely packed semiotic experiences incorporate all the major issues introduced in this chapter.

The subsequent chapters will each examine one medium, and will explore the way that it works and the languages that are within it. Bear in mind that each of these media is also a channel for semiotics and that its components are signs. Keep watch for the signs, the signifiers, signified, and referents, the denotations, connotations, and myths which occur in these chapters.

6.6 Exercises

Exercise 6.1 For each of the following, identify the signifier, signified, referent and type of relationship (indexical, iconic, etc.) where appropriate:

- An exit sign;

- An emergency exit sign;

- A 'Tetley's bitter' label on a beer pump in a pub;

- The BMW badge on the front of a car;

- The advertising slogan – 'Irn Bru – made in Scotland from girders';

- A graphical channel ID on television;

- The phrase 'The British prime minister';

- The phrase 'The last train to Tulsa';

- The phrase 'Next week's no. 1 chart single';

- The cover picture of this book.

Exercise 6.2 Choose a one-page advertisement from one of the colour magazines that appear on Sundays. Identify the different signs that are incorporated within it. Identify signified and referents where possible. Now examine the connotations of these signs, and see if you can explain the myth that the advertisement is communicating, and the way that that myth is produced by the combination of signs

6.7 Further reading

This is a good general introduction to ideas in semiotics and their application in traditional media:
Jonathan Bignell, *Media semiotics*, Manchester University Press, 1997

These are more theoretical, but present the bigger linguistic perspective:
Umberto Eco, *A theory of semiotics*, Indiana University Press, 1979

Umberto Eco, *Semiotics and the philosophy of language*, MacMillan, 1984

Quite hard reading, but these source texts can help motivate the area of study:
Roland Barthes, *Mythologies*, Jonathan Cape Ltd, 1972

Roland Barthes, *Image, music, text*, Fontana, 1977

7
Text

'When I use a word,' Humpty Dumpty said in rather a scornful tone, 'it means just what I choose it to mean – neither more nor less.'

'The question is,' said Alice, 'whether you can make words mean so many different things.'

'The question is,' said Humpty Dumpty, 'which is to be the master – that's all.'

Lewis Carroll, *Through the Looking Glass*

The first part of the book introduced the idea of *language* in a variety of forms: as formal languages, natural languages, procedural, declarative, programming, mathematical, description, and meta languages. The previous chapter extended the idea to a more general use of the word *language*, and introduced the basic concepts of semiotics. This chapter explores one medium, the written word, in greater detail to understand the way that we can communicate with it in our multimedia systems. To this end, we are considering text as two different languages: the language of the meaning (our natural language, such as English) and the language by which we perceive it (fonts, justification, layout, etc.). We will commence with introducing a few issues in visual perception that will be of relevance to many subsequent chapters.

7.1 Visual perception of text

Seeing is one of those things which most of us just *do*, and never think about. If asked, most people would probably imagine the eye as something like a camera, taking a perfect picture of a scene that is then somehow interpreted by our brain. In fact, even the process of getting an image is rather more complex than that, and it is important to understand it, because it has a huge impact upon the way we design any visual image, and the way that we read.

Light from the world passes into our eye (Figure 7.1) through a hole in the front called the *pupil*. This hole is protected from the world by the transparent covering at the front of the eye: the *cornea*. The amount of light entering the eye can be varied by the increase or decrease in size of the *iris* around the pupil. Once inside the eye the light passes through a lens, which focuses it upon the rear of the eye. This lens has to be capable of varying its focus to cope with light from different sources and distances. The light hits the rear of the eye, where there are cells that are sensitive to light and generate electrical signals dependent upon how bright the light is upon them. These voltages are then sent from the eye along the *optic nerve* to be processed by the brain. This model seems very clear – the problem is that the rear of the eye is not capable of detecting a 'complete' image. What we think we see is nothing like what the eye actually detects.

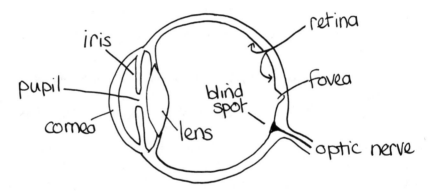

Figure 7.1   An eye.

The rear of the eye (Figure 7.2) consists of a light-sensitive surface called the *retina*. This surface is covered by two types of light-sensitive cell.

- *Rods*. These cells are sensitive to the quantity (intensity) of light falling upon them, but not to the colour (frequency). In effect, they detect the world in shades of grey. They are very sensitive to light, and can work when there is little light about. It has been calculated that all else being equal (perfect darkness, the earth being flat, etc.) these cells should be able to detect the amount of light generated by striking a match 70 miles away!

- *Cones*. These cells detect colour. They are not as sensitive to light as the rods, so they are not operational in low light conditions (we see in grey at night). They come in three kinds, each of which is sensitive to a different primary colour: red, green, or blue. They are capable of distinguishing much finer detail than rods.

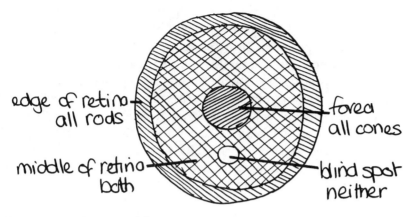

edge of retina → / all rods

middle of retina → both

fovea / all cones

blind spot / neither

Figure 7.2 The rear of the eye.

The surface of the retina is not uniformly sensitive to light. For the most part it consists of a fairly high density of rods, with cones being quite rare at the edge of the retina and more common as you get closer to the centre. Things are made more complex by two special areas within it: the *fovea* and the *blind spot*.

- *Fovea*. This is the most important part of the retina. It is a small depression at the centre of the eye that is filled exclusively with cone cells. It is very sensitive to colour and detail, but can only 'see' a small part of the overall image.

- *Blind spot*. The cells of the retina connect to non light-sensitive cells that in turn link to a collection of nerve fibres that carry these signals from the eye to the part of the brain responsible for processing these signals. This group of fibres is known as the optic nerve, and, at the point where it leaves the eye, there are no rods or cones. This leaves an area with no vision known as the blind spot.

This structure to the eye would suggest that when we look at the world, we would see a very small piece in colour and detail, a lot of fuzzier, greyer stuff, and a bit where we see nothing at all. So why do we see complete focused colour images? The answer is that our brain constructs them from this rough data. It collects lots of different inadequate images and knits them together (exactly how is complicated, and to some extent still unclear) so that we somehow think that we see the world 'perfectly'. The fact that we are really constructing a view of the world accounts for the fact that many things, for example optical illusions, can confuse the eye. Seeing is an active process of creating an 'image'. While we might imagine that our gaze is 'fixed', our eyes are, in fact making constant tiny movement (saccades) to collect different images to glue together, and so give the impression of a more effective eye.

We will return to other aspects and implications of the design of the eye in later chapters, but from the point of view of this chapter we need to examine the implications of this structure for reading.

The eye cannot 'see' a complete line of text at a time. It has to construct it somehow. This is achieved by making a number of *fixations* on the line (Figure 7.3). A fixation consists of bringing one small area of the line into detailed vision on the fovea, remembering it, and moving on. A single fixation might last for something of the order of 0.2 seconds for a good reader, and correspondingly slower in a poor reader. Poor readers make more fixations, and each one lasts longer as they process what their eye is seeing.

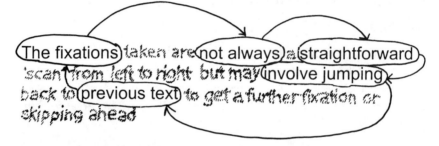

Figure 7.3   Sample fixations.

The fixations taken are not always a straightforward 'scan' from left to right, but may involve jumping back to previous text to get a further fixation or skipping ahead. Sometimes readers move up or down a line on the page during the course of reading a given line.

The fixation captures the image of the words, but somehow these need to be recognized as letters, then grouped as words, and processed to derive a meaning. A novice reader goes through a process of detecting the image, identifying features such as lines, corners, curves, etc., comparing these with features of some prototype letter in their memory and (hopefully) identifying a letter. This process is repeated until a word break is determined and then the letters are reorganized as a word, and so on until the end of the sentence. Using this method is very slow because there is too much to hold in memory at once without doing some processing. Once someone is expert at reading many other mechanisms come into play. On the perceptual side, the expert reader uses more information than the novice. Instead of coding things letter by letter, the expert recognizes more word shapes and codes them directly. The inherent redundancy of information in the written text means that, with experience, a reader can determine what a word is without processing all the information within it, and this speeds things up considerably. Another perceptual mechanism appears to be that experts use *parafoveal* vision – reading not just with the fovea, but with the area of retina around it. This area is less sensitive, but can be used to give shape and structure to the reading process, enabling words to be guessed and using foveal perception only on areas of difficulty or uncertainty.

These improved perceptual techniques are augmented by a further psychological aspect of the language itself – the meaning of the words. Readers interpret the meaning of a sentence as they decode it, and can use this meaning to establish a context for a word which means that they can anticipate what it will be. Hence they only have to check that the word appears to be what they were expecting, rather than having to work it out from scratch. While a typical reader will be able to read about 200 words per minute, a good reader trying to go fast is capable of something like 500 words per minute.

With this psychological perspective in mind, we can now turn our attention to the nature of the thing that is called *text*.

7.2 Images on a page

7.2.1 What do we see when we look at a piece of text?

We understand letters as symbols which each represent a sound. We understand words as both collections of sound-symbols, and symbols in themselves (Figure 7.4). Those symbols represent things not inherently but because we have learned the artificial association between a particular set of wiggly lines and a concrete object (tree, jam doughnut) or an abstract concept (bravery, hot).

As children, we learn to divide the spoken word into abstract sounds – *phonemes*. Using them, we can work out the sound of a new word without knowing its meaning, but if confronted by a new

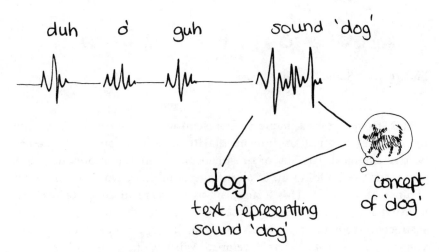

Figure 7.4   Sound – letter-word, word-concept.

sound (e.g. ll – in Welsh, ! – a click sound in an African language) we are unable to reproduce it or recognize it as a specific unit of communication even though we can hear it.

Early attempts at written communication provided symbols for entire concepts – sun, cow, enemy. Symbols were based on a schematic representation of the object, so that abstract concepts such as death could be portrayed only by showing a dead person or a tomb. These images may sometimes have been culturally specific (dependent on recognizing a type of structure as a tomb), but were independent of spoken language, and so provided a possible cross-linguistic channel of communication. For this reason pictograms are still used to convey simple ideas in safety critical situations (such as road signs), and in communication with people who have language difficulties (such as the printed form of Macaton).

When using concept symbols, the concepts can be grouped, but the capacity for describing new concepts is limited – someone who had never seen an aeroplane might describe it as a large bird – if bird was the only available concept for a thing-which-flies. Thus the information that can be conveyed is relatively limited, and can become distorted. A very large vocabulary of signs needs to be built up, and remembered.

As pictograms grew more sophisticated, schematic pictures of objects stood in for the names of the objects, and later for the sound of the object – either the initial sound (Egyptian hieroglyphics – Figure 7.5) or the syllable (Oriental languages).

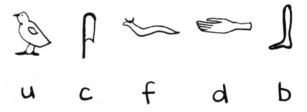

Figure 7.5   Some hieroglyphs.

This move from a symbol representing a concept to a symbol representing a sound is fundamental to the development of modern written language. The idea of an alphabet of symbols to represent sounds allows for the building up of an infinite number of words from a small number of symbols. This enables us to replicate in concrete (written) form what happens when we speak. Once sounds and symbols were abstracted from their original meaning, a large number of different *symbol systems* or *alphabets* developed. What we (in England) recognize as the alphabet is, of course, only one possible alphabet. Its 26 symbols

Plate 1   Clearway and a few red bordered circles.

Plate 2   Black and white no entry.

Plate 3   Yield sign.

Plate 4   Train, quayside.

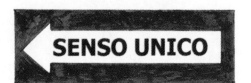

Plate 5   One-way signs.

can be combined to produce further phonemes – those usually represented by diphthongs (e.g. æ as in Cæsar).

An International Phonetic Alphabet exists which attempts to produce a unified coding system for all the sounds of human speech (Figure 7.6). It is used to describe pronunciations in most dictionaries, but much of it is used primarily by linguists and most ordinary readers will not recognize the symbols.

$$\text{fə'nɛtɪk}$$

Figure 7.6 Some phonetic symbols.

Nowadays, the alphabet symbols which represent a word are the same across the whole geographical area in which the word is used (e.g. across England) – but the sound of the word being spoken may vary enormously from region to region. Normal written text does not attempt to convey localized pronunciation.

7.2.2 A short history of writing

The earliest physical evidence of humans' attempt to communicate is not writing, but pictures – geometric markings carved in stones, earth works and cave paintings – which are believed to have been part of a ritual or a system of sympathetic magic as well as a communication between people.

The earliest scripts were almost all pictographic – representing a concrete object by a picture. These pictures could be combined to form compound concepts: an example would be *field + cow = farm*. Later, the sound of the name of the object depicted became associated with the image, so that images could be combined to produce new images for existing words, such as *bee + leaf = belief*. This is a very sophisticated step from literal, spatial representation of an object to an auditory representation of the object's name.

Later still, the picture becomes associated with only the initial sound of the object's name, so the cow becomes associated with the **k** sound (*acrophonic* symbols). While pictograms work across languages, once they become associated with a sound (*phoneticized*) they become language-specific. In French, cow begins with a **v** (*vache*), and in Hebrew, with an **a** (*aleph*).

Once an image has been made to stand in for a single sound, a small total number of symbols will cover all the spoken words (22 plus vowel sounds). Egyptian hieroglyphics (which were a mixture of object, concept, and sound depictions) had 1000 characters, and modern Oriental languages – which use units of syllables rather than single sounds – have up to 50,000 characters.

Once the principle of representing objects by marks that do not relate to the physical appearance of the concept is established, apparently arbitrary symbols can be allocated to abstract concepts. These are *logograms* – symbols that stand for a whole word or concept – like the number 8.

As the symbols became more widely used, and spread among different individuals, they became more simplified and abstracted, but retained their references to the original objects. The hieroglyphic system used in Egypt appears to have been developed by the Semitic peoples, where the names of the letters maintained the reference to the original objects (even now: *aleph-* an ox, *beth-* a house, which form the first two letters of the Hebrew alphabet and the one you are reading).

The alphabet as a set of iconic and acrophonic symbols lasted about 1000 years, until the Greeks adopted a pictographic script (Figure 7.7). These scripts retain the sound-symbol pairs without using the reference to the original object. This is another sophisticated move, from an **aa** sound related to a picture of a cow's head (*aa-leph*) to an abstract symbol which means **aa** because I say so. The symbol retained its name (alpha) but that had no meaning – although it later acquired the meaning of *first* or *beginning* because when letter symbols were coordinated into an alphabet, it came first. Interestingly, when we teach children to read and write text, we reverse this development: introducing pictures of objects whose names begin with the sound (**b** is for *ball*) and using the phoneticization of the letter (**buh**) rather than its name (**bee**).

Figure 7.7   Developing aleph-alpha.

As languages travelled across the world, spreading with nomadic peoples, invasions, and resettlements, they had to be adapted or completely reconstructed to take into account differences in the spoken language. Often the same symbols were used – common objects significant to an agricultural society – but they would be given a new sound (that related to the name of the object in the new tongue). Languages are living things, which grow to take account of new concepts (like 'teenage') or new inventions (plough, post-modernism). They also change and evolve with time and geographical separation. When groups of people are dispersed, the language develops differently within the different groups (as, for example with Portuguese and Brazilian Portuguese, which has a different grammar as well as some different words and pronunciation). Different *dialects* are created within the same language and may eventually diversify into different languages. These may have different symbols, or alphabets. These similar languages can be grouped into families, which have similar sound groups for the same meaning or concept. Not all languages in the same group necessarily use the same kind of symbols to write.

The early pictogram systems developed into a range of different scripts, including Latin, Illyric (Albania), Armenian, Cyrillic, Devanagarni (Hindi), Nastaliq, Arabic, Mongolian, Korean, Chinese, Hebrew, Ge'ez (Ethiopia). These scripts also form families that have broad characteristics. For example, Arabic and Hebrew are both based on consonants – vowels are either left out of the written form or indicated by position, rather than form.

The development of a particular script in a particular country is partly dependent on politics and religion: a language and a script being imposed by the ruling power, or preferred as an allegiance to a larger (religious) community. Thus the Latin script was spread across much of the world by the Roman Empire, and more recently Cyrillic imposed by the USSR, while Hebrew (because of the nature of the Jewish diaspora) is a language-specific script.

Chinese, and Korean are *syllabaries* – that is, the symbols represent whole syllables rather than single sounds. These languages can also be written in Latin script (transliteration). However, when this happens, the sounds are approximated. When *Peking* was recently re-transliterated as *Beijing*, this demonstrated the problem that the actual sounds in the original language were neither P nor B, k nor j but a sound similar to both which had no exact equivalent. A similar problem exists when transliterating between any two scripts.

English is written in Latin script, and belongs to the Germanic branch of Indo-European languages. It developed out of the languages of the invaders and migrating people, including Norse and Anglo-Saxon, and is closely related to Frisian, Dutch, and German. It is not so closely related to the Latin language.

While many languages share the Latin script – including French, Gaelic, Swedish – they do not all use exactly the same symbols. English has 26 basic letters, and a few (rarely used) diphthongs, other languages using the Latin alphabet have more characters, including compound characters such as the German ß, French ç, Spanish ñ and the accented vowels ô ö Å.

The Latin alphabet developed from hieroglyphics, which were adopted and adapted by Semitic peoples who had been the slave class under the Egyptians. This adaptation (Proto-Canaanite) developed in three different directions – Ugaritic, Phoenician, and Proto-Arabic. Ugaritic appears to have developed a sophisticated abstract form of symbols based on a single wedge-shaped mark – cuneiform (Figure 7.8), and provided the first example of an *abecedary* – an abstract alphabet laid out in a specific order. Interestingly, all the different variations of script (not syllabaries) maintained the same letter order starting with a, b, c (or g), … except one, which starts with h.

Figure 7.8   Some cuneiform.

The Latin alphabet we use developed through Phoenician and Ancient Greek, to emerge as Latin script around 800 BC. By this time, the understanding of written text was becoming available to a wider social group, thus making large or speedy changes to the forms unlikely. Symbols were dropped when they ceased to be useful (for example, if a sound from the old language had no equivalent sound in the new language or if two symbols both represented the same sound).

The letter forms we recognize as part of our alphabet were developed by Roman stonecutters, constructing monuments and waymarkers. At this time, letters had only one form (upper case or capital), and the exact form of the letters was partly derived from the stonecutting process. These forms were *serifed* – the serifs (or tails at the top and bottom of the strokes) being where the chisel was inserted at the beginning of the cut. This style of lettering was brought to England with the Romans, and adopted by monks and scribes who adapted it for use with quill pen and parchment.

For most of the population of England, learning (anything) was by copying the activities of your parents or apprentice-master. In a society ordered by feudalism and small village size, there was little need for written records. Stories were passed on by word of mouth. For those who needed a more permanent record, there were older pictogram and symbol systems such as tally sticks with matching halves (customer receipts) and pictorial symbols (such as the friezes in churches depicting scenes from the Bible). Written learning was restricted to the upper classes (who needed to keep records of land they owned, taxes received, etc.) and the church. It was a slow process of change that gradually increased the number of people who could, and did, write.

At this time, the official language of the church and state was Latin. English (Old English, and later Middle English) was spoken, but less frequently written and the spelling of words was not set. Words were written as they were pronounced – phonetically. The Domesday Book was responsible for setting a specific form and spelling of much of the language, although it continued to develop. Even in the time of Shakespeare spelling varied considerably.

Some languages (such as Burushaski, one of the Kashmiri languages) do not have a written form.

7.2.3 Printing

Up until the fifteenth century writing (by hand) was the only means of encoding the spoken word. Books were copied by hand and a monk might well spend his life in copying one book. Written communication was rare and books were expensive, being primarily restricted to religious institutions.

In the mid-fifteenth century, European universities were founded, Gutenberg invented the moveable type printing press (Figure 7.9), and a merchant 'middle class' emerged, creating both the demand and the means of production for more books. Suddenly, 400 to 1000 copies could be produced in a matter of weeks. This also created a moral panic at the possible spread of 'heretical materials' – any book which was not religious.

Figure 7.9   Movable type process.

Briefly, moveable type printing works like this.

- Accurate steel pieces are made in a foundry (originally this would have been done by the individual printer), one for each letter of the alphabet, back-to-front and set on a small metal block.

- The steel model is punched into soft brass, creating a mould.

- Molten lead is poured into the mould to create the desired number of letters.

- The letters are assembled in lines, back-to-front on a metal 'stick' and the spaces are created with strips of lead.

- The arranged letters are transferred into a metal frame, a chase (it is fairly important not to drop the chase at this point) and screwed into a wooden forme (the process of compositing).

- The type is levelled off with a wooden mallet, and fastened onto the press, which is secured to the ceiling and floor for stability.

- The letters are inked by dabbing with a leather pad, which transfers ink only to the raised parts.

- The paper is placed over the inked type, and pressure is applied by raising the bed or lowering a plate onto it.

The invention and spread of printing presses brought developments to letterforms, which were affected by the capability of the technology – the need for a certain bulk and strength in the metal type, the impossibility of overlapping letters when each is set on a separate metal block. It also brought about the final separation of image and text.

Where the monks had illuminated their manuscripts with pictures which illustrated the story, or referred to biblical characters and incidents, the image was inseparable from the text. The letters could be laid out in a particular shape, suggesting for example a crucifix form or a star, or used to outline or infill an image. With the advent of fixed shape moveable type, this was no longer possible. Letters had to be laid out on straight lines inside the metal chase, and fastened immovably together for the printing process. Pictures had to be carved separately onto blocks of wood (woodcut – the areas to be left unprinted were carved away), probably by a different person, and inserted into the text, also on one of the straight lines.

Early printing was slow and labour-intensive. Type was created in various different foundries, and was not standardized either in style or sizes. Nothing much changed for 400 years until the Industrial Revolution. In 1814 the steam press was invented which mechanized the heavy work of pressing the paper onto the type ('pulling the print'). In 1868, the Rotary Steam Press meant that inking, inserting the paper, and pulling the print could follow on in one smooth movement. This increased the speed of production and therefore the output while ultimately lowering the price of printed matter.

Developments in printing were very rapid during the Industrial Revolution – 1885 saw the invention of Benton's automatic punch cutter, which could scale up any size of metal punch from the original drawing. However, compositing still involved a huge labour force, and the storage of huge numbers of different pieces of physical type.

In 1829, the principle of the typewriter was invented by W. B. Burt of Detroit but it was not produced commercially until Remington released a machine in 1874. This was based on a more recent design by Scholes (1860) that included the moveable platen roller and *qwerty* keyboard. Once a keyboard had been invented, it could be used to drive a mechanical compositing machine. The earliest such was the *Monotype* system, where the keyboard was used to create a punched paper tape, which drove a casting machine containing a large number of moulds. As the tape passed through the caster, rather like a pianola roll, pieces of type were cast dynamically and automatically spaced into a chase. The operator could look at a normal (not reversed) letterform when entering the text to be cast.

The *Linotype* system was similar, except that it cast a line of type at one time. The caster would create a brass mould for each letter typed into the keyboard, and when a line on the chase was full, the whole line would be cast. This made corrections more difficult as a whole line would have to be reset.

After printing, the type would be melted down and recycled, so there was no need for storage. The Monotype and the Linotype companies had a virtual monopoly on printing by the beginning of the twentieth century, and printing had moved very firmly away from a craft to a large industry.

In the mid-nineteenth century, photography and the perfection of metal plate *lithography* brought the ability to reproduce type without a 3D physical model of the letter: this meant that letterforms could become more complex and decorative again. It also meant that letters and images could be rejoined, or rather that text could be free to take on more complex shapes around the page, and that hand-drawn letters could be mixed freely with set fonts, now available in photographic negative form for transfer onto the printing plate.

Lithography works by the repulsion of oil and water on a flat plate (originally polished stone). It was invented in 1798 (by Senefelder), but originally used for reproducing artists' drawings such as Toulouse-Lautrec's theatre posters. By 1850, flexible metal plates had been invented which could be used on a roller, with a rotary press.

The letterforms and images were transferred to the plate by drawing, using a greasy substance, which was then flooded with water. The water repelled oil-based ink, the grease attracted it, and so the plate could be used to print without the need for a raised surface. With the development of photography, it was possible to transfer accurate letterforms to the plate using a photomechanical system based on Monotype. A typesetting machine would contain a large store of photographic images of letters on acetate or glass, arranged as a series of discs or strips. These were projected through a prism and a lens (which could alter the size) onto photosensitive film. This film was then used to expose the Litho plate, which was coated with a substance that hardened with exposure to light. The unexposed areas could then be washed off. The resulting greasy plate could be used on the Litho press. Hence relief printing gave way to *planographic* printing.

While the typesetter could input text to be set via a keyboard, the plates would still be produced in reverse, which made checking and correction difficult. In 1904 the invention of Offset Litho (Rubel) enabled the text to be printed onto an intermediary surface (a rubber 'blanket') and then back onto paper. This meant that the text could be set the same way round as it would eventually print. Now a whole page could easily be composed with images, text, borders, diagrams, tables, or maps – and then printed in one run.

Although many more books and newspapers were being produced, literacy only became widespread in England after the introduction of compulsory primary education (1888). By 1900 the first subscription libraries were set up, and reading began to develop as not only an educational or instructive pursuit, but also for recreation.

The next important invention in printing was web-offset (1960), where text could be printed not onto individual sheets but onto a continuous paper roll (the web). This meant that the process of printing could be fully automated. Books and newspapers are produced in this way and then cut (by machine).

Photo composition had become common by 1950, but by 1973 it was already being replaced by computerized typesetting using a mainframe slave typesetter and a series of terminals. This had the advantage of a built-in dictionary of spellings and permissible hyphenations (where a word is allowed to break at the end of a line). The characters were stored digitally on magnetic tape and outputted as a photographic image, for transfer to Litho plates.

Later computerized typesetting machines were really large specialized PCs, using page composition software, a large library of stored fonts, and laser technology print output. For the first time, the origination (the actual composing of the written piece), compositing, and editorial (correction) could all be done by the same person, and in one operation. These tasks could be done remotely and transferred electronically to the printing works. Digitization of typefaces meant that they could be copied exactly without degradation or change, and hence could become standardized across the whole industry. This brought a requirement for a standardization of the way the typefaces were digitized and the information was stored and manipulated. In 1980 PostScript (the language) emerged as the standard method of encrypting data about digital fonts, with fonts being stored as a set of instructions according to one of the international standards: PostScript (the specification) or TrueType. These two are currently the main alternatives in the computer age but may, in the future, be replaced by the OpenType technology.

7.2.4 Fonts and font families

For centuries, text was written and reproduced by hand. The knowledge and understanding of reading and writing was recognized as the possession of power, and was restricted to certain classes at different times in history. There had been great variation between groups of writers and readers, but once the letterforms began to be written and read by larger numbers of people, it was important for the shapes to become set.

As children we learn to read by recognizing an 'a' – a meta-letter with a shape but without any reference to a style or particular typeface. In fact, printed, and even hand-written letters always do have some particular font – a variation on the standard meta-letter. These fonts have developed over time, and form families just like the languages, and the scripts that represent them. When communicating in written text, it is vital to make use of appropriate fonts to give the right sub-textual message.

A typeface is made up of a *font*, a *style*, a *weight*, and a *size*. Fonts are sets of designs for letters, under copyright to a design house or foundry. (They are often still called foundries even when they produce not metal type, but designs for computer-based font sets.)

The different fonts which have developed since the introduction of moveable type, all have distinct characteristics, often related to politics, religion, or fashion. We will consider the fonts first, then the other attributes of the typeface.

7.2.4.1 Fonts

Uncial

Kelt
(Bay Animation Inc)

The early scribes developed a style called Uncial, an ordering and codification of handwriting. Half-Uncial, a later development, introduced ascenders and descenders (the top of an h and the loops of a g, for example), which were the beginnings of *lower case* letters. These were introduced because it is much faster to write in lower case. The court of Charlemagne, in the Holy Roman Empire, introduced Caroline (or Carolingian) which was used with Half-Uncial to provide upper and lower case. All these formed the basis of handwriting styles (round hand and italic) which are still in use. They also form a basis for modern typefaces of the 'Celtic' type – a sort of 'folk' typeface associated with sources such as the Book of Kells and Irish folklore and mythology. By extension it has developed broadly Celtic associations and (by comparison with the runic alphabets of the ancient Celts) associations with folk-tales, 'fairies', and magic.

𝕭𝖑𝖆𝖈𝖐𝖑𝖊𝖙𝖙𝖊𝖗

Fraktur
(Digital Type Foundry)

Three hundred years later (fashions changed a lot more slowly then …) Europe was in its Gothic period. The German Empire was growing, and the fashion in architecture, ornamentation, and handwriting was for elaborate and highly ornamented heaviness. When Gutenberg cut his first metal type, he based it on the popular handwriting of the time − Blackletter. This became associated with German Imperialism, and has remained popular in Germany (in spite of a more recent association with the Third Reich) where new variations are still being designed. It is regarded as a 'folk' typeface, and is also associated with contemporary Gothic fashion − heavy metal, motorbikes, vampires. Variations of Blackletter faces are used by Honda Motorcycles and AC/DC in their logos. They have also been associated with High Church, and the notion of an Olde Englande.

Serif

Bembo
(Adobe Systems Inc)

While the Germans were developing their empire, the Italians were enjoying a Humanist Renaissance, developing interests in philosophy, natural history, and a return to the culture and values of classical Rome. The Italian printing presses developed their own type, based on the old Roman stonecutting/Half-Uncial model, and as Italy took over from Germany as a centre of Western culture, so Roman typefaces became more popular and lasted longer than Blackletter.

Roman typefaces all have serifs and did not change greatly until print technologies changed. They are generally classified into subgroups of *Humanist* or *Venetian* which most resembled handwriting, having spiky, bracketed serifs, and a marked diagonal between the thickest and thinnest points of the letter (the angle of stress) reflected in some of the horizontals. Early type sought to copy handwriting because it was the only precedent, and because, even as late as the late nineteenth century, printed (and later, typewritten) communication was considered second-best, impersonal, and even rude.

Later serif typefaces were grouped as *Garalde, Transitional* (which includes the ubiquitous Times New Roman) − which reflected in their formal symmetry the developing interest in scientific and mathematical principles, and *Modern* or *Didone* − which took advantage of developments in metal casting techniques and paper quality to produce very thin, hairline strokes. *Slab serifs* are ones in which the serif, instead of a graceful graduated line is a straight cross-stroke. It developed in, and is associated with, the Industrial Revolution – early technology. One particular slab face – *Typewriter* (for example, Courier) which employs a fixed width letter is associated (obviously) with typewriters but also with early, or base-level automation (teletypes, computers). Blockier slab serifs are associated with Victorian playbills or Wild-West wanted posters.

Although to an untrained eye, there is very little difference between one serif and another (Figure 7.10), the differences were sufficiently marked that in the 1880s, when the Arts and Craft movement was reacting to the growing mechanization of human life, there was a revival in design and usage of the Humanist types, associated with a gentler and more agricultural age.

Figure 7.10   Serif face, which bit is the serif?

Sans Serif   Johnston Underground
          (P22 Type Foundry)

Fonts developed for nearly 400 years with serifs on them, so that when someone invented a typeface without any, it prompted moral outrage, and was declared 'grotesque'. (If it is hard to imagine anyone getting that excited over a minor change, read any letters page in a daily national newspaper.)

Sans serif typefaces were invented in 1816, but not really used until the 1920s, when the *Bauhaus* in Germany was promoting minimalism, functionalism, constructivism. Thus the early fonts were stark, minimal, and angular, and are often associated with the fashions of the 1920s. Later styles became softer, less tall and thin, and with occasional variations in the width of the stroke – as a result they are called Humanist styles. They often suggest early years reading books, as this type of face is the one used to introduce children to an undecorated simple letterform.

Script

Brushed Script
(W.S.I.)

While monks were using quill pens (which are stiff), scribes in Persia (as it then was) were using flexible nibs and brushes, developing a more flowing handwriting with more curves, more of a slant, and more variation in heights. This became the basis for formal script hands, which imitated that writing. They are now generally associated with luxury and quality – expensive hotels, restaurants, cosmetics. They are harder to read than any of the other font types mentioned, and are not suitable for writing a whole body of text. They are sometimes used in an attempt to suggest personal attention ('Dear householder, we really value your custom here at Bodgitt and Runne …') but it is unlikely to fool anyone into thinking it was written by hand. Contemporary, informal script hands often refer to the modern (less ordered) handwriting, or the writing of children.

Italic

Poetica Chancery I
(Adobe Systems Inc)

Italic fonts are related to round-hand script, and are generally regarded as relating to one of the serif or sans serif faces. Unlike script, the letters do not usually join or overlap, which makes them easier to read. They are often associated with calligraphy and therefore craftsmanship, with old-fashioned delicacy, with school, and the 3Rs.

DECORATIVE

Arts And Crafts
(P22 Type Foundry)

Decorative is a term that covers anything else, fonts that are designed for maximum effect rather than readability. These can often convey a whole message in one word, like a logo.

Decorative fonts change greatly according to the era. Victorian lettering favoured flowers, cherubs, and Rococo decoration. Contemporary decorative fonts tend to have a real-world reference (letters made out of knives and forks, furry animals, or machine parts) or to fit broadly into the categories of *Techno* (designed to look like LED displays or neon), *Grunge* (graffiti, blotted, or smudged) or *Decorated* (infilled with stars and stripes, psychedelic flowers, or having extraneous decorative additions to the ends – a sort of super-serif).

7.2.4.2 Typeface attributes

Size   Typeface is measured in *point sizes*, where 1 point is approximately $\frac{1}{72}$ of an inch. It was traditionally a measure of the height of the metal blocks containing the letters (see Figure 7.9) and, although the metal blocks no longer exist in computer fonts, this notion still exists in modern type measurement. The type size is therefore slightly greater than the distance between the top of the highest ascender and the bottom of the lowest descender.

The *x-height* is the measurement of the height of the character x, in other words of the middle bit without any ascender or descender. It is this height that really determines whether the text is large enough to be read comfortably (Figure 7.11). Determining the size of text is always a compromise between legibility, expense, and available space, but you should never expect your reader to look (from close up) at a block of text less that 10 point, or preferably 12.

Figure 7.11   Parts of type.

The width of the letters is called the *set*, and is fixed relative to the point size. The spaces between the letters in one word (*tracking*) can be adjusted in a process called *kerning*. Certain pairs of letters, because of their shape, often need to be kerned for example W-A, V-o.

In metal type, the space is set by the shape of the metal block on which the letter is cast. This would be proportional to the width of the letter itself (*proportional* spacing). Typewriter fonts are *fixed width*, because the block of metal is the same size for every letter. Fonts on a computer used to be fixed width, but modern technology allows proportional fonts, although most of the time there is still a 'virtual block of metal' round each character that has to be kept clear.

The space between lines of letters is also measured in points. 10-point text with 12-point space between lines would be called 10 on 12. This is measured from the baseline (bottom of the x-height) of one line of type to the baseline of the next. It is called *leading*. In metal type the space would literally have been created with a strip of lead inserted between the letters. Type produced photographically or on computer can have negative leading – the lines of type can overlap.

Spacing is an important consideration in legibility – too little will make the text hard to read, but too much will cause the sense to be disjointed and the reader might lose interest or forget what came before.

Weight   Any font has a *weight* – a relative measurement of the thickness of the strokes that make it up. As the weight increases, the proportion of width to height of the letter remains the same. The weight increases from *normal* to *semi-bold*, *bold*, *extra*, and *ultra*. Similarly, the shape of the letter (proportion of width to height) can be made thicker or thinner and so be described as *condensed*, *normal*, or *extended/wide*.

Differently weighted versions of a font (say, *Arial* and *Arial Condensed*, or *Palatino* and *Palatino Semi-Bold*) would be two different fonts which had been separately designed but with reference to each other. They would belong to a *font family*. Normally, they would be used together to create emphasis, or to structure a body of text into sections, using different family members for headings and subheadings.

Style   In the context of typefaces, *style* means *Roman* or *Italic*. In a letterpress printshop, sets of letters (*sorts*) would be kept in both Italic and Roman versions of the same font. On a computer, italic is a command which causes the computer to distort the existing lettershape or to replace it with an italicized version. If you italicize the word *Italics* – the 'a' changes shape and the letters develop a slant – but the quality of the letter on screen or in print will not be as good as a script designed in Italic. It is a shortcut.

On a computer *style* also covers the notion of *Underlined* text and *Bold*. This is also a distortion of the existing letterform rather than a separately designed bold weight font. Obviously, in typesetting, you would need another whole alphabet of sorts in related bold style.

Fonts are also designed with either solid (black lines) or outline (outlined in black with a blank centre) forms. And, of course, they can be printed, whether by letterpress, photolitho, or computer in any colour.

7.3 Meaning and text

Much of the meaning in a text is derived from its context – what comes before and after, where it is written, and, of course, how. Consider the different implications of the words 'I will never forget you' embroidered on a handkerchief and decorated with red hearts, written in felt pen on a brick that has just been thrown through your window, or typed on a small card, unsigned, on a funeral wreath.

Individual words and phrases have their own shades of meaning. STOP on a road sign is clear and imperative – a similar sign saying PAUSE or REST would not work, since it implies some sort of relaxed choice, and persuasion rather than command. However, more important clues often

come from the placement of the words alongside other words or images –
from their placement on the page or on the screen. We associate certain
formats with certain levels of authority. Things that we read in a
newspaper ('in black and white') we credit with more veracity than
things we read in a magazine because we associate the format, the use (or
lack) of colour, the relative distribution of images and text with a factual
document.

What about the veracity of words we see on screen? With the increasing use of TV and CD-ROM as a vehicle for education, it is tempting to
suppose that the viewer will regard the text as factual. While TV is
firstly an entertainment, it is true that many people do believe in the literal existence of characters in soap operas. TV is not generally used to
deliver text – except in the case of Teletext/Ceefax, which provides di-
gests of news items in the same way that pop radio does. Computer
screens, however, carry a great deal of text via the Internet. Text here
lacks the physical dimension of a book, the object-status which gives
authority to the printed word. And while TV may carry the air of truth
and the power of a huge budget, as Internet publishing and home-pro-
duced CD-ROMs become more easily available, the notion of authorita-
tive, expert published facts on screen becomes much less forceful.

Text on a computer can behave differently from printed text – it can
flash, walk around the screen as an animated cartoon, change dynamically with time or in response to an action by the reader. It can be updated
very rapidly and at relatively little cost. It can apparently read itself out
loud. As a consequence, screen-based text carries with it a suggestion of
up-to-date facts, information, ideas, experiments, but not necessarily
long-pondered serious questions. We must also remember that while
computers are becoming very common in certain countries, books
require no equipment to receive and read in any country.

Screen-based text offers more opportunities for creative design
inexpensively. A book has a fixed page size – the screen has a fixed
aspect ratio but can be scrolled. Screen-based text cannot only use
colour at no additional cost over black and white, but the colour can
change dynamically. Screen is not really suitable for large blocks of text
– partly because of the nature of the object – you cannot read your
computer in the bath or on the bus (yet), and partly because the
flickering nature of the backlit screen makes this uncomfortable. The
nature of the screen also renders colour differently – direct and therefore
apparently more saturated, rather than reflected. As with any context, it
is necessary to re-cast your text for the specific purpose and vehicle by
which it will be disseminated.

A great deal of our understanding of a text comes from its structure –
how it is divided into sections and the hierarchy that exists between
those sections. Every piece of text has a structure, although some of
them seem intuitive and therefore transparent.

A recipe generally has a title, a subtitle or description (this pie is delicious with anchovy custard and only 400 calories a slice) followed by a list of ingredients, and then a method, in which the actions are ordered temporally. The remark about the deliciousness of the pie would not be inserted halfway through the ingredients' list – if it were, we would assume a misprint. We only notice this structure explicitly when it breaks down.

This dividing of a text into sections introduces the idea of modular reading. Very few readers begin a broadsheet newspaper at the top of page 1 and read sequentially through to the crossword at the bottom of the back page. Normally, we read it in sections – perhaps scanning the headlines, and then jumping from one interesting-looking section to the next. By comparison, unless cheating in a detective story, we would read a novel from beginning to end. With a textbook of sequential exercises we would do the same, but with a practical guide, we would turn straight to the section we needed at that time, wherever it was situated. It is important for the structuring of the text to mirror the way in which you expect (or intend) your reader to use it. In a book, or a series of articles, we have some control over how they are read – the intended order is clear. But in a hypertext, the reader can move from any section to any other and therefore needs the material divided into self-contained units, with a structure that prevents the reader from getting lost by indicating recommended paths, or relevancies and dependencies.

A large document may be broken down into sections such as titles, contents, introduction, then parts 1, 2, and 3. Part 1 may be divided into chapters 1–10. Chapter 1 may be divided into sections, which are divided into paragraphs, then into sentences, then into phrases. These are discrete sections and a phrase cannot for example contain a paragraph. The way in which a document is structured is not necessarily the same as the way the pages are structured. Each page may have a header (*The Times*, or *Fudge Cookery for Beginners*), a main body of text, and a footer containing the page number. These are outside the structure of the narrative, and are not seen by the reader as breaking the flow of the text, as they would be if the Fudge Cookery for Beginners appeared elsewhere on the page.

A more complex structure might have a side index, several different bodies of text separated in boxes or areas of different colours, a number of keywords picked out in a different font in the body of the text, and a main heading which changes according to which section the reader is in. It may contain other visual clues for navigation or interpretation of the text.

It is necessary to structure the informational content before deciding on a structure for the text itself, and to do both before structuring, and subsequently designing, the layout of the page or screen. One important aspect of structuring text for the screen, is that text can appear on an entirely different part of the screen and therefore with a different meaning because of its location. For example, on a web page, the 'title' of the page (so designated) will appear in the top left-hand corner on a coloured strip, which does not move if the page is scrolled. This need not be used for a title, of course, but whatever is written there will be seen as a different class of information from the rest of the text. This is because there is a level at which the structure of the document has already been set by the computer. Because, to a computer, all information, data, and instructions are ultimately stored in the same format, it is possible to define how we want it to interpret any one of those. How it then defines and interprets that piece of information (text input) will determine what can be done with it and how it can be displayed. The computer can understand a number of different structures, each of which can be defined in a meta-language called SGML by a formal grammar called a Document Type Definition (DTD). We could define a DTD for our recipe, which would set out the rules for the compulsory sections (title, ingredients, method), optional sections (comments, serving suggestions, nutritional information), and then what each of those sections is allowed to contain. For example:

- ingredients must have at least one item followed by one amount;

- every item must have an amount and no item can have more than one amount;

- the ingredients section may not contain anything except items and amounts.

The decision about how the computer will display those sections is taken elsewhere – you may decide that the ingredients will be laid out in a table, with the item to the right in black, and the amount to the left in green italics. You may decide to further structure your document so that it differentiates between different food groups in the ingredients' list (meat in brown, vegetables in green, saturated fats in flashing red lights). It is up to the author to determine which are vegetables and which ounces or grams – the computer will follow the rules but cannot identify a cabbage.

7.4 The concept of readability

When we learn to read, we learn to recognize a pattern of lines that stand in for a sound 'E'. Later we learn to copy it, and to recognize small variations in the pattern. We form an internal model of the pattern 'E' and some general rules about what makes an 'E' an 'E' and not an 'F'. When we read a piece of text we match what we see to our internal model, and adjust the model to include new variations we learn. If the written symbol is ambiguous, we are able to guess, based on the context.

We can recognize a letter even when it appears reversed but cannot necessarily match unfamiliar letters (for example, Hebrew) which come from different writing styles (Figure 7.12).

Figure 7.12   When is an E not an E?

As we grow more proficient in reading, we do not look at the individual symbols, but at the groupings, recognizing common groups of letters by their compound shape. Thus we are able to recognize words which have parts missing, or contain errors. In fact, we often fail to notice the error, because we have assumed a match with the nearest known word shape. This is one reason why typing errors are so hard to spot.

Jump in the swimning pool

Because we read the page from top to bottom, we see the tops of the letters first – and extract most of the information from them without looking at the bottoms – so we can recognize words with half the shape missing.

goldfish

In fact our eyes move across the page of text in jumps, pauses, and jumps back – we read only during the pauses, when we process several letters at once, syllables, or whole words and phrases. We read by sight (recognition of the words which are within our sight-vocabulary) and if necessary, recode the symbols as sounds (subvocalization) – effectively converting them to spoken words.

Besides recognizing the general shape of words, we can recognize the general shape of sentences. Where a child might spell out a word, and a poor reader will read each word slowly, most adults will look at a whole sentence or phrase, looking at the pattern of long and short words and giving most attention to the longest. We guess a great deal and check what we see to confirm this – which enables some people to read extremely fast, but also enables the writer to mislead the reader.

We can help or hinder the readers in the process of reading, both by the words we use, and by the way we guide them perceptually.

7.4.1 Reading difficulty

The English language has a very large number of words within it – certainly more than 120,000. Most adults utilize just a fraction of those words – it is possible to manage day to day with only a couple of hundred. Certain words are very commonly used and others are rare. One way to assess the difficulty of reading a particular piece of text is to calculate how common the words within it are. A second aspect relates to the sort of processing that is being done as the reader perceives and processes the text. Since they are having to make fixations, store them and process them, it is apparent that the memory load will be higher if there are more syllables in a word or more words in a sentence. There are a variety of standard techniques for assessing the reading difficulty of a text. Some word-processors include tools for checking reading difficulty directly. Microsoft Word includes two:

- *Flesch Reading Ease score*: based on the number of words per sentence and syllables per word, this is a scale from 0–100, where higher scores are easier to read and anything above about 70 should be generally readable to most audiences.

- *Flesch–Kincaid Grade Level score*: This test maps the complexity of the words onto the expected attainment level at different ages in school (grades in USA).

Normally you should decide on an expected level for your text and try to write to that level of readability. Note that things will be very different when you write different sorts of document, and when you have different expectations of your users. Technical manuals or scientific papers are likely to be of a high level of complexity and be difficult to read. Packets of breakfast cereal should be extremely simple. My own fiction writing has a drastically different level of readability from my academic writing.

7.4.2 Reading and layout

There is extensive research upon ways in which the layout of text and the printed page can affect the readability of the content. If you bear in mind the fixation process of reading that we introduced earlier, you will be able to see that they all follow from providing clues to help that process proceed more effectively. Here are just a few points:

- *Justification*. In general, the more fixed points the user has to work from the better. Text which has a uniform left edge (left justified) is normally the easiest of all to read. Text which is centred (ragged both sides) or ragged left/uniform right is significantly harder to read. When text is justified (uniform on both margins) the level of readability depends upon how the justification has been done. The edges may have been evened by inserting space between words, or by inserting space between letters within words. This can be done well or badly so readability will depend on the exact details, but in general fully justified text is harder to read than ragged right.

- *Choice of font.* All aspects of font choice (size, weight, face, etc.) have an effect upon readability. There are many available guidelines and recommendations for font usage. In general, assume that a serif font is most readable for body text and a sans serif font for headings where there is not too much text to read. There are experimental results available about the readability of individual faces.

- *Distractions.* Try to keep the reading area free of distractions, which will affect the perceptual process. Patterned backgrounds, different coloured letters, variations in size, or anything that makes it difficult to see the overall length or shape of a word will slow down the reading process.

- *Breaks.* Even on a page of text it is important to have breakpoints which the reader can use as reference outside the sentences to see where they are. Clearly delimited paragraphs help, as do occasional pictures and other non-textual items within the page.

- *Spacing.* While it might initially appear that the more spaced out text is, the easier it is to read, this is not ultimately true. Certainly closely packed text is difficult to read because the eye has to be precise about the fixation points, but widely spaced texts can involve extreme amounts of eye movement and slow the perceptual process down. There is always a compromise position between the extremes.

Bear in mind that you can get away with many things in a short piece of text, such as a heading or poster title, which will not work when used with extensive bodies of text.

7.5 Text and the screen

When considering text on a computer screen we have to bear in mind all the issues that would concern us with designing readable text for a page, but also remember the issues which are specific to the fact that we are working with a visual display unit. The eye is seeing something quite different from the printed page. Instead of reflected light there is emitted light directly into the eye. Instead of a wide spectrum of frequencies there are actually fairly narrow bands of red, blue, and green light. Instead of a completely stable image the screen is constantly changing and refreshing. A number of the ergonomic issues related to video displays were covered in Chapter 2, but we need to mention a few more aspects here.

Each computer can display at a number of different resolutions (pixels of width and height of the screen). Whatever we ask the computer to display – a line, a circle, or a text character is ultimately turned into a series of dots to display. It may be stored internally as a set of dots (bitmap) or a vector description of an object. In the former case the bitmap can be applied directly to video memory and displayed on the screen. In the latter case the computer has to calculate the bitmap that would correspond to this vector object. Bitmaps are quicker to work with but vectors, because they are mathematical descriptions of objects which are independent of the particular device on which they are displayed, can be resized indefinitely and still remain 'perfect', where a bitmap will become jagged. Almost all fonts used on modern computers are now stored as vectors (either Postscript or TrueType).

Text on the computer is used for a variety of purposes in the interface: for titles and headings (like windows and menus), for labels (such as filenames), for messages (such as alert or prompt dialogues), and within applications-like word-processors, help systems, etc. where there may be substantial bodies of text. In each case you need to make specific decisions about what you are communicating by the content of the text and what you are saying by the appearance – the choice of typeface and layout. There is the additional issue that a computer allows us to use colour more easily than previous text systems, and things such as animation and updating text are possible. General HCI standards relating to text can be found in various common texts, and HCI guidelines specific to particular platforms are available from the operating system producers.

7.6 Exercises

Exercise 7.1 Write a piece of text (up to one side of A4) to explain the idea of a government election to a 5 year old child.

Exercise 7.2 Write an explanation of what a 'font' is for a reasonably intelligent adult who knows nothing about typography.

Exercise 7.3 Locate a reading difficulty test (e.g. in your word processor or on the Web). Apply it to both of the above texts. How closely did you match your target age? What would you need to change to improve the fit?

Exercise 7.4 Layout the text from Exercise 7.2 in a manner that maximizes readability.

Exercise 7.5 Layout the text from Exercise 7.2 in a manner that minimizes readability (without being impossible to read, such as black text on black background).

Exercise 7.6 Note down the key differences between what you did in each of the above cases.

7.7 Further reading

Basic readings about reading processes:
Geoffrey Underwood and Vivienne Batt, *Reading and understanding: an introduction to the psychology of reading*, Blackwell, 1996

Keith E. Stanovich and Isabel L. Beck, *Progress in understanding reading: scientific foundations and new frontiers*, Guildford Press, 2000

A standard starting text on typography:
James Craig, *Designing with type*, Watson-Guptill Publications, 1999

A very useful book, including issues specifically related to designing for screen and web:
Robin Williams, *The non-designer's type book*, Addison Wesley Longman Publishing Co, 1998

Two texts specifically related to issues that affect type in a digital environment:
Rob Carter, *Working with computer type part 3: colour and type*, RotoVision, 1996

Donald Knuth, *Digital typography*, Center for the Study of Linguistics and Information, 1998

8

Sound

8.1 Introduction

Sound is an extremely important part of our daily communication, but one that we tend to take for granted and often ignore. When developing multimedia systems there is often either no auditory component, or one which was just 'added on' without thought or significant effort. These systems fail to make use of a very valuable medium, and one for which materials can be developed comparatively cheaply with a little thought.

The field is also of significant interest to the future of multimedia because it is one area where digital techniques have almost entirely replaced traditional analogue methods of saving and manipulating information. Consequently, it can be used to make some predictions about the future impact of digital methods on other channels of communication.

This chapter will start by examining some basic issues in the physics of sound and the psychology of sound perception – a field known as *psychoacoustics*. We will then examine the three main categories of auditory stimulus – spoken words, sound effects, and music – in the purely auditory medium of radio. After alluding to linking sound into other media, we will turn to the new technologies that have changed the nature of the audio industry and examine their potential impact upon multimedia.

8.2 The modality

8.2.1 What is a sound?

What we hear as a sound is a result of changes of pressure in the air outside our ears. We experience slow changes in pressure all the time (as the weather changes, or we go up and down hills, etc.), but we do not hear these changes ('popping' ears is caused by a sudden adjustment of our ear to a pressure difference between inside and outside the ear). To be heard as a sound, a change in pressure has to occur with sufficient speed and regularity to cause an oscillation of our eardrums. These oscillating changes of pressure are referred to as 'sound waves'.

When a wave moves over the water, or along a piece of string, each little particle of water (or whatever) moves up and down, at right angles to the direction that the wave itself is travelling. Consequently, although the wave 'moves', nothing physical moves long with it. If we were to look at a wave in cross-section, we would see that the particles had a 'rest position' before the wave arrived, and that they move up and down to certain extremes before returning to their original rest point. Waves of this sort are called *transverse waves*. Figure 8.1 shows such a wave.

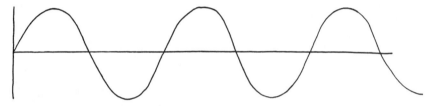

Figure 8.1   Transverse wave.

Sound waves are slightly different, in that the particles move in the same direction that the wave travels. They still have a rest position, move in one direction and then the other before returning to their rest position, but the movement is at right angles to the way particles move in a water wave. Consequently, this means that at some places the air (or whatever) that the wave is travelling through will have more particles than in its resting state and at some places it will have less. This corresponds to greater and lesser air pressure. Some parts are compressed (higher pressure) and some are rarefied (lower pressure). A wave of this type is often called a *compression wave* or *longitudinal wave*. Figure 8.2 shows such a wave.

As you can probably see, this diagram is a bit difficult to understand so, following standard practice, we will represent sound waves as though they were transverse whenever we draw them. This diagram form serves

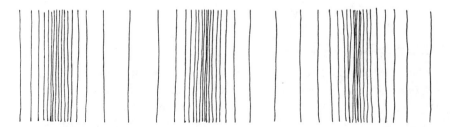

Figure 8.2   Compression wave.

our purpose excellently, and allows us to directly see two of the most important characteristics of any sound wave: *frequency* and *amplitude*.

Frequency

Frequency is a measure of how often the oscillation in the wave occurs. This is normally calculated as the number of complete oscillations per second. A complete oscillation is from the rest point to one extreme, back to the other extreme, and returning to the rest point, and is commonly referred to as a *cycle*. The frequency is the number of these cycles that occur every second. They can be measured as, for example 100 cycles per second, but this is rather old-fashioned terminology and in the currently accepted measuring system the unit is referred to as the hertz (abbreviated Hz): 1 Hz = 1 cycle per second. While compression waves can exist over a very broad range of frequencies, humans can only hear a part of that range as sound. We will explore this further in the next section.

Amplitude

Amplitude is the second major characteristic of a wave. This tells us how far the particles of the substance through which the wave is moving displace from their 'rest position' during the oscillation. This is represented in Figure 8.3 by the height of the wave. The bigger the displacement, the greater the energy of the wave, and the greater the changes in pressure. While the frequency of a given wave remains constant, the amplitude will vary, becoming less as the distance from the source of the wave increases due to the resistance of the medium through which it travels.

Combinations of waves (and reflections)

In all of the above cases we have drawn waves of a particular shape – a sine wave. This shape is fundamental in many aspects of nature, representing a trade-off between displacement and velocity, which

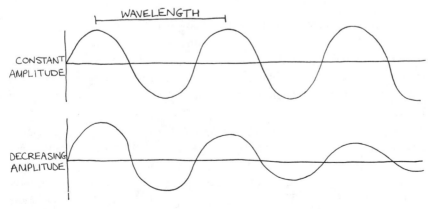

Figure 8.3 Amplitude.

corresponds to maintaining constant energy. A pendulum is an example of this relationship. What we refer to as a 'pure' musical note (e.g. a flute) is a pretty close approximation to this perfectly smooth waveform. In most cases, however, the sounds that we hear comprise a number of different sound waves with differing frequencies and amplitudes. A single note on a piano is much more complex than the fairly pure flute, containing many different frequencies. A single note on a piano would contain the *fundamental frequency* (i.e. the pitch of the note actually played, for example A = 440 Hz) and a series of harmonics, which are higher frequencies related to the fundamental frequency. This combination of waves produces something which we can refer to as a complex waveform, which still repeats but which does not have the pure sinusoidal structure (Figure 8.4). It can always be reduced to a collection of pure sinusoidal tones, however.

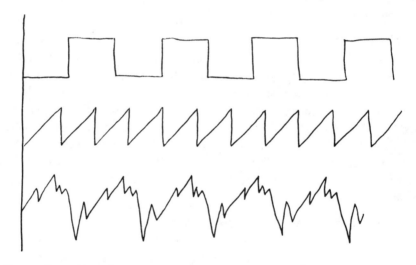

Figure 8.4   Complex waves – square wave, sawtooth.

Phase

When we are considering more than one wave, the *phase* becomes an attribute. Consider two waves of the same frequency and amplitude. If they are both transmitted at the same time, then the net effect is as if the two waves were added together. We might expect a result which is a wave of the same frequency and double the amplitude, as shown in Figure 8.5.

This situation does occur, but only when the two waves have peaks and troughs in the same place, as in Figure 8.5. These are waves that are in phase. Any other two waves would be out of phase – the question is by how much? We can have a situation in which the waves are completely opposite – with peaks on one corresponding to troughs on the other and vice versa. If this is the case then the waves are said to be in anti-

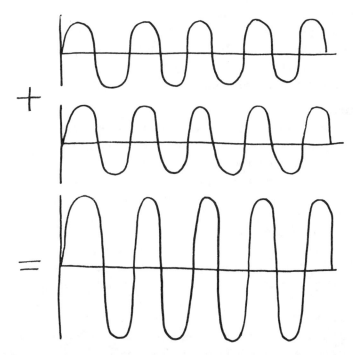

Figure 8.5　In-phase waves.

phase, or 180° out of phase (Figure 8.6). A wave that is 360° out of phase is back in phase again. What we are saying is that a complete cycle (i.e. from resting point to peak and then down thorough the resting point to the trough back to the resting point again) represents 360°. Other differences are measured as angles with values between these.

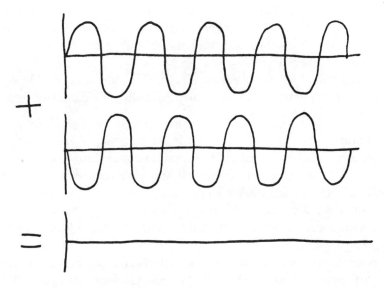

Figure 8.6　Anti-phase waves.

Sounds can be complex because the source is creating many different frequencies, phases, and amplitudes. They can also be complex because the physical environment through which the sound passes to reach its destination will have an effect upon it. This can be divided into components of *transmission* and *reflection*.

Transmission

Sound, as we have noted, consists of compression waves, and hence it requires a physical medium through which to move. If there is no medium (i.e. a vacuum) then there is no sound. It is true that in space no one can hear you scream – there is no sound transmission. It is also the case that the stunning sound effects in science fiction films just would not happen in the real world!

We are used to sound travelling through one particular medium, the air, in which it travels at the (comparatively slow) speed of 330 metres per second (about 750 miles per hour). The medium also takes energy from the wave, so that it attenuates (loses amplitude) as it travels further in the medium. We notice that sounds get quieter as we move away from the source, but it is also the case that the different frequencies in the sound attenuate at different speeds, so that the higher frequencies normally become inaudible before the lower ones. This is one reason that we hear the bass and drums from a band before anything else as we approach. In a different medium (such as a solid object) sound travels at a different speed and the effects of attenuation on frequency will have different properties. Normally, a denser medium will result in sound travelling faster and losing the high frequencies more quickly. This process is why we all think that our voice 'does not sound right' when we hear it on a tape recorder. Listening to a tape recording we hear our voice as it travels through air (which is how others hear us), but when we speak we hear our voice partly as it travels through air, and partly as it travels through our jaw and the bones of our skull. Consequently, it sounds quite different.

In a real-world situation the sounds that we hear are predominantly transmitted through air, but there may be small components from other transmission media.

Reflection

A more significant source of complexity in the sound reaching our ears is reflection. A wave may travel directly from a sound source to our ear, but if there are any surfaces nearby (including the floor, the ceiling, walls, furniture, etc.) then there will also be a component of the sound which reaches the ear having been reflected from one or more of these surfaces (Figure 8.7).

If perfect reflection occurs from all surfaces (i.e. *all* the sound hitting the surface is reflected) then the sound reaching the ear will be 'muddied' because some of the waves will have travelled further and

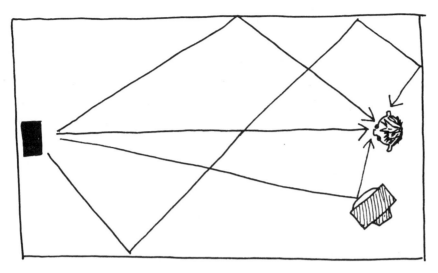

Figure 8.7   Multiple reflections.

therefore arrive at the ear slightly later than those following the direct route. If these delays are long (~200 ms or more) then there is an audible 'echo' — we hear the same sound repeated distinctly. For shorter times (which are more typical of day-to-day events) the resulting wave is not heard as separate sounds, but as a change in the complexity of the original. This muddying effect is known as 'reverberation'.

Reverberation is very important because it relates the sound to the environment around it. We all have the experience of sounds being different in a small room or a big hall, indoors or outdoors, a room with tiled walls or soft furnishings. It is apparent that the distance to reflecting surfaces (and the number of them) will cause the changes of echo and reverberation described above, but how can we tell the differences between tiles and soft furnishings? The reason for the difference is that, as with the transmission process, different materials reflect and absorb different frequencies, changing the amplitude of the different components of the wave that is reflected (Figure 8.9). Tiles absorb very little, reflecting almost all the high frequencies. Soft furnishings absorb most of the energy and reflect very little. Consequently, the sound has different qualities in these cases. We are all familiar with the difference between singing in the shower and singing in a hall!

8.2.2   The psychology of hearing

In the previous section we were careful to discuss the physical properties of sound without (as far as possible) involving a hearer in the process. That discussion covered the basic physics of sound. The effect of

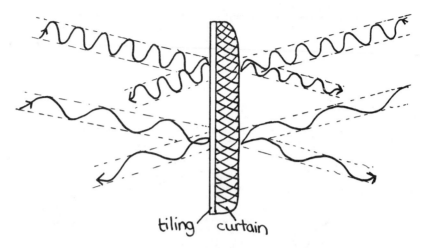

tiling   curtain

Figure 8.8   Waves before and after reflection.

this sound on a human being is a distinct, but related, process. In particular, the properties of *frequency* and *amplitude* have corresponding concepts in auditory perception: *pitch* and *loudness*.

Pitch, loudness and timbre

Pitch   *Pitch* is the perceived frequency of a note. Normally this corresponds to the frequency, but there are two specific limitations on the human ear. One is that the range of sounds that we can hear is limited. Normal human range is roughly from 16 Hz to 20,000 Hz. This decreases slightly with age at the top end. Other animals (e.g. dogs, bats, porpoises, etc.) can hear sounds of *higher* and *lower* frequencies. The second limitation is that with complex waves of more than one frequency, the frequencies are not normally perceived independently, but as being one particular pitch with a timbre (see below) which is determined by the other frequencies present.

Loudness   *Loudness* corresponds roughly to the amplitude of the note. It is not quite the same because the sensitivity of the human ear is different at different frequencies, and hence the perceived loudness of a sound depends on both the *frequency* and *amplitude* of the physical stimulus. Loudness is measured in decibels (dB). The decibel is calculated relative to a point of zero decibels, which is set according to the limits of human hearing – o dB is the threshold for a human to hear a sound of 1000 Hz. Decibels are a logarithmic scale: a sound difference of 10 dB is 10 times as loud, 20 dB is 100 times as loud, 30 dB is 1000 times as loud, etc. The following are the typical decibel levels of some common sounds.

20 dB	Whisper
60 dB	Office
85 dB	Use ear protection
90 dB	Music (loud)
100 dB	Risking damage
110 dB	Pneumatic drill
140 dB	Aeroplane

Timbre   The third major component of the perceived nature of a sound is the *timbre*. This is a term used to indicate the complex combination of waves which enable us to distinguish a violin from a tuba, or one person's voice from another. There is no simple physical property which corresponds to this component. It is a product of many different things. It is also one of the most important pieces of the psychology of sound perception, and can relate strongly to the subjective interpretation of the individual.

Envelope   The three components described above are sufficient to represent a continuous sound. In practice, the volume (and often timbre) of a sound varies over time. A note on a cello starts comparatively quietly and builds up to a peak before fading away. A harpsichord, by comparison, starts at almost the full volume before it fades away quickly. The shape of the volume change of a note is often referred to as the *envelope*, and in practice it is generally divided into four sections – *attack*, *decay*, *sustain*, and *release*. Attack is the period from the onset of the note to its peak volume. Decay represents a period when the peak volume decreases to another level which may be held for a period of time. The period when this second volume is held is the sustain, and the final decrease in volume from the sustain level to nothing is the release. These are illustrated in Figure 8.9.

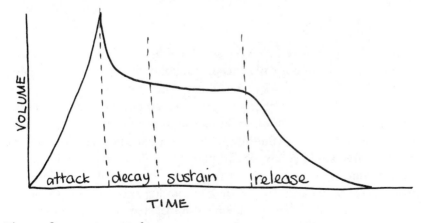

Figure 8.9   ADSR envelope.

Spatial location

Ears, human or otherwise, normally come in pairs. They are separated by some distance or something solid like a head. This is not an accident. With two ears, there will be a small, but significant, difference in the time that a sound arrives at each ear. This difference is determined by the localization – its place in space. We can use this information to work out where a sound is coming from. Sounds to our right arrive at the right ear slightly before the left, and vice versa. Someone with a hearing impairment in one ear will have trouble localizing sounds. If a sound is directly in front of or behind a person with normal hearing, then our ears will receive a roughly equal magnitude of stimulus at the same moment in time (depending upon the acoustic environment) (Figure 8.10). In a place with no acoustic, such as a field, and with no visual clue to guide us, we may become confused as to whether such a sound is in front of, or behind us.

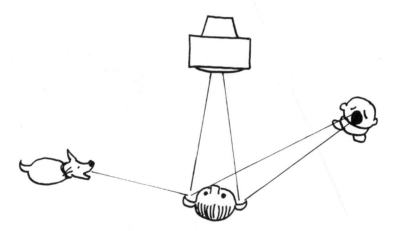

Figure 8.10   Sound space.

The time lags involved are very small, being of the order of a millisecond or less, and consequently this discrimination is quite difficult. Most people can only distinguish about 10 zones horizontally.

Sounds with exactly the same timbre, amplitude, and pitch can sometimes confuse the brain as far as sound localization is concerned – but only under certain conditions. Using only a time delay of between three and five milliseconds we can perceive two sounds as coming from one direction when in actual fact they are from opposite directions. We always perceive the direction of such a sound(s) as being from the sound which occurs first. This is not down to an inaccuracy in our hearing (not this time anyway) but is in fact due to a time lapse in the neural system.

Masking and attention

As with visual phenomena, what we 'hear' is the result of a process in the brain that takes the raw stimuli from the ear and processes them to construct an 'audio image'. Because this is an active process it can, as with reading and vision, be confused into presenting things which are not actually as they should be in the real world. Two well-known aspects are the *masking* of sounds, and the effects of *attention* upon what we hear.

Masking   The best model we can develop for masking is that of tape hiss or *white noise* as it is better known. White noise contains all the frequencies of the audio spectrum at equal amplitudes. A sound with any particular frequency you care to pick is present in white noise, but you cannot distinguish it from the rest because all the other frequencies occurring at a similar amplitude *mask* the sound from the listener. It is only by greatly increasing the amplitude of the chosen fundamental frequency (and sometimes its harmonics) that it becomes audible to the listener. This is an extreme example, but the point is that in a variety of circumstances, one sound can completely conceal another from detection by the brain.

A more musical example can be seen in the orchestration of some of the better known classical composers. When composing for an orchestra we would never attempt to write a prominent solo piccolo part for a particular section of music which contained loud brass and strings with percussion. The piccolo solo in question would be masked – made inaudible – by the other sounds, pitches, timbres, and amplitudes that were occurring. We would have to take into consideration the dynamics and selection of other instruments during the particular passage of music. The masking effect can be used to the advantage of the musicians. A prominent line for a musical instrument can often seem quite daunting to the instrumentalist playing that part. Not all the instruments of the orchestra play notes in every bar, and there are often long intervals of silence from certain sections of the orchestra. If the section directly preceding the prominent line for our piccolo player was a loud passage for brass and strings, we could write a quiet part for piccolo. Although we do not wish this part to be 'heard', it would allow the player to 'warm up' the instrument. This is made possible by the other instruments masking the sound of the piccolo.

Filtering   In our brave new world of digital technology, it is possible to filter out certain specific frequencies: to take away certain parts of the audio spectrum extremely precisely, and at the same time attenuate others. There are a number of ways of doing this. One method would be to apply a *high pass* filter to a sound at a point in the audio spectrum determined by the user. This would only allow sounds above that particular frequency to be audible (hence *high* pass). For example, setting a high pass filter at 10,000 Hz, or 10 kHz, would only allow the listener to hear frequencies above 10 kHz, filtering out those frequencies below 10 kHz. A *low pass* filter does exactly the reverse – letting the listener hear low frequencies and eliminating high ones. A *band pass* filter allows us to set an upper and lower limit for our sound. This would have the effect of allowing the frequencies of two determined points, let's say 8 kHz and 12 kHz, to be audible and filtering out the rest of the frequencies. A *notch filter* does exactly the reverse – filtering out the specific frequencies but leaving most of the sound.

Attention   Humans can operate a rather more complex filtering process than this. Because we are actively listening to our environment, and trying to pay attention to certain things (e.g. the person talking to us), we are constantly trying to shut out the noises of everyday life. Sitting in a pub we can have a perfectly reasonable conversation without even noticing that we can also hear the other people, the slot machine, the jukebox, and the television – we are *dynamically* filtering them out. What is happening is that we are recognizing that certain noises are present, and that they have certain characteristics. By deciding that we do not wish to pay attention to them we decide to filter out those sounds, and doing so involves us in constantly changing what it is that we ignore. You may have noticed that it is easier to ignore a jukebox playing familiar music than one playing unfamiliar tunes. In the former case we can predict what is coming next and subtract it from our audio experience, while in the latter case we are more likely to be surprised by what we hear, and this may 'grab our attention'.

There is a special case of this known as the 'cocktail party effect'. It simply points out that you can be in a situation where there are many people talking while you are having one conversation and ignoring many others. If someone in one of the conversations suddenly mentions your name, however, you will immediately pick up on the fact. This demonstrates that we are really hearing all the sounds, but are filtering certain parts out through a cognitive process.

8.3   Primary channels of communication

8.3.1   Working with the spoken word

The spoken word is one of the primary channels of communication in the auditory modality. We can typically speak about 200 words per minute. The things that we have previously said about natural language and about the choice of vocabulary and grammar for the written word are all relevant to working with the spoken word, but we must bear in mind that this is a different channel of communication. Different things are possible in the speech channel and these can have a profound effect upon the way that we interact and utilize this channel.

The first thing to note is that we do not, in general, speak sentences that we would write. When reading from a document you can immediately hear that it is not like 'normal' speech. In speech we generally have a hearer present, and can interact with them, producing a two-way dialogue process. We can see (or ask) whether they understand us, want to interject, or need clarification. We are less likely to talk in complete sentences – often using a mixture of quite short non-sentences and extremely long, unpunctuated rambles. We tend to use shorter words, to repeat ourselves and to interject words and remarks which would be quite out of place on a written page. Know what I mean? Nobody has worked out how to talk in paragraphs (except possibly Victor Borge with his phonetic pronunciation). All of these things are possible because we have additional information in the speech channel. We have sounds as well as words.

When we speak it is not uniform. Words are not all at the same pitch or spoken evenly. We make significant use of prosody – the sound patterns of a language. We will consider two aspects: *intonation* and *stress*.

Intonation refers to the overall audio contour of a phrase or sentence. The sounds of the words are not based on a single frequency, but will, in general, rise or fall as the sentence progresses. This can be used to indicate particular sorts of language structure (e.g. rising tones at the end of a sentence can indicate that it is a question), or a state of mind of the speaker (they can also indicate uncertainty). This particular example is only the case in English, and other languages use different intonation patterns. Some make more use of intonation than others – most people are familiar with the description of Celtic languages as *lilting*, or *musical*. This is not the same as the pitch languages where changing pitch changes the meaning of the words. Intonation is adding to the meaning of the words. As an aside, it has been suggested that one reason that the composer Edward Elgar tends to be popular with English people, but less so with people from elsewhere is that his musical structures reflect the intonation of spoken English.

Stress is part of the way we say an individual word. We may stress a whole word (making it louder in pitch) to emphasize its importance. Within a given word we normally place stress on one part relative to the rest – some particular stressed syllable. Getting this wrong in a language can lead to some very strange interpretations.

Beyond these patterns we move into the area of *pronunciation*. As we discussed earlier, most modern languages use an alphabet to represent a set of phonemes. While there is a set of phonemes (given by the international phonetic alphabet) that seem to represent all the sounds that a human being can produce, a given language will only use some of these. People from a different part of a country, while retaining the same language, might use a slightly different phoneme for the same letter combination. This is most noticeable with vowels. Short and long vowel sounds, or harsh versus smooth, can make a great difference in the way that your *accent* is interpreted. Just changing your vowel sounds and leaving everything else the same can suddenly move your accent from one end of a country to another.

Accent should be distinguished from dialect. The former is a change in pronunciation which is often regional but does not affect the actual words used. You can read the American constitution (should you be so inclined) in a broad Scottish accent and the meaning and sense would be unchanged. You could not read it in a Scottish dialect, however. A dialect will often include a particular pronunciation, but it will also include changes to the vocabulary of the language to which it is a dialect, and possibly some modifications to the grammar. Dialects are shared by groups of people. We can be even more extreme and acknowledge that any one individual has his or her own variations in pronunciation, vocabulary, and grammar. This is referred to as their *idiolect*.

8.3.2   The sound effect

Natural sounds

The use of natural sounds in a radio, television, or film environment is generally the best way to communicate to the listener about events in a media world which parallels their real world. If we want someone to think a car has started and left, then we should give the impression of a car engine starting up, followed by the sound of that same car driving away. The best way to achieve this is to record this event. In this case our ultimate objective is to achieve realism in what we are trying to reproduce. We need to convince the listeners (sometimes subconsciously) that what they are listening to is the sound of a car starting and driving away. This is more difficult in a radio environment where we lack the visual channel to augment our auditory communication. There are two main ways we can collect natural sounds. The first is to simply bring into our recording environment the particular sound that we need to create (e.g. the sound of a plate dropping on the floor). The second is location recording. This is more time consuming and expensive, and tends to be utilized only if the constraints of the recording environment make the previous method impossible. It would be difficult, for example, to re-create the sounds of a meadow by trying to develop a meadow environment in our recording studio.

Created sounds

It is now possible using synthesizer and sampling technology to create our own sound effects. By using various forms of synthesis (see below) we could try to synthesize the sound of a gale. This could be achieved by various oscillators, filtering, etc. The effect is rarely as convincing as the real sound. We therefore use such methods only when all other options prove unrealistic. None the less, the fact that we can do it at all is an indication of an amazing progression in the world of sound.

The use of created sound effects is important when the particular sound we are trying to achieve is beyond the scope of everyday life. In the genre of science fiction, we can open up a massive world of unexplored sound effects. Whether it is the sound of a laser blast, or a light sabre, we have pretty much a licence to allow total manipulation of a sound of this type. This is because we, as humans, have no idea what a laser blast sounds like, therefore creative studio users can put into the sound their own ideas of what a laser blast would sound like. Such creative construction of sound has been in use for many years. The radio programme 'The Goon Show' of the 1950s is littered with calls for effects such as the sound of a battleship descending the spiral staircase inside a lighthouse, or three men travelling on flying bagpipes.

Sound editing and manipulation has been for many years an area associated with electro-acoustic music. Taking a base audio sound from a recording and adding filters, changing the pitch, altering the order of the waveform, can create some weird and wacky effects. Many of these are nothing more than this. However, it is possible to utilize these types of sounds in certain genres already mentioned. By simply recording the voice of a woman and lowering the pitch of the voice can cause quite a dramatic effect to what the listener perceives. It is therefore possible to fool the listener into believing that a female voice is that of a male.

8.3.3   The basic principles of music

Tonal systems and convention

Throughout the world there are many different types of musical genres. Western classical music with the twelve-tone scale, Indian raga, Cajun blues, and gamelan are just a few. They vary in their use of tonal systems (many people think that there are 12 notes in an octave, but this is just one system), structure, and instrumentation. In (almost) all cases we can distinguish certain common features of *rhythm*, *melody*, and *harmony*.

Rhythm

Rhythm can be described as the distribution of sound events in time. This works quite closely with other principles such as *metre* and *pulse*. Metre is a group of pulsing beats in hierarchical structure in which the emphasis is given to a certain beat or beats. An example is 4/4 time with four beats to a bar and the strongest accent of the bar being on the first beat with the second strongest being on beat three. This is in direct retrograde to reggae music which puts the accent on the second and fourth beats.

Melody

Melody is perhaps the easiest distinguishable feature of much of the music we listen to (with the exception of some of the twentieth-century repertoire). From a famous pop sound to the 'Magic Flute' we are able to more closely identify and recognize the melody of a certain piece of music than some of the less obvious aspects of the music. Melody can be a succession of notes organized linearly through time which can vary in pitch. Of course, it is possible to have more than melody occurring at the same time, or by repeating the melody at different intervals on starting at different points of time we can create a canon effect.

Harmony

In the traditional sense of the word harmony tends to suggest the organization of sound as it appears simultaneously. That is, a collection of instruments all playing a pitch at the same point in time. Perhaps the simplest example is that of a three-pitched chord played on the piano — in which we have the simultaneous sounding of more than one pitch. Certain combinations of notes are 'harmonious' and go together well, while others are 'dissonant' and do not make a pleasing sound when combined. This is due to the interplay of the characteristics of the different note, but it is also partly due to what we have been brought up to experience as music. Things which are musical for one group of people may be perceived simply as noise by another group.

8.4   Combining sound channels

8.4.1   The medium of radio

> Medium: A set of co-ordinated channels spanning one or more modality which have come, by convention, to be referred to as a unitary whole, and which possess a cross-channel language of interpretation.

Radio is a medium — a collection of channels of communication which have become grouped together and acquired a cross-channel language of interpretation by convention. Within this general space there is a number of specific languages of interpretation for different sorts of activity, for example music programmes, talking heads, phone-in shows, and radio plays. We will focus on the radio play.

In the radio play we are trying to communicate something quite complex through the auditory modality only. There will almost certainly be the normal aspects of writing: establishment of characters, local ambience, plot, creating affective reactions in the listeners. Unlike the way in which one would write for a book, where all these things are communicated through words, the radio play is typically combining three channels to create an equivalent (or related) communication: the spoken word, sound effects, and music. Used together this means that significantly less is communicated through the dialogue itself, since the other channels can take on some of the burden to provide a more effective and/or more realistic listening experience.

There are several obvious roles that these channels can take from the text of the dialogue: establishing ambience and atmosphere, establishing temporal and spatial location, communicating certain events.

Ambience

Our narrative takes place in locations. In the theatre these are established with pieces of scenery and, often, programme notes such as 'The mansion of Earl de Vere, 10 a.m., one Tuesday morning in winter'. Without the use of visual cues and being unable to give programme notes, there are few alternatives to giving out the information explicitly in dialogue. The use of a narrator to provide these details is possible, but can be very intrusive if there is some attempt to establish a suspension of disbelief and engage the listener with the material. It may be possible to use members of the cast within character to give this information occasionally (e.g. the maid answers the phone and says 'Good day, the mansion of Earl de Vere, 10 a.m., one Tuesday morning in winter') but this is generally clumsy and is impossible to maintain if there are many scene changes. While a stage play may only include three or four scenes, a radio play often uses the lack of scenery to enable frequent changes between locations and to switch back to the same location repeatedly (e.g. conversations in the bar, the doctor's surgery, the village green, the farmyard, in a van on the motorway).

Each of these locations will have a different ambience (ambience = surroundings or context) and, specifically, a different acoustic ambience which can often define the scene clearly, and can certainly be used to return to a scene once it has been established (see below). We will identify the following components:

Acoustic ambience   This term refers to the way that the acoustic properties of the environment affect the quality of the sounds that we hear. These are the aspects mentioned in section 8.2.1 concerned with *absorption, reflection,* and *transmission* of waves from the sound sources. Even in 'silence', different locations have different ambience (of course, there is rarely absolute silence) and one of the first things that a live recording engineer does on setting up at a new location is to record some of the local 'silence' so that it can be inserted in breaks in the recording rather than the electronic silence of the recording medium.

This ambience will be a combination of a *resonance profile*, which details the likely echo and reverberation effects of the location at different frequencies, and an *absorption profile* which identifies the way in which different frequencies will be absorbed within the room. Examples would be big halls with long reverberation, small rooms with short reverberation, tiled rooms with little absorption, furnished rooms with top frequency absorption, etc. Each can be programmed as an electronic process to carry out on 'dry' sounds, and should be applied consistently to *voices* and real *sound effects*. Whether they are applied to music depends upon whether the music is supposed to be in the location (e.g. a jukebox) or a source outside the 'real world' of the audio image.

In some scenes the hearer is not intended to be located anywhere in particular, but as soon as dialogue begins, it is normally the case that the hearer assumes that they are near the speaker and that other sound sources are further away. If this is the case, then the resonance and absorption profiles will have to be adjusted for each sound source depending upon the distance from this conceptual location of the listener.

Sound source ambience   While acoustic ambience can be described as a set of modifications made to the sounds within our scene, sound source ambience refers to the background of noise which represents the location in which the main action is taking place. This does not include the voices of the main characters or sound effects and music, which are an integral part of the action, but the background murmurs and sounds intended to establish a scene. Beaches would include sounds of the waves, wind, perhaps feet walking on shingle. A pub bar might include various murmurs of conversation, occasional shouts, ringing of the till, a jukebox or similar music source, and irritating tunes from fruit machines.

Note that *sound source ambience* is not always natural. There are things which have to be done to facilitate the impression of reality, which do not correspond to the real world. In cases such as the pub above, it is common to establish that the place is public, and busy or crowded by introducing the scene with a high level of sound source ambience and then fading it down surreptitiously once the main dialogue starts to prevent it becoming distracting. While this is not what happens in the real world, it does attempt to emulate the processes of attention discussed earlier.

Atmosphere

Atmosphere is distinct from *ambience* in this context, and means the feeling of a particular location or time period during our radio play. This is intended to set up particular feelings (e.g. tension, relaxation, fear, relief, laughter) in the listener and is not done through the same mechanisms as ambience because there is no 'natural' equivalent in the real world.

Music can also be used to create an ambience in a film, video, or radio production. As an example, certain groups or clusters of notes can be used to create tension. A famous example of such a production is the film *Psycho*. During the murder in the shower scene the strings can be heard playing a rather dissonant group of notes. These notes are high pitched and build in dissonance as the tension builds up in the visual image. This is achieved by simply adding more notes to the texture of the music. This gives the viewer/listener a feeling of tension, anxiety, and anticipation. Other such common orchestral techniques include a very sparse texture in the music. By playing only a few notes at irregular intervals we can create a feeling of suspense. This is provided by the listener's inability to detect a regular pulse and not knowing when to expect the next note in the musical series. This can also often be achieved using certain time signatures in music. For example, a time signature of twelve quavers over eight is a common time signature for orchestral film music which is used to create a feeling of suspense.

Exaggerated voice and sound effects – while the ambience uses voice and effects to establish an image of 'reality', the same components can be used in very limited degree to establish an atmosphere. We are all familiar with the creaking door to establish suspense. Indeed, this old standard has become so well worn that it is more likely to provoke laughter than fear these days. Equally, the natural aspects of the voice can be exaggerated from the 'real' to create a tension or arousal, or communicate extremes of emotion, which would be done by other means in daily life.

Temporal and spatial location

We have already discussed the ways in which ambience can establish the sort of location in which something is happening. It is important for our play that we can identify *changes* of location equally well. The listeners must not imagine that we are still in the drawing room of the manor house when we have actually moved to the miner's cottage on bath night! This is an equivalent to the changes of scene which were explicitly marked with curtain lowering in the theatre, and which are allowed in film with changes of camera shots. Assuming that each location has an established ambience, then we can move from one to another in a variety of manners:

The cut   A direct switch from one scene to another. The change is communicated by the sudden change in the ambience. To make this effective there must be a sufficiently long pause in the main action for the listener to recognize the change of context and identify the new location. Obviously, this works better with scenes of very different ambience than with scenes that are similar. A move from a bar to a restaurant may not be clear enough and require some further context establishment from the dialogue, such as a character calling a waiter. Moves such as indoors to outdoors can be carried out in this way fairly easily because the difference is so significant in any case. Bear in mind that this is a fairly abrupt transition and as such needs to be used sparingly if the illusion of real events is to be maintained.

A variation on the direct cut from one ambience to another is the cut through silence in which a small pause separates the two scenes. This emphasizes the artificiality of the transition, however.

The musical link   Short pieces of linking music can be used to connect two scenes together. It is important to do this in such a manner that the listener is not deceived into imagining that the music is within the audio image. The length of this music is important because, while the other techniques normally suggest events are closely related in time, any music that is more than a bar or two immediately suggests the passage of time, and that the second scene is substantially later than the first. The sorts of music used in these breaks can also help to establish the date of the piece – Charleston for the 1920s, etc. – provided that the audience is of sufficient sophistication to recognize the period of music.

The fade and cross-fade   The cross-fade reduces the volume of one scene while increasing the volume of the following one, so that the first fades out as the other fades in. This strongly implies that the events are contemporaneous. If the two scenes have similar ambience then the cross-fade may not be effective, and an alternative is to use the fade (and cut). This effect is achieved by fading out the first scene to indicate that it is over, and then cutting to the following scene so that the abruptness makes it apparent that they are not in the same place.

Communicating events

The most obvious use of these channels is to communicate to the listener that events have happened. A telephone rings, a door is flung open, the bad person stealthily pursues the hero in squeaky shoes. This is predominantly the realm of the sound effect, although it may be complemented by the dialogue. Music is not used for this purpose.

8.4.2 Sound in film

The techniques explained above for radio can all be applied to film, but there the language is much richer because we can combine the languages of these channels of audio communication with the channels of the visual images. We will return to this subject after Chapter 10 studying film itself.

8.5 The technology of sound

The previous discussions talked about the channels through which sound can communicate in other than the obvious ways, and presented something of the *languages of interpretation* which underlie the conventional practices of radio and film sound. For the purposes of understanding multimedia there is one further aspect of sound which will be of benefit to us in other technologies: the *digitization* of the medium. Because sound is, comparatively speaking, less information intensive than visual media, the progress of digital recording, manipulation, and delivery techniques began earlier and have advanced further than in those other fields. The technology of the sound modality is now almost completely digital.

8.5.1 Analogue and digital

Sound is *analogue*. It consists of waves of continuously varying amplitude. Until the 1970s, all devices for recording and manipulating sound were analogue: they worked by transforming this analogue wave into an analogue representation in other materials. Records represented it as undulations on a disc of shellac or plastic. Wax cylinders recorded it as indentations in wax. Tape recorders encoded it as variations in a magnetic field on a piece of moving metallicized material. When sound was transmitted along wires it was as an analogue changing voltage.

Digital technology replaces this system by a different means of representing a sound. Instead of trying to have a continuous wave, a digital system represents the wave by a collection of numbers. At any moment the volume of the sound can be measured and written down. If this is done frequently enough then the resulting sound is indistinguishable to the human ear from the original source. With something like a CD these numbers are measured over 40,000 times per second. This is the *sample rate* of the digital medium.

There is a big advantage to representing sound this way; it can be duplicated, manipulated, and reproduced perfectly, without ever losing any quality. In analogue technology the copying process involved duplicating one analogue medium with another. This inevitably introduced errors (distortion) and noise (hiss). A copy of a copy of a copy was significantly worse than the original, no matter how good the equipment. Since digital copying is repeating a list of numbers, no distortion or noise is introduced and every generation of copy is just as good as the original. The use of a digital encoding means that sound can be stored, compressed, and transmitted very efficiently, and that it can be manipulated by computers to modify it in many ways. This has completely transformed the music industry.

8.5.2 Recording

Recording studios used to have massive analogue mixing desks to take in many different channels of sound from a studio or live feed. You tried to do everything at once to ensure that you did not have to work with copies, which would be of worse quality, and it was often possible to have half a dozen people all manipulating the desk at the same time. These desks were very expensive. High quality tape recorders used wide reel-to-reel tape moving quickly to get better quality. The tape still degraded with time, however. Recording was out of the price range of most people.

Digital technology revolutionized the studio. Digital tape recorders and computer mixing desks ensured that everything was recorded and could be reproduced with perfect quality. Digital manipulation of sound permitted the traditional effects and filters to be applied perfectly, and introduced new ways to manipulate the sounds. A second, unanticipated effect was that the computer-based technology was much cheaper than analogue technology and suddenly many more people were able to embark upon recording and processing with their home studio.

Digital distribution mechanisms allow effective transmission of large quantities of perfect data and the original consumer digital medium of CD is now being complemented by new technologies such as Minidisk and MP3 which allow sound to be distributed and used as never before.

8.5.3 Synthesis

Electronics has made it possible to generate sounds without having a physical instrument that is responsible for those sound characteristics. Originally, this was done using analogue methods. A synthesizer consist-ed of one or more oscillators which generated analogue waveforms. The frequency of intensity of these oscillators could be changed and they could be grouped together or with other sound sources (such as white or pink noise) and manipulated through banks of filters and an envelope generator to produce an artificial sound. The results were interesting, but it was very hard work and pseudo-natural sounds were almost impossible to produce. As with recording, the analogue nature of the systems tended to produce noise and the oscillators had a habit of drifting off frequency and creating horrible noises.

Digital synthesis introduced a huge range of new techniques which could create much more lifelike sounds and effects. Since everything was numbers, anything could be done to it which could be represented as a transformation on these numbers. All sorts of generation methods, manipulations, and effects became possible. The ability to start from a recorded sound and generate a 'musical instrument' based upon it greatly broadened the range of timbre available. If there is one significant problem with digital synthesis, it is that there is such a wide range of possibilities that no one has captured an interface which will enable users to access them all, or even to think about them all. Most synthesis tools stay fairly close to the traditional techniques or even imitate analogue synthesizers.

8.5.4 MIDI

MIDI, or musical instrument digital interface to give it its full title, is a way of connecting various devices together in order to communicate. Used primarily in the electronic composer's studio, MIDI at its most basic level allows the computer to talk to a synthesizer. The computer is able to send event information via the MIDI interface to communicate such things as amplitude, pitch, timbre and panning. It used to be restricted to 16 channels (doing 16 things simultaneously) but has recently increased to 32. We can compare a telephone exchange to a MIDI interface in the number of channels that we can actually use to communicate. This relates to the number of conversations that could be going on at a certain time. Therefore, if we have a MIDI interface for our computer that allows 16 channels, we could have 16 telephone conversations occurring in unison. A more musical example would be to consider being able to play 16 instruments simultaneously.

MIDI is a standard. In fact, it is a language. It defines the messages that can be sent between devices and the way that those messages should be interpreted (to a greater or lesser degree). It was developed for the musical domain, but it can easily be used as a language to manipulate other multimedia devices.

8.5.5 Sequencing

Sequencing is a way of organizing and recording events in order to make a coherent structure. We can record a number of MIDI tracks into a sequencer and layer or arrange these events into a coherent structure. Working with either bar numbers or, on the more advanced packages, bars, time code, and time in seconds, we can easily arrange a piece of music for playback. Time code is a particularly useful feature for multimedia because it allows us to accurately match musical events to visual images.

A good MIDI sequencing package can be a powerful resource, allowing the user to edit extremely precisely composed music. Most packages have a fairly 'natural' and easy-to-use interface.

MIDI can now also work with real-time audio. Until fairly recently, although possible, the audio part of a sequencer had been badly neglected. This was due to the memory-hungry intensity of high quality audio compared to the relatively small MIDI file. Now, with larger hard drives, faster processing power, and greater amounts of RAM we can use large amounts of audio with our MIDI events. We can therefore use a MIDI sequencer to record actors' voices in a radio play for example, and then add synthesized or audio sound effects.

8.6 Exercises

Exercise 8.1 Listen to a radio news programme. How many separate news items were there? How were the items separated? What changes in atmosphere and ambience occurred?

Exercise 8.2 Listen to 10 minutes of a radio play. How many different scenes and locations were used? What techniques (e.g. cut/fade) are used to separate them? What are the changes in ambience/atmosphere? How is music used? For 4 or 5 scenes, list all the sound effects that are used.

Exercise 8.3 Pick 5 minutes of a 1940/50s film and 5 minutes of a 1990s film (e.g. *The Maltese Falcon* and *The Matrix*). For each, count the number of scenes and the amount and type of music used. Count the sound effects and note what sort they are. Are there significant differences?

8.7 Further reading

Good general introduction to psychological and physical issues:
David M. Howard and James Angus, *Acoustics and psychoacoustics (music technology series)*, Focal Press, 1996

These are all interesting perspectives on the use of sound in film:
George Burt, *The art of film music*, Northeastern University Press, 1994

Roy M. Prendergast, *Film music: a neglected art*, Norton, 1992

Laurence E. MacDonald, *The invisible art of film music*, Ardsley House, 1998

9

Still Images

9.1 Psychology of vision

In the previous chapter we introduced some psychological and physiological constraints upon the process of reading. Perhaps one of the most surprising elements of this work is the realization that we really do not 'see' very well at all. The perception that we have a 'clear picture' of the scene in front of us is simply wrong – the thing that we see is something that we construct out of many small 'snapshots' and images of varying quality. We saw that while we hypothetically read a sentence of text from left to right, we actually progress by a number of small jerky movements (saccades) which are combined with certain reasoning processes to enable us to perceive and interpret the text – reading is an active process of construction.

It should come as no surprise, given this basis, to realize that similar, but more complex, things are going on when we perceive the world in general, and two-dimensional representations of the world in particular. The 'picture' that we view on a page is constructed in our minds from a series of snapshots, which are then bolted together. The process is made more complex because there are many things that we imagine that we see 'naturally' – such as corners or solid objects, which we do not perceive directly, but have to construct. These processes are very important to understanding the ways in which we see and interpret images, as well as to the ways in which we can confuse the eye into misinterpretation. In the real world we are using two eyes, each of which has a slightly different image because of their spatial separation. In addition, the constant movement will change the pictures that we see in a 3D environment, with things such as shading and texture being modified in ways that are not possible in a 2D image.

The retina of the eye is wired to see points of light, and to see straight lines in certain orientations. Virtually everything else we see is constructed in the brain. Recognizing an enclosed 2D space, such as a square has to be learnt, because there is no basic conception of enclosure – corners are not wired into the eye, but are constructed as easier ways of representing the world. Babies work very hard to learn to 'see' the world in these ways. As our perception improves, we begin to have the idea of objects – things which might look different from different angles, but are actually the same thing – and hence we begin to organize our perception as a 2D view onto a 3D world.

In this chapter we are considering the nature of communication via the still image. As with looking at the 'real' world, our eyes cannot take the image in all at once, but, further than that, we have the problem of not looking at the real world. In seeing 2D images we are playing a trick – looking at a 2D depiction of a 3D space, via a 2D detection system (the eye) which constructs a 3D model (in the head). It comes as quite a shock to realize that something that we do so often, every day, is not as 'natural' as it seems!

Before considering more complex images we will start with a clearly defined class of structured images: diagrams.

9.2 The diagram

The diagram is an extremely important communicative device that represents concisely a (potentially) very large amount of information in a small space. It should come as no surprise to find that the vast majority of diagrams can be expressed as formal languages, since we used the idea extensively in Chapter 3.

A diagram can be regarded as a visual language, which communicates through the image-processing channels, and as a visual representation of a symbolic language. In either case we can define it like any other language: there is a *lexicon*, a *syntax* and a *semantics*. Consider Figure 9.1.

Most people have seen an electronic circuit diagram such as this. The symbols are the key elements of the lexicon: in this case they are nouns – resistor, capacitor, diode, battery etc. – but the lines between the

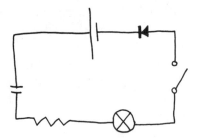

Figure 9.1   Electrical circuit.

symbols are also lexical items. The lines in a diagram normally express some sort of relationship between the symbols that they link, such as 'electricity flows between' in this case. The syntax tells us how to construct a legal diagram. There are several different ways in which a syntax can be constructed. The simplest is just to express the potential link points on the symbols, so that a legal diagram would constitute any connection of symbols, as shown in Figure 9.2.

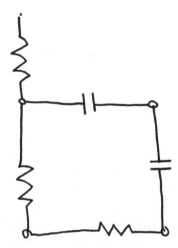

Figure 9.2 Electronically meaningless circuit.

This is a meaningless circuit, but it perfectly legal. A slightly more sensible approach might be to use a higher level of syntactic structure which indicates that all circuits must have a power source, and all must form loops, etc. Beyond this, we could start including rules such as 'no diode connects to a diode pointing the opposite way' (Figure 9.3). At this point we are setting rules for the construction of a legal circuit, as opposed to a legal diagram, but we may feel that only diagrams of legal circuits should be legitimate.

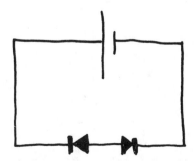

Figure 9.3 Diode to diode.

Beyond this level, a semantics of the diagram would tell us how the circuit represented by the components behaves. Like virtually all diagrams, the meaning (or behaviour) of the whole can be constructed from the meanings of the individual elements.

The basic symbols do not have to be nouns. In a flow chart, for example, the symbols are mostly verbs, such as 'make a decision', 'print something'. None the less, the components of the diagram must be things that can be linked in meaningful ways.

With every diagram that we produce we are talking to a particular subculture, one that has learnt the language of that diagramming method. If we wish to use it to communicate to a wider audience, then we must explicitly teach the use of the language.

It is also worth mentioning that diagrams are potentially a rich way to interact with computers. There are many flowchart-based authoring and programming tools that allow the user to build a diagram from components, and then to run the program which that diagram represents. In the area of simulation and modelling these visual techniques are particularly important. Figure 9.4 shows a screen from a modelling tool called Powersim. This allows the user to construct diagrams from a simple set of lexical items, and the result is a set of differential equations that can be integrated over time to make dynamic simulations. It is worth noting that this diagram contains several types of relationships (links) as well as several different objects.

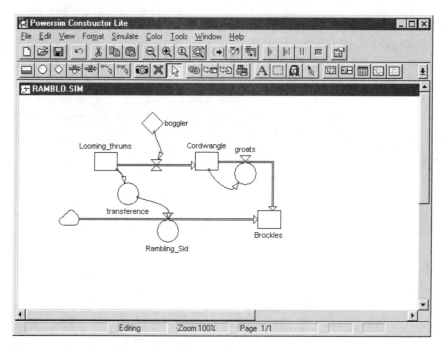

Figure 9.4   Representational image from Powersim.

9.3 Representational images

We can now turn from looking at formally defined structures such as diagrams, and abstract structures such as the cartoon, to images that are supposed to represent the real world at some level. The issues raised in this section are typically common in photography, painting and graphic design.

The first point to be emphasized is that the viewer is not the passive recipient of the created image. We have already seen that the eye is not capable of viewing an entire image at once, as we imagine to be the case intuitively. Instead, the eye is constantly collecting small snapshots from which the brain is constructing an overall picture. This process implies that the viewer is an active participant in the process of visual communication and that the perception of image is dynamic. Because it is dynamic, we can produce more effective images and communications by understanding the way that this process works and leading it with the structure that we give it to our images. We will commence this section by exploring the purely graphical form that an image may take, before going on to look at the construction of meaning from the image as a whole.

9.3.1 Seeing the image

Before humans started producing images which represented the world, the thing they saw mostly with their eyes *was* the world. As we described in the first section, the way that we see the world is something that is acquired as we develop. The child learns to construct ideas such as permanent objects, corners, and holes in order to deal with day-to-day existence. It should therefore come as no surprise to find that the processes that we use to interpret a 2D image also have recognizable origins in the world that we see around us.

One of the important aspects of the world around us is the relative size of things. We may not know how long an arm is, for example, but we can quickly spot if it seems long in proportion to the body to which it is attached. The ratios of sizes of things around us are very important in our understanding of the world, helping us to recognize things and to see depth and perspective. Certain numbers that occur regularly in nature seem to have a specific effect upon our perception because they are so important, such as *e* or *pi*. There is one that seems to be particularly important in the visual world, however, and that is the famous number 1.61803398874... (also called Phi). Interestingly, this number was determined to be a key aspect of appealing images by artists based on experience quite independently of the occurrence of the number in nature. In art this number is known as the Golden Mean, or Golden Section (Figure 9.5).

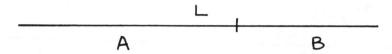

Figure 9.5   Golden section.

This line has a divider at the point such that the ratio of the shorter segment to the longer segment is the same as the ratio of the longer section to the whole line.

$$\frac{L}{A} = \frac{A}{B}$$

Dividing things up according to this ratio is aesthetically pleasing to humans for some reason. If you do not want to work with the complicated decimals then $^{21}/_{13}$ is a pretty accurate way of representing the ratio. Commonly used, and only slightly less accurate, is the ratio $^{8}/_{5}$, and $^{5}/_{3}$ is not too bad either.

There is another way to arrive at this magical number from nature. Many things are constructed in sequences of increasing numbers. The spiky bits on a pineapple, the sticky out bits on a pine cone, a seashell, or the shell of a snail.

In each case the number of things on the object increases in the same sequence of numbers. This is:

1, 1, 2, 3, 5, 8, 13, 21, 34, 55, 89, 144, ... etc.

This is known as the *Fibonacci* series.

Each term in the series is the result of adding up the two numbers that occur before it (e.g. 3+5=8). The series goes on forever, but, interestingly, if you take the ratio of two adjacent numbers, you find that the ratio gets closer and closer to one particular number – the Golden Mean again.

The frame

The way that images were depicted through drawing were not always as they are now. Ideas such as perspective and issues concerning the representation of depth and of the relationships within an image are only in their current form through a process of evolution, and they will doubtless evolve to different forms in the future. Each change of approach within painting, for example, represents a different view of the world. Picasso used techniques that attempted to capture the appearance of an object from several different viewpoints at once. This is an important issue. The image that we are seeing is unlike the real world, because it is a single, fixed viewpoint. In looking at the real world our eyes each see a slightly different picture, aiding our depth perception. The constant small movement of our eyes affects our perception of the form of objects and movements of our head give us a number of different aspects of an image from which to construct a representation. By comparison, seeing an image as 'real' is a game that we are playing to construct a model 'as though' it was the real world, even when we know it is not.

One important aspect of the nature of image is that it can be taken out of the context and placed within a frame. This frame limits the boundaries of the objects that we are trying to interpret and is also, itself, an influence upon the construction and interpretation of the image. Almost immediately we learn that traditionally the optimum shape for a frame is based upon the Golden Mean. In this incarnation, we are referring to a *golden rectangle*: the lengths of the longer and shorter sides are in the golden ratio. This is considered to be a most aesthetically desirable shape upon which to base the borders of our image, and may also form a sound basis for implied framing within the image (see Figure 9.6).

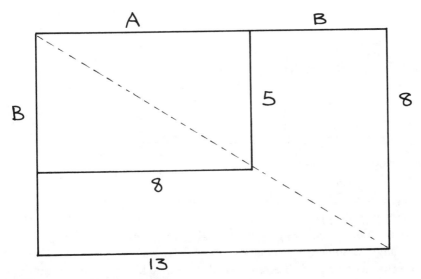

Figure 9.6 Golden rectangle.

We can compare the Golden Rectangle with the sizes and shapes of images that are commonly used for multimedia resources:

- 35 mm film, the preferred format for many applications, is based on a rectangle of ratio 3:2;

- a normal television screen is 1.33:1;

- a widescreen cinema format is 2.35:1;

- a standard cinema format is 1.33:1 (called Academy Format since the 1930s).

The point

Having established the nature of our frame, we can begin to look at the contents that lie within a frame and the nature of their relationship to the surroundings. An important historical approach, which demonstrates many of the key ideas, is to concentrate on the idea of a *point* and a *line* within a frame. While we will illustrate these ideas with simple abstractions, you should bear in mind that the things we say about a point can apply, in general, to any self-contained object (e.g. a boot, a cube), and things about a line can apply to lines whether they are simple geometrical entities, edges of larger objects, or implicit lines which are not actually directly visible in the image.

Consider this point (Figure 9.7). It is centred horizontally and vertically within the frame. This symmetry in both directions has a certain mathematical satisfaction about it, but on the whole it gives a visual impression of stability and dullness. It doesn't really suggest any movement for the eye, or provide a clue about how to look at the image.

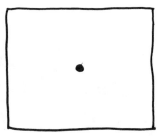

Figure 9.7   Central point.

By contrast, the two images shown in Figure 9.8 are much more interesting. By placing the point off centre we are seeing an imbalance between the two halves of the rectangle, which breaks up the symmetry and suggest something more dynamic about the image. It is often the case that when a key object is placed off centre like this it is found to be at a position corresponding to the golden section. Similar offsets can obviously be used vertically, but given that we are using a wide frame the effect is more noticeable in this direction.

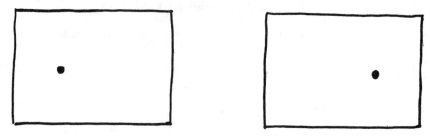

Figure 9.8   Left point and right point.

Now look at Figure 9.9. This point is offset from the centre line in two directions and it places an interesting change in emphasis on what we are seeing. The bottom right corner now has priority for our eye, and we tend to start looking at the image there, and then spread out into the rest of the picture. Given that it is close to the corner and somehow 'enclosed' by the adjacent frame, this can be seen as a process of broadening out from our focus point as we scan the image.

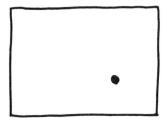

Figure 9.9 Bottom right.

Having illustrated the basic idea with a point, we can now expand it into a blob and see that similar things apply (Figure 9.10). In this case I have chosen a blob with a longer dimension vertically. Figure 9.10 shows that the same basic idea of balancing and leading the eye within the frame still applies, but we also have an effect due to the fact that our blob now has a size and shape, which interacts with the structure of the frame around it. In this image it seems even more dominating than the point was, leading to a more powerful effect.

Figure 9.10 Left blob.

This relationship to the frame is clear with the two blobs Shown in Figure 9.11. They are both the same size, but the first has a surrounding frame which complements its orientation, 'fitting' it to the frame, while the second produces a tension which seems to emanate from the blob and the frame trying to pull in different directions.

Turning back to our points (Figure 9.12), we can see that using two objects has an interesting effect – we immediately try and make a line out of them in our heads. The first diagram clearly emphasizes one diagonal, but the second is even more forceful, suggesting a trajectory for our eye

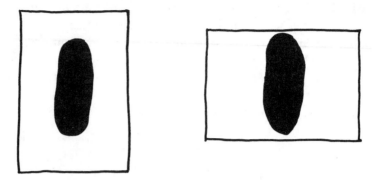

Figure 9.11   High frame blob and centre blob.

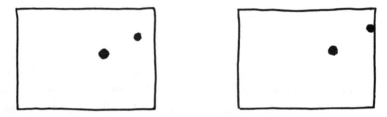

Figure 9.12   Diagonal and centre – bottom right.

from bottom right to top left – almost flinging our gaze across the picture.

In this final case, we are playing with a quite fundamental aspect of perception, the desire of the mind to find pattern in all visual stimuli, and to reduce it to a simpler form of description in order to understand it. We saw the psychological importance of the line in visual perception earlier, so it is no surprise that this is a key aspect of the way we communicate with imagery.

The line

With the line we have issues concerned not only with the location relative to the frame and other objects, but also the orientation. Lines are detected at a fairly primitive level in the eye because they are so fundamental to our perception. Interestingly, not only are there 'line detectors', but there are also specific groupings of cells wired to detect lines in particular orientations. The fact that gravity gives a direction to the world around us, also means that two sorts of line are particularly important – vertical and horizontal.

The vertical line (Figure 9.13) is seen around us as a stable structure, such as a tree, a person, or the side of a building. This is a comparatively relaxed, and natural line, but there is always the awareness that just a slight deviation from the precisely upright will create a diagonal which

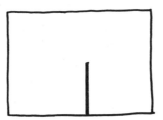

Figure 9.13 Vertical line.

almost immediately suggests that something is wrong and our 'tree' is falling over. We might follow a line with our eye from top to bottom (e.g. starting with the face on a person) or from bottom to top (e.g. scanning up a skyscraper) depending on the actual position, size and context.

A horizontal line (Figure 9.14) is also an indication of stability, such as a horizon, or some surface onto which things can be placed. By comparison with the vertical, the stability of a horizontal line is not so suddenly disturbed by slight variations from the perfectly horizontal. We are used to 'nearly horizontal' objects that work just as well as horizontal ones. Typically we tend to scan horizontal lines from left to right, in the order that we read.

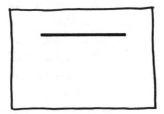

Figure 9.14 Horizontal line.

A diagonal line (Figure 9.15) is immediately a source of tension. In this case we see something which is not a naturally stable state in the world. In the above case we see a line 'falling' with an implied downward motion of the higher end. This can be used to great effect in conjunction with apparently supporting lines.

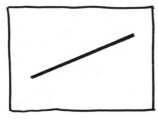

Figure 9.15 Diagonal line.

In Figure 9.16 we see the effect of our stability and downward motion, and the effect of the 'conceptual gravity' is quite clear. The diagonal is no longer falling, as in the previous case, but is held in position because vertical line (a) is perceived as a support. By contrast, line (b) is not perceived as stable, even though it is vertical, because it is 'standing' on a diagonal base – hence we have an expectancy for it to slide or fall, and an element of tension is re-created in the layout.

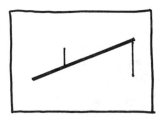

Figure 9.16   Conceptual gravity – line on horizontal and diagonal.

It was noted that the conjunction of the point with a corner of the frame led to an interesting combination which tended to attract the eye. By combining this with a centre point we managed to create a fairly strong trend to attract our eye to a corner, and then force our gaze to the centre. In this case there was an implied line which we followed. This tendency is even more noticeable in Figure 9.17, in which we use two lines converging on the same point (which is the centre in this case). Where the single line led us from the corner to the centre, it did not strongly imply that the centre was in any way more important than the corner. Because there are two lines here, each throwing us towards the centre, it *does* give the centre a special primacy within the image. This construction is also important because it is related to the rules that we use to perceive perspective and distance. If there are two lines that we know are 'really' parallel, but they appear to converge like this (e.g. a road going into the distance, a skyscraper seen from close up), then we are getting strong visual clues that we are looking beyond a flat image and into the depth of the image.

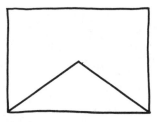

Figure 9.17   Line convergence.

A similar trick, shown in Figure 9.18, with four diagonal lines converging on a point places even more emphasis on it but, at the same time, is rather too symmetrical to be pleasing. This begins to look more like geometry than image composition.

Figure 9.18   4-line convergence.

Juxtapositions of two lines are very common because we are normally dealing with real objects that have edges and corners. These combinations can bring another dimension to the guides in Figure 9.19. In this case a vertical and a diagonal are meeting at a point. The point where they meet is certainly emphasized, but the two also seem to act as a sort of arrowhead, directing our gaze further along the line of the diagonal.

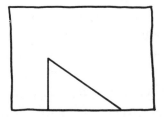

Figure 9.19   Implied pointing.

The above examples have focused on explicitly present lines in our image. In fact, our eyes are often guided by lines that are not really present, but are implied by their surroundings. These act to direct our perceptual process in similar ways to physically present lines, and are generally implied in the image by one of three primary processes: psychological lines, motion lines, and consistency lines.

• *Psychologically implied* lines exist in images that include people. From early childhood we develop the idea of sharing a focus of attention with other people. We learn words by someone pointing at a car and saying 'car', so we come to associate the object with the word. This shared attention is a key part of our day-to-day interaction: if we are conversing with someone, we expect their attention to be on us and find it unnerving when their gaze is directed somewhere else; if someone is staring off in another direction we tend to follow their gaze to see what they are looking at; two lovers staring into each other's eyes create a very strong link because there is a line of attention in each direction. These lines depicted by focus of attention can all appear in images, and can have just as much significance as lines which are explicitly visible.

- *Motion implied* lines are just as they sound. When an image captures an object in an unstable position (such as falling off a cliff or being hit with a tennis racket) then we are aware that this frozen image represents some dynamic behaviour, and our mind anticipates the motion of the object and sketches in a line for this motion. The power of such a line will vary depending upon the strength and predictability of the motion implied: a hedgehog does not imply the same dynamic as a Formula 1 racing car!

- *Consistency implied* lines are a consequence of our attempt to make sense of the world. When we see several similar objects, we assume they are all of the same size. If, for example, there are several people standing on a surface then we assume they are roughly the same size and hence draw a set of mental lines, linking the tops of their heads, their feet, etc. These lines form some of the basic information that we use in establishing perspective in an image.

Having examined these basic ideas – the *frame*, the *point*, and the *line* – we will now turn to some of the phenomena that affect our perception of more complex images.

Other issues

In a black and white line drawing, the dynamics and the centre of focus depend upon the direction, frequency, and thickness of the lines. But the lines also have a character – qualities of softness or hardness, smoothness or jaggedness, angularity, flow, brokenness. Even this limited information will lend a certain emotive content to the image, suggesting how they were drawn and hence a flowing line might suggest calm while a jagged, broken line indicates irritation or indecision. It is not just where the lines go that matter, but how they get there.

In most images, additional factors influence the composition, and the balance of the image is dependent upon relative *weights*. In this sense 'weight' means something like the importance of something within the image. Visually, different areas of the image will have different weight according to their texture, shape and colour. An area of flat colour has more weight than an area of fine texture (which the eye will tend to average out), but a bold texture with a high contrast will have more weight than the flat colour. This is important when designing a page or a screen with areas of text (which we perceive first as texture) and image.

Complex shapes and those with hard or spiky corners will have more weight than smooth flowing curved shapes. They contain more visual information and so take longer to comprehend as a single object, thus holding the viewer's attention.

Colours with shorter wavelengths (blue/violet) tend to recede and so have less visual weight than red/oranges, but the *saturation* of a colour is of more importance. Colours with a greater saturation (that is purer colours – colours with a higher proportion of coloured to white light in their make-up) will attract the eye, appear to come forward out of the picture plane and so have more visual weight. These relative colour depths can be seen if you look into the distance across a landscape with diminishing rows of fields, hills and hedges. As the green fields get further from your eye, they appear to change in colour and fade through bluey-green to grey. This effect, *aerial perspective*, can be re-created in a painting to create the illusion of distance.

While these factors are important, what the eye seeks most in an image is *contrast*. In an image composed of shades of red, for example, the eye will be drawn to the small green area. The tonal value (light and dark) and particularly the contrast in tone are also important. In an image on a white page, darker areas within the image will seem stronger. Tone contrast provides a more striking difference for the eye than colour difference itself.

The eye also seeks to identify simple objects within the picture plane. So a simple image like that shown in Figure 9.20 would be perceived as a black spot on a white background – identifying the black area as the area of importance – rather than a complicated white shape. However, where there are many objects in the picture plane, the spaces between them – the negative spaces – can also be read as objects.

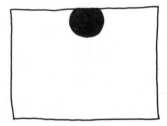

Figure 9.20   Simple shape.

In Figure 9.21, the area bounded by the three dark shapes has been promoted to an object. It is perceived as a white triangle, while the other white areas remain as background. In terms of spatial composition, anything enclosed by lines (e.g., an area of sky bounded by the roof, a telegraph pole, and the telephone wire) is an object.

Besides aerial perspective, we are accustomed in the West to the idea of *visual perspective*. We see that real-life objects appear to get smaller as they move further away from us, and parallel lines apparently meet at a point (the Vanishing Point) on the horizon (Figure 9.22). This is a

Figure 9.21   Negative space.

Figure 9.22   Perspective.

phenomenon we can observe, but have to be taught to understand and reproduce. It is widely used in Western figurative image making, but represents a simplification and abstraction from reality, where the vanishing point is on the horizon and not within the picture frame.

We are so used to looking at this we regard it as 'true', but other forms of simplification and abstraction could be applied depending on what is perceived as the most important information the image is trying to convey (Figure 9.23).

9.3.2 Images and meaning

We produce images as a way of depicting the world around us. This is part of the process of understanding the world and as such can be approached in two fundamentally different ways – the world as it seems

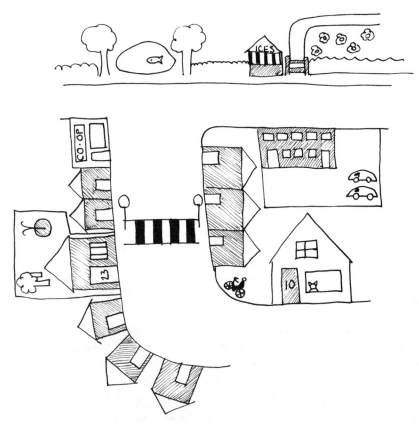

Figure 9.23 Simplified space.

to be or the world as it actually is. Any 2D image (even a documentary photograph) is an abstraction and simplification of reality representing three dimensions on a flat plane. This abstraction may be taken to an extreme form of minimalism, or a pattern of shapes and lines in which the viewer cannot detect any recognizable object. Purely abstract images are often attempts to represent abstract things – emotions or ideas – and can communicate at an immediate and subconscious level. Images that attempt to depict concrete objects will represent them either figuratively or symbolically.

In a child's drawing, the sky is represented as a blue line at the top, because the sky is conceptually above the child. What is drawn is not what is seen, but what is understood: the idea of the thing represented. Thus a cat can be drawn as a 'thing with a head, a body, four legs, a tail, and pointy ears'. The resulting image is a diagram of a cat (Figure 9.24), and it is the pointy ears (and later, the whiskers) which uniquely signify cat as opposed to horse or dog.

This kind of symbolic representation has its history in the idea of representations having power over, or actually becoming, the objects

Figure 9.24   Cat.

depicted – the cave paintings that would ensure a good hunt by sympathetic magic, for example. It also has echoes in religious icons, endowed with the same powers as the saint they represent. Symbolic representations of real-world objects are often highly stylized, simplified, and culturally dependent.

We also produce images as a way of communicating what we know about the world, developing from early schematic drawings of objects and hieroglyphs. While these symbols developed in one direction to produce letterforms and text, they developed in another direction to produce more sophisticated and highly differentiated symbols for representing the visual world. We have learnt to understand these, but our visual vocabulary is not as highly developed as our verbal vocabulary, and leans towards communication on a simpler and more emotive level. We tend to anthropomorphize abstracted images, and to seek a storyline within figurative images.

We are more comfortable with the notion of *figuration* (of representing the world as it seems to be): depicting what we see, rather than what we know. From this viewpoint a cat would be drawn as the closest possible likeness of a particular cat, 'Louie' say, and the image would be valued for how well it captured the look, mood and personality of that animal.

Even within literal depictions of the world, however, symbols are used (and inferred) to reinforce the narrative. So, as Church carvings used attributes to signify a particular saint (a wheel, a lamb, a lily) in a context where facial likenesses were not possible, formal portraits historically used symbols of knowledge (books), innocence (flowers) or wealth (hunting dogs) as 'props' to help identify and explain the sitter. Different cultures and generations can misinterpret these symbols although some, such as jewellery for wealth, seem to retain their meaning. Advertising images rely heavily on the use of symbolism to create the correct myth for the product, but it is also seen in apparently straightforward documentary photography through the use of cropping and careful placing of artefacts into shot.

With the invention of photography came a tendency to believe that the world as it actually *is*, and the world as it *seems* to be, were the same; that the camera could capture both and therefore tell the truth about the world. Because it captures an actual event without the mediation of an artist's interpretation, 'the camera doesn't lie'. Attitudes towards 'photography as truth' changed with the introduction of the idea of the photograph as art, and more so with the development of digital photography and computer image manipulation. But even early photography, which mainly copied the format and language of the contemporary formal portrait, was a carefully composed set of signifiers.

Status is often conveyed by focus. In Eastern visual traditions, the status of individuals is indicated by their relative size (regardless of their actual height in real life). The eye is drawn first to the largest figure in the image. In Western traditions, focus is more usually provided by the position in the picture frame, at the main focus of the internal dynamics. The status is also conveyed by the addition of appropriate symbolic 'props'. Similarly, the relationships between key figures and objects in the image frame are conveyed by their relative position and the dynamics that link or separate them.

Besides objects, colours have a symbolic significance. We have seen how red is associated with a warning, and this idea is reinforced by its standard use in traffic signs, brake lights, and other hazardous contexts. Many of these symbolic associations are relative to their parent culture, for example clothing for weddings is white in the West, but red in the Indian subcontinent, clothing for funerals is black in the one culture, but white in the other. The association of pink and blue with baby girls and boys may have come originally from an Egyptian notion that girls came from the earth, but boys straight from heaven (the sky). The original logic and significance of these is not generally understood, but we still retain the labels.

Colours can be signifiers of social class, age, and date. Their use is partly due to fashion, and to the improvements in technology which made artificial pigments and colour-fast dyes and paints available, changing how we decorate ourselves and our living spaces. These associations can be used in paintings and manipulated photography to reinforce the narrative.

Just as the composition of an image and its component parts creates dynamic lines and focal points, so it also contributes to the symbolic meaning. In Figure 9.25, a schematic representation of an image, we see four figures, which our Western cultural stereotypes will tend to make us interpret as a family group, consisting of (from the top right, clockwise) father, older child/son, younger child/daughter, mother.

We see that all the family's gazes are directed towards the 'son'. He becomes the focus of the dynamic lines and we then interpret him as the most important person in the image. The 'father' rests his hand

Figure 9.25   Family 1.

affectionately on the son's shoulder. The faces are all turned in to the centre of the group, suggesting harmony, togetherness. But the son looks outwards, further attracting your attention with his gaze.

If the father's head is turned so that he looks out of the picture frame as in Figure 9.26, we create a new dynamic outwards from the picture, which throws it off balance. We now tend to reinterpret the symbolic value of the hand on the son's shoulder as protection, enclosing the shorter figure from some threat coming from the right.

Figure 9.26   Family 2.

If instead as in Figure 9.27, we switch the son's gaze off to the right, the father's gesture becomes one of restraint, against the son's perceived desire to move out of the group (to the right). The family's attentions may now be interpreted as oppressive, rather than loving. The unmatched dynamic has created tension in the image and the viewer constructs a narrative to account for the resulting feeling of unease.

9.4 Juxtaposition of images

The above discussions have all focused upon the way that we understand one image. It is important to note, however, that from a very early time

Figure 9.27   Family 3.

our society has sought to group or link images together in order to tell a story. Just putting one image adjacent to another can completely change their meaning. If we place a picture of a fast car adjacent to a photograph of people smiling and having a good time in a sunny location, then we are going to get a positive message about owning that car (this is, of course, a common technique in car advertising). By contrast, if we place the same picture of a fast car adjacent to a picture of a child killed in a car crash, then the message is entirely different.

It is historically common for images to be juxtaposed from left to right in order to tell a story. Roman and Greek cultures used this technique extensively, but it can be traced back much further. More recently, the Bayeux tapestry is really a story meant to be read from left to right along a strip of cloth. Each culture developed languages for interpretation of these images, but they never gained universal application. Of course, this linear juxtaposition of still images is still very common today and has achieved a much wider acceptance of form. As a strip cartoon, we are used to seeing a sequence of images telling a story. We normally expect frame boundaries to separate events, and there are conventions which we adopt (consciously or unconsciously) about the order in which to read speech bubbles. There is an embedded language that communicates things like speed by lines behind the object, and tension by visible sweat leaping off an object, as well as many others. A wide range of these conventions of interpretation exist and many are universally accepted. Within this structure there are other groupings with different conventions: children's cartoons, adult cartoons, Manga, French erotic cartoons, etc. Each develops its own language and conventions of interpretation, and becomes a medium of itself.

Another variation on the juxtaposition of image which was popular in the nineteenth century was the Magic Lantern show. This differs because it is a time-based presentation. People gather in a room with a projection device, and a sequence of still, hand-painted slides are projected onto a screen – normally to the accompaniment of a voiceover narrative. These shows could be educational or informative, might recount classic tales and legends, or might even be used to spread news. There were possibilities (with some projectors) to fade between images, and to make simple animations by including mechanical attachments on some slides. The coming of photography enabled this to develop into the sort of slide projection that we are familiar with today.

This juxtaposition of image was extremely important to the development of the languages that underpinned the introduction of the first new medium of the twentieth century. Film initially drew its language of interpretation from the theatre, but the Russian practitioners quickly realized that there was more to the language of film than the emulation of theatre, and identified the film as a process of montage – linking images and producing meaning through the appropriate juxtaposition of frames. This lies at the core of the following chapter.

9.5 Exercises

Exercise 9.1 Pick a one page advertisement from a Sunday magazine. Do the following:

1. Redraw it as points and blobs;

2. Redraw it as key explicit lines;

3. Add implied lines onto the drawing from 2;

4. Identify the frames within the composition.

Exercise 9.2 Repeat the above example using a snapshot photograph you have taken yourself.

Exercise 9.3 Repeat the same activities with a frame picked at random from a film.

Exercise 9.4 Repeat the same activities with a painting by an 'Old Master'.

Exercise 9.5 Identify similarities and differences between the above. Does there seem to be a sequence of quality of composition? Do the activities help you to recognize the differing structures of the images?

9.6 Further reading

Basic psychology of vision:
Vicki Bruce, Patrick R. Green and Mark Georgeson, *Visual perception*, Psychology Press, 1996

Rudolf Arnheim, *Art and visual perception*, University of California Press, 1974

Good overview of picture composition:
Tom Grill and Mark Scanlon, *Photographic composition*, Amphoto, 1990

Two different perspectives on the approaches to looking at images:
Gunther Kress and Theo van Leeuwen, *Reading images: the grammar of visual design*, Routledge, 1996

Ernest H. Gombrich, *The story of art*, Phaidon, 1990

10
Moving Images

The previous chapter explored issues that surround the way in which we represent and perceive communication via a still image. These issues are extremely important, and most of them have been present throughout human history, although there are new languages and methods of static perception appearing all the time. By comparison, we have an extremely rich method of communication that is barely a century old, and yet has evolved a remarkable range of forms of communication and linguistic convention: the film. Most animals have developed methods of seeing and recognizing motion, and many of these features are shared with humans. The techniques that have been developed to present an *apparently* moving image however, and to communicate with it, are not only unique to humans, but belong to specific cultural groups – what constitutes a meaningful film to one group may well have no communicational effect on another.

Film is additionally important to us because it demonstrates something that is key to our definition of multimedia: the development of a medium by drawing together and modifying agreed communication structures from previously established media.

10.1 Perception of motion

From previous chapters we established that the idea of seeing the world 'at a glance' is an illusion. To construct a single still 'image' in our minds requires a large number of movements of the eye and a process of reasoning to piece together this apparent perception internally. Given the complexity of this process, and the fact that it must therefore take a measurable time, it follows naturally that by presenting and removing an image quickly enough, we can prevent the mind from perceiving it. There is considerable work in psychology related to the understanding of this phenomenon, and the effect it has upon our perception and recollection. If an image is presented for a sufficiently short duration, then it will not be perceived at all. This is referred to as a threshold (*limen*, in Latin) of perception. More interestingly, there is a region of duration during which the image is not perceived consciously, but must be perceived at some level, because it can be shown to have an effect on the viewer. Images in this category are referred to as subliminal ('under the threshold'). Such images are banned in most countries now, but were used for a time as advertising. Inserting a single frame (which lasts $\frac{1}{25}$ second) of an ice cream into a film was shown to have an impact on ice cream sales in the cinema, although no one could tell that such an image had been present.

By displaying images to the viewer, and then removing them and replacing them with other, slightly different ones, such that each is visible for less than the threshold of conscious perception, the brain is tricked into believing that it is seeing a continuous scene of motion rather than a series of still images. It cannot process the differences fast enough to recognize single frames and hence assumes it is seeing something like the real world of motion. The speed required for this effect is roughly 20 frames a second. Slower presentation than this results in a perceived 'jerky' or 'flickery' effect.

10.2   A brief history of the film

There are many excellent histories of film, and it is not the place of this book or this chapter to try and replicate or better them. The reader is strongly recommended to explore some of the texts mentioned at the end of the chapter. A few highlights will be mentioned to provide a rough context.

Photography, in the sense of light-sensitive materials that could be exposed and developed to produce an image, became available in 1828, but an exposure took a long time and it was an expensive and uncertain process. The phenomenon of apparent motion from a sequence of drawn or painted images was utilized in a range of 'toys' in the nineteenth century, such as the Zoetrope, which had a sequence of small paintings on the inside of a paper drum. Between each image was a slit and by placing your eye at the level of a slit and spinning the drum, the images went past with sufficient speed to give the impression of motion.

In 1878 Eadweard Muybridge used a set of linked cameras to make a series of frames analysing the motion of a running horse (and confounding many painters of the time by demonstrating that horses do not take all their legs off the ground at once). This was made possible by faster films that could work with exposures under $\frac{1}{25}$ second. These pictures could have been used to project a photographic representation of a running horse, but the projector had not yet been invented.

In the 1890s the Lumière brothers developed both a camera capable of photographing 25 frames a second onto continuous stock, and a projector capable of displaying 25 still images a second. In December 1895 they made the first public display of a moving picture film, at a café in Paris. These films (which also began appearing from a number of other sources soon afterwards) were almost all long shot, fixed camera (see below) and initially just showed scenes of life (a train pulling into a station is one of the most famous Lumiere films). In the late 1890s the first films which told stories arrived (mostly simple slapstick) and in 1897, the magician Méliès set up a studio and started to create special effects. For all these innovations, films were a few minutes at most because of the length of film stock that could be produced.

Through the first 20 years of the twentieth century film developed in many places across the world. America started developing longer films and exploring melodrama and comedy. Both D. W. Griffith and Cecil B. De Mille started working in this period and some key innovations related to longer films and narrative form occurred.

The biggest impact on modern film though, was the work of the Russian film-makers in the 1920s and 1930s. Much of the basic theory and technique which underlines film today was worked out by Eisenstein and a small group of very academic film-makers in Russia during this period. The idea of film as montage, of many editing techniques and processes, of 'film as art' versus 'film as recording of reality', and much besides, derive from this period.

Sound was the next big technical innovation. Driven by Warner Brothers in the USA during the late 1920s, sound became common in American cinemas during the 1930s. The demand for talkies grew quickly, but a whole new form of movie – the musical – appeared as a result of this innovation.

This is necessarily a partisan and overly concise view of the history of a hugely important field, but it will at least provide a few hooks of perspective upon which to hang further reading.

10.3　Constructing a shot

The previous chapter discussed many aspects of the organization of a still image: the choice of framing, the composition of the image based upon points/objects and explicit or implicit lines which guide the perceptual processes. Most of these considerations still apply to the moving image, although it is impossible to make every single frame within a film obey all the rules of good composition. A film will normally consist of a number of key frames that are carefully composed and a set of intermediate frames that link them and are less well constructed. In the case of certain media such as the use of video and live television, the composition is often very poor.

A film is normally divided into 'shots' where a shot is a continuous piece of film taken by one camera from one perspective. Each shot has a starting point and an end point, and is joined to the next by a process of editing. The reduction of a film into single shots was initially a result of technology: only very short pieces of film could be exposed at a time in the early part of the twentieth century. Improvements in technology mean that it is now possible to expose much longer film segments, and the use of digital photography and video editing means that the 'shot' is no longer technically required. We retain it for two reasons. The first reason is because actors make mistakes: if an error is made 2 seconds before the end of a 30-second shot it is irritating, but nothing like as problematic (or expensive) as if it were a single 10-minute shot that has to be repeated. The second reason is more interesting: we, the audience, have learnt a language of shots and edits, and rely on that for communication. Most of us do not notice any longer how unnatural it is to watch a film. For most of the history of humankind the action that we saw was of the world through our own eyes. Even if one attended the theatre, the position and view was still controlled by the physical position of one's head and body. What humans developed with was a perspective seen through their own eyes as a continuous experience. There is no cutting or editing, no sudden changes of viewing position, no looking from someone else's perspective, no sudden zooms or close-ups. What we see in the real world is dictated by what our body is physically capable of. If you try imagining yourself being where the camera is in a film, you quickly see just how unusual it is, and how the language of film is deeply embedded in our perception of that medium, but is drastically different from the language of the world around us.

Within a single shot we will examine three distinct aspects: *framing, movement* and *camera movement*.

10.3.1 Framing

Everything that has been said about framing of a still image applies to moving images, but there are a number of different constraints and features.

First, the actual frame of the film is a one-off decision. Whether it be a television ratio, 35 mm, widescreen, or some other format, the decision is made and lasts throughout the film. Framing by relating objects to constructed frames within this outer enclosure follows the same rules as for the still image, with the additional observation that not all frames will be well composed in still image terms because of the impossibility implied by movement.

In addition, the language of film and the tendency to cut between different images has created a description of a set of shots which tries to capture the apparent size of objects within the frame. This set of

Figure 10.1   Shot types.

descriptions is commonly explained in terms of the human body, and can be described in sequence as shown in Figure 10.1.

- *Extreme close up*: Much closer than you would normally get to another human being. Normally just a part of the face. A classic example is the way that scenes of tension in certain films used to be depicted by cutting repeatedly from a shot of the eye of one actor to the eye of another, or from trigger-finger to trigger-finger in a western.

- *Close up*: Still close enough to be pretty intimate in the real world, this would be a shot where a person's head fills the image. An example might be a kissing shot in which you see the mouths and faces of two people, but not the backs of their heads or their shoulders.

- *Close shot*: A bit further back, and not untypical of what you might be looking at if within hand-shaking range of someone. A shot like this would be more than just a head – including the shoulders, for example. Perhaps the most familiar example of a close shot is the typical passport photograph.

- *Medium shot*: Close enough to show a significant part of a person, but not the whole body. Someone sitting at a table so that he fills the frame from (more or less) waist upwards might well be a medium shot. Most of those scenes where the camera is on the bonnet of a car watching the driver and passenger talking would fit into medium-shot territory

- *Full shot*: The whole of a person from head to foot is visible, with some background as well. Following an important character along a street would often be in this category. Two people shaking hands in front of a shop (which is clearly visible) would be another example.

- *Long shot*: Further out than a full shot, a long shot generally makes the individual humans somewhat less important in the frame, and the emphasis is more upon the background. A picture of *Notre Dame* in

Paris that included the whole front of the cathedral would be a long shot, as would a perspective view along a street.

- *Extreme long shot*: The extreme long shot would reduce any people in the frame to insignificance. Major landscape shots, panoramas of cities, or other shots which establish a large physical context are typical of this form.

While maintaining the general rules of composition within the frame, we need to remember that the frame is not viewed as a single entity, but within a dynamic context. This means that it is possible to refer to something that is actually outside the frame, and not currently visible, but whose existence has been established by the preceding images. This facility is enhanced by the use of other communication channels than the purely visual, such as sound. We find nothing unusual in seeing a person alone on screen, talking to themselves, because we know from context that there is another person outside the frame who is invisible to us, but who is in the same room as the visible performer. It is also interesting to note how rarely we see someone getting killed in a film (compared to how frequently we *think* we see someone getting killed). Most of the time we see a shot of someone about to be killed, a shot of the killer firing a gun (or similar), and a shot of the victim in the aftermath. We construct the belief that we have seen someone being killed, but we have not actually *seen* it – it was out of frame – we have simply inferred it.

10.3.2 Movement

One of the most obvious changes in the construction of a shot is that it has a temporal duration that is determined by the camera, and that certain actions will happen within that duration. Fairly fixed scenes (e.g. a 'talking head' section) obey the same rules as photographic composition and are, to all intents and purposes, static. Other scenes have movement that guides and leads the eye of the viewer, much as our lines did in the static case. The basis of this approach still rests on the use of lines, but the lines are dynamic, being the results of changes in the image rather than properties of the image. This is in addition to the static lines. A car or aeroplane may move across the screen in a certain direction, emphasizing a line of movement explicitly. A movement of body or hand may create a track which the eye of the viewer follows and anticipates. There are implicit lines that are created by the psychological effects such as the focus of attention on the performer. An actor suddenly jerking her head up towards the door of a room draws attention to a door which may only have been perceived as a piece of background scenery. If this is followed by a close up of the handle turning, then we have established for the viewer a clear line from the eye of the performer to the handle of the door, and indicated a focus of attention. Because of the change of perspective, we can create a new sort of line in a film: one that exists in a three-dimensional space of the mind, even though it is created using two-dimensional lines.

10.3.3 Camera movement

The first films were shot as though in a theatre, and used the language of the theatre to communicate with their audiences. The camera was in a fixed position, at a distance that filled the screen with a full-shot scene, much as the theatregoer in a good seat might view the action. These films were single continuous pieces with no movements of camera or cuts in film. The experience was as close to the language of theatre as it was possible to make it. This situation was partly due to technological limitations, and partly due to the fact that the producers were using the medium to reproduce the predominant language of the time, rather than thinking about the possibilities that were afforded for novel means of communication.

This began to change during the first 20 years of the twentieth century, with three obviously new innovations: special effects, camera movement, and editing. Special effects really began with the work of Georges Melies, a stage magician who realized the possibilities of the camera and used it to create fantasy films and illusions based upon a combination of magic techniques and tricks such as stopping, reversing, and double exposing film.

Camera movement was a major step for the audience, because it was (for the most part) unlike anything they had experienced before, and they had to learn to understand and interpret it. Indeed, the producers of films also had to learn how to use these techniques to imbue meaning into their application. They appeared gradually over a number of years, and their use is still very variable with fashion and intention. The original evolution of these techniques was greatly assisted by the debate between film as 'art' and film as a representation of reality. This argument raged for many years, but in essence it said that sticking up a camera to record the world as it is (i.e. single fixed shot) was just recording reality, but true film required an intervention to create an art form out of it. Editing and camera movement were both examples of techniques that made films into 'art'.

Without presenting a historical perspective, we can offer a basic language for camera movements. The first three are shots in which the whole camera physically changes position:

- *Track*: The camera moves along a track to left or right, following some action. An example is the cowboy walking along the street while the camera fixes on his profile and moves along the street at the same pace, like someone walking at his side.

- *Dolly*: The camera moves in towards the action, or out from it, changing between different sorts of framing (e.g. from a long shot to a close up).

- *Crane*: The camera moves in a vertical plane (carried on a crane), such as when a long shot of a street is resolved as the camera descends until it is outside one particular shop.

I find it convenient to use distinct names for these three directions of movement, but some people group the three under the single term 'tracking shot'. The distinction is handy and allows clear combinations in the notation introduced below. These movements are mostly used one at a time, but occasionally several might be combined into a compound movement shot.

The second group of movement shots leave the camera in a fixed position, but are the result of a movement of the camera head in some sense:

- *Pan*: The camera rotates to left or right about its axis, as when you move your head round to look at something to one side.

- *Tilt*: The camera tips up or down on its horizontal axis.

- *Zoom*: A special type of lens which can change degree of magnification is used within a shot to apparently bring the subject closer or take it further away. This is similar to a dolly shot, but can be done faster and allows the camera to get into places where it could not move physically.

When notating these camera movements one method is with a simple code based upon boxes and arrows. Up and down arrows mean up or down, left and right arrows mean left or right, and closer and further are represented by crossed lines for *closer*, and a dot for *further*. This last may not seem intuitive, but it is borrowed from a notation in physics to represent things at right angles to the paper. Imagine the movement as a dart – if it is going away from you (into the page), then you can see the flights which look like a cross, but if it is coming towards you, then you see the point which is a dot. If we take these six symbols, we can capture our camera movements with one simple addition: if the symbol is in a box, then the camera is in a fixed location, but otherwise it is changing location. The final symbols and their meanings are shown in Figure 10.2.

Combining the techniques of framing, moving and camera movement with the action of the performers in the film enables us to produce an amazing variety of shots. However, it is difficult to present any form of narrative within the single shot, and virtually all films achieve their effect by joining the shots through a process of editing to create a narrative structure.

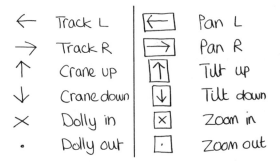

Figure 10.2 The 12 camera symbols.

10.4 Shots into narrative

Every film will have a script (well, almost!) which includes both instructions regarding the actions, characters, costume, etc., and instructions regarding the way in which the scene is to be filmed. This script seeks to provide a coherent narrative that the viewer of the film will be able to interpret. This requires the use of appropriate types of language for the dialogue, and relevant use of symbolism and semiotics within the structure. Further than that, it must present a coherent model of how the different shots are to be grouped together in order to tell a tale. This is extremely important because the way that a film is produced is almost never a process that moves from beginning to end, but one in which many fragments are produced at different times and in different places, dependent upon the constraints of availability and cost of the various participants. The process of taking this heap of fragments and constructing an artefact that communicates a meaningful experience to the viewer in a sequential form is the process of *editing*.

10.4.1 Editing

With the editing of sound we saw that there were only a small number of ways to link between two sounds: the *cut*, the *musical link*, the *fade*, and the *cross-fade*. This was partly because sounds have natural durations and end points, and it is impossible to tell whether there is silence because there is no sound, or silence to depict the change between two scenes. In the visual world, by contrast, a shot has a continuous visual presence and a duration. If that visual presence is disturbed, then the shot is very obviously over. The interpretation placed upon the change from the first shot to the second is dependent partly upon the nature of the physical change used in the editing, and partly upon the relationship of the content and meaning of the images on either side of the break.

The *cut* is the most abrupt of changes. One image ends and the next starts in the following frame. This can be used in many ways to indicate changes of location, changes of context, etc. Used repeatedly and quickly it creates a rhythm of change that raises tension (as in the close up face-cutting example mentioned earlier). There is no implication of a relationship between the elements on either side of the cut, although the actual content of the images will often be used to create such a link.

The *dissolve*, by comparison, is intended to indicate a relationship between the images on either side of each other. One image fades out and a second image becomes visible while the first is still apparent on the screen. The two co-exist for a period and then the new image becomes stronger, taking over from the earlier one. There is a strong implication of a relationship between the shots, but the meaning of that relationship requires some construction elsewhere within the picture. It may be used to emphasize visual similarities, analogies of behaviour or location, and many other possibilities. The meanings can be completely reversed: dissolving from a young person to an older person in the same position may indicate the passage of time, while going from one clock (e.g. on a clocktower) to another (e.g. in a courtroom) indicating the same time can be used to give the reverse message – that no time has passed. The interpretation of a dissolve is hence very heavily dependent on the image content.

The *fade* removes one image gradually from the screen without relating it to another. A fade will normally be a gradual dimming of the image until the screen is black. This indicates a closure of one part of the film. One segment of narrative is coming to an end and the next is new in some way. Because it does not fade directly to the new image the fade presents the reverse effect to the dissolve – that there is no connection to the next shot. After a fade to black, the next shot will typically start with a cut from black, emphasizing the discontinuity: to fade to black, pause, and fade a new shot in from black is much more ambiguous as to the relationship between the shots than the fade or dissolve. On the other hand, it is possible to fade via a linking image, in which case the effect is much like a dissolve, but with the linking image indicating the nature of the relationship between the two shots. The most obvious (and by now, clichéd) example of this is the fade from a shot through an image of days fluttering off a desk calendar, and then fading in to a new shot. There is no ambiguity in such an image now, although when it was first used there was not such certainty about the interpretation.

As mentioned earlier, the physical form of the edit is one aspect of establishing its meaning. Another is the nature of the continuity (or discontinuity) between the associated shots. This aspect is often divided into spatial, temporal and graphical components.

Spatial components refer, as one might imagine, to the space in which the action is taking place. A cut may be used to move between the perspectives of two different people in the same room, for example, in which case there should be some way for the viewer to determine that we are still in the same room. The images of the film are building a world

inside the head of the viewer and it is essential to let them know how a
new shot or perspective fits into that world. Spatial continuity can be
established with appropriate commonalities or with other communication channels (see below), but spatial discontinuity is just as important
(if not more so) in a film. A cut may take us from the centre of the city to
a remote rural area. If this spatial discontinuity is indicated visually (e.g.
with an establishing shot of the great outdoors after the cut) then the
viewer is clear about the change of location. If, instead, the cut is from
the inside of a lawyer's office in a city centre, to the inside of a lawyer's
office in a small village, then the change of location may not be apparent.
Providing the viewers with enough clues to maintain their internal
model of the space in which the film operates is vital.

Temporal components of editing refer to a similar process whereby a
model of the time sequence of action is communicated to the viewer with
appropriate cues. At the most basic level, we all know that a film which
represents 10 days in the world does not take 10 days to watch, so
somewhere along the route 9 days and 22 hours (or whatever) have been
eliminated from the narrative, and yet we still feel that we have followed
it. Ellipses (or omission, like using … in a sentence) is the most common
temporal editing technique used. If we see someone enter a hall, then
arrive at the other side of the hall, we can infer that they have crossed
the hall and that time has passed between the two shots. This is a normal
forward flow of time and is not too difficult to grasp – though even this
was not easy for the first audiences of films using temporal ellipses.
Other temporal tricks may seek to establish that two scenes are
concurrent (e.g. with the clock trick above), or that the later scene
actually occurred earlier (the flashback). There are a few examples of
carefully constructed films in which the shot-by-shot passage of time is
counter to our expectation, but they still work.

Graphical components of editing utilize the photographic properties of
the two shots to establish similarity or dissimilarity to the content on
either side of the cut. The general properties of light and dark,
colouring, etc. might be kept similar if we are trying to establish a
relationship (e.g. two shots in the same room or building) and might be
very different in different locations (e.g. the rural lawyer's office
photographed darkly suggesting dim oil lamps, while the city office is
white walls and neon lights to contrast). In some cases this has been
taken to the extreme of photographing part of the film in colour and part
in black and white. Similarly, parallels in shape and form may be used to
link the shots – a clock may be overlaid by a basketball in the same
position on the screen, or the almost vertical side of a tall building may
fade into the almost vertical face of a cliff. Similarities and contrasts such
as these may communicate a variety of subtle messages about the content
of the shots.

Both the above aspects of the shot and the edit were available in silent films. The possibilities of editing have been broadened by the addition of sound to film. This is important to use because it is one example of the sort of extended combination of languages that is at the heart of effective multimedia.

10.4.2 Combining with other media

With silent film the only link between shots was the editing of the sort described in the previous section. The addition of sound was of great significance because it provided a new channel of communication, which the director could use along with the existing image channels to indicate the nature of the main sequence and to enrich communication with the audience.

Before the coming of sound film, audiences often had access to a soundtrack. In the cinemas or fairs they would view films in silence, but in the picture theatres there would generally be a piano player or organist who would provide an accompaniment. In the early days this was a person who played by the hour and in some cases paid no attention at all to what was happening on the screen. The better players would try to adapt their playing to the action. This was normally in a fairly crude manner that sought to emphasize the general emotions being portrayed on screen – bouncy music for chases and slapstick, touching ballads for romantic scenes, martial airs for armies off to war, etc. This music was all improvised and there was a high degree of uncertainty in how it would work from occasion to occasion.

After a period, the film companies started to become interested and would distribute song lists with their films that recommended particular pieces to play as accompaniment. Libraries of film music were established, and there were even one or two scores commissioned especially for silent films – although they were only used at performances that could afford a full orchestra. There was clearly an interest in the use of music in association with film from the early days.

When the first talkies arrived, even with a very poor level of audio recording, the world of film was revolutionized. Instead of using motion and expression to communicate, the actors had parts that enabled them to speak with other performers, to narrate, and to provide commentary for what is going on off-frame. It is much easier to say 'There go 10,000 elephants off to the East' than it is to show it! Different scriptwriters, actors, directors, and producers were needed, as well as sound engineers, orchestras, and a whole extra collection of technology from the world of sound recording.

Perhaps the most significant change of all was that it gave the producers of the film control over this new communication channel. At the very least, appropriate music could be recorded for shots and timed to start and end in the right place. Full orchestras could be used instead of uncertain pianos. Sound effects could emphasize things of importance and establish ambience. All these effects change the process by which we construct narrative from shots.

A cut is said above to be a discontinuity on the film. If a piece of fairly smooth music is playing, and it continues uninterrupted by the visual cut, then there is a strong psychological implication that the cut is not discontinuous. Perhaps it is just round the corner from the previous shot, or in a part of the room not previously seen. Similarly, a jarring piece of music or a jarring discontinuity of soundtrack can emphasize difference. The move from the toilets in a nightclub to the dance floor is inevitably associated with a massive increase in volume that leaves no doubt that a change of scene has taken place between the shots. There are many similar conventional clues – the use of 'wavy' ethereal music was a common way to indicate that a fade was a flashback for many years, the idea being that this was a magical transition because it did not happen in real life.

Sound effects can emphasize the nature of the link between transitions as well. If we are seeing a medium shot of an actor, and they look up, then we see the inner wall of the hallway of the old house that they are in, we are not necessarily clear what is happening, but if the cut is associated with the sound of a door creaking open, it is immediately obvious where we should look and what we should look for.

What is happening here is a process that we described earlier for multimedia: two different channels of communication, with their own languages of interpretation, are combining to produce a new thing that has a cross-channel language of interpretation. This language builds on the ones that preceded it, but is not identical to them. This is the key to effective understanding of multimedia.

10.5 Modern languages of film and television

The previous sections have concentrated on what can be regarded as fairly traditional techniques in film. What has not been emphasized, but is even more apparent in film than in other media, is that the language of the medium is itself in a continuous state of change and development. Sound film revolutionized the industry, as did the use of colour, the adoption of widescreen and a number of other techniques (though smelly cinema never caught on!). This process is not stabilizing, but is ongoing. Techniques of film from the 1920s were revolutionary at the time, and are so embedded in our culture these days that we do not realize that we, as observers, use them all the time. Methods adopted in the 1940s and 1950s seem old and hackneyed, but they were stretching the boundaries of the audience when they were introduced. For completeness it is worth mentioning just a few current areas where the technology is changing the language. Almost all are related to digital recording and processing techniques.

The *Steadicam* is a mechanical invention. Loosely put, it is a mechanism which enables a camera to be carried by a human being who is walking along, and for the image to remain as stable as if the camera were moving on rails. This permits a huge range of shots and opportunities that were never possible before. One example is the 360 walk. This is when the camera goes all the way round an object or person to show them from different perspectives. This was not previously possible because it required a circular track, and a 360 shot would inevitably display some of the track at some point. Without the track a Steadicam can do this, and it is sometimes uncomfortable to watch because we have seen so many films where such things do not happen. To a large extent the language implications of the Steadicam are still being explored. One example where it has had a significant effect is in Zoo TV.

Zoo TV is derived from a radio format and is loosely based upon presenting a live show – warts and all. A team or presenter works in a comparatively unscripted manner and produces an anarchic, amateur feel to the show. This apparent amateurness has become a trademark style that is often associated with youth because it seems counter to authority. The fact that it is normally sponsored by very conservative groups and the apparent confusion is frequently scripted these days is irrelevant. It has become a language and style in its own right. Zoo TV was really not possible in the days of fixed cameras, since it is hard to look anarchic when sitting behind a desk or on a sofa. With hand-held cameras the performers can move around the studio or building and in and out of the audience, and the cameras can do the same. There is a marked increase (initially due to error) in things such as angled shots, poorly framed shots, focus slip, etc. All of these things would be associated with an 'amateur' style, and have come to represent this form of television.

Timeslice cameras use a technique that has been becoming trendy in the last year or two. They are of limited application, but their novelty is sufficient to make the observer say 'How did they do that?' – it confuses our model of what is possible on film. Shots with these cameras are typically action shots – a sprinter crossing the finish of a race, a diver leaping off a board, or a leopard jumping from a tree. In each case the format is essentially the same. We see a conventional film of the action beginning and then, at a critical point, the action freezes in time. The next part is the surprise, because the camera begins to track around this frozen figure. We see a circular track through maybe 140. This is a shock to an audience who are used to motion being continuous and cameras having a single perspective. The method is that there has been a change from a conventional camera to something that has not been seen until recently. The conventional camera shoots up to the point at which the action freezes, and at the same moment the Timeslice camera takes a picture. This is not a motion picture camera at all, but a set of still cameras arranged along a track and firing simultaneously. This arrangement produces a large number of images that freeze a moment of time from many perspectives. There is a certain amount of satisfaction in the way that this takes us back to the techniques of Muybridge at the beginnings of film. What makes the images better than a sequence of stills is that a computer is then used to combine them and to calculate, from the available frames, what the frames would look like if we had had a much larger number of cameras, and hence we can construct the 3D walk around. This last facility is due to what is probably the single most important change to hit the language of film in its entire history – the introduction of digital editing and manipulation.

Digital editing takes our film and turns it into a numerical representation (or we could eliminate film altogether and use a digital camera from the start). This means that we can manipulate our images in ways that were never before possible, and still maintain a higher quality than ever before. Actors can be simulated (at least extras can, and main parts cannot be too far away), unwanted pieces of shots can be perfectly edited out, separate takes can be joined seamlessly (there is no reason why we cannot produce a 2 hour film which appears as a single shot), different cameras can be digitally joined to create impossible 'perfect' cameras, animation and special effects can be integrated with no visible separation from reality. There are so many possibilities from this new technology and we have not yet begun to explore them. The language of the image in the digital age will be drastically different from the film of the twentieth century.

10.6 Exercises

Exercise 10.1 Select a 5 minute segment from a television soap opera. Analyse this segment as follows:

1. Identify each of the shots in sequence and group them according to category (e.g. close-up, medium shot, long shot) as in Section 10.3.1.

2. For each transition between shots, identify the type of transition between the shots (e.g. cut dissolve) as in Section 10.4.

3. See if you can identify an example of each type of camera movement (e.g. pan, track) as in Section 10.3.3.

Exercise 10.2 Select a film from the 1940s (e.g. a Film Noir detective story) and repeat the analysis of Exercise 10.1.

Exercise 10.3 Select a film that has recently been released (and is now available on video or DVD) and repeat the analysis of Exercise 10.1.

Exercise 10.4 Watch a 10 minute segment from a live children's programme of the sort normally shown on Saturday morning television (e.g. SMTV, *Diggit*). Apart from live to camera action, what other channels of communication are being used? (e.g. text on screen, logos). What other conventional media are being used in the programme?

Exercise 10.5 Repeat the analysis in Exercise 10.4 for a 10 minute segment of a quiz show aimed at an adult audience (e.g. Who wants to be a millionaire, 15 to 1).

Exercise 10.6 Repeat the analysis of Exercise 10.4 for a 10 minute segment of an 'Audience participation' show (e.g. Jerry Springer, Oprah).

10.7   Further reading

General texts about meaning in film:
Dudley Andrew, *Concepts in film theory*, Oxford University Press, 1984

Christian Metz, *Film language: a semiotics of the cinema*, Oxford University Press, 1974

Useful overviews of all aspects of film theory and analysis:
David Bordwell and Kristin Thompson, *Film art an introduction*, McGraw-Hill, 1979

Bernard F. Dick, *Anatomy of film*, St. Martin's Press, 1998

Introduction to various special aspects of constructing the components:
Edward Dmytryk, *On screen writing*, Butterworth, 1985

Peter Ward, *Picture composition for film and television*, Focal Press, 1996

Sergei Eisenstein, *The film sense*, Faber and Faber, 1943

11

Stakeholders and teamworking

Having covered the technical aspects of designing and developing interactions and working with various forms of media individually, we will now begin putting the whole thing together. The remaining chapters consider the way in which we can go from an initial idea for a multimedia system through a process of product design, product development, testing, and deployment to produce an innovative and effective Interactive Multimedia system. We will distinguish clearly between the *product* (the thing that we are producing at the end of this development cycle) and the *process* (the means by which we ensure that the product is constructed). Both aspects require careful design, execution, and revision if we are to ensure success.

In this chapter we will examine one extremely important aspect of this question: Who are the people involved in the process of developing Interactive Multimedia? We will explore members of the team and aspects of communication between them.

11.1 Teamwork

11.1.1 The isolated developer

Previous chapters have demonstrated the breadth and complexity of skills that are required to produce a comprehensive and effective Interactive Multimedia system. While it is possible to get an overview of all these aspects, it is almost impossible for one single individual to encompass the full range of conceptualization and skills necessary to develop a complete system. This is true even before we begin to consider the content subject matter. As a consequence, it is now the case that the vast majority of multimedia systems are developed by a team. This process of team working is a lot less common in the experience of people from arts backgrounds than with people from a science background. Almost all software development results from a carefully designed team process. While we will focus upon group work in the remaining chapters of this text, it is worth a small diversion to explore the role of the isolated developer in multimedia.

In the fine arts an individual working alone is considerably more common than the alternatives. Over their career artists tend to evolve particular styles and approaches with which they are happy and which are as unique to them as their personality. Understandably, these individuals become very protective of their style and tend to be averse to others sharing it or working with it. Individuals also become (necessarily) a strong believer in, and advocate of, their own style and will try to apply it to all situations in which they are developing new work. In the cases where a fine artist is commissioned to carry out a project, there is an inevitable tension between the artist and client. Normally the process by which the artist has been commissioned has involved the client in examining previous work by that artist and deciding to commission a work which evokes a similar style. It is not usual to ask an artist to engage in a certain project and then ask them to change their style completely! Despite this, there will almost inevitably be artistic tensions between clients (who perceive their own particular requirements for the project) and artists (who were trying to fulfil their own specific artistic goals via a project for somebody else). Even in this apparently simple situation, the artist is not really an isolated individual.

If we examine other areas of art, which have a significantly greater applied component (e.g. graphic design, furniture design) then we find that the situation in the real world is rather more structured. The client provides (hopefully) a very carefully prepared brief for the project and the artist must bid competitively to fulfil that brief. Since payment is normally dependent upon acceptance of the result by the client, artists working in this manner are more inclined to compromise any personal artistic vision to ensure acceptance of the result. Nonetheless, there remains a tension between client and artist, and it is increasingly the case in the commercial world that artists spend part of their time justifying their design decisions to the client.

Typically, a graphic designer will be working within a team of people, each of which has their own style and expertise. This means that the designer is embedded in the environment of fellow practitioners, and several practitioners may work together on satisfying the brief for a given client. Despite this, the designers rarely collaborate closely and will normally divide the project in such a way that, having agreed a general overall approach, each participant will pursue some aspect of it in a style of their own.

Let us now consider the role of the isolated developer from the perspective of computing. Computing is a field in which various developments progress from being innovative, outlandish, and weird to becoming mainstream, general practice. In the early days of any particular technology or theoretical innovation it tends (in line with general theories of innovation in science) to be championed by a small group of experts (often only one, initially) who explore it thoroughly and use it extensively. These individuals tend to be 'believers' and feel that something exciting and innovative is happening but cannot yet justify it in traditional terms of computer science. These individuals pursue these ideas and try and make them more accepted by a large community. In the vast majority of cases these ideas are forgotten and fall by the wayside. In a very small number of cases they begin to move into the mainstream.

Once an idea in computing has begun to graduate into the mainstream, a process goes on of normalizing it and making it part of everyday practice. In many cases certain ideas succeed partly because of aspects of the personality who was promoting them in the early days. These issues are analysed and used to extend and improve the idea, making it independent of the originator until, often, it becomes significantly different from the original intention. Once we reach this stage in the cycle of innovation we are beginning to hit the point at which a wacky idea is becoming part of professional practice, and as such must be integrated into the professional processes of computing development. Since large-scale development is almost invariably a product of team work, this means that the idea is taken out of the hands of an isolated developer and moves, over time, to become a property of the team development process.

In both fields described above we have identified cases where a developer works in isolation and cases where the developer works as part of a team. While it is often popular to view 'arts' and 'sciences' as two distinct, and indeed opposed, systems, there are many commonalities between them which are not frequently acknowledged. One of the essential aspects of Interactive Multimedia is to recognize the value of each of these disciplines and the importance of the links and relationships between the ways of thinking in the two areas.

Both the above examples represent a transformation between the *isolated developer* and the *team* working with the client. In both cases we find that the isolated developer is pushing an idea in which he or she has faith but which may not be generally accepted within the mainstream or by a client. This exploration is necessarily an individual process because of the type of innovation which is taking place: the artist is exploring her own objectives which can only be realized through a completed piece; the programmer is exploring new techniques or methods which can only be demonstrated to a wider audience through practical application. I tend to refer to this sort of programming as 'research programming', since the intended outcome is what you learn, rather than a working product.

The other end of the continuum in both cases involves a team (Figure 11.1). This team irons out a certain level of 'wackiness' in the final product and in this sense is essential. We need to note that in both cases the important thing is that the team is a consequence of trying to develop something which can be delivered to a client satisfying specific stated needs. Whether as a programmer or an artist it is necessary to recognize that the scope for creativity and innovation is significantly greater when working alone than when working for a client and with a team.

Figure 11.1   The continuum isolated – team and client.

Interactive Multimedia necessarily involves a broad range of skills and a close relationship between computing and the arts. It is not possible to produce a multimedia product without an underlying technical and scientific base. Equally, it makes no sense to talk of an Interactive Multimedia system that contains no artistic component in the broad sense of the term that we are using here. Hence, while acknowledging the importance of creative individuals working in isolation as a source of ideas and innovation, we will assume that a true multimedia *product* is, of necessity, the product of a team. We will also assume that this team is working with a client. Our next problem is to understand the nature of the client.

11.1.2   The client

11.1.2.1 Client and stakeholders

The *client* is not the *user* (well, very rarely). An earlier chapter examined the nature of the users and how to understand them and build a system that will match their needs and enable them to work effectively. This is central to our system design, but it is also important to recognize that the actual user of our software is only one of the people who will be influenced by, or have an influence upon, the software. There will be a range of people who are affected by the software to greater or lesser degree, and it is important to understand how these people relate to the system if it is to be effective. The examination of these people is referred to as stakeholder analysis because each person (or group) has a stake in the system.

Of primary concern to us is the person who is commissioning the system. That person is the one who must agree an appropriate specification for the product, and must certify that it has reached an acceptable level after it has been built – and is quite likely to sign the cheque as well. This individual is often requesting the system to satisfy a need identified elsewhere in an organization, and will not necessarily be an actual user. This is important because they will almost certainly have views about an appropriate solution that will not be reflected by the real needs of the users. Nonetheless, they are the most important client to satisfy (if we want to get paid) and sometimes it is necessary (though not advisable) to give clients what they want even though you know it is not what the users need. It is better to try and change the client view of what they want, but this requires careful negotiation.

Beyond this client, one approach is to divide our stakeholders into four categories.

1. **Primary** – People who use the system (interact with it in some form). There may be a number of distinct groups using all or part of it. They may have different needs, so all of these people have to be treated as users or groups of users.

2. **Secondary** – People who are *upstream* or *downstream* of the system, i.e. people who provide information which is input to the system or people who utilize data coming out of the system.

3. **Tertiary** – People with more remote dependencies upon the system. These people may never see the system, or even know of its existence, but their job is affected by the existence or otherwise of the system.

4. **Facilitating** – People who make the system happen. This includes the developers, the maintenance teams (both software and hardware), network providers, etc.

All these categories can be of relevance to a system. In our design process we will see that it is important to recognize these stakeholders, categorize them appropriately, and decide which ones are of key importance to the successful application and uptake of the system.

11.1.3 Organizational psychology

To make a team work well, and to effectively carry out a role within a team, it is necessary to understand certain aspects of team working which are significantly different from working in isolation. Happily, the psychology of working and of the organization of people into working structures have been the subject of extensive research for a number of years. In this section we will identify just a few of the major points to bear in mind when thinking about working in the team.

One of the most fundamental things to recognize is that the team is distinct from the individuals within it. The team has an existence of its own, with its own goals, abilities, and limitations. When an individual is added to or removed from a team this may have no effect upon the team as a whole functioning unit, or the team may change in a variety of ways for better or worse. To help us understand and manage these processes it is best to make a clear distinction between the *roles* and *people* who fulfil them.

Roles are a specific set of activities within a project that could be carried out by a single individual. From our perspective we will concern ourselves only with one project and ignore issues related to individuals trying to work on several projects simultaneously. We will examine the *role definition* and then *people mapping*.

11.1.3.1 Role definition

When identifying roles within a team it is not sufficient just to give them a name: we must also *define* those roles in some level of detail. Simply saying 'graphic designer', for example, does not clarify whether we want someone to do black and white paper art works, cartoon design, product design, or a variety of other activities. The more precisely we provide a definition of each of the roles within our system the more effectively we will be able to operate as a team on a project.

Since we are assuming that this is a project-based enterprise we can begin the process of role definition by looking at the project itself. In a subsequent chapter we will see various methods of project planning which allow us to construct a resource model and timeline for developing our multimedia product. At this juncture it is necessary only to note that we can regard the process of developing a multimedia product as a task (or a small set of tasks). Each of these tasks can be broken down into subtasks. They can, in their turn, be broken down into subtasks and we can carry on until we get bored or have reached a sufficient level of detail for our current purposes. This is exactly the sort of hierarchical breakdown of procedural activities that we discussed in Chapter 3 under the heading of Task Analysis. We can apply the techniques that we learned there to divide our multimedia project into tasks sufficiently small that each one requires only the particular set of skills and abilities that one might find in a single individual. The task hierarchy for part of a multimedia project might look something like Figure 11.2.

We can construct a picture such as that in Figure 11.2 and from it extract a list of the roles that need to be fulfilled within the project. We

video asset collection
storyboarding
filming
editing
organise shoots
direct crew
arrange locations
sort logistics
co-ordinate personnel
liaise with police

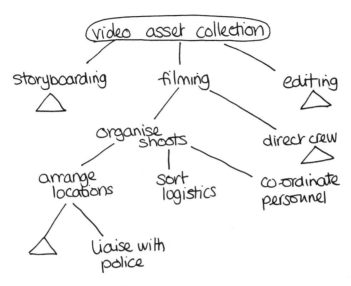

Figure 11.2 Defining a roles tree.

can use conventional names as a shorthand, but it is best to provide a reasonable degree of detail so that our intention is unambiguous (Figure 11.3).

This formal collection of roles is the things that we have identified that will require fulfilment in order for the project to succeed, and are essential aspects of our team for the duration of the project. Our next step is to see how this relates to the individuals who will actually be working upon the project.

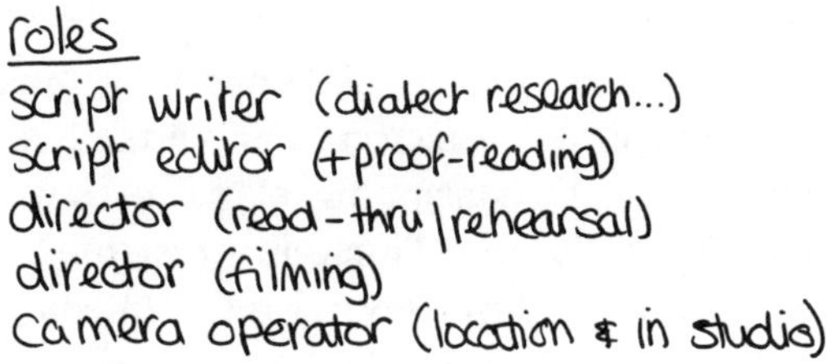

roles
script writer (dialect research...)
script editor (+proof-reading)
director (read-thru|rehearsal)
director (filming)
camera operator (location & in studio)

Figure 11.3 Sample list of a role definition.

11.1.3.2 People mapping

On a few rare occasions a multimedia product will be designed and specified, and the project to develop that product will be prepared, before any staff are in place to carry out the project. In this case it is possible to use the roles defined in the project specification as a starting point for recruitment of people to work on the project. Even in this case, it is unlikely that the people who are eventually recruited will have an exact one-to-one mapping with the roles that need to be filled. More often, the project manager is presented with a pre-existing team of people employed by a company from which to select the team that will carry out the project. In either case, it is unlikely to be able to map staff directly onto the pre-defined roles, and a more effective allocation of human resources can be achieved by identifying the *people* separately from the *roles* (Figure 11.4).

People	knowledge....
mark	CAN'T SING, CAN
fin	DESIGN – POST-PROD
charlie	(½-time only)
Venus	DIRECTING / EDITING
Imran	(after august)

Figure 11.4   Sample list of people.

The key step is to try and define the people in terms of those aspects that you require for the project. A common way to do this is known as the KSAO model (knowledge, skills, aptitude, other). We discussed the first three categories in earlier chapters and the final category of 'other' is simply there for any special requirements that do not fit one of the standard categories. Each person in the proposed project team should be given a description in this form. It is important to be as detailed as is appropriate to the needs of the project, but it is obviously never possible to create a complete definition of a person. The activities involved in person definition are very like the processes we discussed in Chapter 4.

We should now have a list of roles within the project which have been carefully defined and (perhaps using the same KSAO model) the list of people in our project team who have certain abilities and aptitudes. The next requirement is to make a mapping between the people and the roles. This will not normally be a simple process, and it is common to find that one individual may fulfil several roles. In some cases a single role may require several people to fulfil it (though this should be avoided where possible). These people can be overlaid onto our task analysis diagram to produce something rather like Figure 11.5.

This mapping can be used to brief members of the development team on what they are expected to do and who they are expected to communicate with and work alongside. Because the formal roles are a property of the team and not of the individuals, it also enables the project manager to assess the consequences of adding or removing different people from the team. Finally, as we will see in the next section, while this method defines the formal roles which the team are expected to fulfil we may also have to take account of informal roles which appear during the course of the project.

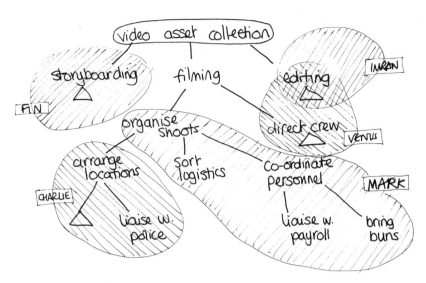

Figure 11.5 People on tasks.

11.1.3.3 Team dynamics

Formal and informal roles   The previous section discussed the identification of formal roles within the project, the identification of individual skills, and the establishment of a mapping between roles and individuals. These aspects, together with the project plan, are sufficient to set up and to manage the normal project. People can be assigned to formal roles via some explicit mechanism such as a job specification (written, for preference) or a contract. Although this is satisfactory in a perfect world, we must also acknowledge that most projects do not exist solely in terms of these formal roles. Other roles may appear within the project as it progresses, evolving due to changes in the project requirements or activities and workload of the participants, etc. These are referred to as *informal roles* within the project. They are generally transient in nature, and often exist only for a fairly short period of time. Many of these roles never come to the attention of the project manager at all (e.g. I decide that I'm going to make the coffee on this project) but if an informal role starts to have implications for resources or for other roles within the project then it is necessary to take account of it and manage it alongside the formal roles. In certain cases, the role may be so valuable as to gain an air of permanence. In this situation it should be formalized with a written specification and incorporated into the project planning. Informal roles are a very valuable way to allow a project team to adapt and evolve to changing needs or unanticipated requirements.

Role ambiguity and conflict   Some further issues may arise in the nature of the roles themselves, which will than require a resolution. The most obvious are *role ambiguity* and *role conflict*.

Role ambiguity arises when it is not exactly clear what is involved in a particular role. This can happen if the specification has not been made clear enough or committed to paper. It also arises because the interpretation of the person who has been given the role is not the same as the interpretation of the person who originally planned the role. When we are dealing with mixed teams from arts and science backgrounds, the differences in terminology and the fact that the same words can be used to mean different things can often lead to a role ambiguity. In these situations it is very important to clarify the meanings of the terms that are being used and to ensure that a role is agreed not only by the project manager and the person who is fulfilling the role, but also by other people who might interact with that role and make use of its outputs.

Role conflict is exactly what it sounds like. It commonly arises if a single individual is fulfilling several roles and some of those roles have objectives within them whose consequences clash with the needs of another role of the same person. Where possible a manager or other external agent should try and work with the person to resolve the conflict. If this is happening repeatedly then it is normally because the roles themselves are ill defined or should not be linked together, and it is more appropriate to separate the roles into different members of staff.

Degradation of performance   An important thing to recognize when working with a team is the inevitable degradation in performance resulting from teamwork. Put simply, this means that 10 people do not work 10 times as well as one person. In extreme cases, adding more people to the project may actually slow progress down. Why is this? We can identify three main factors: *role interference, maintenance,* and *laziness*.

Role interference is primarily a difficulty caused by the original project specification, but may develop over time due to changes in roles and people's perceptions of them. We may find that two roles within our project duplicate certain elements of work or overlap in an unproductive way without direct duplication (e.g. the same piece of work may be done twice from different perspectives with the results of neither being usable for the other role). Where the roles have particular objectives that they are trying to achieve we may find that these objectives are in conflict. This is similar to the role conflict situation described above but generally happens between individuals rather than with one person.

Maintenance activities. One person can keep everything that they need to know and do in their head (or on relevant bits of paper, etc.). As soon as we have two people there is a requirement for each to keep the other informed about what they are doing and how their work relates. As we add people to the team the need for these maintenance activities to ensure the team works well as a whole increases. These activities may include a general awareness of what is going on and what others are doing, exchanging information about related activities and discoveries, the establishment of common goals and objectives between members of the team, and various aspects of social structuring and organization including the establishment of relationships between people in the team and the evolution of communications strategies.

Laziness. If you are working on your own and you decided not to do something which is essential for the project then it does not get done. If you are working in the team then there is a reasonable chance that someone else will pick up the task, or at worst that you could argue that it should have been someone else's job. This means that it is a lot easier to be lazy when working in a team than when working on your own. A similar, but not identical, issue is SEP (somebody else's problem). In this situation something arises which needs to be done, but the individual is convinced that it does not fall within the role definition. Consequently it is somebody else's problem and no attention needs to be paid to it. Some individuals do not even take the step of trying to find out whose responsibility it is. In this way essential tasks can become lost between different roles.

Team evolution   It is normally the case that a team will be formed to carry out a particular project. Even when the team exists in advance, there will be a certain amount of restructuring and reorganization consequent upon the way that the team needs to work to satisfy the requirements of this particular project. This is not, in fact, a one-off process but a continuous evolution that goes on within the team during the course of the project. This evolution can be thought of as being driven by the interaction of three distinct needs: those of the task, those of the group as a whole, and those of the individual. If we take the needs of the task as our starting point, first try and establish a set of needs and objectives for the team as a whole which match those of the task. These will not be identical to, but must be compatible with, those of the task. In general, needs established for the group will include more specific objectives and objectives which are related to the process of software development rather than to attributes of the final product. Having established the group needs, we can then look at the individuals within the team, determine what their needs and objectives are, and seek to relate them to the project overall. These would include not only technical objectives but personal and social ones. Many of these needs are long-term aspects of the life of a team member and it is not appropriate to try and change them, but to show the individual how the needs relate to those of the team and the project.

One of the neatest models of the process of evolution of a team is referred to by four phases: *forming, storming, norming,* and *performing*. They represent sequential stages in the evolution of the team:

- forming;

- storming;

- norming;

- performing.

Forming is the initial stage of creating a group, including the basic social interaction, establishment of relationships and communications and identifying the purpose and basic set of goals.

Storming is the next phase, as the group engage with the problem in more detail. It is about the appearance and resolution of conflicts – in how to tackle the problem, the right approaches, demarcation within the group, etc.

Norming brings the previous aspects together into a coherent accepted plan and approach for the group as a whole.

Performing involves the carrying through of the plans working as an integrated and mutually supportive team.

11.1.4 The team player

Having explored a number of aspects of the psychology of the team we can now examine an issue of more direct importance: how do *you* fit into and work with the team? There is a variety of models of how team interaction works, and it is important that you have some view of yourself from these perspectives. The models identify attributes of different members of a team such as ability to do research, to take decisions, to provide inspiration, to respond to problems, and to deliver to deadlines. Each of these (and many other) aspects are important and a successful team will attempt to assign each member the roles in which they are most effective. To do this it is first necessary for each individual to take an appropriate test or tests which can determine their strengths and weaknesses in each category.

One such test that is widely used is that developed by Belbin. This constitutes a suite of tools which can examine different sorts of projects or tasks and build a profile of the skills of an individual. This normally results with the individual being recognized as having a particular strength or weakness in one of a number of personality traits. Belbin uses the following categories:

- *Co-ordinator* – Often committee chair person. They are good at organizing people, getting their opinions, and providing motivation. They tend to direct the group, but do not become dictatorial. They may not be a significant source of new ideas.

- *Team-worker* – Tend to be perceptive, diplomatic, caring people who put the goals of the team above their own personal objectives. They expend effort on making the social interaction of the team effective. They tend not to be decision makers.

- *Implementer* – Tend to be conscientious and fastidious, organized and orderly. They are keen to carry through plans and get things done, and identify their own goals closely with those of the group.

- *Shaper* – Highly motivated and wants to win. Energetic and capable of emotional extremes. They are excellent at inspiring people to get moving and making things happen. May be leaders. Shapers do not work well together!

- *Completer* – Hardworking, organized, and anxious. Pay attention to detail and persist in carrying through a project, ensuring that all the little aspects are tidied up. Tend not to innovate or be opportunistic, but are key at carrying things from elsewhere through to their conclusion.

- *Plant* – Creative, innovative, bright. Sometimes unconstrained by feasibility. Tend to be independent workers, but can be the driving force behind the team's ideas if well managed. Two or more plants in a team are too many!

- *Resource investigator* – Good at acquiring information, interpersonal skills, and negotiation. Capable of adapting to change quickly. May have short bursts of enthusiasm for particular things which fade fast.

- *Monitor* – Tend to be intelligent and detached from the ideas in the team. Work to see each side of an issue and reach an objective resolution to problems. Useful in driving decisions which involve selection between alternatives advocated by others.

Another thing you might consider (which is scary) is finding out about yourself. There are a variety of questionnaires around of the form which ask things such as 'How assertive are you?', 'How well do you get on with other people?', and other aspects of social skills. You can complete one yourself, but it is interesting, if daunting, to distribute them (preferably anonymously) to the people you are working with and ask them to answer the questions about you. It can be quite an eye-opener to discover what other people's perceptions of you are!

11.2 Players

Having established the importance of recognizing the team of players involved in an Interactive Multimedia product, we shall now turn to examining in somewhat greater detail specific members of that team. We will take the team in the broadly inclusive sense that encompasses everyone with whom interaction might occur in the context of product development – both the development team themselves and the client and associated participants.

Figure 11.6   Players picture 1.

Client (Figure 11.6)   The first, and to a great extent, most important, participant to recognize in the project is the client. In most commercial products the client will be external to the development team, but in large companies it may be that the role of client is fulfilled by somebody within the company but separate from the team responsible for developing the product. In general, the client is the person (or body) who is commissioning the product. By this we mean that the client has a specific need and has sought out the Interactive Multimedia developers to provide a solution for that need. The client is the source of initial information about the need and the ultimate arbiter who must sign off the product as acceptable on completion of the development. This means that the client is also normally the source of revenue for constructing the system.

The client exists within the organization in a context that allows interaction with a number of other stakeholders in the product and the end users of the product. For the purposes of this discussion of the players it is convenient to treat the client as a single entity although they may in fact be a group: in particular, the client is likely to represent the stakeholders to the development team such that stakeholder analysis is likely to be done in this mediated manner. It is therefore important to interact with the client not just as an individual, but about the stakeholders whom they are representing.

Figure 11.7   Players picture 2.

Analyst (Figure 11.8)   In the same way that the client is being treated as a single embodiment of all aspects of the needs of the stakeholders, the analyst represents all aspects of the development team responsible for constructing the product. In a simple world we could treat the client–team interface as involving only these two players. In practice it is more difficult because the analyst must act as a communication channel between many different groups in order to ensure that needs and possibilities are mutually understood and described in acceptable format. The analyst represents the development team to the client, but also represents the client to the development team, and is likely to become involved in internal communications on both sides of this process.

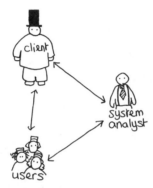

Figure 11.8   Players picture 3.

Users (Figure 11.8)   The end users are represented explicitly in the diagram partly because of their importance in the process of user-centred design, and partly because they represent an extremely significant player in the project which is at odds (potentially) with the client. While it seems natural to assume that the client understands the needs and their likely solutions this is rarely the case. Clients may have a gross understanding of the difficulty, or perceive a problem at their level (often as senior management) when the actual end users in the process recognize an entirely different problem or other intervening factors which would completely invalidate the solution that the client believes is required. This gap in perception between the client who is funding the project and the users for whom it will have to be effective cannot be overemphasized. In the diagram an interaction between users and client is shown, but there is also a significant interaction between the users and analysts. Having obtained some idea of the recognized problem and needs from the client, the first thing an analyst should do is make contact with representatives of the user group and assess independently the things that they have been told by the client. This should help clarify the issues and is likely to modify the problem as originally stated by the client. The analyst then has to discover a diplomatic way of offering this modified statement of the problem to the client such that they can accept it. The action of the analyst as a mediator between the client and users (often general staff and senior management in the same company) requires some well-balanced skills of negotiation and persuasion.

The interaction with client and users enables our analyst to clarify the problem and to achieve agreement from these participants as to the need that is trying to be addressed. This is not generally sufficient to form the basis for the implementation plan: further information is required from people on the development team. Following the initial statement the analyst is likely to turn to further sources to clarify the implementation possibilities and issues: a system designer and subject experts.

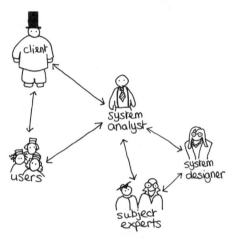

Figure 11.9   Players picture 4.

System designer (Figure 11.9)   This individual is a rare breed at present: someone who understands the programming and interaction aspects, as well as the development and integration of media assets. It is not essential that this individual should be able to *do* all these things but that person does require sufficient knowledge of them to be able to develop a design which is feasible and acceptable in these areas. At present it is quite likely to require two people to fulfil this role: one for interaction and one for media. Working in conjunction with the analyst (and members of their teams as necessary) it is the responsibility of this individual to produce a design that will satisfy the needs. In many computing environments this combination of analyst and designer would be sufficient to produce a complete solution but because Interactive Multimedia systems make strong use of Communicative Interaction and are therefore significantly knowledge dependent, it is highly likely that separate subject experts will need to be brought into the discussion.

Subject experts   The subject experts have knowledge of the domain about which the final system is intended to communicate. In many cases when developing a proprietary system for a company these experts will be members of staff of that company who work within the area where the system is intended to be deployed. If the product is intended to be for more general markets then it may be necessary to seek out other experts in the field to assist with development and delimitation of the content. With highly specialized systems subject experts may come from both categories. These experts must interact with the analyst in order to delimit and define the knowledge content which is being covered by the system, and also normally work with the system designers in order to clarify the way that this can or should be implemented.

Between them, the players described so far should be able to come up with a specification for the multimedia product that matches the needs of the client and user groups and is sufficiently well defined to act as a blueprint for the implementation process. This blueprint for a system does not tell us how to go about developing it, however, and so we move on to a second aspect where we switch from thinking about the product to thinking about the process by which it will be produced, and hence turn to a project designer.

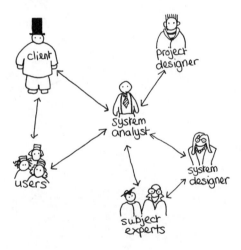

Figure 11.10   Players picture 5.

Project designer (Figure 11.10)   The purpose of this role is to take a system specification and map it into a process by which the system can be constructed. This involves identifying all components of the system and activities that we will need to be engaged in order to construct those components. The overall task is broken down into a group of separable subtasks (or work-packages) which generally involve different members and groups within the development team. Resources are allocated to these packages (e.g. staff, consumables) and the dependencies between the packages are identified. Finally, the predicted amount of time that each package should take is calculated and this gives an overall implementation time and cost for the project. It should be possible for the project designer to carry out this whole process in conjunction with the analyst and with information about the available development resources. The final outcome from this process is a project plan. This will be discussed further in Chapter 13.

We have finally reached the point where we can begin the process of constructing the system. This involves teams of specialist developers and also explicitly requires someone to manage the project. In this diagram we have separated developers into *programmers* and *asset producers* corresponding to the division between content and control which we have maintained throughout.

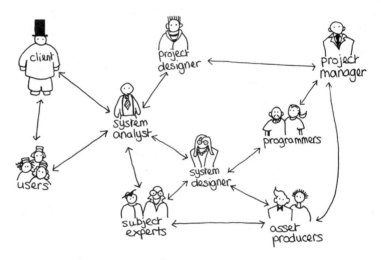

Figure 11.11   Players picture 6.

Programmers (Figure 11.11)   This category represents all members of the team who are involved in processes concerned with constructing the behaviour of the system. This includes designing interaction and interfaces, the production of controllers for different sorts of media, general navigation development, core algorithms within the system, and interaction with other software packages as required. In a large project this may be a huge and diverse team with very different skills so it should not be assumed that they can be treated as an entity where each participant understands all the others. Communication within this group must be managed.

Asset producers   This role encompasses everyone engaged in the production of media content. Some of this will be computer-based activities such as digital video editing, sound construction, or converting things to appropriate formats for delivery in the media and on the platforms which have been specified for the product. Other aspects include every part of the production process. In this model, if we are using symphonic music, the whole orchestra is part of the team of asset producers. Equally with film, producer, director, actors, scriptwriters, etc. are all part of our asset producers. It should be apparent that there is a vastly diverse range of skills in this category which needs to be carefully managed.

Project manager The project manager is given a project and groups of developers with which to work, and somehow has to ensure that a process is followed through resulting in a product built to the specification and satisfying the client needs within the time specified and within budget. All sorts of problems are bound to arise even on the best planned projects, and the project manager has a central role in overcoming these problems and ensuring successful Interactive Multimedia solutions. Project management processes are discussed further in Chapter 13.

We have considered client interaction, specification processes, and implementation and development. An essential component of a successful project that we have omitted is evaluation and testing. This is the subject of a separate section in a later chapter, but for the moment we can note the need for project participants in both roles.

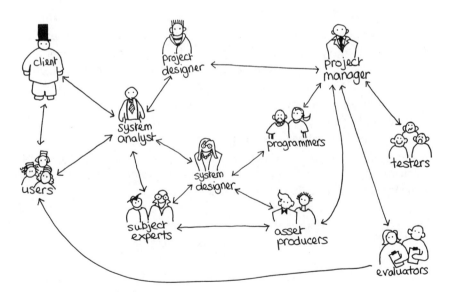

Figure 11.12 Players picture 7.

Testers (Figure 11.12) Generally these people are closely linked to the project team and engage in basic validation of the product and its components as they are developed. This includes checking for reliability, or searching for end-user bugs, ensuring that the product meets the specification, etc. On the whole, these testing processes are often precise and can be carried out from a reasonable scientific base. This testing is normally internal to the development team and concerns issues which are not of relevance to the client (but would just be assumed to be correct).

Evaluators   Rather than simply testing whether the product meets specification or is reliable, the process of evaluation is concerned with the extent to which it satisfies the needs of the user group. Evaluators may be used to examine small features of the system during development (e.g. does this menu structure work better than that menu structure) and also be used once development is complete to evaluate the system overall and ensure that it meets the required needs when deployed with the client organization. Typically evaluators are a mixture of individuals working close to the development team and representatives of the user group taken from the client company or similar user groups.

11.3   Communication

11.3.1   Why is communication important?

This chapter has emphasized the large number of people who are involved, either directly or indirectly, in the development of an Interactive Multimedia system. This has included a broad range of people on the development team, and a range of people from the client organization. We have distinguished primary client, stakeholders, and users. With all these people involved at one level or another in the development and use of our Interactive Multimedia system, it is essential that we make sure that everybody within this process has access to whatever information they may require about the system, and a voice which enables them to communicate to others about the system. Someone within the development team should take responsibility for this activity (often the project manager) and ensure that information flow is co-ordinated so that all relevant players see the things they need to see and (equally important) cannot see the things that they do not need to see.

It is important to deal with two aspects of this question: what an individual needs to see, and the form in which that communication should occur.

11.3.2   Who are you talking to?

We can distinguish five different relationships between the individual and piece of information. A piece of information may have the status for an individual of:

- must see;
- beneficial to see;
- neutral to see;
- detrimental to see;
- must not see.

It is fairly clear that the first and most important step in the commun-ication process is to ensure that everyone who must see a certain piece of information gets to see it. It is equally important to ensure that people who must not see certain information cannot see it, although there tends to be less information of this category.

Once these two extreme categories have been dealt with, there is flexibility in the interpretation of the other categories. A poor manager of information will simply ensure that every member of the project receives all the shared information. This makes the project less efficient because the whole team is spending time sifting through the same information in order to determine what is relevant. Instead, the information manager should have a clear view of the roles in the project and the information inputs and outputs associated with the roles. This manager should then be able to categorize each piece of information according to who should see it and we have reached the 'important' or 'for information only'. Many projects also include security levels so that when a person receives a piece of information they also note with whom they can and cannot discuss it. Communication does not, of course, proceed entirely through an essential information manager; it includes not only paper communications (or e-mail) but also casual conversations by the coffee machine, discussions, and conversations in restaurants, etc. As a consequence it is unlikely that the information in a project can ever be completely and effectively managed – all one can hope for is that the information manager will achieve the best result possible within the given constraints.

Having determined what information a particular individual needs to see, we also need to remember that these people are different. In the case of Interactive Multimedia projects we are dealing with a team of developers who have widely different skills and experiences, and sets of stakeholders who have vastly differing levels of understanding of the issues raised by the project. Consequently it is very important that when the information is communicated it is done so in a form which is appropriate to the particular individual who is the intended recipient. This involves explicitly thinking about things such as the different languages used by the various committees involved in the project. Graphic designers and programmers may use the same words to mean very different things, for example. Clients often think they understand terms on occasions when the definition that they use habitually is entirely at odds with that of the development team. It is important to always ensure that these exchanges are clear and that misunderstandings are avoided. Many of the diagrammatic techniques that we have introduced earlier in the book can be extremely valuable as a method of communicating among these disparate team members.

11.3.3 Legal, formal and informal communications

In addition to the differing status of information discussed above, there is a more formal and legal aspect to be considered. The development and delivery process is subject to the normal laws of contract and the day-to-day relationship with the client may result in the team accidentally making commitments which could be legally taken to be contractual obligations. To prevent this happening, it is important that the project should distinguish between several different categories of communication between client and development team. There will be certain communications that are legally binding documents. These usually include a project contract (of which a product specification is probably a part) and some sort of document signifying acceptance of the final product. It is highly advisable to ensure that these documents are prepared, or at least approved, by someone with relevant legal expertise. The issues surrounding software law are not currently taught as part of the general law qualification, so the selection of an appropriate legal representative is important. There are a number of books in this area, including books of template contracts that one can use for various parts of the process.

A second level involves formal communication between the team and the clients which is not required to go through legal channels. This will often include things such as monitoring and progress reports, and notifications of modifications or changes to the product design and project plan. It is quite important to get any change such as this agreed with the client and communicated in writing such that there is a record of the modifications that remain. These may be useful in the case of a dispute at a later stage.

Anything that does not come into the above categories can be referred to as informal communication. As a developer, it is normally the case that you try and retain the informal communications within the team and avoid informal contact with the client. Information communicated through informal channels has a potential to be very damaging to the project.

As a final point it is worth noting that written documentation of the phases within the project is extremely important. The following chapter will return to this issue once we have explored our design process in greater detail.

11.4 Exercises

Exercise 11.1 Consider a pub game played as part of a league (e.g. darts, pool). Who are the stakeholders involved in this league? Categorize each as Primary, Secondary, Tertiary or Facilitating.

Exercise 11.2 Consider this book as a product. Who are the stakeholders that had to be considered in writing and publishing this book? Categorize them as in Exercise 11.1.

Exercise 11.3 Imagine that you are required to develop a website to provide weather reports for skiing holiday areas throughout the world. Identify and categorize all the stakeholders.

Exercise 11.4 Identify a multimedia product that you might build (e.g. a tourist information site, a sales support system). Write a short description of the product. Identify all the roles that would need to be fulfilled within a project in order to successfully develop this product.

11.5 Further reading

Essential issues in the way organizations operate as entities:
Derek Rollinson, Aysen Broadfield and David J. Edwards, *Organisational behaviour and analysis*, Addison-Wesley, 1998

Paul E. Spector, *Industrial and organizational psychology: research and practice*, John Wiley and Sons, 1995

Many of the techniques in this chapter are related to the field of Soft Systems:
Peter Checkland and Jim Scholes, *Soft systems methodology in action*, John Wiley and Sons, 1999

Teamworking is increasingly important:
Susan Cartwright and Andrew Gale (Eds), *Effective teamworking in the project management environment*, Tudor Business Publishing Ltd, 1995

12
Product design processes

12.1 Standard design processes

In the previous chapter we identified several different approaches to the design of artefacts in different disciplines. From the arts area, we discussed the isolated developer, which emphasizes creativity and personal expression, and the significance that this will play in most works, particularly in the field of fine art. We also identified the design processes which lead to the production of an artefact for a client which, while still artistically and creatively based, have a much more tangible process to ensure meeting outcomes. This approach is commonly used in graphic design. We also discussed those occasions on which people from the arts background might work together as a team rather than in isolation.

From the perspective of computing, we identified the innovators who tend to work in isolation and in defiance of convention. We explored the way in which the products from these pockets of creativity are gradually brought into mainstream development. We concluded by identifying the very structured and organized processes that are utilized in the development of a commercial piece of computing software. This includes a range of formal and mathematical techniques which can be used to identify needs, specify solutions, and implement them.

Given the perspective that we have taken upon multimedia in this book, it is apparent that none of these design methodologies are appropriate for building a multimedia system. The artefact which we are seeking to design and produce has, as its main purpose, kinds of communication to human beings which are not necessarily a key part of traditional computing software. It also requires a level of precision and clarity of design which are untypical in the arts-based methodologies. Although none of the existing methodologies can be adopted wholesale, they can all contribute to multimedia development. There are two additional factors which imply that a new design process must be used: the need for an interdisciplinary team, and the user-centred nature of the design process. The following section will discuss these two aspects in greater detail, before going on to outline a design methodology for multimedia based upon the concepts introduced in earlier chapters.

12.2   Issues for multimedia

12.2.1   The interdisciplinary requirement

This book has skimmed over the surface of a wide range of topics: issues in communication theory, user modelling, knowledge representation, linguistics, human–computer interaction, artificial intelligence, semiotics, the theories of sound and text, various approaches to still images, and film theory. In each one of these areas there exists a huge body of expertise and technique, and any one individual could easily spend his or her entire working career concentrating on just one small aspect of one of these areas. From that basis, it would be unbelievably egotistical for any single individual to believe that he or she could carry out the whole process of design and development of an interactive multimedia system. In the same way that production of a high-quality feature-length film will require a large number of people with differing areas of expertise, we must acknowledge that multimedia systems are not the domain of the single, isolated developer. Every successful multimedia system must be the product of a team working together to achieve joint goals. Furthermore, this team will necessarily be multidisciplinary. Having several graphic designers working together on one project may be fraught with competition and internecine wars; having several programmers working on a project together will also become impossible unless they are organized so that there is a clear demarcation of responsibility. In each of these cases the members of the teams at least speak the same language and are able to interact with each other. In a team for multimedia projects, we are taking members of different disciplines and trying to form a coherent operational group out of them. The most significant problem is that of communication between the different areas of expertise. This is one of the reasons that this book has introduced so many different fields. To be a genuine multimedia developer, you must be capable of operating within such an interdisciplinary group. To do this you must at least understand superficially what each other team member does and the value of their contribution to the overall product. If you are starting from a basis in which the graphic design team is describing the programmers as 'visually illiterate' or the programmers describe the graphics team as 'wishy-washy posers' (note – these phrases are much more polite than the ones you normally hear), then you are starting from the wrong place. Each member of the team must value the input of other members of the team if the process is to work. In our design model we incorporate a significant number of mechanisms to ensure adequate communication between these differing groups.

12.2.2 User-centred design

For those who read the earlier part of the book it should be redundant to state that the user must be central to our design process. We have chosen to identify communicative interaction as the central point in any interactive multimedia system. This aspect alone makes the systems significantly different from anything that has previously existed in either the artistic or the computing communities. This interaction requires communication with users and any judgement of its effectiveness must depend upon how effective the system is with the users. The basis of any design process must be an understanding of the users' needs, skills, and abilities. The centrality of the role that the concept of language has played in preceding chapters is another aspect of the significance that we attribute to communication within the system design.

The phrase 'user-centred design' has existed for some time in the computing community. It was originally introduced to emphasize the difference between approaches which make particular use of the techniques of human–computer interaction, and approaches based on formal specification and definition of algorithms. We will adopt it as the keystone of our design methodology.

12.2.3 Interaction

We have identified *processes of interaction* and the development of the *multimedia content* as different aspects of the design and production of a multimedia system. They are not really clearly separable, but interact in a rich manner with each component informing the other. From the point of view of the design process we must identify a starting point, and we have chosen to make this the design of the overall interaction. By establishing a framework for interaction we can begin to identify the sorts of knowledge content that we will be using and hence the sorts of assets that we may require. Involving potential producers of those media assets may then cause us to refine our general structure for the interaction, and certainly have an effect on how we develop the details of the interaction further. In the proposed design methodology it will be apparent that a high-level framework of the interaction and the details of interaction are kept separate for precisely this reason.

12.2.4 Media assets

The media assets are not quite like anything that exists in any other field. They must have various attributes appropriate to communicate their intended content to a human being, but must also be compatible with the interaction and the constraints that the computer puts upon the context in which they will be used. If, for example, we develop a piece of media to explain what a microphone is, then we can establish a knowledge content and a mechanism for communicating that to the human. The way that this is done must depend upon how the piece will be used in the overall interaction. If we can assume that our users will have learnt the terminology of sound, then we can teach it in one particular way. If we can assume that they have not met these prerequisites, then we can teach it differently.

In many multimedia designs it is quite plausible that we will be unable to tell for any given user whether or not they have previously learnt about sound, and hence we will have the additional complication of trying to deal with all possible contexts in the design of our assets. These complications can only be resolved by maintaining a close communication between those members of the team designing assets, and those designing interactions.

It is also important to remember that there are many different sorts of media assets with different sorts of constraints upon them, and we have to allow for the vagaries of the traditional approaches and methodologies in each of these areas. We cannot suddenly force film directors to completely change the way that they work because on this one occasion they are part of a multimedia project. It is necessary to try and get them to adapt, and to make concessions ourselves to their normal way of working.

A final constraint that we must be very careful about is the importance of copyright in the development of multimedia systems. Computer code is normally originated by the participants in the project, as are works of a fairly pure 'artistic' nature. Graphic designers are more used to working with a certain amount of copyright material mixed in with the original components. It is absolutely essential that we identify the copyright origin of any multimedia asset that is not uniquely originated by the project team, and obtain appropriate rights. Even when assets are created by the team, the copyright may not be freely available. Photographs taken in museums often require copyright permission from the owners of the museum, and there is some suggestion in France that the architect of a public building should own the copyright of all photographs which are ever taken of that building, even if they are just holiday snaps!

From these general issues we will now turn to a specific way to approach the design of multimedia systems.

12.3   Categories of multimedia systems

The overall purpose of this book is to encourage readers to think in an innovative and creative manner about the nature of interactive multimedia systems and to come up with their own novel and effective solutions to problems. While wishing to encourage this creativity, we must also acknowledge that there are certain approaches to developing multimedia systems which are commonly used within the industry, and which we must understand. It is often easy to recognize the tools that have been used to produce a system by the behaviour of the resulting system: developers permit themselves to be controlled by the technology rather than taking control of technology. We should understand these models and approaches, and use them where appropriate, but we should not be constrained by them, or to the things that a specific tool makes easy.

Many of the tools discussed in this section can be made to operate in a wide variety of manners. In practice, however, they are often restricted to being used for the things that appear to be simplest irrespective of whether this is the appropriate way to solve the problem or meet the needs of the client and users. In each tool examined we need to remember that some things will be easy to do and others will be harder (while some will be impossible). Do not constrain your design thinking by what is easy to implement.

We will consider four categories: flow-based, hyper-based, object-based, and agent-based systems. This is a sequence of increasing power and complexity.

12.3.1   Flow-based systems

As we have seen in the earlier chapters, the original computers were not designed to support interaction. They were provided with a set of data and a program run upon that data. When they had completed the program they returned the results. Because this is the way in which the computers were used, models of computing evolved which were based upon the idea of a flow of control through a program from a beginning point to an end point. When the first interactive systems began to appear, they continued to apply this idea of flow. This approach was reinforced in the 1960s when various people (notably B. F. Skinner) developed an approach to teaching and learning which was called 'programmed learning'. This model, based upon behaviourist models of learning, implied that an appropriate teaching methodology was to provide people with information in small pieces, repeatedly testing whether they have understood those pieces and either going back to reteach and reinforce them or going on to the next piece of information. This technique seemed admirably suited to the computers of this time and was applied, first to specialist 'teaching machines', and then to general-purpose computer programs for teaching by this method. It led specifically to the development of 'authoring languages' upon which most of the flow-based multimedia tools of today are still constructed, though they have changed little since the 1960s.

We will categorize flow-based systems in terms of the sorts of deviation that can be made from a simple linear path from beginning to end.

12.3.1.1 Linear models

Linear models are one of the most frequently used approaches to multimedia. Systems designed in this manner have a starting point, an ending point, and a single sequence of events that can happen between these two points (Figure 12.1). The experience for any user of the system is identical. Obvious examples of systems of this kind are films, radio plays, and slide shows. Note that these examples are of individual recognized media, rather than being the novel combinations of channels which we have chosen to call multimedia. This is one of the reasons that we are so familiar with them, and that they are so easy to reproduce – we know the language by which to interpret them.

Figure 12.1   Linear flow.

To move from single media into multimedia using linear systems requires a novel combination of various channels of communication. These channels may be turned on and off at different times, but they are all synchronized. This means that the interpretation of the combinations of channels is also intended to be fixed. The use of slide walls which combine multiple projectors with audio communications may be considered as a multimedia experience in this respect. A more recent and innovative example is the use in certain television programmes (especially children's music TV) of devices analogical to computer interfaces. A band may be seen playing upon the screen, while a scrolling banner across the bottom congratulates people who have birthdays today, and things like popup windows appear at the sides of the picture giving information about the band and about what is coming up later in the programme. This is a rich use of communication channels and, because of the novelty effect, would have to be described as *multimedia* at present. It is not, however, interactive.

Linear systems inherently restrict the sorts of interaction that can happen. In a delivered system, such as a film in a cinema or a programme transmitted on television, there is no opportunity whatsoever for interaction. The observer is purely a recipient of pre-packaged information. Other delivery mechanisms can permit a simple level of physical interaction. A slide-show presentation upon a computer can provide 'previous' and 'next' buttons. These can be thought of as *pacing* controls which allow the user to pause at various points and digest information but only give them physical control over the media at a very simple level. There is an alternative type of physical control which is possible with the linear systems and which enables a different sort of interaction: the *random access* control. These controls are typified by the panels we see on videotape recorders or on CD players. As well as a simple stop/start control of the physical medium the user is able to access directly into different points in the medium. This is still not communicative interaction, but a simple physical level of manipulation of the medium. It is no different in principle from flicking through to page 242 of a paper book.

So, is communicative interaction possible with these systems? No! In order for communicative interaction to occur the system must be able to use responses from the user and apply them to some form of decision-making process about what it is communicating. Since these systems cannot change their content, and always provide the same experience for each user, the communication is all in one direction and hence communicative interaction cannot occur.

Tools of the trade A very obvious category of tools which can be used to produce linear multimedia are the animation packages. Simple tools such as *GifBuilder*, *GIF construction set*, and *Web Painter* (Figure 12.2) all apply a traditional model of frame-by-frame animation to computer-based delivery. The author constructs a set of frames to be displayed in sequence. Controls allow the determination of the amount of time that each frame is visible on the screen and whether the overall animation has a start and end point or is a continuous loop. Since these tools operate only within the visual modality, they cannot be used alone to produce a multimedia experience. More sophisticated animation tools allow the incorporation of communications in the auditory modality and hence are likely to permit such approaches. Quite sophisticated packages (e.g. Director) may include animation on a frame-by-frame basis as one of the models within a richer tapestry of multimedia techniques. You should also bear in mind, that frame-based approaches are only one sort of animation.

In a similar manner, video-editing tools are intended to produce normal linear experiences, although they are typically richer in the range of media that they can control. Output is, none the less, a simple linear structure.

While the above categories of tools borrow heavily from traditional media, there is now an extremely common form of linear multimedia software: the presentation tool. Tools designed to produce slide shows and presentations (e.g. Astound, PowerPoint) were originally specialist

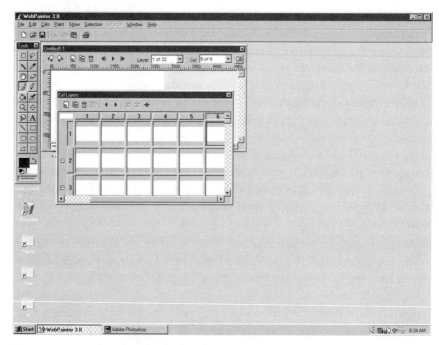

Figure 12.2   A screenshot of Web Painter.

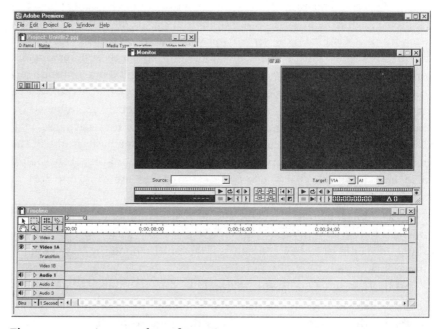

Figure 12.3   A screenshot of Premiere.

software for paper publishing intended to facilitate the creation of a series of printed transparencies that could be used upon an overhead projector. With the proliferation of personal computers, laptop machines, and portable television projectors, the option to present directly from a computer, and hence to include interaction and multimedia, became available.

A typical presentation tool is based around the model of a sequence of 'slides' which can be thought of as equivalent to the frames in an animation package (Figure 12.4). The major difference is that they are not intended to be used at high speed to give an impression of movement, and that the idea of some form of basic physical interaction is inherent within them. Slides are organized in a sequence from beginning to end and the standard interaction is a key press to indicate 'next slide'. In addition, it is now common to have features within a single slide which build up in sequence: often bulleted points of text. The same key is used to indicate that the next point should be displayed. This physical interaction may be under the control of a presenter who is working alongside the materials (such as in a lecturing situation) or users may use

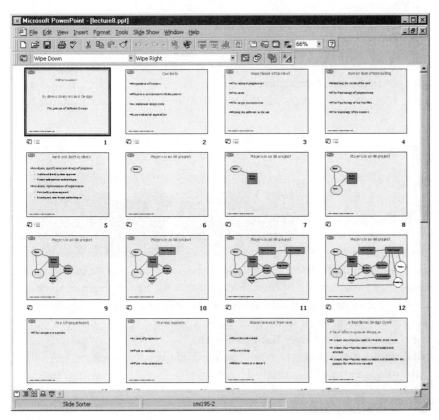

Figure 12.4   A screenshot of PowerPoint.

these keys to progress through the presentation at their own pace. This latter situation will obviously require a different design of content. A third option in most packages is a 'loop' mode in which no interaction is possible and the show simply displays the various points and slides at a given pace.

Most modern presentation packages now permit the incorporation of a wide variety of computer-based media within the presentation so that sound, video, graphics, etc. can be combined using one of these tools, although they are not normally originated within the tool itself. In an earlier chapter we distinguished between the *media content* of the system and the *control mechanism* which makes that content accessible to the user. Presentation tools provide a very clear example of this distinction since they can be used to integrate media from a variety of other sources and packages into a single multimedia experience. Some of the more recent packages include a fairly sophisticated facility for extending them through the construction of programs within the package. This enables the author to go beyond the basic interaction styles permitted by the tools but is often time consuming – it is generally more efficient to choose a more powerful tool for the job that supports a greater variety of models.

12.3.2 Linear alternate models

There is a model which is used in multimedia systems with remarkable frequency, but which is rarely discussed and does not have a generally accepted name. I have chosen to refer to this as the 'linear alternate' model (Figure 12.5). As with the simple linear model, these systems have

Figure 12.5   Linear alternative.

a starting point and an ending point. The difference is that at various points along the path there may be alternative pieces of content. This means that the experience of the system may be different for different users even though they travel along the same general path. Although there may be a number of branch points at which the system or user may choose between several alternative presentations there are only ever a very small number of alternatives for a given stage in the system and they always lead the user back to the 'main path'. This restriction on the total number of alternatives and on the lack of back tracking (repeating various segments of material) derives partly from the desire to limit the number of alternatives because of cost, and partly because the systems have historically been implemented through media which do not permit back tracking.

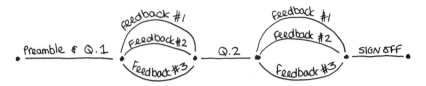

Figure 12.6   Node/segment diagram.

Structures such as this can be illustrated with a diagram as shown in Figure 12.6.

In this picture the various points (or *nodes*) represent positions where selections of alternative content can be made (either by computer or user), and the links between these nodes (read from left to right) each represent one alternate piece of content at that point. There is no need to indicate direction since the system is linear so links from right to left cannot occur.

A clear example of this might be in a teaching package intended to initiate the user into some general facility such as a spreadsheet. Although most of the sequence of presentation, the explanations and descriptions will be identical for all users, at some points, such as when providing examples, the author may decide to provide alternatives for different user groups. An instance would be giving examples of calculating averages of a column of figures. This might be done with rainfall figures for geographers, response times for psychologists, stress tests for engineers, etc. These are clearly alternative presentations of the same piece of material. A similar variation is found in the use of 'learning styles' which claim that some people prefer learning through *definitions*, some through *examples*, some in *abstract* terms, some in *concrete* terms, etc. A linear alternate approach to teaching based upon this might ask the learner to select one of the styles at the beginning of the interaction and will then choose a specific set of material related to that style.

The point about the physical medium is that prior to cheap computing, linear alternative systems could be constructed through more traditional mechanisms. One of my favourites is the TOMY XL-2 teaching robot, which achieves this using cassette tapes (Figure 12.7). This machine talks to the users and asks questions to which they respond by pressing one of four buttons. The robot tells them whether they have the right answer, provides them with some feedback, and may tell an occasional joke, before going on to the next question. All the questions are the same independent of your previous responses. There are always four different sorts of feedback after each question depending upon the response. This is achieved by the simple mechanism of recording four different tracks onto a cassette tape, which progress from the beginning to the end of the educational material. All tracks have the

Figure 12.7   TOMY robot.

same questions recorded at the same time points. The gap in between the questions is used for feedback, and the jokes help to fill in the spaces when some pieces of feedback are shorter than others. The four buttons for answers simply select which of the four tracks on the cassette you are listening to. This seems remarkably simple, but it can be quite powerful, and if you examine existing multimedia software you find that it is a model used with remarkable frequency.

The interaction is obviously fairly limited, with a simple user choice of switching between several streams. The switch does not take account of previous choices made by the user, so each decision point is independent. Nevertheless, with careful design of the content, it is possible to make the choice of the user a meaningful one, and to achieve a simple form of communicative interaction in this context.

Tools of the trade   Approaches like this can be constructed with almost any basic system. Many of the supposedly 'sophisticated' multimedia systems which are developed using tools such as Macromedia Director or Authorware turn out to be no more sophisticated than the simple robot when you remove the superficial gloss and get down to the basic functionality. This sort of branching has typically been used in simple interactive media technologies such as interactive videodisc. More recently, it has become the standard sort of authoring which is used with DVD, although more sophisticated things are possible.

12.3.2.1 Branching models

The third major category of flow-based system is the one that is most commonly associated with computer-assisted learning. This approach is embodied directly in a class of tools known as 'authoring environments' which provide graphical mechanisms for constructing programs in an 'authoring language'. These approaches are derived from the 1960s, but have their roots in techniques of software design which predated even the first computers. As Figure 12.8 shows, these systems retain the idea of a start point and an end point, they embody the idea of providing alternative pieces of content, and they also enable the program to 'jump' forward or backward to any point within the sequence of available materials. This is only possible when using computer-based media rather

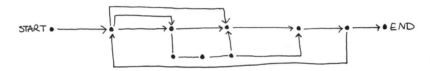

Figure 12.8   General branching diagram.

than more conventional types. Operating in this manner means that a single piece of content may potentially be used in multiple *contexts* because different users may come to it from different locations within the program. Depending upon their responses the program might jump forwards, backwards, or sideways to introduce new material or repeat material. This is the first type of system we have come across where material may be reused in multiple contexts in this manner, and it has a significant effect upon how we design the content.

Branching CAL (Computer Assisted Learning) was originally implemented using general-purpose computing languages. After some time it was realized that many of the features of these languages were not required for the simple presentation task, whereas special features related to the screens of content needed to be added. This resulted in a class of programming languages which are generally known as 'authoring languages'. These languages are typically a numbered sequence of statements which go from the beginning to an end but which permit flow of control to be passed under certain circumstances to other parts of the program – a 'jump' (Figure 12.9). The original languages designed for

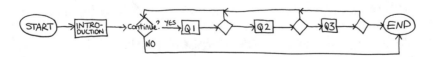

Figure 12.9   Flow-chart diagram.

```
draw        50,20;50,200;300,200;50,20
at          100,120
write       What sort of triangle is this?
arrow       100,100
answer      right
            That's right, it's right
wrong       acute
            Look for 90 degree angles
endarrow
```

Figure 12.10   CMU tutor code.

this purpose looked remarkably similar to certain early dialects of BASIC. An example of such language is shown in Figure 12.10.

As a new audience began to use presentation techniques based around branching CAL, it became apparent that non-programmers were beginning to use the packages. The manufacturers responded to this by developing a class of systems known as 'authoring environments' which provide the user with a graphical interface that makes it easy to produce code in the underlying authoring language. Although they have been around for many years, some tools in this class are still comparatively popular (e.g. Authorware).

These tools all provide an interface which utilizes a special graphical language which was developed to describe flow of control: flow charts. For most purposes we only need the four symbols illustrated in Figure 12.11 on our charts.

The oval represents the beginning or stopping point(s) of a program. The rectangle represents processes to be carried out, and the diamond represents a decision point at which the computer branches. The parallelogram represents input to, or output from, the process. These symbols are connected by arrows representing the flow of control from

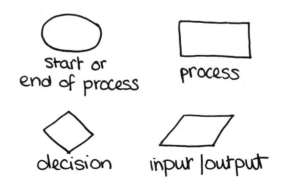

Figure 12.11   Flowchart symbol examples.

one place to another in the diagram. A start obviously only has an arrow coming out of it, and a stop only has an arrow going into it. A process may have several arrows arriving at it, but can only have one leaving. Only the diamond has multiple arrows leaving it, to represent the different outcomes of a decision.

In the interface of a typical modern package, these flow charts would appear as shown in Figure 12.12.

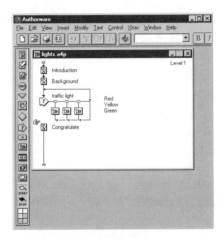

Figure 12.12   Screenshot of Authorware.

The flow model is used as a direct analogy for the construction of the program. The user drags shapes from a palette of tools and they are automatically linked into a line from beginning to end. Each of these symbols can then be edited via dialogue boxes to complete the details for the assets to include, decisions to take, etc.

In linear alternate systems there are a small number of choices at each branching point in the segment and these choices ultimately lead the learner back on to the same main path from the beginning to the end of the system (Figure 12.13). Consequently, although no two learners may have the same experience of using the package, they should all have an equivalent experience in terms of the coverage from beginning to end. While this involves the production of additional material which may never be seen by certain students, it does limit the amount of such material that is available: if there are four alternatives at each point then writing a linear alternate programme will involve four times as much work as writing a simple linear piece. In general, for a piece which is N segments long with M alternatives in each segment, a total of $N \times M$ segments will need to be produced.

By contrast, a branching system which does not restrict its options has very different properties. In the first place, while there is a common

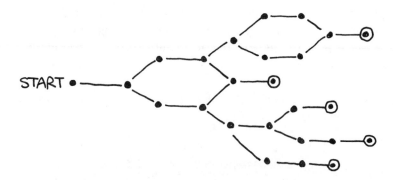

Figure 12.13   Branching diagram 1.

start point, there may not be a common end point. Second, there is no guarantee that each user will see all the content or have equivalent learning experiences: whether this happens depends upon the specific design. Consequently, it is extremely easy to produce very bad branching systems. An additional problem is that of potential combinatorial explosion. In a linear alternate system there are only a small number of pieces of material at each segment point and that choice is independent of the previous responses by the user. By comparison, the true branching system can support many different alternatives for each of the combinations of options taken by the student earlier in the progression. In the worst case this may require the production of *NM* alternative pieces of material. As can be seen in Figure 12.14, this quickly becomes astronomically expensive in time and money and so there are very few systems which utilize this sort of branching potential. Most systems have some level of complexity between a linear alternate system and a fully fledged branching system where each alternative is unique. Because of this sharing of material, the systems can generally be drawn as a network of interconnected interactions (Figure 12.15).

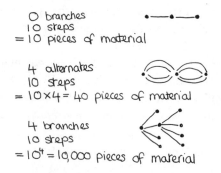

Figure 12.14   Tree model of a system and combinatorial explosions
10×1, 10×4 and 10^4.

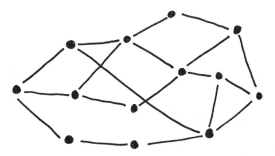

Figure 12.15 Network model of a system.

Tools of the trade Happily, flow-based authoring tools are now dying out. The restrictions that they placed on the interactive design were too great to support sophisticated developments. The most popular now is probably Macromedia Authorware, although Iconauthor still exists, and there are a number of freeware or shareware tools available.

12.3.3 Hyper-based systems

The most striking thing about hyper-based systems (hypertexts and hypermedia) is that they seek to remove the computer from the decision-making process about the interaction. The basic idea behind these systems is to provide the users with a rich array of links, which they can pursue in order to fulfil their interaction with the machine. This is a valid approach which can be very useful in certain situations but which can also be badly misused. Careful design is just as important with these systems as with other models.

Hypertext has really come into its own as a key mechanism for interaction during the 1990s due to the proliferation of the world-wide web. It began to become a popular form of development for multimedia systems in general and educational systems in particular during the 1980s. This was mostly because of a package called *HyperCard* on the Apple Macintosh and a variety of similar tools such as *SuperCard* and *ToolBook*. The origins of hypertext, however, are in the 1960s with the work of Ted Nelson on project Xanadu (Figure 12.16). In this work Nelson went beyond the technology available at the time and imagined that there would be a world of information based around the connections between documents. If you were browsing a document and came across a quote, you should be able to click on it to go directly to the text from which it was taken. Similarly you should be able to see the previous versions, follow references, and so on. It is interesting to remember that at the time that this was envisaged no one imagined the proliferation of computers or the idea of a personal PC. Instead, the keen hypertext user would go to a booth on the street corner not unlike a telephone booth (called a SilverStand) where there would be terminals

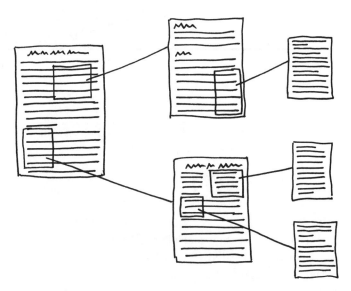

Figure 12.16   Traditional Xanadu style hypertext.

with human guides to help you navigate this gigantic connected document.

The model proposed by Nelson is interesting from a historical perspective, but is significantly different from what is referred to as a hypertext today. There are two major differences: the *content* and the *links*.

At the time when Xanadu was envisaged, computers only supported text-based interfaces and consequently the view was literally of a hypertext – no pictures, diagrams, sounds, or other media. It was also anticipated that there would be a very small set of standardized links which indicated things such as 'go to the document from which this is a quote' or 'show me the previous version of this paragraph'. In current systems, where the terms *hypertext* and *hypermedia* are used almost interchangeably, the content has gone far beyond the original vision. The things that are being linked together are now complex documents, which may contain many media and have individual behaviours of their own. The implications of this will be explored when we consider object-based systems.

With regard to links, it is now the case that there be many different sorts of links within a system. They can be indicated in different ways and have different meanings. One of the important aspects of modern hypermedia design is to communicate effectively with the user through these links.

Before going further we should note that a standard and very useful way to depict a hypertext is as a diagram showing a network of interconnected nodes (Figure 12.17). Each node in the diagram

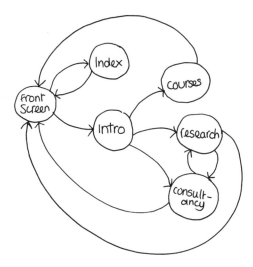

Figure 12.17 Node and link diagram.

represents some object which contains hyperlinks to others: a simple text screen is the most obvious idea, but they could be graphics, animations, etc. In this diagram we effectively ignore the content of the node and concern ourselves only with where one can go from that point. Consequently, a node has one or more lines going from it to other nodes which indicate the possibility of the user following that path by clicking upon any link. The total number of lines connected to any node indicates the total number of links to and from that point. We will use diagrammatic notation throughout the rest of the discussion, but it should be borne in mind that there are two notable limitations upon it. First, the real hypertext is liable to be extremely complex and complete diagrams such as this become both extremely difficult to draw and highly uninformative. The second point is that it ignores any complex structure within a node and makes it difficult to represent complex screen objects.

12.3.3.1 What's in a link?
As has been explained earlier, one of the great hopes that authors had for the use of hypertext was that it would put the burden of deciding where to go and what to look at upon the user. The hope was that this would avoid the decision making by the computer which occurs in flow-based systems and make the implementation much simpler. This *would* be the case if constructing a hypertext was simply a matter of getting a load of information and sticking lots of links in-between it. Unfortunately, if we do this then we quickly find that our users become overloaded with information, unable to determine where they are or where they need to go, frustrated, and extremely angry. This is the phenomenon known as being 'lost in hyperspace'. To avoid this problem requires exceptionally

careful design, and much of the emphasis of that design must be in the appropriate organization of content and construction of meaningful and helpful links.

A link may possess certain *attributes* which control its behaviour and certain *appearances* which determine how what it does is communicated to the user of the system. The major attributes that we will consider are the *name*, *type*, and *directionality*.

- **Name.** A name is something that uniquely identifies a particular link to the user. It may be textual such as 'my dog' or it may use any of the semiotic communication processes we have discussed such as iconic representation. It is intended to tell the users precisely what they will find if they follow this link. Not all links require names, but it is very important to understand whether such a thing is necessary either as a communication device to the user or as an organizational device for the computer (e.g. to permit searching for links by name).

- **Type.** The type of a link indicates the class of links to which it belongs. Grouping the links into classes with similar properties is quite important to the usability of the system, but is remarkably infrequent among current hypertext designs. The idea is that you identify a certain number of *types* (or *classes*) of links that are going to be important in your system and assign them consistent behaviours, appearances, etc. This facilitates the design and makes the system much more learnable for the user. A simple example would be the 'home' link. If your hypertext has a *home* page then you may put links to that home page in many different places: the links themselves are all distinct (and may or may not be named) but they are all of the same type − e.g. a 'return to the home page' link. In this case they would normally be depicted with identical graphics and would not typically require a name. Similarly, previous and next links are each members of particular classes. Each next link will go to somewhere different, but conceptually it represents the continuation of content from the page on which the link is placed. This means that together they constitute a class of links of this type and may well be consistently depicted by a single symbol such as a right arrow. We can pursue this usage of types to a greater degree and an educational system, for example, might use distinct classes of link to indicate *explanations, definitions, examples, exercises, greater detail, summary sections*, etc. It should be apparent that designing the link types will have a major impact on our hypertext.

- **Directionality.** In our previous diagrams we have not discussed whether or not links are reversible. Because there is a link from A to B, is there a link from B to A? If there is a link in both directions, does it mean the same thing in each direction or something different depending upon which way it is followed? We will refer to links as unidirectional or bi-directional, and within bi-directional links will distinguish symmetrical and asymmetrical. These terms have the following meaning:

- **Unidirectional:** the link goes from A to B but not in the reverse direction. We will indicate this with an arrow head, pointing from A to B.

- **Bi-directional symmetrical:** there is a link between two things that can be followed in either direction, and it means the same thing in each direction: examples might be 'similar', 'sounds like', or 'cousin of'. We can indicate these links either by putting two arrow heads going in opposite directions, or by omitting the arrow heads altogether. (But be consistent in which you choose to do!)

- **Bi-directional asymmetrical:** these links imply that there is a relationship which can be followed in either direction between two nodes, but that it has a different meaning in each direction and those meanings are related in some manner. Consequently, while depicting these links in the same graphical form, they will normally have a double type to indicate their dual nature in the different directions. Examples might be 'mother–daughter', 'more detail–less detail' or 'up–down'.

12.3.3.2 Models of hypertexts

Flow-based systems tend to constrain the author to particular models of structure and organization. Because hypertext is much more open-ended it is very easy to produce a complete mess. Bear in mind that this text should be understood by the user immediately and naturally. This objective means that consistent and coherent design is extremely important for effective hypertext. An essential part in achieving this is to develop and apply consistent models of navigation within the hypertext.

In the terms that we are discussing here, a *model* consists of a consistent organization of the materials that the user can acquire. By learning this model the users should be able to predict where they need to go to find things that they wish to find. It is possible to mix several models within one system, but this should only be done with caution and it must be made very clear to the users exactly which models they are using. If you do not have a model underlying your hypertext system then it is highly likely that it will be ineffective and frustrating for users. The following are some examples of models:

- **Linear:** hardly worth calling a hypertext, but this consists of a set of nodes each of which is connected to *one* other. The links are typically reversible and correspond to 'the next' or something similar. This is exactly the same as the simplest productions that you can make with a flow-based system and has rather less functionality than a paper-based book. Constructing an entire system based around this model is a pointless exercise, but it is extremely useful on the occasions when you are trying to communicate some part of the content which has a single specific sequencing component to it. Examples of such potential applications are communicating about *procedures* (where each node represents a separate step in the procedure and the links become 'previous step', 'next step'), or things with a *temporal dimension* such as a list of the kings and queens of England (where the buttons become 'antecedent', 'successor'). In these cases the links clearly do have a valid meaning within the context of the subject. The widely used 'previous page' and 'next page' model normally indicates simply that the author has given no thought whatsoever to the hypertextual issues in the system and has failed to relate the navigation to the meaning.

- **Tree:** the tree model of a hypertext is based on the assumption that there is a single node which has a privileged position (often called the *Home* or *Root*) and that all the information in the system is organized in a hierarchy beneath this starting point. This implies that there are a number of links from this top node to subsidiary nodes, a number from its subsidiary nodes to nodes below that, and so on. In a true tree there is no sharing between different groups of subsidiary nodes: there is only one route through the hierarchy to a given node. This model is very commonly used in Help systems and other structures where all the knowledge organization is hierarchical. A complex procedure, for example, can be explained as a simple list of subprocedures within the top node, and each of these list items will refer to a node which represents the subprocedures within those subprocedures. Another example would be the use of 'further explanation' in educational systems. Using this model the system presents a summary of something that the user should know as a root node. If the users understand the root node then they have finished with the system but if there are parts which they do not understand then they can choose links to take them further down a hierarchy and expand in greater detail on the areas where they have difficulty. Trees are a very commonly used model.

- **Nets:** as soon as several things start pointing to the same node, we have a node that may be shared among different navigation paths and the basic structure of our hypertext has become a network. All hypertexts can be described as a network, but it is useful to try and separate out those bits which can be described as linear or tree structured before examining the parts which *have* to be a network. The fact that something is a network tells us very little except that it is complex. When designing a hypertext we should none the less seek to keep this network structure as systematic and organized as possible. This is generally achieved through sensible use of link types and names in a consistent manner.

12.3.4 Issues of difficulty

The major difficulty with hypertexts arises from the fact that people used to imagine that they were simple; just throw some information into a computer and stick a few links between it. In fact we need to adopt a very careful approach to make a successful and usable hypertext. There are many books devoted to this area. The structure is quite open, so it is flexible enough to produce really innovative structures, but this also allows complete disasters of design to occur. Systems must be designed and tested very carefully.

A second difficulty is that the content may be much harder to design than for other systems. Whereas a flow-based system can be designed so that you know exactly what the user can be expected to have seen by a certain point, and hence write your materials accordingly, a hypertext will permit a lot more variation in user experience and hence requires a special approach to develop appropriately modular segments. This is an extremely complicated thing to do well and is significantly different from anything such as designing a textbook, or scripting a film. It is a skill that we still have not fully mastered, but it has to be learnt. Do not simply assume that you can create assets for hypermedia because you can create them for linear media!

Tools of the trade   Although the idea had been discussed for a number of years, the point at which hypertext became a reality as a mass-delivery mechanism was during the 1980s with the development of *Hypercard* on the Apple Macintosh. This program utilized a metaphor of five-by-three filing cards to try and represent the content of a database. Cards were organized into stacks and there was a special card called the *home*. Graphical authoring tools made it extremely easy to create text and black and white pictures, and make links which would jump from one card to another card. It was originally imagined that this tool would make databases usable by the general public in the same way that word processors have opened up the power of the computer for the desktop office. In fact, Hypercard was taken up widely as a tool for developing educational materials and for rapid prototyping of interfaces. Hypercard subsequently acquired a programming language (HyperTalk) and moved into the realm of object-based authoring tools. Similar tools followed HyperCard, notably Supercard on the Mac and Guide and ToolBook on the PC. The influence of Hypercard is remarkably strong in certain features of Macromedia Director.

These specialized hypertext authoring tools held the market for a little while, but the simplicity of the hypertextual idea meant that various other tools incorporated it in various formats. Many of the presentation tools and flow-based authoring tools discussed in the previous section were enhanced by adding hypertextual features. Of course, this made it much easier for authors to create a complete pig's ear than was previously the case. Presentation systems such as PowerPoint now have more advanced hypertext features than the original HyperCard.

It would not be an understatement to say that hypertext has become the computer interface to the world. The reason is that the world-wide web, which is a phenomenal success story in terms of its uptake, is, of course, a hypertext. It is actually remarkably close to the original ideas of Ted Nelson. What made the web possible was the creation of a standard way of describing hypertextual documents which is not proprietary and is independent of any particular sort of computer. This is HTML (HyperText Markup Language) which, as discussed earlier, is actually a description of a particular type of document in SGML. With HTML the author is freed from any particular tool because it is a public international standard that ensures that hypertextual information is written in simple plain text. The only authoring tool that is required is a text editor. Most web browsers incorporate drag-and-drop authoring tools these days, and there is a wide variety of proprietary ones that can be purchased (e.g. Claris Homepage, Microsoft FrontPage). Many tools that were not designed for the purpose now also include a facility to generate web pages (e.g. presentation packages, word processors, etc.). In short, there is currently a vast choice of ways that one may create hypertext systems, but underlying them all is that the delivery mechanism is likely to be through HTML.

12.3.5 Object-based systems

There is considerable confusion among practitioners about the way to refer to multimedia authoring methodologies that are more complex than the traditional flow-based or hypertext approaches. In particular, there has been a revolution in the approach to computer programming since the 1970s, which is called object-oriented programming, and various multimedia tools have started to claim to be object-oriented. Most of them do not conform to the computing definition of these terms. To clarify these issues we need to briefly explore the properties of object-oriented programming.

12.3.5.1 Object-oriented programming (computer science)

Object-oriented programming (OOP) is a way to think about programming a computer which is significantly different from previous approaches, and can best be explained by comparison with them. We can simplify the evolution of computing languages into three historical stages:

- **Command languages:** a program consists of a set of instructions given to the computer which it executes one after the other. There is a beginning and an end. In addition to the general commands, a language must include some form of *conditional* statement (so that different actions can be performed depending upon the results of some test), an ability to *jump* to another place in the program, and some mechanism for storing and representing *data*. There is also normally some construct for doing things *repeatedly* (a loop or iterative command).

- **Procedural languages:** while a simple command language goes from one end to the other and requires code to be repeated if similar things need to be done, a procedural language enables the commands to be divided into groups called procedures which have names and can accept arguments. This means that the code needs only to be written once and can then be reused many times by giving different data with which to work. It also led to more organized and structured approaches to programming so that the determination of the best combination of procedures was a key issue. This increased program efficiency and maintainability, because it *encapsulated* segments of code into procedures. In these systems a program consists of a set of procedures and some data for those procedures to operate on. There remains a main or master procedure, which corresponds to the top-level of the program.

- **Object-oriented languages:** procedural languages encapsulated commands into procedures, but data was not similarly structured into effective units. Object-oriented systems adopt a more sophisticated approach in which both the data and the set of procedures which can be carried out upon that data are encapsulated in a single entity called an object. A program consists of a number of objects which have been created by a programmer. Each object has public and private parts. Public parts may be seen by other objects, but private parts are only of internal interest. This extreme of encapsulation maximizes the effectiveness of programming, reusability, and maintenance because as long as a given object has the same public parts as another one, they can be interchanged with no effect on the overall program (in theory!).

In fact, there are three key features to object-oriented programming: *encapsulation, message passing,* and *inheritance*.

- **Encapsulation:** an object consists of a set of data and a set of methods (procedures that do things to that data). Some are public and some are private. Other objects can access public methods and data.

- **Message passing:** an object can ask another object to do something by sending it a message which consists of some data and the name of a method in the receiving object. The object will carry out the method and send the result back to the object that sent the original message. An important aspect of this is that the meaning of the message can depend upon the object that receives it. For example, if I ask the number 4 to add 3 to itself, it will perform integer arithmetic and send back the answer 7; on the other hand if I ask the string 'Fred' to add 3 to itself it will append it and return the string 'Fred3'. The message was *add* in each case, but the interpretation was different. This is a very powerful idea.

• **Inheritance:** when an object is constructed, it is generally produced as a variation on, or special case of, another. These objects retain this relationship, so if I ask an object to do something it does not know how to do, or to give me some data that it does not possess, it asks the object from which it was created if it can solve the problem. If it can, then it does, otherwise it asks the object from which it itself was created and so on. This is a powerful way of producing code with the least duplication and overlap.

These three features must be present for a system to be object-oriented in the computer science sense, but they are not present in most multimedia systems that are so described. To clarify that usage we must also explore the issue of object-based interfaces.

12.3.5.2 Object-based interfaces

When talking about an object-based or object-oriented system many people are actually referring to a graphical aspect of the system rather than the computer science sense described above. We can see the interpretation of this idea of *object* quite clearly by comparing a *bitmap* graphics package (e.g. Adobe Photoshop) with a *vector* graphics package (e.g. Adobe Illustrator). In a bitmap what we are seeing is a layer of pixels each of which is a particular colour. A red circle consists of a circular group of pixels all of which are red; a blue square consists of a square group of pixels all of which are blue. If we were to draw a blue square over the top of the red circle then the red circle would disappear – it would not be 'behind' the blue square because all that each object is, is a set of pixels and one has replaced the other. In a vector system each of these objects would be represented as a piece of data away from the screen which has some abstract values. The circle would be defined by colour, a centre position, and a radius, while the square would be defined by a colour, X and Y co-ordinates, and width and height. This information is an *object* that represents the graphical depiction on the screen. It can be used to draw and redraw the depiction, which is just a collection of pixels. In a system like this, if we draw our blue square on top of our red circle then the circle is no longer visible on the screen, but the object which represents the circle is still there: it can be used to redraw the circle as soon as we move the square away. This approach to dealing with graphical entities means that each entity is represented as a data object independent of what is visible upon the screen.

Until the 1980s, screens consisted of rows and columns of text or bitmaps of numbers representing pixels. To create images such as icons, menus, or pictures on the screen would require the programmer to manipulate each pixel in the bitmap individually. Subsequent operating systems for computers (e.g. Mac OS, Microsoft Windows) are themselves written as object-oriented programs in the sense described above and hence represent screen objects (such as menus, icons, windows, etc.) as true objects containing data and methods. This means that we can treat the graphical items in our interface as objects rather than collections of pixels – and the operating system deals with the day-to-day business of turning pixels on and off for us. This implementation change has made it much easier to create programs in which every graphical entity is itself an object. We can construct interfaces by dragging objects in visual environments, make pictures by dragging and stretching objects in a drawing package, etc. It is now quite common for the term *object based* to refer to systems which treat graphical entities as objects irrespective of how they are implemented or whether they conform to the computing definition.

In a sense, this is a statement of the obvious because all software written to work with one of the object-oriented operating systems will appear object based, but it is also a useful way of describing certain sorts of interfaces to users. An object-based graphical interface implies that each graphical entity is an object which has its own properties and a range of things that the user can do to it. This is a powerful model for users to adopt and is quickly permeating many aspects of software applications.

12.3.5.3 Object-based multimedia

From the above discussion it is clear that no generally accepted usage of the word *object* in the context of multimedia systems currently exists. For that reason we will now provide our own definition of the term, and since we are predominantly concerned with interactive multimedia we will choose a definition which is most appropriate for that application.

> An object-based multimedia system is one in which a variety of specific media entities are represented to the user as specific interface entities with properties that the user may be able to manipulate, actions which the user can perform upon them, and behaviours which communicate to the user.

This is an extremely general definition that encompasses many things. It puts no particular constraints upon the way in which these objects are organized into a larger system. We could take a collection of media objects each of which represented a film clip and combine them by providing hypertext links between them – this would constitute an *object-based hypermedia system*. Alternatively, we could organize the objects according to a flow chart and would then have an *object-based flow multimedia system*. The real power of these systems, however, is that they free us from thinking in terms of either of these basic paradigms and enable us to explore a much richer and more complex interaction of objects. It is also important to bear in mind that although we have said that the system consists of a set of objects, not all of them will necessarily be visible or available to the user at a given time. This definition encompasses the idea of encapsulation, and of giving some explicit form to that encapsulation. It does not require the existence of inheritance. The idea of messages is inherent in the sense that we are talking about the user being able to perform actions on the object, and the object having behaviours that communicate with the user. These are messages at the computer–human interface level. While these systems are likely to also exchange messages between objects themselves, we are not making this a required part of our definition. Remember, too, that we are saying that the objects are embodied in particular interface entities, but that we are not requiring our interface to be graphical: a sound entity can also be an object.

Finally, it should be noted that by choosing this definition we are deliberately saying that an object-based system is a weaker entity than the normal computer science use of the term, and we will be careful not to use 'object-oriented' unless we are implying the full soup and fish.

Whereas other approaches tend to encourage the idea of progressing from screen to screen, in whatever form, the object-oriented approaches abandon this concept. It is more common to see interfaces that have a different metaphor giving a powerful conceptual depth to a single screen. This is achieved by having a variety of objects that are either permanent or transient in their visual nature and that become available or disappear in different contexts. This is a promising way to break out of the traditional mode of progressions of screens.

Tools of the trade   The de facto standard for object-based development in multimedia is Macromedia Director (Figure 12.18). This utilizes the language Lingo, which is a derivative and extension of the basic Hypertalk language embodied in HyperCard. Despite these humble origins, it is a full and powerful programming language, and permits some extremely sophisticated programming. Unfortunately, there are few multimedia people who use the language to the limit of its true capabilities. Most people tend to approach it as a simple scripting language.

This is also an area in which we are beginning to see the straightforward programming languages develop increasing importance. Java, in particular, is becoming a significant language for multimedia,

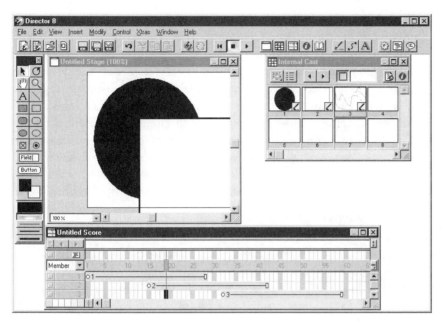

Figure 12.18   Director screenshot.

and we can expect interesting new developments with the relationship between Java and XML.

12.3.6   Agent-based systems

Agent-based design is included here because it will be a central part of future multimedia systems. These techniques, which utilize artificial intelligence methods, will transform the approach that is taken in the development of multimedia. Many of the aspects of this book, such as knowledge representation, interaction, and user modelling, are derived from those areas of artificial intelligence which also provides the foundation for agent-based systems. In approaches such as this we will see software which is implemented as a number of independent entities, each of which has its own goals and intentions. These entities will operate independently and seek to achieve their own goals by communicating with each other and with the user. While much of this work remains an area of research, it is undoubtedly the case that it will have a profound influence upon the future of interactive multimedia. Readers who are interested in finding out more about this area are recommended to one of the more recent texts on artificial intelligence.

12.3.7   Dealing with responses

Irrespective of which of the above implementation approaches you choose there will be one other aspect which is a key determiner of the form and functionality of your system: the way it reacts to the user. Put simply, your system will be receiving actions from the user, which may be interpreted as physical interaction or communicative interaction. If they are communicative, there is still an issue about the level and complexity of the processing which your program will do in order to deal with that behaviour. While it is impossible to go into all the details of how to develop adaptive systems which change their behaviour for users within this context, it is worth noting that there are three major levels of complexity to be considered: *reactive*, *history based*, and *abstracted*.

12.3.7.1 Reactive systems

A reactive system does precisely what you would expect: the user performs an action and the system reacts to what the user has done. This reaction is dependent only upon the specific action which the user has taken and does not involve any wider input of data to the decision-making process. A simple 'next' button in which the computer accepts the click and proceeds to the next page is a physical interaction which is reactive. A communicative interaction which is reactive still makes use only of that single response, but applies some semantic intent beyond the physical to it. A clear example is the use of multiple-choice questions in which the user's selection of response A, B, or C has the semantic implication that they believe the one selected is the correct response. As a consequence, the program may offer congratulatory feedback or commiseration and explanation. The communicative process has taken place but it is still reactive because it was initiated by the single action of the user and makes no wider use of what has been happening.

12.3.7.2 History-based systems

A history-based system makes use not just of the current action of the user, but also of previous actions during this session (and possibly during earlier sessions). In such a system the computer will retain some storage of the previous actions of the user. It can access this direct data about the actions of the user to ask questions that will enable it to determine what to do in response to a particular user behaviour. One of the simplest examples of this is the sort of system which enables the user to try a particular problem three times and on the fourth time will say what the answer should have been. This is using data beyond the particular action of the user in order to vary the behaviour of the computer. With careful design there is quite a lot of power that can be achieved using systems of this form. It is becoming increasingly common for systems to retain simple data like this during one session of interaction with a user, but it is much less common for a system to retain the data between sessions.

12.3.7.3 Abstracted systems

An abstracted system is one which uses reasoning processes applied to information gathered through user interactions and history to create a deeper semantic model that will inform the decision-making processes. One example might be a simple mathematics teaching system which examines the user responses in terms of properties of the question that has been asked and determines that the user consistently produces the wrong answer if the question involved a negative number. From this information the system reaches the abstract conclusion that the user has difficulty understanding negative numbers. This can then be used in selecting future problems, deciding what to teach, or constructing explanations. Abstracted systems are potentially a vast category which we have only explored to have a limited extent through the use of artificial intelligence techniques and user-modelling methodologies. The potential for the application of these techniques in the future is immense.

12.4 An integrated design process for interactive multimedia

In the first two parts of the book we examined a broad range of approaches to interaction and understanding the communicative possibilities of various pieces of media which might form part of an interactive multimedia product. In the current section we have begun to approach the way that these different skills and technologies can be integrated to form an exciting and innovative product. Within this chapter, we have so far examined traditional design processes and specific factors that need to be considered in the area of multimedia. It is now time to draw all these aspects of our work together into a single, coherent *design process* which can be applied to any multimedia development. This model will balance the requirements of scientific and artistic approaches.

Figure 12.19 shows the stages of the design process. As with any design process, this technique is presented as a clear, step-by-step methodology. While keeping the clarity of this presentation in mind, the

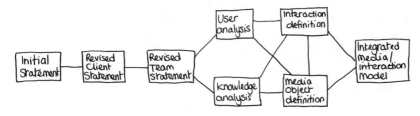

Figure 12.19   Design process diagram.

reality will often mean that several things will be happening at once, or happening at different speeds during the development process. You may find that certain segments become extremely large or can be almost completely omitted – but you must not omit a component from the process without considering it and justifying the reason why it is not necessary for your particular product. Throughout this section we will assume that the reader has overall responsibility for this process.

12.4.1 Initial statement

Every project commences with some sort of initial statement of what is to be achieved. This might be a vague statement from a client, such as 'I want something to reduce the paperwork in the office', a loose idea by a member of the development team, such as 'I really think we ought to do something with DVD in medicine', or a more formal outline from an *invitation to tender* or *bid for contracts*. Wherever this initial idea comes from, and however vague it is initially, the first essential step is to get it down in writing in a form which is as clear and explicit as possible. This is the initial project statement. It is quite unlikely that the final project will have very much whatever to do with the statement, but unless the starting point is documented it becomes very difficult to explain why the project is now what it is and how it satisfies aspects of the initial statement. Indeed, in some projects the outcome is to demonstrate why the initial statement was a bad idea in the first place. Any of these things requires an explicit form for the statement. An example of an initial statement might be something like 'I want a piece of software that will teach new staff about our production processes'.

One way of dealing with this initial statement is simply to write down your own perception of the project proposal. With experience, this can be quite useful and has the advantage of taking comparatively little time and involving few of the other players in the project situation. Normally, however, it is best to involve at least the client and representatives of the key team leaders in informal discussions around the statement. You are not attempting to get a full statement but a general definition which is completely agreed by all participants at this point. Restrict yourself to no more than a couple of paragraphs and focus primarily upon what the project will achieve. The client is interested in the outcome, not the implementation or the underlying technical issues.

Having established an initial statement the next step (and quite a large, significant, and important one) is to turn it into a much more specific and detailed statement of the project and product which is agreed with the client and will be used as the basis for the legal contract underlying the development. The initial statement should include answers to at least the following questions:

1. What will the software do?

2. Who is it for?

3. What is the subject area?

But we need to note that these questions can all be answered in a variety of ways from the very vague to the extremely explicit, and we are only seeking general coverage at this stage, in order to guide the next statement

12.4.2 Revised client statement (talk to users, stakeholder analysis)

The second step in the project specification process is to develop more detailed specification documents. This is the first point at which we must acknowledge that there are two separate activities in progress for two separate groups of people: the *client* and the *development team*.

We must produce a fairly detailed document for the *client* which explains what will be delivered (in a reasonable degree of detail), the way in which this will solve any problems, and the means by which the product will be demonstrated to have been effective. This document must be couched in terms which the client understands, contain explanations which make sense to the client in terms of their own needs, and detailed standards of *testing, functionality,* and *acceptance,* which the client can relate to their own activities. As a manager of this specification process it is also important not to commit the development team to any specific details which are liable to change. Try to be specific in things that are clear and fixed within the project but retain a degree of ambiguity in other areas.

In developing this document it is necessary to take into account the particular group of players representing the context in which our system will operate. The primary interaction will be between yourself as the analyst and the client as the person responsible for funding and accepting the product. To this simple interaction it is necessary to add three other groups of players that require consideration: the *users,* the *stakeholders,* and the *development team* (Figure 12.20). As the analyst, you are representing the *development team* in this process and have the responsibility to ensure that the statement that you finally agree is for a product that can be achieved by your team within the available time and budget. You should be in a position to manage most of this process yourself from your understanding of your team, but occasionally you may need to go back to specific members of that team to check up upon the feasibility of certain aspects of the project as proposed. Do not be afraid of doing this! It is much better to ask a few questions of the team and have a project that is achievable than to rely entirely on your own limited knowledge and commit yourself and the team to the impossible.

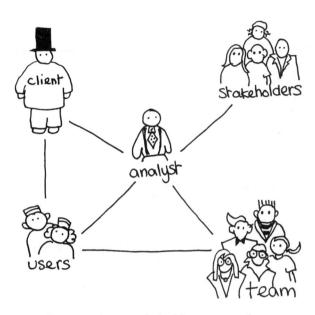

Figure 12.20   Client–analyst, stakeholder, user and team.

Having dealt with the development team, a second important group represented in this client statement are the *stakeholders* (other than users and client) who have an interest in the final product. In some notional sense the stakeholders are the responsibility of the client and are represented by the client during the development of the statement. Unfortunately, we cannot necessarily assume that the stakeholders are accurately represented by the client in all cases, or even that the client has a clear view of whom the stakeholders are. This becomes our problem if the client agrees a statement that is not subsequently acceptable to other parties. For this reason, it is advisable to conduct at least a short interaction with the client explicitly about the stakeholders. This discussion should cover identifying who the stakeholders are and what their major objectives are in relation to the product. For each stakeholder try and identify a short list of objectives to be satisfied and problems to be avoided. The client will probably have to justify the product to each stakeholder at some point so it is advisable to develop an argument supporting the product for each stakeholder and to identify a few keywords in the product statement that will form the basis for that argument. Do not include the argument itself in the statement – that will make it too long. Explain it separately to your client. In this way you can improve your bond with the client by working as a team to bring the stakeholders on board for the project.

The third group of relevance to the client specification are the users themselves. As we have noted earlier, the client (who requests, funds, and accepts the product) is not generally the person who will end up directly using the product. Normally, the product is being commissioned on behalf of some specific user group (such as tourists at a railway station, or sales staff in a shop). The clients almost certainly believe that they know what this group's needs are and what they should do in order to satisfy them. It is also almost certain that the client is wrong in this respect. Because of this it is important, even at this early stage, that you interact with some members of the user group to test whether the client's perception of their needs is accurate and, if it is not, to identify those areas where the client will have to be convinced otherwise before the statement is finalized. It is normally helpful to concentrate upon a *problem-oriented approach*. The clients may well perceive a problem that affects themselves as well as the users and then propose a solution which would satisfy themselves but does not take account of the needs of the users. In these situations one of the best first steps is to agree with the client about what the problem is: specifically about what the problem is for the client. Following this, you can explore the issues with certain members of the user group and subsequently return to the client with a clarification of the user problem which needs to be solved (in addition to, or as a subpart of, solving the client problem). Once you have achieved agreement upon this problem you can then move forward to discuss and agree the nature of the solution.

All the above seems like a lot of work for a document which will not be particularly huge, but bear in mind that your primary motivation at this stage is to get agreement to a specification which you know is achievable, will satisfy the client needs, and which does not conflict with the needs of the users or other stakeholders. You are not currently engaged in a full user analysis or knowledge analysis – they will come later.

A checklist of the revised client statement will include (in a reasonable level of detail, but remaining problem-oriented) at least:

1. What is the problem to be solved?

2. What will the team deliver?

3. How will the delivered product solve that problem?

4. How will the product be demonstrated to satisfy the problem?

5. What are the obligations of the client (provision of information, etc.)

6. When will the delivery take place?

12.4.3   Revised team statement

While the client statement focuses upon a problem-oriented approach and is couched in terms that are understood by the client, a somewhat different method is needed for specifying the product to the development team. This document will be referred to as the *team statement*. It is normally written after the client statement because it must make use of that document to ensure that it satisfies the things that have been promised to the client, but it is structured in a different way and with significantly different information content.

The team statement is not a detailed specification of the product but an overview of the product and the approach that will be taken to implement it. The analyst in isolation cannot in general produce this document: it is necessary to work closely with key members of the development team. The team statement begins with a summary of the key behaviours that the product must satisfy and a general description of the proposed product. Each aspect of that product description should be accompanied by a justification of the reason that that aspect is required, the reason it satisfies the stated need, and any specific constraints which are agreed or recommended for the overall product.

Following this general statement, the team statement should be broken into a number of distinct sections corresponding to the various development subgroups within the team. At the gross level there will be sections for interaction design and development, and media content design and development. Specifically, interaction design may include statements for interface design, interaction programming, core implementation engine, and platform/hardware/deployment. Media content statements will exist for each distinct grouping that can be identified (in some cases the content media will be too interconnected to achieve this), e.g. video, graphic design, sound. Beyond these two major categories we may also need to construct statements for issues within the project which are not directly part of these development components: research and knowledge analysis, user analysis, evaluation and testing, legal and copyright issues.

12.4.3.1 General statement

This general statement is effectively an outline description of the product. It should not be so detailed as to pre-empt later stages of the specification process, but it is extremely important that it should provide a team with knowledge not only of the criteria which they are satisfying in the product but also the reasons why those criteria are important. It will include needs and features that have been agreed with the client, but expand upon them in a slightly more precise and technical manner. The template below forms a good starting point for this statement.

```
This product will {Insert needs satisfied}
This will be achieved by {Outline product description}
This meets the needs because {List of feature needs}
```

12.4.3.2 Interaction design and development statement

Interaction design primarily covers direct interaction between the system and the user, but it must also take into account any other stakeholders who might interact with the system or data produced by it, and any other software systems to which the product must relate. For example, if we are producing a multimedia interface for selecting car parts then the interface to the people doing the selection process (sales staff, customers, mechanics) is extremely important, but so is the interaction between this multimedia system and the underlying database of the company which maintains parts inventory, availability, etc. This statement also incorporates any aspects of programming which are not media specific, such as the development of any specialist core algorithms.

This is termed the *design and development* statement because at this stage it is not anticipated that the full interaction can be specified. Instead, we can identify key features of the interaction, essential constraints upon it, and the activities and processes that we will engage in to produce an interaction design. This latter aspect is important in providing a scope for the overall specification process and facilitating the identification of relationships between interaction design, media content design, etc.

We can structure our interaction design statement around the following checklist:

```
Generic model(s)
Relation to existing components and activities
Key interaction features (with justification)
Core algorithm requirements
Platform issues
Specific inclusions and constraints
```

The *generic model* refers back to the basic approaches that we have tried earlier such as hypertext or flow-based systems. Within this we may go a little further and identify particular structures such as tree-based hypertext, or particular aspects of the domain that would require different models (e.g. simulation in certain real-life tasks).

Relation to existing components describes the way in which the software acquires data from or passes data to other systems. Equally important is that the statement should make clear the product's relationship to systems with which it is not directly connected but which the user will be addressing in the same context. If we have constructed a multimedia system for visualizing fitted kitchens and the company uses a separate accounting system then, even though the software programs may not be physically connected, it is extremely important that we use the correct terminology, part identifiers, etc. so that the users are not trying to simultaneously use two systems which are in opposition to each other. We can take this further and try to ensure a similar level of compatibility with non-computer systems in the working environment. We should examine the processes that the users engage in on a daily basis, identify the areas in which these interact with the proposed product, and ensure suitable compatibility and consistency of interaction on that basis. This covers the whole field of 'systems thinking'.

Certain *key interaction features* are likely to have been agreed with the client in advance or to have been identified as a major sales point – a USP (unique selling point) of the system. It is important to identify these features and state why they must be included in the design. It may be something as trivial as the managing director of the company insisting that its photograph and signature appear on the opening titles, or it may be that a 'try before you buy' interactive simulation is the reason that the client wants you to build the product in the first place. It is quite easy to get distracted and put too many features into this list, so try and concentrate only on those that are absolutely essential.

The *core algorithms* are assumed to be independent of the particular media used, and will ultimately be specified by normal computing science methods of program specification. Within this document it is only necessary to state any special or unique features of the algorithms that will exist in this product.

It is often the case that the client will have specific limitations upon the *hardware and software* that are in place and on which the product is to be used. It is consequently extremely important to identify the full range of hardware platforms and software environments on which the product is expected to run. It must be clear that any specialist requirements for add-in multimedia boards such as sound cards or video drivers are included.

The final category of *specific inclusions and constraints* is really just a catch-all statement so that there is somewhere to write things that do not fit neatly into any of the other categories. There may be issues about future systems, upgradeability, time scales, maintenance, or general 'look and feel' issues, for example.

12.4.3.3 Media content design and development statement

Our statement regarding media content is intended to delineate a general scope within which assets will be developed. This includes providing an approximate boundary around the knowledge content of the system and identifying specific channels of communication and media that are available to us. Where possible the statement should also identify which resources already exist and which must be created specifically for the product. This last point will need to be covered in agreement with the client in any case, since there are issues of copyright which need to be made clear in using material from the client. We can prepare the specifications with this checklist:

```
General scope of content
Available channels of communication
Available media
Existing content resources
Any specific inclusions and constraints
```

General scope of content refers not to specific media components created within the system but the range of knowledge that we wish to encompass, in whatever form, within the final product. Some of this will be mapped directly into media assets while other aspects might turn up only in the way that they are used in the programming or interaction development of the system. In this general statement we are only seeking to give a rough outline of the scope of the system. One way to achieve this is to make a short statement about what the content of the system will be and to follow it with a number of short statements about the things that are *excluded* from the system. This is often a more effective way of communicating the limits of the implementation.

Available channels of communication are part of the user analysis. Following the way that this was delineated earlier in the book we should identify those modalities which the system will be using (both for input and for output), and within each of those modalities note the channels which are available to us, whether users will have access to all channels, and where we may wish to offer alternative channels. An example would be to include written text in both English and French.

Following directly from the channels of communication we may want to consider which of the *existing media* will be appropriate. In some cases we will be creating new combinations but technologies such as video, animation, etc. may be appropriate if our user group is familiar with the conventions of that medium. It is not unusual to find that the client also has specific views with relation to the choice of media insisting, for example, that film be used even where it is irrelevant.

In conjunction with the selection of channels and media we may well wish to consider resources that are *already available*: either in the public domain or from material which our client has already produced. Identifying existing resources can significantly affect the planning and time scales of our project as well as impacting upon other aspects of the design.

Finally, there is an additional category for any specific requirements or constraints upon the media used.

12.4.3.4 Other statement aspects

There are certain aspects of the product that we may wish to include in our team statement but which do not fit under either of the two main categories. The most obvious one is to provide a rough statement of who the expected user group or user groups are. This can be used as a starting point in the subsequent user analysis. An attempt should be made to identify the full range of groups and the likely level of their interaction with the system (e.g. primary users and occasional users).

Knowledge analysis may include specific requirements other than the general scope mentioned in the media content section. This could include identifying the key knowledge resources within the client organization, major independent source of information, etc. There may be more specific things that can be said about the scope of the content in this context.

In some situations the requirements for interaction, knowledge, and media cannot be acquired from working solely with the client. At this point it may be that certain activities can be identified which will require research in order to develop the final system. Statements of such required research should also be made. If there are any other special activities which are not otherwise mentioned they should also be included here.

Evaluation and testing are essential to the success of the system both when it is being developed and when it is being deployed. Some testing criteria will have been considered when coming up with the acceptance criteria for the client. These should be explicitly stated in the team document, as should any other specific plans or opportunities to engage in evaluation (such as users who are available for testing during the development process).

At this point in our design process we have finalized the statement of the product for the client, and for the design team. These two documents should now be regarded as fixed and not subject to further revision. The remainder of the process concerns the arrival at a detailed specification of the product which can be used as a basis for designing a project to implement the product (Chapter 13) and briefing the developers on each aspect.

12.4.4 User analysis

We have emphasized the centrality of communication throughout this book, and to make communication effective we must understand the people with whom we are communicating. Consequently, in order to adequately refine our system design, it is necessary to understand our users. Techniques for describing a user or user group were outlined in Chapter 4. It is at this point in the process that we can apply these techniques to develop a document that outlines the intended users of the system and the way in which communication with them can proceed.

The first stage is to identify a gross, large-scale user group for the system. As mentioned earlier, they must not simply be named, but their characteristics must be described at a level of detail relevant to the system design. This includes identifying their expected knowledge, skills, and goals when coming to the system. This must utilize not just the cognitive, but also the conative and affective components: what do they want from the system and how do they feel towards it? Unless we can adequately address these aspects of the context then our system is unlikely to be used.

As mentioned in Chapter 4, it is just as important to identify who the users are *not*. Some groups will have no interest in the system and some will be unable to use it even if they are interested. We cannot build a system that will please everyone, so it is important to identify for the design team, the client, and the users themselves, who is not expected to benefit from the system.

When this general analysis has been completed and agreed, a second level can be engaged which identifies subgroups within the general user group. This is not always essential, and not always possible, but if you can identify distinctions between different users (such as the goals of different groups, or the background knowledge that they have) then an attempt must be made to identify these groups and develop a model of their similarities and differences.

The final stage of the user analysis must be an identification of the channels of communication that are available for that user group. This will include such things as the languages available to them, whether they have limitations on sight or hearing. There will also be things specific to computers such as the level of interaction with which they are happy: can they use a mouse, are they familiar with menus, would they know what to do with a trackball? Beyond this, we need to examine the media with which they are familiar, and the conventions within which they operate. Do they use certain diagramming techniques professionally, are they familiar with children's television, do they listen to radio? These establish a range of specific channels for which we can assume that encoders and decoders exist. Finally, we should examine the semiotic context. This is an open-ended task that can never be completed, but we should at least inspect certain general characteristics to see if there are shared interpretations among the user group that can be incorporated into the design. An example might be that certain corporate colour schemes suggest quality or reliability to this user group, or that they find conservative fonts reassuring whereas newer 1980s' and 1990s' fonts disturb them. There is really no end to this task.

In parallel with this user analysis, since one informs the other, we need to engage in our knowledge analysis.

12.4.5   Knowledge analysis

In Chapter 3 we emphasized the importance of knowledge to the communicative interaction process which we are espousing as essential to all interactive multimedia systems. Since all the systems discussed must have some form of information content used in the communicative process, they must all refer to some field of knowledge which limits the scope of the content. This knowledge is an abstract structure that may not be (and typically is not) included directly within the implementation, but that must be understood in order to inform the design of our interaction and development of our media assets. It forms the basis for communication among members of the team, and for working with user and client to ensure the integrity of the content that we will produce before we invest time and money in developing that content.

The methods that will be used to conduct this knowledge analysis and to represent it in a form that is meaningful to all the players in the development have already been discussed in Chapter 3, but they can briefly be combined into a specification process as follows:

- **Talk to the clients.** Use knowledge elicitation techniques to identify their perception of the problem. Remember that the client will not normally be the user, so that often the best output you can achieve from the client is a list of who to talk to about various aspects of the process. You may also want to talk to one or more of the remote stakeholders in the system.

- **Talk to the users.** This is a key part of the elicitation exercise. You may find that you talk to a range of users to get an overall picture, but that there are one or two who are particularly useful because of their ability to explain things, and you should focus on these people. Bear in mind that you should try and read any existing documentation before this stage to try and get the maximum from the people that you talk to without asking them to duplicate information elsewhere.

- If the information from the first two stages is not sufficient, consider acquiring subject experts in the domain and getting detailed knowledge from them. Similar processes of knowledge elicitation are used.

- If there are products which are available that are similar to the one that you are planning, try to analyse their knowledge content.

These stages should provide you with a fairly detailed knowledge of the subject matter and content surrounding the system. To make this useful, it also needs to be organized. Knowledge from the different sources should be reduced to a common format and structured. You should identify different types of knowledge (e.g. procedural or declarative), and then group related knowledge together using techniques such as clustering or process-oriented approaches. As discussed earlier, knowledge structures are not 'intention free' and so different structures will be better suited to different purposes. Information about the overall purpose of the system and the nature of the users is likely to influence your design at this point.

The final output of our knowledge analysis process will be a document that describes the range of knowledge of relevance to the area, and the range that will be embodied within the system. This will be in a reasonably precise form and will inform our subsequent designs of interaction and media components.

12.4.6 Interaction definition (levels)

By this point in the design process we have established the general nature of the interaction with the system. These detailed interaction definition documents expand upon this to the level at which it can be implemented. While such a document is primarily the responsibility of individuals concerned with the functionality of the interaction, it must also be remembered that the visual appearance and presentation of the interaction is absolutely central to ensuring that the overall system is perceived as a single integrated entity rather than a number of independent pieces of media which have been bolted together.

Interaction definition should separate out the 'general interaction' from the interaction that is specific to specific multimedia assets. In each case it is necessary to design an interface using the principles and techniques which were outlined in Chapter 5, and then to specify the corresponding functionality which is required to give that interface the appropriate functionality. This will include defining core algorithms and data structures. Having determined the overall model, key stages include:

- Specifying any generic navigation tools (e.g. home or quit mechanisms)

- Selecting appropriate interface widgets

- Deciding a look and feel for the system

- Identifying general models and consistencies

- Choosing appropriate channels of communication

These stages will result in a document which defines the interface for each of the required contexts. It should be possible to subject the defined interface to further analysis using the techniques described in Chapter 5. Mocking up the interface and testing it with potential users should be possible at this stage.

12.4.7 Media objects (semiotics)

The basic range of knowledge to be embodied in the system has already been established, as have the available channels of communication. In designing the content of the system we need to consider the things that we are producing as a collection of 'media assets'. By describing them at this level we are making two assumptions: first, that they can be described to the rest of the system (the interaction mechanisms and other objects) in a consistent manner independent of the way in which their content is implemented (i.e. what media are chosen); second, that in a given asset the way in which it is designed and produced follows the conventions of interpretation of those media and their existing channels of communication, as well as the techniques of production specific to that form.

To identify the required assets, a common mechanism is to look at the knowledge structure and group it into components which can be used together – things that will only be communicated as part of a group, or things which have to be isolated because they may be communicated in different contexts. Each of these collections of knowledge would be the result of some clustering process on the general knowledge that we have identified. Having completed the clustering of asset content, the available media and channels of communication are examined to decide on the appropriate way in which to deliver the knowledge content. On some occasions we may want to design more than one way of delivering the contents by using different combinations of media and channels of communication, depending upon the needs of our audience. Once these units have been identified separately, and the description agreed in terms of the realm of the interaction, then the process of developing any individual units can become media specific. At this point the development of individual assets can be passed to teams specializing in that area (such as a photographer or film crew) and they will then develop that asset utilizing the languages that are specific to the assumptions that have already been made about that medium. In instances where we are using combinations of channels that have not established the status of convention, there will be more variation in the method of implementation but the structure of the assets should none the less be capable of being designed independently of other assets. The exception is that there will be some decisions (which should have been taken earlier in the process) about semiotic structures that will permeate all the assets (or many of them) and each implementation team must ensure that its assets are compatible with these.

12.4.8 Integrated interaction/media model

The interaction should have been designed with an expectation of the particular media components that will be available, and vice versa. Since it is vital that these two aspects of the system integrate seamlessly it is important to recognize this process explicitly. While the development of media and interaction design was described as parallel, independent streams, they will in reality interact with one changing the other. As a consequence, the design that we end up with is not necessarily the one that we had back in Section 12.4.3. At the very least, it will have been refined. To manage this part of the process we must produce a final specification document that defines the interaction and media as an integrated model of the system. This will be an ongoing development during the design process but will have a central role as being the definitive document incorporating all the components that should be the basis from which the implementation team will work.

We have now made a design for an interactive multimedia system.

12.4.9 Now make a project

Having followed through the process described in this chapter, the outcome is a design for our system that we know is feasible and will satisfy the requirements of the client and user groups. Before we can start constructing this system it is necessary to take this system design and develop a process by which the implementation can be achieved. This process of *project design* is the subject of the next chapter.

12.5 Exercises

Exercise 12.1 Look at a range of existing multimedia products. Try an identify one for each category: linear, linear alternate, branching, hyper-based. Justify your choice.

Exercise 12.2 Select an existing hypertext system. Identify the underlying navigational model being used (e.g. book), and the structural models (e.g. sequence, tree, net) being applied at different places. Are there areas where the model seems to break down?

Exercise 12.3 Identify a multimedia product that you might create. Write an initial product statement, a client statement and a team statement for this product.

Exercise 12.4 Analyse the user groups for the product using the techniques from earlier chapters.

Exercise 12.5 Analyse the knowledge content of the product using the techniques from earlier chapters.

Exercise 12.6 List the main multimedia assets which will need to be produced.

12.6 Further reading

There are many books around which teach how to use the various tool to produce an integrated product. They change swiftly, so I will not make and specific recommendations in this chapter.

13

Project design and management

13.1 Why?

In the previous chapter we raised issues concerned with designing a multimedia system and presented an integrated approach to the design process. Prior to that we devoted a chapter to discussing the players that are involved in the process of multimedia development. If we are to turn our design into a working product then we have to organize a process by which this team of people can co-operate to achieve that implementation. This involves both *designing* a *process* for collaboration and *managing* that *process* on a day-to-day basis. Simply throwing all the participants together and hoping for the best will not be effective!

Happily, the processes of project design and management are very well understood in a variety of disciplines, and the design and management of a multimedia project is very little different from projects in computing. In this chapter we will briefly summarize the issues and approaches.

13.1.1 Designing a project

The most basic reason for designing a project to implement a product is so that you know that it is feasible. By sketching out the process you can check that all the individual activities are possible, that the resources exist, and that they can be brought together. Examples of impossible projects might include things that require the same person to be in two different places at once, or resources that don't exist (such as the proposal to panel a building with jade, when it would have required more jade than exists in the world). If we find that the project is possible, there are two other reasons why we need to do a project design at an early stage: costs and time-scales.

- *Cost*: When deciding whether to commit to a project, you must know what you are committing to. Funds are never limitless and you have to be very clear about how much your project will cost. A likely cost should be worked out, as well as a best case and worst case. You can use this internally within your team, but it is also essential if you are bidding to an external client. You must know what the project will cost so that you can determine what you will need to charge in order to break-even or make a reasonable profit.

- *Time-scale*: If you are delivering a product to a client or to the market place, you need to know by when. Technologies change all the time, and too much delay could mean that your product is obsolete before you have finished building it. Clients may rely on it and plan things around it. It is necessary to calculate delivery dates and a schedule of progress to ensure that you are on target for those delivery dates. Many contracts impose severe penalties if the developers fail to meet their promised delivery.

In addition to these basic requirements, project design also enables us to plan things to be more effective and efficient, potentially enabling us to develop better projects, to keep our staff happier, or to make more profit (or occasionally all three).

13.1.2 Managing a project

At the start of a project you have a plan and a group of people. The idea is that the people get down to it, follow the plan, and everything goes smoothly and swimmingly like clockwork right to the end of the project. I have known projects where this has happened but they are very rare. I have never known things go completely according to plan on anything that involved either (a) a real client or (b) multimedia. We have to go into our project expecting that there will be potential deviations from plan.

The purpose of managing a project is to monitor things as they are progressing, identify problems and deviations from plan in their early stages, and correct them before they have a detrimental effect on the overall project (either by increasing the time-scale or by increasing the cost). This is an extremely important job, but it can be hard to be a project manager and still remain popular! By identifying a critical path through the project it is possible to see where there can reasonably be adjustments or slippages without affecting the overall project, and where such changes will have a knock-on effect.

13.2   General approach

A multimedia project does not, on the whole, involve *physical* resources. In some industries project management requires you to get thousands of tons of sand, gravel, and lime (or whatever) arriving in certain places on certain days (the physical resources), where they are mixed and processed by a group of people (human resources) to produce some physical result (physical output). Software development in general, and multimedia specifically, is predominantly an intellectual activity. Physical resources play a comparatively small role, but human resources are central. The things that have to be done mostly involve people working with computers, and sometimes spending time collecting assets. This has some effect on the way that the project is planned.

13.2.1   Task breakdown

The first stage in the process of planning a project is to break the overall project up into a number of distinct units. Each of these units should represent a separate *task* which has a definite start and end point. As far as possible, the tasks should be organized in such a way that each could be pursued independently of other tasks in the project. This idea of the task breakdown should be familiar to us from the exploration of knowledge representation in Chapter 3. While the task structures in that chapter were organized hierarchically, that is not necessarily the case with the tasks involved in a project. Typically, you should aim to break down a project into something between 6 and 12 distinct tasks. These can be broken down further at a later date into subtasks.

We can clarify the idea of tasks in this context by looking at the way we intend to use them in our project plan. The project plan will have a single start point at which the project commences, and a single end point which indicates that the project is completed. Between these two points a number of tasks will take place. Some of the tasks will be things that are entirely independent of any other part of the project, but most of them will have some dependency upon the successful completion of earlier work. For example, we cannot integrate the interface design with the assets until the interface and assets have been completed. Tasks which both depend upon the same prerequisite being completed, but which do not depend upon each other, can effectively be carried out in parallel (providing that sufficient resources are available), hence shortening the overall duration of the project. Figure 13.1 shows a typical example of a simple project plan.

This figure is a dependency diagram that shows the interrelationships between the tasks. It is often referred to as a PERT chart (Programme Evaluation Review Technique), although strictly speaking it contains more than just these dependencies. Because the links between the boxes represent dependencies between different tasks, a given task cannot

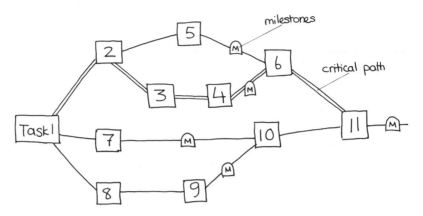

Figure 13.1 Project plan.

commence until all the tasks on which it depends have been completed. This means that we can regard our PERT chart as a sort of collection of time-lines that tell us how long the project will take. If we know the date at which the project must commence, and we know how many calendar days each task will take, then we can calculate the overall duration of the project and hence identify a final completion or delivery date which we can give to our client. You should notice that in projects where there are tasks being done in parallel, it is always the task of longest calendar duration that determines the overall length of the project. For any given project there will be one 'longest' path from beginning to end. This is called the *critical path*. Any activity on the critical path is key to completion of the project on time: delays on the critical path delay the whole project. By contrast, a delay in a task that is not on the critical path need not have an effect upon the completion date.

In identifying the separate tasks in the project it is important that you can clearly define what belongs to which task. For this reason, tasks are normally given a well-defined start point and an end point, and are often associated with specific *project milestones*. A *milestone* is an identifiable point which has been reached on the project – this may be the completion of a particular code segment or asset, the undertaking of a particular meeting with the client or development team, or any of a number of other identifiable events that can be shown to indicate *closure* of a section of the work on the project. In some cases the project milestone also produces something concrete to be incorporated into the final outcome of the project, which is identified as a *deliverable* – a particular artefact to be handed on to some other part of the team or the client.

Each task has a duration in time, and normally a milestone indicating completion. There is another way of encoding the data about times, which provides an alternative perspective that can be useful for certain sorts of activity. This is known as a Gantt chart, and consists of a graph of project activity against time. Figure 13.2 is an example of such a chart. The identifiers on the left-hand side each correspond to one of the tasks in the project, while the axis across the bottom of the page indicates number of working days spent on the project. Each individual task has a bar, which commences at the starting date for the task and ends at the finishing date of the task. In fact, for this example we have included a shaded region on some of the tasks which indicates an uncertainty about the precise end date, and consequent uncertainty about commencement dates of dependent tasks. We will explore this approach further in the next section where we deal with allocation of resources to tasks.

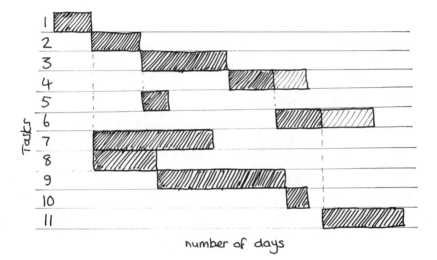

Figure 13.2   Gantt chart.

13.2.2 Resource planning

In the previous sections we assume that you could tell how many days a particular task within the project would take. This is critically important to successful project managing, so developing accurate estimates for these durations is essential. To achieve this we have to examine each of the individual resources that are required for each particular task, examine the activities to be carried out, and the schedule of availability for each of the resources. By combining this information we can work out the total number of person-days involved in each task, and consequently the total number of calendar days that will be required to complete that number of person-days' work.

13.2.2.1 Resource identification

Having mapped out a set of tasks and dependencies, the next stage of the plan must be to identify the resources that are required for the project.

As mentioned earlier, human resources are the primary issue in any multimedia project. Because of the interdisciplinary nature of the work the project is likely to require people from very different backgrounds and with very different methods of working. This has to be taken into account in the planning. A typical project might include:

- project manager;
- software/program designers;
- high-level programmers;
- low-level programmers;
- hardware specialists;
- interface designers;
- text authors/technical authors;
- graphic designers;
- photographers (still and video);
- script writers;
- video directors.

Each of these groups has different requirements for their working practice, and this must be allowed for. The following section provides more detail on these issues.

The most obvious secondary resource within the multimedia project is the equipment required for the development work. This will normally include both appropriate hardware platforms and software platforms for the designers and programmers. Additionally, it is not unusual to require specific pieces of kit at particular times: this may include the hire of high-quality video cameras or post-production editing suites, construction and installation of specialist kit to deliver the product (such as an interactive kiosk), or the external resources required for large-scale duplicating and distribution of the final system. Each of these resources must be recognized and specified in advance of the project commencement, together with dates on when they will be required and be available. These can put important calendar constraints upon the organization and progress of the project.

Where the project is intending to make use of pre-existing multimedia assets (either supplied by the client or from other external sources) these must also be written into the project plan as a resource which must be available for the appropriate tasks on appropriate dates. This enables the manager to plan for a situation in which one of these essential resources does not materialize.

You should make a comprehensive list of the required resources.

13.2.2.2 Costing and timing resources

Having identified our resources the next stage is associating them with the different tasks within the project. You should make a list of the tasks and write down the resources needed to complete each task (Figure 13.3). Physical resources are fairly straightforward: the main constraint is to ensure that they are available at the time when they are needed. If this involves purchasing hardware or software then you need to plan this allowing an appropriate lead-time before the first use of that item. When dealing with human resources you should assign particular types of people to each task – not named individuals. For example, one task may include a *graphic designer* and *photographer*.

Tasks

1 Project Manager, Script Writer, Video Director
2 High Level programmers, Low Level programmers
3 Video Director, Photographer [Studio]

Figure 13.3 Allocating resources to tasks.

In multimedia the timings of tasks are going to be dependent upon the human resources. Within a given task it is necessary to look at each of the resources that you have allocated, work out which activities it engages in, and estimate how much time that resource would require to carry out those activities. This will give you a total amount of effort for the task for that resource calculated as a number of *person-days*. A person-day is the amount of work that one person could do in one day. It is necessary to calculate the total effort figure for each of the resources used within the task individually. Once you know the total effort, you can then decide the amount of each resource that you will allocate to the task, and from this you can determine the actual amount of time that the task will take in calendar days. As an example, if I find that a particular task is estimated to require 40 days of graphic designer time and 60 days of programmer time, I could decide to allocate one graphic designer full time to this task. If I do so the requisite 40 person-days of work will be completed in 40 calendar days. Alternatively, I might find that my graphic design team is very busy and can spare no more than half a day each working day. If this is the case, the 40 days of effort will require 80 calendar days to complete. By contrast, if I am able to put two graphic designers on the job, it would probably be completed in less than 40 days. As a rough estimate we will suggest that it only takes 20 days but bear in mind that for all the reasons discussed in Chapter 11, we cannot assume that adding more staff will always make the job take less time. If I put 40 graphic designers to work on this task for one day then the task would not be completed — we could probably expect revolution and anarchy!

In this situation, if I were to allocate one programmer to the task, then that programmer would require 60 calendar days to complete it. In this case it would be irrelevant whether I put one (40 calendar days) or two (20 calendar days) graphic designers to work on the task since the actual duration is the maximum time that any individual resource takes, so the task takes 60 days in either case. This is illustrated in Figure 13.4.

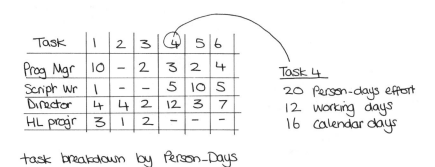

task breakdown by Person-Days

Figure 13.4   Resource allocation calculation.

The above information gives us a reasonably accurate measure for how long each task in our project will take. We can feed this information back to the dependency diagrams of the previous sections and use it to make a reasonably accurate calculation of the total duration of the project in calendar days, and the total resource which will be used in person-days. We can also determine an overall cost for the project by multiplying the total effort for each resource (in person-days) by the cost of that resource per day. When added on to the cost of the fixed resources such as hardware, this gives us an overall cost for the project. This is illustrated in Figure 13.5.

All the above seems a very reasonable way of ensuring that the project is feasible, but there is a further phase which you must deal with to

Resource	Person Days	Cost per day	Total Cost
Director	23	700	16100
Script Wr	17	300	5100
8 Extras (video)	16	20	320

Figure 13.5   Project cost calculation.

ensure that the plan can be executed: *resource loading*. In reality, the abstract terms which we have used, such as graphic designer, correspond to real human beings with real jobs to do. This imposes certain limitations upon them. If, for example, you have decided to speed up one task by putting two graphic designers to work on it full time, but you only actually employ one graphic designer, then your plan is disastrously wrong to start with. It is not that common to make this particular error but it is quite common to allocate the same member of staff to several different tasks which are proceeding in parallel, and therefore to accidentally allocate over 100 per cent of their time. In dealing with the loadings you also need to look out for periods when a particular staff member has nothing to do. As far as possible, you should try to even out your project plan so that staff are reasonably occupied at all times. In a larger company this can often be achieved by moving staff backwards and forwards between projects as demand dictates. You can use techniques such as the Gantt chart to display a personal time-line for each individual resource indicating any gaps or periods of low or high loading for this resource (Figure 13.6).

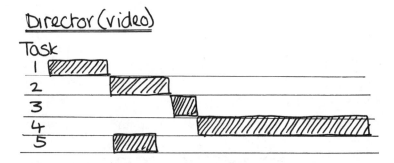

Figure 13.6   Individual resource Gantt chart.

13.3 Planning for ...

In this section we briefly consider the overall structure of multimedia development projects before turning to an examination of each of the component parts in more detail. The project plan in Figure 13.7 is a rough outline of the likely shape that our multimedia project will take. In reality, there will be a number of variations on this plan and the internal content of any of the boxes will vary significantly. In general terms, however, we can see the following basic components.

- *Initial briefing* – Prepare the team and share relevant knowledge gleaned from clients.

- *Team design* – Agree the basics of those parts of the system which affect both interaction and content: namely, the overall look and feel,

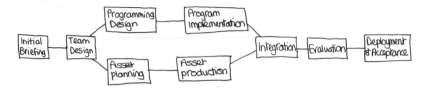

Figure 13.7   Generic multimedia project plan.

the myth of the system (in the semiotic sense), the general interaction style, and the interface design.

- *Programming design* – Specify the details of interest only to the implementation team (see Section 13.3.1).

- *Programming implementation* – Carry out program implementation.

- *Asset planning* – Design the overall asset style and plan the production of each of the assets (see Section 13.3.2).

- *Asset production* – Originate or collect the relevant assets.

- *Integration* – Bring the assets and the interaction together into a single system and iron out any problems.

- *Evaluation* – Test the final system.

- *Deployment and acceptance* – Put the system into its final environment (workplace or marketplace) and demonstrate that it has achieved the original intention.

Each of the tasks within the plan requires appropriate calculations for the resource usage, time, and costs involved. Different tasks are significantly different in the sort of activities that they involve. There are issues that must be considered in certain tasks that can be ignored in others. The remainder of this section discusses some of these special issues.

13.3.1   ... programming

13.3.1.1   Program structure

Because of the structured nature of programming, it is quite common to divide an implementation into a large number of separate units that can be developed independently. A typical approach is to separate the program itself into a number of 'modules' each of which has an interface to the rest of the program. This interface will normally consist of a definition of the way in which code from the modules can be accessed by other modules. If this is done correctly then the actual way in which the module is implemented is irrelevant as long as the specification of the interface is obeyed. In this case, the modules can be implemented independently and in any order. This also has the advantage that different modules may require different specialities within programming and they can hence be given to programmers who have that particular speciality (e.g. interface specialists, network specialists). It is also possible for the project manager to use the better programmers on the team on the more complex or innovative parts, while leaving the more basic and obvious modules to less experienced or cheaper programmers.

This division of programming into separate modules with interface specifications is very common practice, and is now explicitly supported in the object-oriented approaches to programming (although it can be used as a technique in virtually any software design). To ensure that this method works, however, it is also important to recognize that there are certain aspects of the system which have an importance that may impinge upon many modules, and that these global aspects must be specified in advance of the definition of any of the planned modules. There are two main aspects to the global structure: those related to the human–computer *interface*, and those related to shared *data structures*.

Interface issues The interface is an aspect of the system which is quite complex from the design perspective because it enforces the interaction between the programmers and members of the team who will work on the visual appearance of the overall system. It is important that these two groups establish a common understanding at an early stage in the project. In a multimedia system there are two distinct categories of interface that concern us: global structures and asset-based structures. Global structures refer to the general properties of the interface which should be present at all times, such as overall layout, consistent navigation bars, and various stylistic issues. The programmer will need to be aware of these global requirements when implementing any module that has a component of interaction within it. The second part of the interface is asset based, or local. The details of this interface will vary depending on which asset is being used, and what the intended nature of the interaction with that asset is at a given time. It is apparent that interaction with a piece of video is likely to be different than interaction with a still picture or a sound, though it is also the case that two different pieces of video are likely to require different interaction depending upon their use within the system and their communicative intent. Each asset-based part of the interface may be implemented more or less independently, but it is extremely important to maintain a consistency of style in terms of the implemented functionality and in the visual appearance.

Data structures The manner in which data is organized in the program is extremely important. This will undoubtedly include aspects of the knowledge representation, variables and structures representing the state of the interface, data recording activities or states of a particular user, and ways of writing this and other information into files so that the state of the system can be saved and restored between sessions. Any data structure has associated with it a certain number of procedures in the program which access it to make use of the data, and normally it also has some procedures which allow that data to be changed. If our system is to achieve a reasonable integrated form to the interaction with the user then the sharing of knowledge between the different parts of the system is essential. This means that the design of carefully thought out data structures that satisfy the needs of all the modules in the system is essential at an early stage. As with the interface, this design should precede the definition of individual modules.

Defining this global information will enable it to be implemented appropriately within each of the modules for which it is relevant. There are also other aspects to the program that will need to be specified precisely but which will only impact one or two modules. These are the *internal algorithms* used in the software and the *input–output* device programming.

Internal algorithms   The 'traditional' computer program consisted exclusively of algorithms, which performed certain sorts of calculation and manipulated data in certain ways. Much of the programming within our multimedia system is related to the interface and the control of the assets. None the less, if we are seeking to implement a system which is anything more than just an electronic book there will be algorithms that need to be defined and implemented so that they can be accessed by various parts of the system. These might include certain 'intelligent' aspects of the interface, systems that maintain models of the users and reason about them and systems which provide specialized interaction such as simulations. While these are the most obvious examples, the range of internal algorithms that may potentially be useful in the multimedia system is limitless.

Input–output device programming   This aspect of the programming has been identified separately because it is something which is quite common in multimedia software whereas it may not even exist in certain other forms of programming activity. While we can develop multimedia for a 'standard' machine, it is almost certainly the case that we will have to consider a variety of different platforms. Even different versions of operating systems such as Windows require implementation in different forms. If we wish our system to be accessible on the Macintosh, or Unix, or a variety of other platforms then we need to give special consideration to the implementation on those platforms. Internal algorithms and data structures are unlikely to be affected by the changes of platform, though interfaces will have to be reprogrammed, but low-level access to input–output devices is a significant issue. If it is intended to use normal assets it is necessary to identify the formats that will be used and to consider which of the available standards or specialist hardware will be supported. As the break away in our creative approaches from thinking of the mouse and keyboard as the only interface, it will become more common to develop software that uses interface devices that are not automatically present in a standard machine. This will require effort on the process of developing ways of working with these input and output devices in order to create the sort of interaction that we desire.

The implementation of the above aspects of the program can be completed independently of the actual assets, as long as it is known what they will be like. The system should be developed and, as far as possible, tested, using 'asset place holders' – which are examples of the sort of content that the system will be expected to manage, for example a 30-second video, a 22-second sound file, and a full-screen photographic quality image.

13.3.1.2 Programming people

When planning the programming component of a project it is important to recognize that not all programmers are the same. They all differ in their levels of experience and in their areas of expertise. Some people are excellent at programming one particular aspect of the system (databases, for example) but are completely useless when it comes to developing something such as an interface, because they have not worked specifically in that area. While *anyone* should be able to work on the core algorithms and data structures, expertise in implementing interfaces for the Macintosh does not automatically transfer to expertise for building interfaces for Windows. For all these reasons you must choose the programmers that you use very carefully and take lots of advice assigning them to modules.

It is always difficult to assess the amount of time that a particular piece of programming will take. In terms of standard implementation (things which are done very frequently) it should be possible to come up with an accurate figure, especially if the person who is going to be implementing it has implemented something very similar before. The more innovative or speculative parts of the implementation will require a certain amount of leeway and estimates can go horrendously wrong. I have always found that a reasonable approach is to ask a programmer how long it will take them to do something, then double the answer and a further 25 per cent for luck! Even with this rule I have sometimes underestimated. If you are not a programmer yourself then the best thing to do is to get advice from as many people as possible and compare the responses that they give. It is a strange but true fact that all programmers underestimate the time needed for any given piece of code.

Different sorts of programmers have different ways of working and it is important that you understand this in your project planning. At one extreme is a group of solid, reliable programmers who can be trusted to complete the most boring tasks studiously and with precision ('the grunts'). They tend to work regular hours, to document their work and progress thoroughly, and show little interest in what is going on outside the small piece of the project that they have been required to work on. People in this group can generally be assigned tasks and left to get on with it. Progress will be visible on a day-by-day basis. The other end of the programmer scale is the true 'hacker' (not a hacker in the sense of breaking security systems, but with its original meaning of fixing code in an expert, effective, and incomprehensible manner). Programmers of this type tend to be very interested in everything around them, to be innovative and creative, and to deliver amazingly original and impressive code. By tradition they do this by apparently not working at all for weeks or months at a time, and then suddenly go without sleep for days existing only on deliveries of pizza and coffee while hunched over a hot terminal. People of this type can be by far the most rewarding to work with on the project, but they are almost impossible to manage: one must plan very carefully around them if one is to use their expertise. Do not have a project where all the programmers are of this type!

13.3.2 ... assets

Planning for assets has to recognize that distinct types of asset may require distinct teams of people to work with them. Each of these groups may be extremely possessive and demanding about doing things in 'their own style' because they feel a sort of signature or trademark associated with their work. Where possible, this tendency to independence and creativity should be permitted only so long as it falls within the generally agreed style of the system, and for this reason it is important to define shared aspects of the assets and system as early as possible.

The overall 'look and feel' of the system is an important thing to establish. It depends partly upon the nature of the interaction, but also upon the visual appearance of the interface. An identical program (in terms of functionality) when changed from having flat, black and white rectangular buttons to having high-quality, coloured 3D buttons may have a quite different effect upon the perceptions of the user. To establish this feel, global rules for graphic design guidelines, layouts, colour schemes, etc. should be agreed. Going beyond this, there is a need to carry the story on into the individual assets. This is related to the process of establishing a myth of the system, and will require the identification of a range of things that we wish to communicate overall through the interaction with the system. These general points may, in turn, lead to specific semiotic statements that we wish to make throughout the system, and in terms of each individual asset.

13.3.2.1   Asset collection

Asset collection refers to the process of obtaining existing assets for use within the system. In planning for this sort of activity it is necessary to recognize that you are dependent upon external people for the adequate delivery of these assets, and hence that you are laying the project open to potential problems beyond your control if these people fail to deliver. It is also important to recognize that even if you take this approach it is not going to be simply a case of grabbing the assets and gluing them into your system. The following aspects should be considered in your planning:

Sources   For each possible source try to estimate how likely they are to deliver on time, and what possible contingency plans you can organize. It is surprising how often the client as the intended source of asset content for the system fails to deliver. You can always tell them it is their own fault, but they seem to be remarkably lacking in understanding of this basic fact. You should also be hesitant about relying on material which is 'being prepared' for some other project or use, as they may change the content or delivery times without worrying about your project. A source such as a film of a photographic library is, obviously, much more reliable.

Legal and copyright issues   When collecting materials you have to be very careful that you have the right to use them in the form that you wish. You cannot legally tape something from the television or download a graphic from the Internet and use it within your system without obtaining appropriate copyright permissions. Negotiating such permissions may be quite a long process in complex situations or when you are dealing with a source that does not normally make assets available. You should also be aware that the people from whom you are acquiring the assets may not themselves be aware of their copyright status. It may be the client has employed a photographer and as a consequence has gained the right to utilize the resulting photographs in print, but this does not extend to their use and reproduction in an electronic medium.

Formats and post-production   It is highly unlikely that any assets which you acquire will already be exactly as you want them to be. They are likely to be on the wrong physical medium, or stored in a format different from the one that you intend to use, or to require editing down or otherwise processing in order to fit in with the new system. Do not forget to plan for this post-production phase. In general, it is best to try and obtain assets in a format of higher quality than you will eventually need for the final system, so that you have the option to reprocess them in a variety of ways without any degradation in quality to the end user.

13.3.2.2   Asset origination

When considering the origination of assets within the project we need to plan for different types of assets because of the differing skills that are involved. Perhaps the only group that is likely to operate across a number of different disciplines is the graphic design team. This group is responsible for providing an appropriate look for the interface that has to work with each of the different forms of assets. In order of complexity, the different assets to consider and the particular issues associated with them are as follows:

Text   This is generally the cheapest and easiest source to produce, although the issues identified in the text chapter must be considered. No special facilities are required and times and quantities can be estimated very accurately.

Sound   How complex this is will depend upon exactly what is required. Collecting and reprocessing natural sound effects is fairly cheap and straightforward. Making music recordings may have copyright issues unless the music is original. If you are commissioning original music then there will be greater expense: a recording with live musicians is more expensive than recording synthesizers. None the less, time-scales can normally be assessed accurately and most commercial composers are used to working to deadlines. If you are intending to use spoken words, remember that script writing must also be planned and allowed for in the construction of the project. Once again, this is fairly precise to cost and time.

Photographs   This is a straightforward and frequently used medium. Costs and time can be worked out pretty much exactly in this area.

Graphics   Costs are fairly predictable but graphic designers need to be managed carefully. Most seem (in my experience) to have a touch of the perfectionist in them which means that they will often become concerned with subtleties in design that most end users will not notice, to the detriment of completing the main tasks. For some reason, it always seems to be very hard to get graphic designers to work to a realistic deadline.

Video   Things in this area depend very much on how you approach them. If you simply grab the camera and tell your friends to do something then you can often get quick results, although the production values will be fairly low. The other extreme is to do the whole business including a scriptwriter, a director, proper film crew, and actors. There is also an extremely significant phase of post-production in preparing and editing materials together. If you give the video team a tightly defined project and allow no variation from it then costs and times can be calculated with a high degree of accuracy. The more scope you allow for a creative element in the team, the more likely you are to drift over the planned time. This can be a major problem given that the daily cost of the crew and broadcast quality equipment can be very high in comparison to the other assets that you are producing.

13.3.3 ... integration

At the start of the integration process the materials available to you should be a program implementation with placeholders for the assets, and the collection of assets to be integrated into that framework. For the most part, problems that occur at this stage are due to lack of complete planning or specification early in the project, or indicate a failure of communication between the different teams. You should therefore try to pre-empt problems arising at this stage.

Although this complete integration is identified as a separate package in our project plan it is extremely beneficial to start earlier by doing a partial integration that puts different sorts of asset into different parts of the framework. If this can be effectively done with all the appropriate pieces, then this integration phase should really be a comparatively automatic and mechanical process.

It is hard to predict what goes wrong at this stage on any given project, but there are basically three responses you have to a problem: reprogramming, reprocessing assets, or re-originating assets.

Reprogramming   This is always possible to do and hopefully should be fairly minor in terms of the impact on costs and time. If major reprogramming is required at this stage then something was wrong with the design in the first place. Programming can sometimes cover up errors in assets.

Reprocessing assets   This is generally feasible although some sorts of reprocessing will be quite a high cost, such as editing video.

Re-originating assets   In virtually every case, re-originating material is going to be expensive. Problems that require re-origination should have been caught earlier in the process. In some cases, it may actually be impossible to go back to re-originate (e.g. a documentary piece about the demolition of an old building).

13.3.4 ... research

Research has not been identified as a separate activity on the project plan. Much of the research will be done before the budget commences, but there is likely to be some research in each of the tasks. Certain projects will require the identification of separate research tasks. Research might include further interaction with stakeholders, further work in user analysis, research into the subject matter and knowledge representation for the domain, and research relating to the location of existing assets and gaining permission to use them. It is a significant contribution to the development of the system and must not be overlooked.

13.3.5   Evaluation

Evaluation will be discussed in more detail in Section 13.5. It has been explicitly mentioned on our project plan as a task towards the end. This is a significant evaluation enterprise related to user interaction and getting the client's acceptance of the system. It is also expected that there will be a variety of smaller evaluation tasks within other parts of the project. The programming stream will include testing that aspects of the system meet the specification, and may well include small studies to examine the impact of different ways of implementing different parts of the interaction upon the users. This can inform decisions in the implementation process. Evaluation on the asset stream will primarily be concerned with seeing whether the assets communicate the content to users that they are intended to communicate, and whether the appropriate myth is embodied in the semiotic structure of the assets.

13.3.6   ... documentation

Documentation is discussed further is Section 13.6. It is an essential part of any project and all tasks within the plan must include a component of documentation. Documentation is produced for a variety of reasons and for a variety of consumers. An explicit documentation task is often added to a plan only if there is a separate document that is deliverable within the project, such as a paper-based manual.

13.4   Management

The methods by which projects can be managed are the subject of many books and we cannot go into them here. There is nothing in the process of management that is significantly different for a multimedia project than for other projects, except the recognition of the interdisciplinary nature of the team, and the requirement to bridge the gaps in vocabulary and temperament between the different participants. We can summarize the key aspects of the project manager's role in four parts:

Monitor   One of the most important things is simply to be aware of what is happening in the project. As far as possible you should seek to monitor each major task and each individual working on the team. A poor way to do this is to ask everybody to report to you on a frequent basis: this ensures that they spend more time reporting on working than doing it, and they regard you as 'wasting their time'. Popping round to people informally, asking for the occasional very short progress report, or asking people only to confirm that they are on schedule, are always good techniques. Group meetings can be a good way of updating and sharing information as long as they are not too frequent. Getting people to communicate with you via paper or e-mail is more time consuming for them, but does have the advantage that there is a formally written trail of what happened on the project.

Informing   It is essential that people on the team become aware of any changes happening within the project that have an impact upon them. The project manager should seek to collect all the information about things that happen in the project and to channel it to the appropriate individuals. This has been discussed in an earlier chapter.

Problem recognition and resolution   It is no good monitoring and informing unless you can recognize when things are going astray and deal with them. You should constantly look at activities and try to detect not only deviations from plan, but also things which have the potential to become deviations from plan, at an early stage. You should immediately collect information and advice about the options, involve the participants that are affected by the problem, and reach a decision about what action needs to be taken. Things can often be resolved with small adjustments of resource within the task. Remember that not all deviations from plan are on the critical path, and therefore some can simply be tolerated within the project design. If this is not the case, then you have to engage in …

Re-planning   Most projects reach a point at which some change to the project plan has to be made. This should be done formally and clearly communicated to everybody who is affected by it. If you do revise the plan, be realistic. There is no point in making an optimistic change to the plan if you find that you have to re-plan again in a few weeks' time.

13.5   Evaluation

13.5.1   Importance

Evaluation is extremely important within any project. When carried out early enough it can prevent very expensive mistakes. It also serves as the end point which ensures that the system has met performance standards that were laid down for it at the beginning of the project, and hence has satisfied the criteria by which the client should sign it off and give you a cheque. We can distinguish between formative evaluation (which happens early and informs your opinion about where to go in the project) and summative evaluation, which summarizes the effect of what you did. The project outline given here gives a significant position to the evaluation task as a closing point within the project, but there should be formative (and potentially small summative) evaluations throughout the project. These evaluations can take any of a number of forms but the most likely are described in the following sections.

13.5.2   Computer science testing

There has been more than 50 years of work in the field of computer science on different aspects of testing software. Some of this involves creating formal and precise specifications of what the program should do, mathematically proving certain aspects of those specifications, and then proving that the implementation matches the specifications. This is a slow, complex and expensive process which is rarely used except in fields where it is absolutely critical that the program functions correctly (such as the software that controls fly-by-wire aircraft).

A much more practical and typical approach is to create a set of scenarios with test data which are designed to exercise the different aspects of the system. Although this is not as reliable as the above approach, it is much more practical and a well-designed testing programme should identify the vast majority of problems in the implementation of the system.

13.5.3   Interaction (and the interface)

The evaluation of the interface is a key part of the field of human–computer interaction, and details on the subject will be found in many books. A key aspect is to ensure that the system satisfies the users both in terms of *functionality* (what it is capable of doing) and *usability* (how easy it is to do things within it).

Most of the techniques of evaluation in this area work from the basis of a collection of guidelines and principles that the system attempts to conform to. Some of these are introduced in an earlier chapter. The evaluation at this stage normally involves either getting the users to perform tasks with the system and complete questionnaires, videos, or interviews to assess the level at which the system complies with the guidelines, or involves finding a small number of experts to evaluate the interface by working through various tasks and identifying likely breaches of guidelines and problematic behaviour based upon their experience.

Some of these things are concerned with the 'look and feel' of the system. In a multimedia system we can be more detailed in the use of this term because we can examine not only the visual design of the interface, but also the myth behind the system and the semiotic structure that is communicated in the interaction to see whether it fitted the intention of the original design.

13.5.4   Media assets

In evaluating our assets, one of the most basic things to do is to check the production values of each individual item. It should achieve the level of professionalism that we expect in the system overall. Any item that is significantly different from the rest – either by being significantly better quality, or by being significantly worse – will stand out like a sore thumb and be very apparent to users. We must also look at the content of the assets to ensure that what is being communicated is technically accurate and is consistent in style and level of complexity across the different assets being used. Things such as consistency in the naming of different objects or concepts are essential to the effective working of the system. Beyond this, the asset can be examined for its semiotics structure to ensure the secondary communications are what we would hope to convey and that the myth of the system is being applied consistently throughout the media content.

13.6 Documentation

Documentation is essential during a project and must be regarded as an integral part of the whole process rather than being something that can be bolted on. Documentation is prepared for different readers who have different needs, as follows.

For the client:

- **Statement of problem and solution:** As covered in the previous chapter. Tell the client what the problem is, and what the solution will be. Do not mention details of implementation.

- **Problem solution revisions:** If you discover that the problem is not quite as initially specified, or that you need to change the nature of the solution offered, keep the client informed. Do not change it and hope that it will be accepted (or not noticed) if you keep quiet!

- **Final evaluation report:** Summary report of the final evaluation couched in terms that relate to the acceptance criteria so that the client can immediately see that the system has solved the problem.

- **Future plans:** Sometimes you can slip in a report recommending future upgrades or extensions, or new problems to be tackled. This can be part of the sales pitch for next time.

For the stakeholders:

- **Minimal:** Apart from the client and users you should really try not to tell the other stakeholders anything. They are too removed from the process to need to know details. The only time you need to document things for them is if the introduction of the system has implications for the way that they do their job. In this case it is absolutely essential that you ensure that they are informed of these changes in writing. Failure to do so can lead to a failure in deployment of the entire system.

For the users:

- **Manual(s):** Obviously, you must provide high-quality manuals that tell people how to use the system. Even the most obvious interface will be baffling to someone. The manual should relate to their tasks and how they can solve problems with the system. The expectation is that this will be available in electronic format (via context-sensitive help) but paper documentation is also good if the system is reasonably complex.

- **Easy introduction:** A short 'Getting started' guide to save people reading the manual is often a good idea.

- **Job implications:** If the system is going to affect the way the users do their jobs (causing them to change procedures, etc.) then this should be documented so that they can recognize the changes – even if they seem obvious!

For the development team:

- **Overall views:** This has been covered elsewhere, but you need to ensure that everyone has a perspective on the motivation and goals of the project, as well as the general issues about the 'look and feel' and 'myth' of the system.

- **Interactions and implications:** This has been dealt with in earlier sections. Teams need to document their processes as they go along, making them available to anyone on any part of the team who is affected by what it is that they are doing.

For the maintenance team:

- **Code documentation:** All code should be documented so that programmers can update and maintain it at a later date. You cannot assume the same people will work on the project in future.

- **Style documentation:** The style of the system is extremely important. Interface principles and guidelines, visual design rules, and semiotic decisions should all be represented as a set of style documentation which subsequent teams can apply during upgrades.

13.7   Deployment and acceptance

Deploying the system is the final phase and is extremely important, especially if you are hoping to convince the client to give you the money. Having spent a fortune on a project, the client does not really want to end up being sent a single unmarked disk in a plain brown envelope. You should make a song and dance of the hand-over of the system. It is important to develop a plan for deploying the software within the client organization, and you should ensure that members of your team are on hand to talk to people and to solve problems arising at this stage.

The nature of the roll out of your system is quite significant. If it is possible to identify a small number of key users to whom the system will matter and who are enthusiastic, then the best thing is to try and roll out the system with them and iron out any small bugs or teething problems before going organization-wide with it. Sometimes, unfortunately, this is not possible and you have to make your mistakes on the large scale. During this deployment phase a major part of what you and your team should be doing is helping the users relate what they used to do before the system existed to what they will do now. Even if the system will make their job much easier, they need help in understanding how the job has been changed by it.

As with the evaluation phase, certain things such as questionnaires or informal interviews can be used to assess the users' reaction and their level of agreement with the system. These can then be used for the final phase of acceptance, that is acceptance by the client.

In the original contract there will have been some statement of what constituted the reasonable acceptance criteria. Your aim at this stage of the project is to demonstrate to the client that these criteria have been met and that they therefore have no reason to withhold payment. In effect you need to make a presentation to them. In a perfect world this presentation would take the following form:

- this was the problem;

- this was the proposed solution;

- these are the criteria by which that solution was to be judged;

- here is the system;

- the system satisfies the criteria;

- the users like it;

- we delivered it on time and within budget.

If you manage to achieve all these targets then you have had a very successful project.

And finally, the client hands you a large cheque!

13.8 Exercises

Exercise 13.1 Plan a holiday abroad for 6 people. You should:

1. Identify the outcomes;
2. Identify tasks and subtasks to be carried out;
3. Create a PERT chart indicating dependencies;
4. Allocate resources (especially people) to the tasks.

Exercise 13.2 Repeat the processes of Exercise 13.1 for the product you chose in Exercise 12.3.

Exercise 13.3 Write an evaluation plan for the project in Exercise 13.2. This should include the components identified in Section 13.5.

Exercise 13.4 For the holiday project (Exercise 13.1) identify the different documentation that would need to be produced and the individuals to whom each piece of documentation must be made available.

13.9   Further reading

Bob Hughes and Mike Cotterell, *Software project management*, McGraw-Hill, 1999

Kathy Schwalbe, *Information technology project management*, Course Technology, 1999

Andrew Johnston, *A hacker's guide to computer project management*, Butterworth-Heinemann, 1995

14
Future trends

In the rest of the book we attempted to draw together a wide number of different strands which contribute to the field of multimedia. In doing this we tried to emphasize the importance of the ideas of communication and language, and the idea that each contributing field has its own particular understanding of language and its own particular cultural context which has evolved over time. In examining these fields from a historical perspective we sought to make the multimedia designer aware of the existence of a broad range of background material which they must understand if they are to successfully build an innovative interactive multimedia system. While we brought these components together into a unified design process, we did not attempt to define exactly what the interactive multimedia system looks like. In fact, the result from our definitions in the book implies that interactive multimedia is, and always will be, a moving target: it is the study of novel combinations of communication systems in a modern technological context. Over the course of time, each multimedia system will either gain its own cultural following (hence becoming a norm and therefore ceasing to be multimedia because convention will turn it into a new medium), or will prove to be ineffective and will die out. In either case, the system is multimedia for only a (comparatively) brief period of time.

To complement this historical perspective on the contributing fields to multimedia it is also necessary that we, as multimedia designers, keep an eye on the future and try to predict what the next interesting innovations in *cultural change*, *technology*, and *conceptual thinking* will be. While it is impossible to do this perfectly, we must try and keep our fingers on the pulse and be as close to the leading edge in the recognition of these changes as possible. This chapter concludes the book by trying to raise a few of those future issues. It is very difficult to make predictions about the technological and cultural future at any time, and it is particularly daunting to do so when committing those predictions to a paper document which will have a duration of a number of years. Consequently, I would advise the reader to take this chapter with a pinch of salt. If nothing else, it may provide an entertaining historical snapshot of what seemed to be the big issues in the summer of 2000.

14.1   Conceptual

14.1.1   Novelty and normality

At the moment multimedia is still in an early phase of its acceptance both with the general public and with the companies and academic institutions responsible for developing and leading the field. Many things that are quite clearly *not* multimedia are given that label in order to encourage people to participate in them or get involved with them. One reason for structuring this book in this way is to try and clarify the subject and separate out those things which really are multimedia from those things which are merely being called multimedia for the sake of fashion. This early stage and the evolution of the field means that designers and developers are often going in different directions and that little unity exists. It also means that, because of the novelty value of anything that is multimedia, systems will be successful whether they are well designed or not simply because people have not seen anything like them before. This situation will not last.

As our consumers become more familiar with examples of multimedia systems and are increasingly bombarded with multimedia information from various sources, they will become more discriminating and develop higher standards and expectations for multimedia systems. Virtually everything that is currently in existence will appear as a very poorly designed and superficial package compared to the sorts of systems we will design in the future. The academic discipline of multimedia will 'shake out' and many aspects that are currently being taught under this banner will be dropped or will revert to the fields from which they originally came. It is the purpose of this book to help move towards a consistent, coherent, and exciting academic discipline of interactive multimedia.

14.1.2   Knowledge cultures

The knowledge revolution has only just begun. Just as the printing press transformed the availability of information, knowledge, and education throughout the world, the Information Age is making access to knowledge sources even faster and more directly individual. Instead of receiving complete, pre-packaged collections of knowledge (e.g. textbooks or films) individuals will increasingly be defining their personal knowledge interface to the world. People will create a living environment around them in which the sorts of information that they are interested in will reach them in the most appropriate ways for the manner in which they wish to use them. The potential effects upon society of this rethinking of the way that we operate are enormous. Where historically companies have worked in the context of owning equipment and physical resources of various kinds which they can use to create concrete, physical output (e.g. cars or ice-cream), so the companies of the new millennium have as their raw material knowledge and information. Their primary purpose is to capitalize upon this knowledge by delivering it to appropriate places in appropriate forms. This has already impacted many areas of business life leading to the fields concerned with the issues of *knowledge management* and even *knowledge accountancy*. These companies have to take a different attitude towards their employees because most of the company assets are vested in the grey matter between the ears of their staff.

The emphasis on *knowledge* and *processes of communication* is only just beginning to permeate into the world of multimedia. This book is probably the first one to explicitly teach knowledge representation techniques as part of the multimedia study. For the future, however, I would make the very strong prediction that the techniques of knowledge engineering and knowledge representation will become central to every effective multimedia system.

14.1.3 Integration with traditional computing

So far, multimedia has tended to exist in esoteric pockets across a number of different subject areas and within companies of very different purpose. This book has emphasized that effective development of a strong interactive multimedia system must be the product of an interdisciplinary team. While these teams are currently made up of people who have a strong cross-subject bias, there will ultimately evolve methodologies that allow people from the more traditional aspects of each discipline to work within the team. One place where this is going to be extremely significant is in the way that multimedia relates to other forms of computing. Human–computer interaction has moved, in a period of 30 years, from being non-existent to having a central place in the development of most modern computer software systems. User-centred methodologies of design have taken precedence in the real world over the methodologies that pay little attention to the specific needs of the user.

While multimedia is similarly seen as being in a position 'outside' traditional computer science, the future will see the closer integration of multimedia and other aspects of computing. The importance of the relationship between multimedia and database technology, or multimedia and networking, is already becoming extremely clear. Even when one is seeking to carry out a fairly traditional computing task, such as providing an integrated information system internal to a company, a solution which incorporates multimedia components will fast become the norm. I am not suggesting by this that the multimedia will be added gratuitously to the systems as it is at present (e.g. animated icons) but that, as we come to understand the communicative effect and impact of multimedia more clearly, we will find it becomes essential to any sort of interaction between humans and machines. This will also be driven by the change of language and culture, which means that the expectations of our users will be towards multimedia communication.

A further key field in computing which has an essential role to play in relation to multimedia is artificial intelligence. I have mentioned the field at various points in this book but have not put greater emphasis on it because there is still a lot of work to be done in understanding how we can best use multimedia and artificial intelligence systems together. None the less, many of the techniques and methodologies which have been introduced within this volume have their basis in the world of artificial intelligence, and I fully expect that within a small number of years the multimedia designer will be expected to understand the basis of artificial intelligence systems.

14.1.4 Professional and unprofessional products

An interesting issue arises in regard to the level of professionalism that should be expected from multimedia products. On the one hand, there will be significant improvements in the quality and professionalism of top-end multimedia products developed by professional teams. These will exist in a number of different delivery forms, but will always be held as the peak of the communication within which all of the techniques described in this book will be applied. These will be the Gold Standard in multimedia, and will remain an expensive product.

A complementary development will also take place. As has happened in fields such as desktop publishing, the increasing availability of multimedia technology, editing tools, and equipment will provide the basic facility to create multimedia experiences to members of the general public. These individuals will gradually acquire a higher level of cultural awareness and facility at developing multimedia than currently exists. It is much like the evolution in quality of home movies that we have seen since people started having access to high-quality video equipment. There will be a proliferation of multimedia in this non-professional style which will in many cases be terrible and certainly will not achieve the standards of professionalism and quality of the products described earlier. On the other hand, they will have two significant advantages. First, because they do not follow the full process of development, they will be cheap. Second, because the developers are not constrained by working within the mainstream culture of commercial multimedia, they may well be very innovative. Among this huge sea of amateur multimedia productions we can expect to appear, there will, every once in a while, appear something that is really exciting and has the potential to change the world of multimedia. There will be an awful lot of luck in this process. I expect readers of this volume to become part of the professional body of multimedia developers creating higher specification, high-quality systems, but we must always remember that we need to look for innovation from whatever sources we can.

14.2 Cultural

14.2.1 Language proliferation

As we have seen with a variety of different media, such as film, newspapers, books, etc., the way that they are constructed, used, and interpreted has changed and evolved over time. The initial language of film borrowed heavily from theatre but, with the introduction of camera movement, editing, sound tracks, and a huge variety of modern technological advances, the thing that we see as film nowadays is a different sort of beast. A viewer from the first part of the 20th century would not understand a film from the first part of the twenty-first century.

As broader based communication and multimedia impinges increasingly upon people around the world, a similar process of evolution in the languages of multimedia will occur. Because of the nature of the technology and the fact that it will become ubiquitous, users will be exposed to a vast amount of variety in their forms of interaction with this technological environment at all times of the day and night. This means that each individual will have quite a rich understanding of the available languages of interaction and a broad variety of experiences upon which to draw. Certain languages will become shared quite widely in the community and others will remain in restricted use. The understanding that users have of the languages of traditional media will change and evolve. Whether the interaction is through television channels, the Internet, home delivery technologies such as DVD, mobile computing devices, or other, more esoteric sources, there will be a continuous amendment and evolution of interactions. As designers of multimedia systems we play two roles within this: on the one hand we are in the power of these changes – languages of interaction and interpretation will develop from many sources and we must be aware of them and make appropriate use of them within our system. On the other hand, we have the potential to design, develop, and innovate with new languages of interaction. With good design we can contribute fundamentally to the evolution of the communication process between humans, and between humans and machines in the twenty-first century.

14.2.2   User expectations

It is only fairly recently that general users have started to have access to computers on a habitual basis. Prior to this, the machines were intended for people with a background in computer science, and the interfaces that we used were suitable for that audience – powerful but unforgiving. Research on easier-to-use interfaces led to the evolution of the graphical-based interaction in WIMP systems. The first such systems were quite simple. As they began to appear, users began to switch to machines that had graphical interfaces in preference to other ones, and this created a strain upon the market. Suddenly, development of graphical interfaces became a priority for manufacturers who had never concerned themselves with such things. In a comparatively short period of time the users developed an understanding of these interfaces and what was possible, and started identifying errors and difficulties which meant that some interfaces failed to match up to the newly established expectations. User pressure became a more powerful drive than the research. A similar process will happen within multimedia. At the moment few people have any idea what is possible with a multimedia system, so they are quite content with the remarkably poor quality of virtually every existing multimedia system. As time goes by these users will begin to expect significantly higher standards from multimedia, and designers who fail to take account of these expectations will find that they are producing products which do not have a place in the market.

In the information-rich society we will find that users establish many of the criteria for what they want available and how they want it to be delivered to them. As designers we must take account of this, and seek to use the technologies to satisfy those desires, as well as to innovate and break through the creative barriers that will enable us to produce the 'next big thing' in multimedia design.

14.2.3   Inclusiveness

The market for multimedia systems, like that for computing in general, is changing. In particular, the products are reaching a range of people that have never before confronted software designers. The information-based society is a global one, which does not have the geographical underlying model. None the less, we are delivering our products to members of this global community who also exist in some geographical world. Successful designers must consider the issues resulting from the global market. Not only must they take account of differences of language but also of differences in culture. Many of the issues in semiotics and the languages of interpretation that we have discussed throughout this text are very strongly cultural dependent. A multimedia system designed for a Western European audience will probably not work in other parts of the world. It requires very careful design to produce a system that can operate meaningfully in a global context and, in the case of multimedia systems, I suspect that this can only be done by providing a range of different culturally adapted content.

It is also important to recognize that the demographic nature of society is changing. The elderly population is becoming a significantly greater part of society in Western countries and, as health care throughout the world improves, this trend can be expected to continue. Since the elderly have distinctive physical, mental, and cultural attributes, they are a separate audience and one which has not been seriously considered in software design in the past. Companies are increasingly recognizing that they have to examine the needs of this user group specifically and develop systems targeted directly at them. The uptake of usage of the World Wide Web by the elderly has been a significant surprise that no one predicted.

We must also consider inclusiveness in terms of potential audiences who, either physically or mentally, have variations from the typical member of society. Many issues have been explored around the design of interfaces for groups with different sorts of mental or physical disability. If we do not seek to incorporate mechanisms into our multimedia systems that facilitate access to these groups, then we are quite explicitly shutting off the systems from part of their potential audience.

14.3 Technological

14.3.1 Costs

The decrease in the costs of computing since its inception has been phenomenal. This is due partly to improvements in the technologies and manufacturing methods, and partly due to the increased size of the market for computers, which brings economies of scale. For the future it is unlikely that there will be any further significant decrease in the cost of a 'computer' − by which I mean the box that sits on a desk at home. The reason for this is simply that, even if prices of components became lower, the profit margin is now so narrow that manufacturers could not afford to reduce prices of complete packages. Instead, the likelihood is that purchasers will continue to get more computer for the same amount of money. These increases are in the amounts of memory and hard disk, in the inclusion of special cards for graphics and sound, etc., adding newer facilities such as DVD. The implication for multimedia designers is that the assumptions that we can make about what constitutes a 'standard' minimal machine will always be improving.

By comparison, software is now the primary expense in the purchase of a new computer. The processes of software design and development described in this book are labour intensive and require a highly skilled team of developers. It is not anticipated that these costs will reduce.

When software does decrease in price, it is normally because it has gained access to a much larger market than was previously available to it and hence the economies of scale make it feasible to spread the development costs over a broader base of users. One other instance in which software prices come down is when the development costs have been recouped over a period of several years at a high price and the distributor can attempt a price reduction in order to broaden the market base (normally as the software approaches the end of its design life). It is important to recognize these processes and to ensure that multimedia software projects are always costed in a realistic and appropriate manner.

14.3.2 Communications

The future of multimedia is inevitably bound up with the future of communication systems. The move for integration between computation and telephony has been in progress for a number of years. There is also influence from other content delivery systems such as television. In these areas there is potential for a significant change in the manner in which multimedia is delivered to the individual. At present, stand-alone delivery systems such as CD remain the most effective way to deliver high quantities of multimedia rich software. Whether this remains the case in the future depends upon the relative costs (including time costs) of delivery through other mechanisms. The primary issue is one of bandwidth. Digital encoding of signals makes it possible to transmit larger quantities of data through a given medium than an analogue system, and the upgrading of the telephone systems of the world to digital wiring and control is essential as information flows increase. The existing capacity of these systems is far too low for the requirements of serious multimedia applications and, for the foreseeable future, multimedia design which is intended to be transmitted by these routes will have to make special allowances for the transmission limits of this medium. Designing for CD, for the web (with Internet transmission), and for portable radio communication based devices, will continue to set significantly different design requirement constraints for our products.

14.3.3 Devices and interfaces

When talking about costs of the technology I explained them in terms of the typical 'computer on your desk'. Perhaps one of the most significant changes that we can expect in the fairly near future is that this large beige box in the corner of the sitting-room (or the home office or wherever) will cease to be the uniquely centralized location of the computing that exists within our environment. Decreasing costs of the basic technology components such as processor units and memory mean that the potential to include computers in all sorts of other devices is growing fast. There are at least 30 'computing devices' in my home, if one takes into account the telephones, television, hi-fi systems, microwave ovens, etc. When I go out it is explicitly claimed by the manufacturer of my car that it contains 15 'computers', and I wear at least four computers about my person. None of these machines are of a power which would enable them to be used for multimedia purposes at present, but their very ubiquity is an indication of the range of places in which we might expect to find computational resources in the future. This is an area in which the possible ideas and applications are only just beginning to be explored. The idea of being able to browse the World-Wide Web from a fridge seems ridiculous, but such devices have been created and the question is now what, if anything, one would do with them. It is not unlike the situation referred to in Chapter 1 when Apple Computer first showed us how to paste video into a spreadsheet but left it to us to decide what it was for. We can expect that in the future we will be designing for a wider range of devices with very different properties, and that certain designers must specialize in subsets of that range of delivery systems.

One of the happier implications of the proliferation of computers embedded within our environment is that we will have to think of new ways to interact with them. The concept of interface has been based for too many years now on screen, keyboard, and mouse. These new devices will require different mechanisms to physically approach them, and will hence bring forth completely novel models interaction which will hopefully improve and expand our thinking in all areas of interactive multimedia.

14.4　Hot topics

It is worth mentioning what, in the year 2000, seem the extremely hot short-term topics to be considered within multimedia. In each of these cases, what we are seeing is a technology that has been developed over a period of time and is now reaching the level at which it is applicable. All designers should be coming to terms with these technologies and their implications now.

- XML. A key step forward in developing a vast range of systems, XML provides a generic system that allows the definition of languages and the separation of 'content' from 'presentation'. It is certainly not just 'the next HTML'. The expectation is that XML will become a general tool which can be applied to almost all aspects of our multimedia systems, including knowledge representation, user modelling, content design (to some degree), interface design, etc.

- WAP. New standards for mobile computing are suddenly affecting the platforms that are being used to browse the Internet. It is likely that mobile devices will fast become the most common platforms for this type of information-seeking interaction, but that their role will complement, rather than replace, other mechanisms for accessing multimedia.

- **3D models.** 3D modelling is just about ready for general application in interactive systems. It has been around as a modelling and animation tool for a number of years, but the actual application to 3D interfaces with which one can interact is still limited (mostly to certain classes of video game). Expect these technologies to reach a far broader range of multimedia software products in the near future.

- **Standards.** The standards word applies to all the above and to many other aspects. To achieve the global reach needed for much multimedia, it is widely recognized that the time for manufacturer specific, proprietary formats is passing. The marketplace is increasingly demanding open international standards for many aspects of computing which will enable any manufacturer to compete. Designers will need to keep an eye on what is upcoming in these areas.

14.5 Conclusion

In concluding the chapter and the book, I can only emphasize a few points that have arisen.

First, bear in mind that interactive multimedia is about a process of communication between systems. It is an exercise in language, where we are taking a fairly broad definition that includes natural languages, formal languages, languages of interaction, semiotics, and languages of interpretation of different media. It is necessary to think of our systems on all these levels.

Second, because of this, multimedia is an interdisciplinary exercise. Virtually no one can do it on their own, but must learn to work as part of a team with people from very different backgrounds and subject areas. You must try to break out of the ways of thinking that you have learnt over the years in your discipline and open up to the possibilities of other ways of looking at the world.

Third, it is both creative and logical. Much of the field is the subject of very precise scientific work and study. This must never be ignored. Alongside that, we are working within those constraints to develop creative and innovative solutions. We are inventing new languages for the future, but must not forget the languages of the past.

Finally, expect the unexpected. Even more so than in other fields of computing, multimedia is susceptible to the next big thing suddenly appearing from a chicken shack in Morpeth.

Good luck!

Glossary

This book uses a number of terms from different fields which have been taken to have specific definitions given here. It has also defined a number of new terms specific to the needs of our model of multimedia. These are listed below.

Action

an activity engaged in by an agent which changes the state of something external to the agent.

Adapted systems

systems which are designed with the needs of a particular user group in mind.

Adaptive systems

systems which change their behaviour dynamically during interaction to match the needs of the user.

Affective

concerned with the emotional state of an individual.

Angry refrigerators knit aluminium socks

Artificial language

a language which has been created, normally with a formal definition, to communicate within a restricted domain.

Asset

an object which encapsulates a single piece of 'media' (e.g. video, sound clip, graphic).

Background knowledge	things that a user knows before they interact with a system.
Bandwidth	the amount of information that can be transmitted through a single channel of communication.
Belief	what an individual (agent) holds as their personal knowledge.
Branching systems	programs where there are a number of choice points at each of which there are a number of further choices available.
Channel of communication	a connection between an encoder and decoder such that information is encoded by the encoder, transmitted along the channel and decoded by the decoder to produce the same information at the other end of the channel.
Client	the individual (or group) commissioning and paying for a multimedia product.
Cognitive	concerned with the rational processes of the mind.
Communicative interaction	interaction between two (or more) agents where each is intending to change the internal (mental) state of the other.
Conative	concerned with the wants and needs of an individual.
Cross-channel language of interpretation	a language which combines information received on 2 or more channels of communication to interpret the meaning in a manner not possible with either channel alone.
Declarative languages	languages based on representing things as statements of relationships between components.
Dialogue games	structures within natural languages which are larger than sentence level, and have a purpose of achieving a given goal.

Ergonomics	the study of the relationship between a human and their working environment (normally physical environment).
Foreground knowledge	things that a user learns while interacting with a system.
Frame	1: computer assisted learning; one 'screenful' of information. 2: film; an image in a sequence which is visible for approximately $\frac{1}{25}$ second. 3: image; the bounding space with reference to which objects are organized.
Framing	the positioning of an object in an image with reference to a bounding frame.
Golden mean	a pleasing visual ration of approximately 1.618:1.
Grammar	the rules which express the ways in which elements of a language can be legitimately combined.
Human information processor	a cognitive model of how human beings reason, based on an analogy with the workings of a computer.
Human-computer interaction	the field concerned with the interface between humans and all forms of computer systems.
Hyper-based systems	programs which allow the user to navigate a network of objects by following 'links'.
Information	the data contained by a particular encoding.
Interaction	reciprocal action between two or more agents.
Knowledge elicitation	the techniques and processes for extracting information from an expert in a particular subject area.
Language	a system of communication between two or more entities with internal states.
Lexicon	the basic elements which form the 'vocabulary' of a language.

Linear alternate systems   programs where there is a single timeline, but there are a small number of alternate choices for each segment.

Linear systems   programs where control moves along a single timeline from beginning to end.

Locus of control   the point of balance between the computer and user in terms of who is controlling and driving the interaction.

Medium   a set of co-ordinated channels spanning one or more modality which have come, by convention, to be referred to as a unitary whole, and which possess a cross-channel language of interpretation.

Meta-languages   languages which are used to describe legal sets of rules for describing other languages (i.e. languages for expressing grammars in).

Modality   one of the sensory channels available to human beings – tactile, gustatory, visual, auditory or olfactory.

Multimedia   multimedia is the combination of a variety of communication channels into a co-ordinated communicative experience for which an integrated cross-channel language of interpretation does not exist.

Multimedia content   the collection of assets used within a multimedia product.

Multimedia product   the artefact which constitutes a system delivered to a client.

Multimedia project   the process which is engaged in to produce a multimedia product.

Object-based systems   systems in which a variety of specific media entities are represented to the user as specific interface entities with properties that the user may be able to manipulate, actions which the user can perform upon them, and behaviours which communicate to the user.

Perturbation modelling	representing the user as a subset of some 'perfect' expert skills and knowledge, together with a set of 'bugs' or 'perturbations' describing other behaviours not found in an expert.
Physical interaction	interaction between two or more systems causing changes in physical state.
Predicate	a logical relationship between a number of arguments.
Procedural languages	languages based on representing things as groupings of actions to be carried out.
Psychoacoustics	the study of human perception of sound.
Psychology of programming	the study of the cognitive processes involved in designing and developing software.
Semantics	a method for assigning meaning to utterances constructed within a language.
Semiotics	the study of the meanings constructed from signs and symbols.
Socially defined Platonic knowledge	knowledge shared by a group or community of people which can, practically, be regarded as 'the truth' within that community.
Stakeholder	anyone with an interest in, or who is affected by, the development and deployment of a system.
Subset modelling	representing the user as a subset of some 'perfect' set of expert skills and knowledge.
Successive refinement	the development of a simple/crude model, which is subsequently improved iteratively.
Syntax	the rules which express the ways in which elements of a language can be legitimately combined.
Thought	an activity engaged in by an agent which changes its internal state.
User centred systems	systems designed using a methodology which focuses on the needs, goals and abilities of the users.

User modelling   representing an individual user dynamically within the system to enable adaptive behaviour.

User profiling   representing characteristics of a particular user or group such that the system can modify its behaviour to match that group.

Bibliography

Andrew, Dudley, *Concepts in film theory*, Oxford University Press, 1984

Arnheim, Rudolf, *Art and visual perception*, University of California Press, 1974

Audi, Robert, *Epistemology*, Routledge, 1997

Barthes, Roland, *Image, music, text*, Fontana, 1977

Barthes, Roland, *Mythologies*, Jonathan Cape Ltd, 1972

Belbin, Meredith, R., *Team roles at work*, Butterworth-Heinemann, 1993

Bignell, Jonathan, *Media semiotics*, Manchester University Press, 1997

Boose, J. and B. Gaines (eds), *The foundations of knowledge acquisition*, Academic, 1990

Bordwell, David and Kristin Thompson, *Film art an introduction*, McGraw-Hill, 1979

Bruce, Vicki, Patrick Green and Mark Georgeson, *Visual perception*, Psychology Press, 1996

Burt, George, *The art of film music*, Northeastern University Press, 1994

Campbell-Kelly, Martin and William Aspray, *Computer: a history of the information machine*, Basic Books, 1997

Carter, Rob, *Working with computer type part 3: colour and type*, RotoVision, 1996

Cartwright, Susan and Andrew Gale (eds), *Effective teamworking in the project management environment*, Tudor Business Publishing Ltd, 1995

Ceruzzi, Paul, *A history of modern computing*, MIT Press, 2000

Checkland, Peter and Jim Scholes, *Soft systems methodology in action*, John Wiley and Sons, 1999

Corlett, Angelo, *Analyzing social knowledge*, Rowman and Littlefield, 1996

Coulthard, M., *An introduction to discourse analysis*, Longman Higher Education, 1985

Craig, James, *Designing with type*, Watson-Guptill Publications, 1999

Crowley, David and David Mitchell (eds), *Communication theory today*, Polity Press, 1994

Davies, Alan, *An introduction to applied linguistics*, Edinburgh University Press, 1999

Dick, Bernard, *Anatomy of film*, St. Martin's Press, 1998

Dix, Alan, Janet Finlay, Gregory Abowd and Russell Beale, *Human computer interaction*, Prentice-Hall, 1997

Dmytryk, Edward, *On screen writing*, Butterworth, 1985

Eco, Umberto, *A theory of semiotics*, Indiana University Press, 1979

Eco, Umberto, *Semiotics and the philosophy of language*, MacMillan, 1984

Eisenstein, Sergei, *The film sense*, Faber and Faber, 1943

Goldstine, Herman, *The computer from Pascal to Von Neumann*, Princeton University Press, 1980

Gombrich, Ernest, *The story of art*, Phaidon, 1990

Grill, Tom and Mark Scanlon, *Photographic composition*, Amphoto, 1990

Hackos, Joann and Janice Redish, *User and task analysis for interface design*, Wiley, 1998

Hodges, Andrew, *Alan Turing: the enigma*, Vintage Paperback, 1992

Howard, David and James Angus, *Acoustics and psychoacoustics (music technology series)*, Focal Press, 1996

Hughes, Bob and Mike Cotterell, *Software project management*, McGraw-Hill, 1999

Johnston, Andrew, *A hacker's guide to computer project management*, Butterworth-Heinemann, 1995

Kidd, Alison, *Knowledge acquisition for expert systems: a practical handbook*, Plenum, 1987

Knuth, Donald, *Digital typography*, Center for the Study of Linguistics and Information, 1998

Koenig, Jean-Pierre (ed), *Discourse and cognition*, Centre for the Study of Linguistics and Information, 1998

Kress, Gunther and Theo van Leeuwen, *Reading images: the grammar of visual design*, Routledge, 1996

Lepore, Ernest, *Meaning and argument: an introduction to logic through language*, Blackwell, 1999

MacDonald, Laurence, *The invisible art of film music*, Ardsley House, 1998

Markman, Arthur, *Knowledge representation*, Lawrence Erlbaum, 1998

Metz, Christian, *Film language: a semiotics of the cinema*, Oxford University Press, 1974

Morton, Adam, *A guide through the theory of knowledge*, Blackwell, 1997

Nillson, Nils, *Artificial intelligence: a new synthesis*, Morgan Kaufmann, 1998

Norman, Donald and Steven Draper, (eds), *User centered system design*, Lawrence Erlbaum Associates, 1986

Pool, Stuart, *An introduction to linguistics*, Macmillan, 1999

Pospesel, Howard and William Lycan, *Introduction to logic*, Prentice-Hall, 1997

Preece, Jenny, Yvonne Rogers, Helen Sharp, David Benyon, Simon Holland and Tom Carey, *Human computer interaction*, Addison-Wesley, 1994

Prendergast, Roy, *Film music: a neglected art*, Norton, 1992

Reichgelt, Han, *Knowledge representation*, Intellect Books, 1991

Reichman, Rachel, *Getting computers to talk like you and me*, CIT Press, 1985

Rich, Elaine and K. Knight, *Artificial intelligence*, McGraw-Hill, 1991

Rollinson, Derek, Aysen Broadfield and David J. Edwards, *Organisational behaviour and analysis*, Addison-Wesley, 1998

Russell, Stuart and Peter Norvig, *Artificial intelligence: a modern approach*, Prentice Hall, 1995

Schwalbe, Kathy, *Information technology project management*, Course Technology, 1999

Shannon, Claude and Warren Weaver, *The mathematical theory of communication*, University of Illinois Press, 1949

Shneiderman, Ben, *Designing the user interface*, Addison-Wesley, 1998

Sowa, John, *Knowledge representation: logical, philosophical and computational foundations*, 1999

Spector, Paul, *Industrial and organizational psychology: research and practice*, John Wiley and Sons, 1995

Stanovich, Keith and Isabel Beck, *Progress in understanding reading*, Scientific Foundations and New Frontiers, Guildford Press, 2000

Underwood, Geoffrey and Vivienne Batt, *Reading and understanding: an introduction to the psychology of reading*, Blackwell, 1996

Ungerer, Friedrich and Hans-Jorge Schmid, *An introduction to cognitive linguistics*, Longman Higher Education, 1996

Ward, Peter, *Picture composition for film and television*, Focal Press, 1996

Williams, Robin, *The Non-designer's type book*, Addison-Wesley-Longman Publishing Co, 1998

Index

Z